Frommer's

Hong Kong

by Beth Reiber

Macmillan • USA

ABOUT THE AUTHOR

Beth Reiber worked for several years in Tokyo as the editor of the *Far East Traveler.* Now a freelance travel writer, she has written articles for such publications as *Travel Holiday,* the *Los Angeles Times,* and the *Chicago Tribune.* She is also the author of Frommer guides to Japan, Tokyo, Berlin, and St. Louis and Kansas City.

MACMILLAN TRAVEL

A Simon & Schuster Macmillan Company
1633 Broadway
New York, NY 10019

Find us online at **http://www.mcp.com/mgr/travel** or
on America Online at **Keyword: SuperLibrary.**

ISBN 0-02-861126-8
ISSN 1045-9332

Editor: Charlotte Allstrom
Production Editor: Amy DeAngelis
Digital Cartography: Ortelius Design and Devorah Wilkenfeld
Design by Michele Laseau
Maps copyright © by Simon & Schuster, Inc.

SPECIAL SALES

Contents

List of Maps

AN INVITATION TO THE READER

In researching this book, I discovered many wonderful places—hotels, restaurants, shops and more. I'm sure you'll find others. Please tell us about them, so we can share the information with your fellow travelers in upcoming editions. If you were disappointed with a recommendation, we'd love to know that, too. Please write to:

Beth Reiber
Frommer's Hong Kong, 4th Edition
Macmillan Travel
1633 Broadway
New York, NY 10019

AN ADDITIONAL NOTE

Please be advised that travel information is subject to change at any time—and this is especially true of prices. We therefore suggest that you write or call ahead for confirmation when making your travel plans. The authors, editors, and publisher cannot be held responsible for the experiences of readers while traveling. Your safety is important to us, however, so we encourage you to stay alert and be aware of your surroundings. Keep a close eye on cameras, purses, and wallets, all favorite targets of thieves and pickpockets.

WHAT THE SYMBOLS MEAN

✪ Frommer's Favorites

Hotels, restaurants, attractions, and entertainment you should not miss.

⑤ Super-Special Values

Hotels and restaurants that offer great value for your money.

The following abbreviations are used for credit cards:

AE	American Express	EU	Eurocard
CB	Carte Blanche	JCB	Japan Credit Bank
DC	Diners Club	MC	MasterCard
DISC	Discover	V	Visa
ER	enRoute		

Introducing Hong Kong

Every time I go to Hong Kong I feel as if I've wandered onto a movie set. Perhaps I'm an incurable romantic, but when I stand at the railing of the famous Star Ferry as it glides across the harbor, ride a rickety old tram as it winds its way across Hong Kong Island, or clutch the side of the funicular as it groans its way up to Victoria Peak, I can't help but think I must have somehow landed in the middle of an epic drama where the past has melted into the present. So many images float by—wooden boats bobbing up and down in the harbor beside huge ocean liners; narrow streets and old crumbling buildings next to modern high-rises; old Chinese pushing wheelbarrows as Rolls-Royces glide by; abacuses being sold alongside pocket calculators. Certainly it's one of the most vibrant cities in the world. But that isn't all.

A British colony until 1997, Hong Kong was founded as a place to conduct business and to trade, and it has done so aggressively and successfully ever since. The world's third-largest financial center after New York and London, Hong Kong is the "Wall Street of Asia," with banking, international insurance, advertising, and publishing among its biggest concerns. Hong Kong is also the world's leading exporter of toys and garments and is one of the biggest manufacturers of watches and electronics.

But what makes Hong Kong truly unusual is its British and Chinese cultures, which exist side by side and yet have remained distinctly different. The British influence is evident everywhere in Hong Kong, from its schools to its government, from rugby to double-decker buses, from English pubs to three-piece suits. Yet though the city was molded by the British, it remains overwhelmingly Chinese, with Chinese medicine shops, street vendors, lively dim sum restaurants, old men who take their caged birds for walks in the park, and colorful festivals.

Little wonder that as a duty-free port, Hong Kong attracts about 6.3 million visitors a year, making tourism its third-largest industry. Shopping is one of the main reasons people come here, and at first glance Hong Kong does seem rather like one huge department store. But there's much more to Hong Kong than shopping. There's wining, dining, and sightseeing, and there are even isolated places to get away from it all. The more you search, the more you'll find. Before long, you, too, may find yourself swept up in the drama.

1 Frommer's Favorite Hong Kong Experiences

- **A Dim Sum Breakfast:** Nothing conveys a sense of Chinese life more vividly than a visit to a crowded, lively Cantonese restaurant where trolleys of dim sum are wheeled from customer to customer. A great way to start the day.
- **A Ride on the Star Ferry:** To reacquaint myself with the city, one of the first things I do on each return trip is to hop aboard the Star Ferry for one of the most dramatic 7-minute boat rides in the world.
- **A Tram Ride:** Take a double-decker tram ride from one end of Hong Kong Island to the other for an unparalleled view of life in the crowded colony.
- **A Trip to Victoria Peak:** Take the tram to Victoria Peak, famous for its views, followed by a 1-hour circular hike and perhaps a meal. Don't miss the nighttime view, one of the most spectacular and romantic in the world.
- **Shopping in Stanley:** Stall after stall of jeans, accessories, silk clothing, bathing suits, tennis shoes, and more makes this a shopper's paradise.
- **A Visit to the Tailor:** Nothing beats the thrill of having something custom-made to fit you perfectly.
- **Strolling on Nathan Road:** Open-fronted clothing boutiques, jewelry stores, camera shops, tailors, tourists from around the world, international cuisine, huge neon signs, and whirling traffic combine to make this boulevard Hong Kong's most famous shopping street.
- **An Excursion to Lamma:** An excursion to this outlying island will do your soul good. Start with the ferry trip, followed by a hike across the island, perhaps some swimming at a beach, and finally a meal of fresh seafood at a waterfront restaurant.
- **Aw Boon Haw Gardens:** Few things in the world are more bizarre than the "Tiger Balm Gardens" of Chinese mythological creatures, all gaily painted and some rather grotesque.
- **The Family Insight Tour:** This organized tour, offered by the Hong Kong Tourist Association, is a fascinating look at local life, with a visit to a family home in one of Hong Kong's many government-subsidized housing estates.
- **A Walking Tour of the Western District:** Produce, bolts of cloth, snakes, ginseng, Chinese herbs and medicines, a historic temple, and antiques are just some of the things you'll see while strolling through one of Hong Kong's fascinating neighborhoods.
- **Browsing Antique Shops on Hollywood Road:** Whether you have several thousand dollars to spend on Ming dynasty heirlooms or just a couple of bucks for a snuff bottle, there's something for everyone in the many antique shops lining this famous Hong Kong Island road and from outdoor vendor stalls on nearby Cat Street. A sightseeing bonus is Man Mo Temple, Hong Kong's oldest temple, on Hollywood Road.
- **The Horse Races:** Join thousands of spectators at Hong Kong's favorite sporting event between September and May.
- **Dining with a View:** Enjoy Chinese or continental cuisine at one of Hong Kong's many restaurants that offer spectacular views of either Kowloon (with its glowing neon lights) or Hong Kong Island (with its skyscrapers and Victoria Peak).
- **Happy Hour at a British Pub:** End a busy day of sightseeing and shopping by rubbing elbows with Hong Kong's working population as they take advantage of happy hour prices in British pubs throughout the city.

- **Temple Street Night Market:** Highlights include shopping for casual clothing, music cassettes, toys, and accessories; enjoying a meal at a *dai pai dong* (roadside food stall); and watching amateur street musicians.

2 A Look at the Past

Stone, bronze, and iron artifacts indicate that Hong Kong Island has been inhabited since ancient times. More than 100 Neolithic and Bronze Age sites have been identified throughout the colony.

Hong Kong's modern history, however, begins a mere 150 years ago, under conditions that were less than honorable. During the 1800s the British were extremely eager to obtain Chinese silk and tea. The Chinese, however, were not interested in anything the British offered for trade. What's more, the Chinese forbade the British to enter their kingdom, with the exception of a small trading depot in Canton.

But then the British hit upon a commodity that proved irresistible to the Chinese: opium. This powerful drug enslaved everyone from poor peasants to the nobility, and before long the country was being drained of silver traded to support a drug habit. The Chinese emperor, fearful of the damage being wreaked on society and alarmed by his country's loss of silver, declared a ban on opium imports and confiscated the British opium stockpiles in Canton. The British responded by declaring war and then winning the struggle. As a result of this first Opium War, waged in 1841, China was forced to cede Hong Kong Island in perpetuity to the British in a treaty it never recognized.

The tip of Kowloon Peninsula and Stonecutters Island were added to the colony in 1860. In 1898, after having fought the second Opium War to force China to open its doors to trade, Britain decided it needed more land for defense and dictated a lease for the New Territories, including 235 outlying islands, for 99 years, until 1997.

When the British moved in to occupy Hong Kong Island in 1841, the prospects for developing a thriving port did not look rosy. Although it had a deep and protected harbor, no one, including the Chinese, was much interested in the island, and many in the British government considered its acquisition an embarrassing mistake. Lord Palmerston, Queen Victoria's foreign secretary, dismissed Hong Kong as a "barren island with

Dateline

- **700 B.C.** Seafaring people of Malay-Oceanic stock set up floating communities in Hong Kong.
- **960–1500s** Pirates roam the seas around Hong Kong.
- **1514** Portuguese traders establish a base on Hong Kong.
- **1841** Hong Kong is granted to the British in perpetuity as an outcome of the first Opium War.
- **1846** Hong Kong's population is 24,000. First horse races held at Happy Valley.
- **1860** Kowloon Peninsula and Stonecutters Island are added to the colony. Population reaches 94,000.
- **1865** Hongkong and Shanghai Bank founded.
- **1888** The Victoria Peak tram is completed, reducing the journey to the peak from 3 hours to 8 minutes.
- **1898** The New Territories are leased to Britain for 99 years.
- **1900** Hong Kong's population is 263,000.
- **1910** The Kowloon Railway is completed, linking Hong Kong with China.
- **1911** The Manchu dynasty is overthrown; refugees flood into Hong Kong.
- **1938** 500,000 Chinese refugees flee into Hong Kong.
- **1941** Japanese forces occupy Hong Kong.

continues

- 1946 The British resume control of Hong Kong following World War II.
- 1949 Chinese–Hong Kong border closed by Communists.
- 1950 Mass influx of refugees following the fall of Shanghai to the Communists. Population of Hong Kong reaches 2 million.
- 1953 Public housing program begins.
- 1967 The Cultural Revolution in China leads to riots of protest in Hong Kong and pro-Communist riots.
- 1972 First cross-harbor tunnel opens.
- 1978 Vietnamese refugees pour into Hong Kong at a rate of 600 a day.
- 1979 Hong Kong's Mass Transit Railway subway system opens.
- 1984 China and Britain sign an agreement on the future of Hong Kong after 1997, when Hong Kong will revert back to mainland Chinese rule.
- 1989 Student prodemocracy uprisings and the subsequent massacre at Tiananmen Square in Beijing send shock waves through Hong Kong.
- 1997 Britain transfers Hong Kong to Communist China, in an agreement that allows Hong Kong to retain many of its freedoms for at least 50 years.

hardly a house upon it." What's more, no sooner had the island been settled than a typhoon tore through the settlement. Repairs were demolished only five days later by another tropical storm. Fever and fire followed, and the weather grew so oppressive and humid that the colony seemed to be enveloped in a giant steam bath.

Even though the number of headstones in the hillside cemetery multiplied, so did the number of the living. By 1846 the population had reached an astonishing 24,000. By the turn of the century the number had swelled to 300,000. British families lived along the waterfront and called it Victoria (now the Central District), slowly moving up toward the cooler temperatures of Victoria Peak. The Chinese occupied a shantytown farther west, now called the Western District.

Most of the newcomers to Hong Kong were mainland Chinese, who arrived with the shirts on their backs and nothing to lose. Every turmoil that sent a shudder through China—famine, flood, or civil war—flung a new wave of farmers, merchants, peasants, coolies, and entrepreneurs into Hong Kong. Everyone's dream was to make a fortune; it was just a matter of timing and good *joss* (luck). The Chinese philosophy of hard work and good fortune found fertile ground in the laissez-faire atmosphere of the colony.

Hong Kong's growth in this century has been no less astonishing, in terms of both trade and population. In 1911 the overthrow of the Manchu dynasty in China sent a flood of refugees into Hong Kong, followed in 1938 by an additional 500,000 immigrants. Another mass influx of Chinese refugees arrived after the fall of Shanghai to the Communists in 1950. From this last wave of immigrants, including many Shanghai industrialists, emerged the beginnings of Hong Kong's now-famous textile industry. By 1956 Hong Kong's population stood at 2.5 million.

In 1978 Vietnamese refugees started pouring into Hong Kong at the rate of 600 a day, and a year later more than 550,000 Vietnamese were living in camps around the colony. Finding itself unable to support the strain of additional refugees, Hong Kong initiated a policy whereby illegal immigrants from China (with the exception of political refugees) were immediately returned, and the Vietnamese were sent elsewhere as soon as possible. However, with thousands of Vietnamese continuing to pour into Hong Kong (in 1989 alone, 50,000 Vietnamese boat people arrived there), nowhere else to send them, and thousands more still living in dismal camps, Hong Kong began in 1995 to offer monetary incentives to those who were willing to return voluntarily to their homeland. Subsequent forced evacuations have led to riots and protests from camp inmates and to criticism from around the world. Refugees remain one of Hong Kong's most pressing problems, since few believe Communist China will deal with them more charitably after the 1997 takeover.

Although Hong Kong has long existed as a British Crown Colony administered by a governor appointed by the queen, Britain will transfer all of Hong Kong to Chinese Communist rule on June 30, 1997. According to the Sino-British Agreement of 1984, China guarantees that it will preserve Hong Kong's capitalist lifestyle and social system for at least 50 years after 1997. It will become a "Special Administrative Region," largely self-governing, and its people will retain their property, freedom of speech, and the right to travel in and out.

That's the agreement, but whether Hong Kong will nevertheless undergo a drastic change under Communist China's hegemony is a subject of hot debate in the Crown Colony, especially in light of the brutal manner in which the Chinese authorities quashed the student uprising in 1989. China's response to the rebellion sent shock waves through Hong Kong and led to rounds of angry protest. Nearly half of Hong Kong's Chinese are refugees from the mainland; as one Hong Kong Chinese told me, his family had fled China to escape Communist rule, so why should he remain after 1997? Hong Kong residents were not consulted about their future or the agreement, but, then, this is a colony. In a move that has angered Communist China, Hong Kong Chinese have been granted more political autonomy during the past couple years than in all of the preceding 150 years; some see this as a last-ditch effort to prepare Hong Kong for self rule.

Still, many Chinese with the financial means to emigrate have already done so or are looking for viable new homes. Many of Hong Kong's expatriate community have left as well.

The vast majority of Chinese, however, intend to stay. They hope that China will recognize how much it has to gain by keeping Hong Kong as it is. Actually, Hong Kong has had a strong relationship with China for a long time, and even now depends on the mainland for much of its food and water. China has already invested quite a lot in Hong Kong, with hotels, banks, and department stores. As one of Asia's most important financial and manufacturing centers, capitalist Hong Kong has been and could continue to be quite important to the People's Republic.

3 Hong Kong Today

The Hong Kong I am writing about now is not the same city that existed just a few short years ago and is most definitely not the Hong Kong you'll probably experience. Changes are occurring at a dizzying pace, with relatively new buildings being torn down to make way for even newer shiny skyscrapers, whole neighborhoods being obliterated in the name of progress, reclaimed land being taken from an ever-shrinking harbor, and traditional villages being replaced with satellite towns. Hong Kong's city skyline has surged upward and outward so dramatically since my first visit in 1983, it sometimes seems like decades rather than a year or two must have elapsed each time I see it anew. Change is commonplace, and yet it's hard for me not to lament the loss of familiar things that suddenly vanished; it's harder still not to brood over what's likely to come.

But Hong Kong, founded by the narcotics trade and created to make money, has always been like this. Buildings have always been torn down to make way for the new, land reclamation has been ongoing almost from the beginning, and the population has exploded from a few thousand to more than 6 million in a mere 150 years. There

Hong Kong Region

PEOPLE'S REPUBLIC OF CHINA

Guangdong Province

Lo Wu

Deep Bay

Sheung Shui

Lau Fau Shan

Kam Tin

Miu Fat
Monastery

NEW TERRITORIES

Tuen Mun

Tsue
Wan

Tsing Yi

Discovery Bay

PENG CHAU IS.

LANTAU ISLAND

Victoria Pea

Tai O

Po Lin
Monastery

Pokfula

Aberdeen Harbo

Silver Mine Bay

East Lamma Cha

Cheung Sha

Yung
Shue
Wan

Sok Kwu Wan

West Lamma Channel

CHEUNG CHAU IS.

LAMMA IS.

7 km
4.3 mi

N

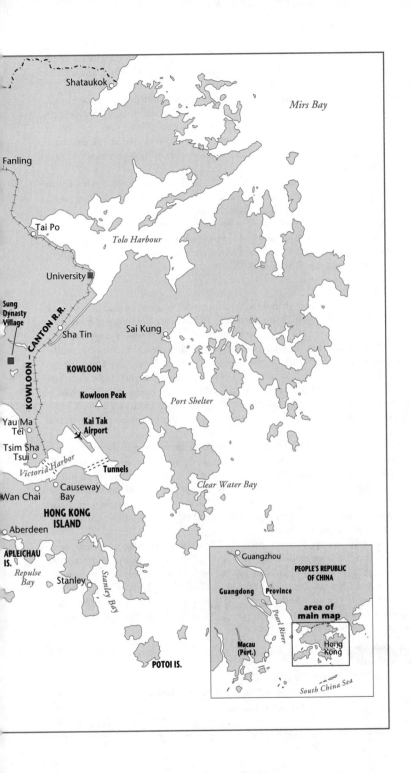

Shataukok

Mirs Bay

Fanling

Tai Po

Tolo Harbour

University

Sung
Dynasty
Village

Sha Tin

Sai Kung

KOWLOON

Kowloon Peak

Port Shelter

Kai Tak
Airport

Yau Ma
Tei

Tsim Sha
Tsui

Tunnels

Victoria Harbor

Clear Water Bay

Wan Chai

Causeway
Bay

HONG KONG
ISLAND

Aberdeen

APLEICHAU
IS.

Repulse
Bay

Stanley

Stanley Bay

POTOI IS.

Guangzhou

PEOPLE'S REPUBLIC
OF CHINA

Guangdong   Province

area of
main map

Pearl River

Macau
(Port.)

Hong
Kong

South China Sea

KOWLOON – CANTON R.R.

are strikingly few monuments or statues to the city's past. Even the city's original settlement, once called Victoria but later renamed (less sentimentally) the Central District, long ago lost most of its colonial-age buildings.

Of course, change is not unique to Hong Kong (even in this part of the world), but the fact that Hong Kong continues its frenzied pace as though there were no tomorrow is especially remarkable. A new airport is due to open soon, new hotels anticipate more tourism, and the cost of real estate has skyrocketed. An uncertain future lies heavily on everyone's mind, but life continues at its same frenetic pace in this teeming, buzzing metropolis.

Despite Hong Kong's modern architecture, the first-time visitor is more apt to notice Hong Kong's Chinese aspects than its Western elements. Ducks hanging by their necks in restaurant windows, bamboo scaffolding, herb medicinal shops, streetside markets, sidewalk vendors, Chinese characters on huge neon signs, wooden fishing boats, shrines to the kitchen god, fortune-tellers, temples, laundry fluttering from bamboo poles, dim sum trolleys, and the clicking of mahjongg all conspire to create an atmosphere overwhelmingly Chinese.

THE PEOPLE

With a population of more than 6 million, Hong Kong is one of the most densely populated areas in the world. Some 98% of its residents are Chinese, and more than half of them were born in Hong Kong. But the Chinese themselves are a diverse people and they hail from different parts of China. Most are Cantonese from southern China—hence, Cantonese is one of the two official languages of the colony. Other Chinese include the Hakka (whose women are easily recognizable by their hats with a black fringe) and the Tanka, the majority of Hong Kong's boat population. Hong Kong's many Chinese restaurants specializing in Szechuan, Chiu Chow, Pekinese, Shanghainese, and other regional foods are testaments of the city's diversity.

The Chinese are by nature a very hardworking, pragmatic people. There are many stories of refugees who arrived with nothing in their pockets, set up a small sidewalk stall, worked diligently until they had their own store, and then expanded it into a modest chain. In a land with virtually no raw materials, the people themselves have proved to be Hong Kong's greatest asset, geniuses at transforming imported raw goods into the electrical equipment, clothing, watches, toys, and other products that have made Hong Kong famous.

Because of its dense population and limited land space, Hong Kong has long been saddled with acute housing deficiencies. The 1992 *Guinness Book of World Records* listed it as the world's most populous colony, with 14,482 people per square mile. About 20 years ago an area of Hong Kong called Mong Kok, in northwestern Kowloon, registered an astounding 652,910 people per square mile. One house designed for 12 people had 459 living in it, including 104 people who shared one room and 4 people who lived on the roof.

Impressions

A barren Island with hardly a House upon it.
—Lord Palmerston, Letter to Sir Charles Elliot, April 21, 1841
A borrowed place living on borrowed time.
—Anonymous, *The Times,* March 5, 1981

Since 1953, when a huge fire left more than 50,000 squatters homeless, Hong Kong has pursued one of the world's most ambitious housing projects, with the aim of providing every Hong Kong family with a home of its own. By 1993, half of Hong Kong's population lived in government-subsidized public housing, a higher proportion than anywhere else in the world.

Most public housing is in the New Territories, in a forest of high-rises that leaves foreign visitors aghast. Each apartment building is approximately 30 stories tall, containing about 1,000 apartments and 3,000 to 4,000 residents. Seven or eight apartment buildings comprise an estate, which is like a small town with its own name, shopping center, recreational and sports facilities, playgrounds, schools, and social services. Each apartment is indescribably small by Western standards—approximately 250 square feet; it consists of a combination living room/bedroom, a kitchen nook, and bathroom, and is typically shared by a couple with one or two children. Each apartment has a single window. But as cramped, unimaginative, and sterile as these housing projects may seem, they're a vast improvement over the way much of the population used to live. They also account for most of Hong Kong's construction growth in the past two decades.

ARCHITECTURE

Most of Hong Kong is what you see when your plane lands at the airport—chrome-and-glass skyscrapers, huge housing projects, miles of glowing neon signs heralding countless open-fronted shops.

But Hong Kong was inhabited long before the British arrived, and some of the precolonial architecture still survives. Many rural villages boast buildings and temples with fine carpentry and wood carving, examples of centuries-old Chinese craftsmanship.

Especially fascinating are the walled villages in the New Territories, some of which have been meticulously restored and turned into museums of traditional lifestyles. These villages were built in the 14th through 17th centuries to protect clans from roving bandits, invaders, and even wild tigers.

Also surviving are some of Hong Kong's temples. One of the oldest is a Tin Hau temple in Causeway Bay, dedicated to the seafarers' patron goddess. Hong Kong's most famous temple, however, is Man Mo, built in the 1840s and dedicated to the gods of literature and war.

Some colonial architecture also remains. One of Hong Kong's most familiar landmarks is the clock tower next to the Star Ferry terminus at Tsim Sha Tsui; it is all that remains of the old railway station that once linked the colony with China and beyond. On the Hong Kong Island side, the former Supreme Court in Central features Greco-Victorian columns and Chinese wood beam eaves. Today it houses the Legislative Council chamber.

For the most part, however, Hong Kong is a jumble of skyscrapers. Construction has been going on at such a frenzied pace that if you haven't been here in 20 years, or even 10, you probably won't recognize the skylines of Central and Wan Chai. Among the most dramatic new buildings are the 78-story Central Plaza, located near the Wan Chai waterfront and boasting an art deco style with eye-catching nighttime lighting; the Bank of China Tower by I. M. Pei; and the Hongkong and Shanghai Bank, designed by British architect Norman Foster and featuring entire floors suspended from steel masts and a 160-foot-tall sun scoop on the roof that uses 480 mirrors to reflect sunlight down into the bank's atrium and public plaza.

Even though Hong Kong's structures are Western, they were built using bamboo scaffolding and constructed according to ancient Chinese beliefs, especially the Taoist principle of *fung shui* (literally "wind-water"), in which harmony is achieved with the spirits of nature. Virtually every Hong Kong Chinese believes that before a house or building can be erected, a tree chopped down, or a boulder moved, a geomancer must be called in to make certain that the spirits inhabiting the place are not disturbed. The geomancer determines the alignment of walls, doors, desks, and even beds, so as not to provoke the anger of the spirits residing there.

Since facing the water is considered good fung shui, when the Regent Hotel was constructed it incorporated a huge glass window overlooking the harbor. While providing people with a great view of the harbor, the glass window also has another much more important function—it allows the dragons that inhabit Kowloon to pass through for their morning bath in Victoria Harbour. Dragons are unpredictable creatures, and who knows what might have happened if they had been thwarted from their favorite path to the harbor due to construction of a new building.

The next best thing, if you can't look out over water, is to bring the water inside, which is why many offices, shops, and restaurants have aquariums. Another way to guard against evil influences is to hang a small, eight-sided mirror outside your window. Other Chinese touches are incorporated in the modern architecture—the Hongkong and Shanghai Bank, for example, is guarded by a pair of bronze lions.

CULTURAL LIFE

If you want to see Hong Kong's Chinese cultural life, simply step outside. Much of Hong Kong's drama is played in its streets, whether it's amateur Chinese opera singers at the famous Temple Street Night Market, a fortune-teller who has set up a chair and table at the side of the road, or a sidewalk calligrapher who will write letters for those who can't. Virtually everything the Chinese consider vital still thrives in Hong Kong, including ancient religious beliefs, superstitions, wedding customs, and festivals.

The first sign that Hong Kong's cultural life is not confined to its stages and concert halls can be seen if you get up early and stroll through a city park, where you'll see Hong Kong Chinese practicing *tai chi chuan* (Chinese shadowboxing), which looks like dance in slow motion. Originally a martial art developed about 1,000 years ago, tai chi chuan today is a form of exercise designed to restore harmony in the body through 200 individual movements designed to use every muscle in the body. Good places to observe the art include Kowloon Park in Tsim Sha Tsui, as well as Victoria Park and the Zoological and Botanical Gardens on Hong Kong Island.

Hong Kong's many festivals feature parades, dances, and observances of local customs. Lion dances, for example, may be performed to the accompaniment of drums, while in the evenings there may be puppet shows or Chinese opera performances.

Of the various Chinese performing arts, Chinese opera is the most popular and widely loved. Dating back to the Mongol period, it has always appealed to both the ruling class and the masses. Virtue, corruption, violence, and lust are common themes, and performances feature elaborate costumes and makeup, haunting atonal orchestrations, and crashing cymbals. The actor-singers train for years to achieve the high-pitched and shrill falsettos that characterize Chinese opera, and the costumes signify specific stage personalities. Yellow is reserved for emperors, while purple is the color worn by barbarians. Unlike Western performances, Chinese operas are noisy affairs, with families coming and going during long performances, chatting with friends, and eating.

In Hong Kong you can also see performances of Western classical music, jazz, pop concerts, ballet, modern dance, and theater.

CHINESE MEDICINE

For most minor ailments, the Chinese are more likely to pay a visit to their neighborhood medicine store than see a doctor. Most traditional medicine stores cater solely to the practice of Chinese herbal medicine, with some cures dating back 2,000 years. The medicinal stock, however, includes much more than roots and plants—take a look inside one of Hong Kong's many medicinal shops and you'll find a bewildering array of jars and drawers containing everything from ginseng and deer's horn to fossilized bones and animal teeth. Deer's horn is said to be effective against fever; bones, teeth, and seashells are used as tranquilizers and cures for insomnia. In prescribing treatment, herbalists take into account the patient's overall mental and physical well-being, in the belief that disease and illness are caused not by viruses but by an imbalance in bodily forces. In contrast to Western medicine, treatment is often preventive rather than remedial.

Acupuncture is also alive and well in Hong Kong, with approximately 3,000 acupuncturists offering their services. With a history that goes back 4,000 years, acupuncture is based on 365 pressure points, which in turn act upon certain organs; slender stainless steel needles are used, which vary in length from half an inch to 10 inches. Most acupuncturists also use moxa (dried mugwort)—a slow-burning herb that applies gentle heat.

RELIGION, MYTH & FOLKLORE

Most Hong Kong Chinese worship both Buddhist and Taoist deities, something they do not find at all incongruous. They also worship their family ancestors. There are ancestral altars in homes, and certain days are set aside for visiting ancestral graves. Many temples have large tablet halls, where Hong Kong families can worship the memorialized photographs of their dead. There are about 360 temples scattered throughout Hong Kong; some embody a mixture of both Buddhist and Taoist principles.

Whereas Buddhism is concerned with the afterlife, Taoism is a folk faith whose devotees believe in luck and in currying its favor. Tao, essentially, is the way of the universe, the spirit of all things, and cannot be perceived. However, Taoist gods must be worshipped and Taoist spirits appeased. Most popular is Tin Hau, goddess of the sea and protectress of fishermen. Hong Kong has at least 24 temples that were erected in her honor. But each profession or trade has its own god—ironically, policemen and gangsters have the same one.

If you look for them, you'll find shrines dedicated to the earth god, Tou Ti, at the entrance to almost every store or restaurant in Hong Kong. They're usually below knee level, so that everyone pays homage upon entering and departing. Restaurants also have shrines dedicated to the kitchen god, Kwan Kung, to protect workers from knives and other sharp objects.

Although not a religion as such, another guiding principle in Chinese thought is Confucianism. Confucius, who lived in the 5th century B.C., devised a strict set of rules designed to create the perfect human being. Kindness, selflessness, obedience, and courtesy were preached, with carefully prescribed manners for how people should interact with one another. Since the masses were largely illiterate, Confucius communicated by means of easy-to-remember proverbs.

But despite the fact that many Hong Kong Chinese are both Buddhist and Taoist, they are not a particularly religious people in the Western sense of the word. They are too practical for that, too busy earning money. There is no special day for worship, so devotees simply visit a temple whenever they want to pay their respects or feel the need for spiritual guidance. Otherwise, religion in Hong Kong plays a subtle role and is evident more in philosophy and action than in pious ceremony. To the Chinese, religion is a way of life and thus affects everyday living.

Almost every home has a small shrine, where lighted joss sticks are thought to bring good luck. In New Year celebrations, door gods are placed on the front door for good luck, and all lights are switched on to discourage monster spirits. On New Year's Day, homes are not swept for fear of whisking away good luck. And during a full moon or major festival, housewives will often set fire to paper creations of homes, cars, or fake money to bring good luck.

But since no one can ever have too much good luck, superstitions abound in Hong Kong. Certain numbers, for example, have connotations. The most auspicious number is 8, because its pronunciation *(baht)* is similar to the word for wealth *(faht)*. Likewise, the most inauspicious number is 4, since it sounds almost exactly like the Chinese word for death. Thirteen is also an unlucky number, so many Hong Kong buildings skip it when numbering their floors.

The Chinese Almanac is another source for finding out which are the most auspicious days for getting married, when to visit the hairdresser, and information on fortune-telling, palmistry, and dates for various festivals held during the lunar year. Its origins date back to 2200 B.C.

To be on the safe side, Hong Kong Chinese will also visit fortune-tellers. Some read palms, while others study facial features, consult astrological birth charts, or let a little bird select a fortune card from a deck.

4 Food & Drink

MEALS & DINING CUSTOMS

Traditionally speaking, Chinese restaurants tend to be noisy and crowded affairs, the patrons much more interested in food than in decor. They can range from simple diners where the only adornment is likely to be Formica-topped tables, to very elaborate affairs with Chinese lanterns, splashes of red and gold, and painted screens. During the past decade, there has been an explosion of a new kind of Chinese restaurant—trendy, chic, and minimalist, many in art deco style.

In any case, Chinese restaurants are places for social gatherings; since Hong Kong apartments are usually too small to entertain friends and family, the whole gang simply heads for their favorite restaurant.

Thus the Chinese usually dine in large groups; the basic rule is to order one dish per person, plus one more, with all dishes placed in the center of the table and shared by everyone. The more people in your party, therefore, the more dishes ordered and the more fun you'll have. Dishes usually come in two or three different sizes, so ask your waiter which size is sufficient for your group.

You shouldn't have any problem ordering, because most Chinese restaurants have English menus. If you want to be correct about it, a well-balanced meal should contain the five basic tastes of Chinese cuisine—acid, hot, bitter, sweet, and salty. The texture should vary as well, ranging from crisp and tender to dry and saucy. The proper order is to begin with a cold dish, followed by dishes of fish or seafood, meat (pork, beef, or poultry), vegetables, soup, and noodles or rice. Some dishes are steamed, while others may be fried, boiled, or roasted. Many of the dishes are accompanied by sauces, the most common being soy sauce, chili sauce, and hot mustard.

The beginning of your meal is heralded by a round of hot towels, a wonderful custom you'll soon grow addicted to and wish would be adopted by restaurants in the United States. Your eating utensils, of course, will be chopsticks, which have been around for 3,000 years and are perfect for picking up bite-size morsels. If you're eating rice, pick up the bowl and scoop the rice directly into your mouth with your chopsticks.

Keep in mind, however, that there are several superstitions associated with chopsticks. If, for example, you find an uneven pair at your table setting, it means you are going to miss a boat, plane, or train. Dropping chopsticks means you will have bad luck; laying them across each other is also considered a bad omen, except in dim sum restaurants where your waiter may cross them to show that your bill has been settled. You can do the same to signal the waiter that you've finished your meal and wish to pay the bill.

As for dining etiquette, it's considered perfectly acceptable to slurp soup, since this indicates an appreciation of the food and also helps cool the soup so it doesn't burn the tongue. Toothpicks are also acceptable for use at the table during and after meals—they can even be used to spear foods too slippery or elusive for chopsticks, such as button mushrooms and jellyfish slices. As in most Asian countries, good manners call for covering your mouth with one hand while you dislodge food particles from your teeth.

A final custom you may see in Chinese restaurants is that of finger tapping—customers often tap three fingers on the table as a sign of thanks to the person pouring the tea.

THE CUISINE

Chinese cooking has evolved over the course of several thousand years, dictated often by a population too numerous to feed. The prospect of famine meant that nothing should be wasted, and the scarcity of fuel meant that food should be cooked as economically as possible; thus, it was chopped into small pieces and quickly stir-fried. Food needed to be as fresh as possible to avoid spoiling. Among the many regional Chinese cuisines, the most common ones found in Hong Kong are from Canton, Beijing (or Peking), Shanghai, Sichuan (Szechuan), and Swatow (Chiu Chow).

Of course, there are many other dishes and styles of cuisine besides those outlined below. It's said that the Chinese will eat anything that swims, flies, or crawls; although that may not be entirely true, if you're adventurous enough you may want to try such delicacies as snake soup, pig's brain, bird's-nest soup (derived from the saliva of swallows), Shanghai freshwater hairy crabs (available only in autumn), tiny rice birds that are roasted and eaten whole, or eel heads simmered with Chinese herbs. One of the more common—albeit strange—items found on most Chinese menus is *béche-de-mer*, which translates as sea cucumber but which is actually nothing more than a sea slug.

If you want to know more about the great variety of Chinese food available, there's an excellent booklet called "The Official Dining and Entertainment Guide," available free at Hong Kong Tourist Association (HKTA) offices.

CANTONESE FOOD   The majority of Chinese restaurants in Hong Kong are Cantonese; this is not surprising since most Hong Kong Chinese are originally from Canton. It's also the most common style of Chinese cooking around the world and probably the one with which you're most familiar. Among Chinese, Cantonese cuisine is considered the finest, and many Chinese emperors employed Cantonese chefs in their kitchens.

Cantonese food, which is either steamed or stir-fried, is known for its fresh, delicate flavors. Little oil and few spices are used so that the natural flavors of the various ingredients prevail, and the Cantonese are sticklers for freshness (traditionalists may shop twice a day at the market). If you're concerned about cholesterol, Cantonese food is preferable. On the other hand, those with active taste buds may find it rather bland.

Since the Cantonese eat so much seafood, your best choice in a Cantonese restaurant is fish. I love steamed whole fish prepared with fresh ginger and spring onions, but equally good are slices of garoupa (a local fish), pomfret, red mullet, sole, and bream. It's considered bad luck to turn a fish over on your plate (it represents a boat capsizing), so the proper thing to do is to eat the top part of the fish, lift the bone in the air and then extract the bottom layer of meat with your chopsticks. Other popular seafood choices include shrimp and prawns, abalone, squid, scallops, crab, and sea cucumber. Shark's-fin soup is an expensive delicacy.

Other Cantonese specialties include roast goose, duck, and pigeon; pan-fried lemon chicken; stir-fried minced quail and bamboo shoots rolled in lettuce and eaten with the fingers; congee (thick rice porridge); and sweet-and-sour pork.

Another popular Cantonese dish is *dim sum,* which means "light snack" but whose Chinese characters literally translate as "to touch the heart." Dating back to the 10th century, dim sum is eaten for breakfast and lunch and with afternoon tea. It consists primarily of finely chopped meat, seafood, and vegetables wrapped in thin dough and then either steamed, fried, boiled, or braised. Dim sum can range from steamed dumplings to meatballs, fried spring rolls, and spareribs.

Many Cantonese restaurants offer dim sum from about 7:30am until 4pm, traditionally served from trolleys wheeled between the tables but nowadays just as often available from a written menu. The trolleys are piled high with steaming bamboo baskets, so ask the server to let you peek inside. If you like what you see, simply nod your head. There are nearly 100 different kinds of dim sum, but some of my favorites are *shiu mai* (steamed minced pork and shrimp dumplings), *har gau* (steamed shrimp dumplings), *au yuk* (steamed minced beef balls), *fun gwor* (steamed rice-flour dumplings filled with pork, shrimp, and bamboo shoots), and *tsuen guen* (deep-fried spring rolls filled with shredded pork, chicken, mushrooms, bamboo shoots, and bean sprouts). A serving of dim sum usually consists of two to four pieces on a plate and averages about HK$20 to HK$35 ($2.60 to $4.55) per plate. Your bill is calculated at the end of the meal by the number of plates on your table or by a card stamped each time you order a dish.

Since I can usually manage only two or three dishes, dim sum is one of the cheapest meals I eat in Hong Kong. I often have it for breakfast with lots of tea. But it's more than just the price that draws me to traditional dim sum restaurants—they are noisy, chaotic, and the perfect place to read a newspaper or gossip. No one should go to Hong Kong without visiting a dim sum restaurant at least once.

PEKINESE FOOD   Many Pekinese dishes originated in the imperial courts of the emperors and empresses and were served at elaborate banquets. This theatrical flamboyance is still evident today in the making of Pekinese noodles and the smashing of the clay around "beggar's chicken." Because of its northern source, the food of Peking (or Beijing) tends to be rather substantial (to keep the body warm), and it is richer than Cantonese food. Liberal amounts of peppers, garlic, ginger, leeks, and coriander are used. Noodles and dumplings are more common than rice, and roasting is the preferred method of cooking.

Most famous among Peking-style dishes is Peking duck (or Beijing duck), but unfortunately a minimum of six persons is usually required for this elaborate dish. The most prized part is the crisp skin, which comes from air-drying the bird and then coating it with a mixture of syrup and soy sauce before roasting. It's served by wrapping the crisp skin and meat in thin pancakes together with spring onion, radish, and sweet plum sauce.

Another popular dish prepared with fanfare is beggar's chicken: a whole chicken is stuffed with mushrooms, pickled Chinese cabbage, herbs, and onions, wrapped in lotus leaves, sealed in clay, and then baked all day. The guest of honor usually breaks open the hard clay with a mallet, revealing a tender feast more fit for a king than a beggar.

For do-it-yourself dining, try the Mongolian hot pot, where diners gather around a common pot in a scene reminiscent of campfires on the Mongolian steppes. One version calls for wafer-thin slices of meat, usually mutton, to be dipped in a clear stock and then eaten with a spicy sauce. Another variety calls for a sizzling griddle, over which thin-sliced meat, cabbage, bean sprouts, onions, and other vegetables are barbecued in a matter of seconds.

SHANGHAINESE FOOD   A big, bustling city, Shanghai does not technically have a cuisine of its own. Rather, it incorporates the food of several surrounding regions and cities, making it the most diverse cuisine in China. Because of the cold winters in Shanghai, its food is heavier, richer, sweeter, and oilier than Cantonese or Pekinese food. In addition, because of hot summers which can spoil food quickly, specialties include pickled or preserved vegetables, fish, shrimp, and mushrooms. Some dishes are rather heavy on the garlic, and portions tend to be enormous. The dishes are often stewed, braised, or fried.

The most popular Shanghainese dish in Hong Kong is freshwater hairy crab, flown in from Shanghai in autumn, steamed, and eaten with the hands. Other Shanghainese dishes include "yellow fish," braised eel with huge chunks of garlic, "drunken chicken" (chicken marinated in Chinese wine), sautéed shrimp in spicy tomato sauce over crispy rice, and sautéed shredded beef and green pepper. As for the famous hundred-year-old egg, it's actually only several months old, with a limey, pickled-ginger taste. Breads, noodles, and dumplings are favored over rice.

SZECHUAN FOOD   This is my favorite Chinese cuisine because it's the spiciest, hottest, and most fiery style of cooking. The fact that its spiciness recalls Thailand, India, and Malaysia is no coincidence, since this huge province (also called Sichuan) shares a border with Burma and Tibet.

The culprit is the Szechuan chili, fried to increase its explosiveness. Seasoning also includes chili-bean paste, peppercorns, garlic, ginger, coriander, and other spices. Foods are simmered and smoked rather than stir-fried. The most famous Szechuan dish is smoked duck, which is seasoned with peppercorns, ginger, cinnamon, orange peel, and coriander; marinated in rice wine; then steamed; and then smoked over a charcoal fire of camphor wood and tea leaves.

Other specialties include pan-fried prawns in spicy sauce, sour-and-peppery soup, sautéed diced chicken in chili-bean sauce, and dry-fried spicy string beans. Most Szechuan menus indicate which dishes are hot.

CHIU CHOW FOOD   A few years ago Szechuan restaurants were opening in droves, but Chiu Chow restaurants are the new trend. The name refers to the people, dialect, and food of the Swatow area in southeastern Canton. Chiu Chow chefs pride themselves on their talents for vegetable carvings—those incredible birds, flowers, and other adornments that are a part of every Chiu Chow banquet.

Influenced by Cantonese cooking, Chiu Chow food is rich in protein, light, and tasty; sauces are liberally applied. A meal begins with a cup of *kwun yum* tea, popularly called Iron Buddha and probably the world's strongest and most bitter tea. It's supposed to cleanse the system and stimulate the taste buds. Drink some of this stuff and you'll be humming for hours.

Two very expensive Chiu Chow delicacies are shark's fin and birds' nests. Other favorites include steamed lobster, deep-fried shrimp balls, sautéed slices of whelk, fried goose blood, goose doused in soy sauce, stuffed eel wrapped in pickled cabbage, and crispy fried *chuenjew* leaves, which literally melt in the mouth.

A Word of Warning: You're safe eating anywhere in Hong Kong, even at roadside food stalls, but don't eat local oysters—there have been too many instances of oyster poisoning. Eat oysters only if they're imported from, say, Australia. The good restaurants will clearly stipulate on the menu that their oysters are imported.

Watch your reaction to monosodium glutamate (MSG), which is used to enhance the flavor in Chinese cooking. Some people react strongly to this salt, reporting bouts of nausea, headaches, and a bloated feeling. Fortunately, in the past couple of years there has been a growing awareness in Hong Kong of the detrimental side effects of MSG; most Chinese upper- and medium-range restaurants, especially those in hotels, have stopped using it altogether.

DRINKS

Tea is often provided whether or not you ask for it, sometimes at a small charge. Grown in China for more than 2,000 years, tea is believed to help clear the palate and aid digestion. There are three main types: green or unfermented tea; black *bo lay* fermented tea (the most popular in Hong Kong); and *oolong*, or semifermented tea. These three teas can be further subdivided into a wide variety of specific types, with taste varying according to the region, climate, and soil. At any rate, if you want more tea at a restaurant, simply cock the lid of the teapot half open and someone will come around to refill it.

If you want something a bit stronger than tea, there are **Chinese wines,** though they aren't really wines in the Western sense of the word. Rather, they are spirits distilled from rice, millet, and other grains, as well as from herbs and flowers. Popular Chinese wines include *siu hing*, a mild rice wine that resembles a medium-dry sherry, goes well with all kinds of Chinese food, and is best served warm; *go leung* and *mao toi*—fiery drinks made from millet with a 70% alcohol content; and *ng ka pay*, a sweet herbal wine favored for its medicinal properties, especially against rheumatism.

As for **beer,** there's Tsingtao from mainland China, first brewed years ago by Germans and made from sparkling mineral water. San Miguel is also very popular. One thing to keep in mind, however, is that excess drinking is frowned upon by the Chinese, who often don't drink anything stronger than tea in restaurants. In fact, one waiter told me that Westerners spend much more in restaurants than Chinese simply because Westerners drink alcoholic beverages.

5 Recommended Books & Films

BOOKS   If you want to read something about Hong Kong before setting out on your trip, I recommend *Fragrant Harbour: A Short History of Hong Kong* (Greenwood, 1977) by G. B. Endacott and A. Hinton, which gives a thorough account of the colony's history from its beginnings to the mid-1960s. Especially fascinating is Nigel Cameron's *An Illustrated History of Hong Kong* (Oxford University Press, 1991), with photographs that show Hong Kong of yore and vividly illustrate how much the colony has changed. Life in Hong Kong during the opium trade is chronicled in Nigel Cameron's *The Cultured Pearl* (Oxford University Press, 1978). One of the best books in recent years is Jan Morris's *Hong Kong* (Random House, 1988), which traces the evolution of the British colony from its birth during the Opium Wars to the present. This book gives a unique perspective on the workings of the colony and imparts an astonishing wealth of information, making it fascinating armchair reading.

Lovers of architecture will enjoy reading Stephanie Williams's *Hongkong Bank: The Building of Norman Foster's Masterpiece* (Little, Brown, 1989), a complete account of the construction of Foster's controversial bank building, which was prefabricated in countries all over the world and then assembled on site.

For an intimate view of Hong Kong, a recommended book is *Hong Kong: Borrowed Place, Borrowed Time* (Praeger, 1968) by Richard Hughes, a foreign correspondent who lived in Hong Kong for several decades and was said to have been the inspiration for several characters in John Le Carré's novels.

Fictional accounts that depict the character of Hong Kong are Richard Mason's *The World of Suzie Wong* (World Pub., 1957) and Han Suyin's *A Many-Splendored Thing* (Little Brown, 1952), an autobiographical account of life in Hong Kong shortly after the Chinese revolution in the late 1940s and early 1950s. James Clavell's *Tai-Pan* (Atheneum, 1966) is a novel about Hong Kong's beginnings; *Noble House* (Delacorte Press, 1981) is its sequel. John Le Carré's *The Honourable Schoolboy* (G. K. Hall, 1977) details the activities of George Smiley, acting head of the British Secret Service in Hong Kong.

FILMS   Novels that have been made into movies include *A Many-Splendored Thing, The World of Suzie Wong, Tai-Pan,* and *Noble House.*

2 Planning a Trip to Hong Kong

Much of the anxiety associated with travel comes from a fear of the unknown. Not knowing what to expect—or even what a place looks like—can give even seasoned travelers butterflies. This chapter will help you prepare for your trip to Hong Kong, but don't stop here. Reading through the other chapters before leaving home will also help you plan your travels. Just learning that Hong Kong has hiking trails and beaches, for example, may prompt you to pack your hiking boots or bathing suit. Keep in mind, however, that things may change during the lifetime of this book, particularly after the Chinese assume control on July 1, 1997.

1 Visitor Information & Entry Requirements

VISITOR INFORMATION

The **Hong Kong Tourist Association (HKTA)** is one of the best-organized and most efficient tourist offices I've come across. They have a wealth of free information available for travelers, including brochures on everything from hotels and restaurants to walking tours and sightseeing. See "Orientation" in Chapter 3 ("Getting to Know Hong Kong") for a complete listing of tourist information offices in Hong Kong itself.

In the U.S. If you'd like information and literature before leaving home, contact one of the HKTA offices in the United States: 590 Fifth Ave., 5th floor, New York, NY 10036-4706 (☎ 212/869-5008 or 212/869-5009; fax 212/730-2605); 610 Enterprise Dr., Suite 200, Oak Brook, IL 60521 (☎ 708/575-2828; fax 708/575-2829); and Suite 1220, 10940 Wilshire Blvd., Los Angeles, CA 90024-3915 (☎ 310/208-4582; fax 310/208-1869).

Around the World There are also HKTA offices at 347 Bay St., Suite 909, Toronto, ON, Canada M5H 2R7 (☎ 416/366-2389; fax 416/366-1098); 125 Pall Mall, 4th and 5th floors, London SW1Y 5EA, England (☎ 0171/930-4775; fax 0171/930-4777); Level 5, 55 Harrington St., The Rocks, Sydney, NSW 2000, Australia (☎ 02/251-2855 in Sydney, 800/251-071 outside Sydney; fax 02/247-8812); and P.O. Box 2120, Auckland, New Zealand (☎ 09/572-2707; fax 09/575-2620).

ENTRY REQUIREMENTS

DOCUMENTS   As we go to press, a valid passport is the only document most tourists, including Americans, need to enter Hong Kong. Americans can stay up to 1 month without a visa. Australians, New Zealanders, Canadians, and other British Commonwealth citizens can stay for 3 months without a visa, while citizens of the United Kingdom can stay for 12 months. If you wish to stay longer or have any questions once you're in Hong Kong, telephone the **Hong Kong Department of Immigration** (☎ 852/2824-6111).

Once in Hong Kong, visitors must carry at all times some photo identification, such as a passport or driver's license.

Note: Although at press time neither the British nor Chinese government had announced any changes in visa requirements, it would be prudent to contact a local Hong Kong Tourist Association office or the Chinese embassy if you plan on visiting Hong Kong after June 30, 1997.

CUSTOMS   At press time, you're allowed to bring into Hong Kong duty free a 1-liter (34-ounce) bottle of alcohol, 200 cigarettes or 50 cigars, and a reasonable quantity of cosmetics and perfumes in opened bottles for personal use.

2 Money

CASH/CURRENCY   The basic unit of currency in the colony is the **Hong Kong dollar,** which is divided into 100 **cents.** Two local banks, the Hongkong and Shanghai Banking Corporation and the Standard Chartered Bank, issue versions of their own notes in denominations of HK$10, HK$20, HK$50, HK$100, HK$500, and HK$1,000. As for coins, they're minted in England in bronze for HK$0.10, HK$0.20, and HK$0.50 pieces and in silver for HK$1, HK$2, and HK$5. In 1995 new HK$10 coins were issued; they will gradually replace the HK$10 note.

Throughout Hong Kong you'll see the dollar sign ("$"), which of course refers to Hong Kong dollars, not U.S. dollars. To prevent confusion, this guide identifies Hong Kong dollars with the symbol "HK$." Although rates fluctuate a little, all conversions in this book are based on HK$7.70 to $1 U.S. (and then rounded off), a rate that has remained fairly constant since the Hong Kong dollar is pegged to the U.S. dollar. If the exchange rate changes drastically, however, plan your budget accordingly. And again, keep in mind that Hong Kong is in such a state of flux, even the currency could change if so ordained by the Chinese.

TRAVELER'S CHECKS   If you want to pay with cash rather than credit cards, your money is safest in traveler's checks, which will be replaced if lost or stolen; traveler's checks can be readily exchanged for Hong Kong dollars at banks, hotels, and currency-exchange offices (banks provide the most favorable rates). Traveler's checks also entail a slightly better exchange rate than cash. Although Thomas Cook and other agencies can issue traveler's checks in Hong Kong currency, I don't think that having such checks is advantageous. For one thing, shops, restaurants, and hotels are not as willing to accept traveler's checks for payment as they are in, say, the United States. Secondly, you can use leftover traveler's checks in U.S. dollars (or your own national currency) for future trips, but leftover traveler's checks in Hong Kong dollars must either be reconverted (which is not financially advantageous, because you lose money with each conversion) or saved for future trips to Hong Kong.

CREDIT CARDS   Many of the smaller shops in Hong Kong will give better prices if you pay in cash with local currency, but you'll also want to take along credit cards

The Hong Kong Dollar & the U.S. Dollar

At this writing, $1 U.S. = approximately HK$7.70 (or HK$1 = 13¢), and this was the rate of exchange used to calculate the U.S. dollar values given in this book (rounded off). While fairly stable, this exchange rate may fluctuate from time to time and thus may not be the same when you travel to Hong Kong. Therefore the following table should be used only as a guide:

HK$	U.S.$	HK$	U.S.$
0.25	0.03	150	19.48
0.50	0.06	200	25.97
1.00	0.13	250	32.47
2.00	0.26	300	38.96
3.00	0.39	350	45.45
4.00	0.52	400	51.95
5.00	0.65	450	58.44
6.00	0.78	500	64.94
7.00	0.90	550	71.42
8.00	1.04	600	77.92
9.00	1.16	650	84.42
10.00	1.30	700	90.91
15.00	1.94	750	97.40
20.00	2.60	800	103.90
25.00	3.25	850	110.39
30.00	3.90	900	116.88
35.00	4.55	1,000	129.87
40.00	5.19	1,250	162.34
45.00	5.84	1,500	194.80
50.00	6.49	1,750	227.27
75.00	9.74	2,000	259.74
100.00	12.99	2,250	292.21

to avoid carrying large amounts in bills. Most shops accept international credit cards, although some of the smaller ones do not. Look to see whether there are credit-card signs displayed on the front door or in the shop. Readily accepted credit cards include American Express, Visa, and MasterCard. Note, however, that shops have to pay an extra fee for transactions that take place with a credit card—and they will try to pass on that expense to you. Keep this in mind if you're bargaining for something (this is discussed further in Chapter 8, "Shopping"), and make sure the shopkeeper knows whether you're going to pay with cash or plastic. All the major hotels and better restaurants accept credit cards, but the budget establishments often don't.

One of the best reasons to carry a credit card is to obtain cash from an automated-teller machine (ATM). Not only do you eliminate the inconvenience of being able to exchange money only during banking hours, but the exchange rate is better. However, commission fees may be higher than those charged for exchanging cash or traveler's checks, so be sure you're going to exchange an amount that will

What Things Cost in Hong Kong	U.S. $
Taxi from the airport to Tsim Sha Tsui	7.80
Metro from Tsim Sha Tsui to Central	.95
Local telephone call	.13
Double room at the Peninsula Hotel (very expensive)	390.00–532.00
Double room at the Kowloon Hotel (moderate)	179.00–312.00
Double room at the Caritas Bianchi Lodge (inexpensive)	103.00
Lunch for one at the Peak Café (moderate)	12.35–25.95
Lunch for one at the City Hall Chinese Restaurant (inexpensive)	8.40–20.80
Dinner for one, without wine, at the Plume (very expensive)	97.40–129.85
Dinner for one, without wine, at Luk Yu Tea House (moderate)	7.15–20.80
Dinner for one, with wine, at Spaghetti House (inexpensive)	10.00
Pint of beer	5.85
Coca-Cola	2.50
Cup of coffee	3.00
Roll of ASA 64 Kodachrome film, 36 exposures	9.00
Admission to the Space Museum	1.30
Movie ticket	7.15
Ticket to Hong Kong Philharmonic Orchestra	7.80–29.85

warrant the fee. To draw money from a Hong Kong ATM, you must usually have a four-digit personal identification number. If you're in doubt, ask your issuing bank for information.

American Express cardholders have access to Jetco automated-teller machines and can withdraw local currency or traveler's checks at the Express Cash machines at all American Express offices (see "Fast Facts" in Chapter 3). Holders of MasterCard and Visa can use ATM machines at the "Electronic Money" machine at the airport and various convenient locations around the city, including the Star Ferry concourses in Kowloon and Central, on Nathan Road, and Connaught Road Central. In addition, the Hongkong Bank also issues cash for holders of MasterCard and Visa, while Citibank serves banking needs of MasterCard.

3 When to Go

Hong Kong's peak tourist season used to be in the spring and fall, but now tourists are flocking to the territory year-round. No matter when you go, therefore, make hotel reservations in advance, particularly if you're arriving during the Chinese New Year or one of the festivals described below. Furthermore, as of press time, no ceremonies had been announced for the transition from British to Chinese rule on June 30, 1997. The historic event is sure to attract Hong Kong fans from around the world.

CLIMATE

Because of its subtropical location, Hong Kong's weather is generally mild in winter and uncomfortably hot and humid in summer, with an average annual rainfall of 89 inches. The most pleasant time of year is late September to early December, when skies are clear and sunny, temperatures are in the 70s, and the humidity drops to 70%. January and February are the coldest months, with temperatures often in the 50s. In spring (March to May), the temperature can range between 60°F and 80°F and the humidity rises to about 84%, with fog and rain fairly common. That means there may not be much of a view from the cloud-enveloped Victoria Peak.

By summer, temperatures are often in the 90s, humidity can be 90% or more, and there's little or no relief even at night. This is when Hong Kong receives the most rain; it's also typhoon season. However, Hong Kong has a very good warning system, so there's no need to worry about the physical dangers of a tropical storm. The worst that can happen is that you may have to stay in your hotel room for a day or more, or that your plane may be delayed or diverted. It has never happened to me, but it happened to a friend of mine—she was glad she was staying at the Regent instead of Chungking Mansion, since she was confined to her hotel for an entire weekend.

Hong Kong's Average Monthly Temperatures and Days of Rain

	Jan	Feb	Mar	Apr	May	June	July	Aug	Sept	Oct	Nov	Dec
Temp. (C°)	15	15	18	22	25	27	29	29	27	25	21	18
Temp. (F°)	59	59	64	72	77	80	84	84	80	77	70	64
Days of Rain	5.6	8.9	10.1	11.1	14.9	14.2	17.5	17.3	14.4	8.6	5.9	3.9

HOLIDAYS

Hong Kong has 17 public holidays a year, including some of the festivals described below. Although some of them are British holidays (and may be dropped after June 30, 1997), the majority are Chinese and therefore are celebrated according to the lunar calendar. Since many shops and restaurants remain open except during the Chinese New Year, the holidays should not cause any inconvenience to visitors.

Public holidays for 1996 are: New Year's Day (Jan 1), Chinese New Year (Feb 19–21), Ching Ming Festival (Apr 4), Easter (Good Friday, Saturday, Easter Sunday, and Easter Monday; Apr 5–8), Birthday of Her Majesty the Queen (June 15), Monday following the Queen's Birthday (June 17), Tuen Ng Festival (Dragon Boat Festival) (June 20), Liberation Day (last Saturday and Monday in Aug; Aug 24 and 26), day following the Mid-Autumn Festival (Sept 28), day following the Chung Yeung Festival (Oct 21), Christmas (Dec 25 and 27), and the first weekday after Christmas (Dec 26).

For dates of 1997 holidays, contact the Hong Kong Tourist Association (HKTA).

HONG KONG CALENDAR OF EVENTS

If you're lucky, your trip might coincide with one of Hong Kong's colorful festivals. Because most of them follow the Chinese lunar calendar, they don't fall on the same date each year. The only time shops and offices close for festival time is during the Chinese New Year, though some in Tsim Sha Tsui remain open to cater to tourists.

Below are the most popular events, including Chinese festivals and festivals of the arts. Other celebrations worth catching include Buddha's Birthday, usually in late May; and the Festival of the Hungry Ghosts, at the end of August, when offerings of food and carefully crafted paper replicas of life's necessities are burned at roadsides to appease the ghosts that are allowed to come back for one day to roam the earth.

January/February
- **Chinese New Year.** The most important Chinese holiday, this is a three-day affair, a time for visiting friends and relatives, settling debts, doing a thorough housecleaning, consulting fortune-tellers, and worshiping ancestors. Strips of red paper with greetings of wealth, good fortune, and longevity are pasted on doors, and families visit temples. Most shops (except those in tourist areas) close down for at least two or three days, streets are decorated, and a fireworks display is held over the harbor, usually on the second day of the holiday. Since this festival is largely a family affair (much like the Christian Christmas), it holds little interest for the tourist. In fact, if you're planning a side trip into China, this would be the worst time to go, since all routes to the mainland are clogged with Hong Kong Chinese returning home to visit relatives. Late January or early February (Feb 19–21, 1996).
- ✪ **Hong Kong Arts Festival.** A month-long celebration with performances by world-renowned orchestras, pop and jazz ensembles, and opera, dance, and theater companies, as well as ethnic music and art exhibitions.
  Where: Arts Centre, Wan Chai. **When:** Mid-Feb through mid-March (Feb 24– Mar 17, 1996). **How:** City Hall, located in Central just east of the Star Ferry concourse, sells tickets to performances, which are priced at HK$50 to HK$300 ($6.50 to $39). For information about the program and future dates, call 852/ 2824 3555; for ticket inquiries, call 852/2734 9009.

March
- **Seven-A-Side Rugby Tournament,** Hong Kong Government Stadium. Known as "The Sevens," this is one of the most popular sporting events, with more than 20 teams from around the world competing for the Cup Championship. A weekend in March (March 30–31, 1996).

March/April
- **Hong Kong Food Festival,** various restaurants and locations around Hong Kong. A celebration of food in Hong Kong, with prizes given to winning cuisines from participating restaurants, street carnivals, theme parties, exhibitions, a waiters' race, and organized food-related tours. For two weeks during late March or early April (Mar 2–17, 1996).

April/May
- **Ching Ming Festival,** all Chinese cemeteries (especially in Aberdeen, Happy Valley, Chai Wan, and Cheung Chau Island). A Confucian festival to honor the dead, observed by sweeping ancestral graves and offering food and flowers. Fourth or fifth day of the Third Moon (Apr 4, 1996).
- ✪ **Tin Hau Festival.** One of Hong Kong's most colorful festivals. Tin Hau, Hong Kong's most popular deity among fishing folk, is goddess of the sea. The celebration stems from a 12th-century legend of a young girl who is believed to have saved her two brothers from drowning during a terrible storm. To pay her tribute, fishing boats are decorated with colorful flags, there are parades, and family shrines are carried to shore to be blessed by Taoist priests.
  Where: All Tin Hau temples, with especially big celebrations at temples in Joss House Bay and Yuen Long. **When:** 23rd day of the Third Moon (April or May; May 10, 1996). **How:** Go by public transportation, but be prepared for the crowds. Organized tours are also available; contact the HKTA.
- ✪ **Cheung Chau Bun Festival.** Unique to Hong Kong, this weeklong affair is thought to appease restless ghosts and spirits. Originally held to placate the unfortunate souls of those murdered by pirates, it features a street parade of lions and

dragons and Chinese opera, as well as floats with children seemingly suspended in the air, held up by cleverly concealed wires. The end of the festival is heralded by three bun-covered scaffolds erected in front of the Pak Tai Temple. These buns supposedly bring good luck to those who receive them.

Where: Cheung Chau Island. **When:** Usually late April or early May, but the exact date is chosen by divination (check with the HKTA). **How:** Ferry to Cheung Chau; expect huge crowds. Organized tours are also available; contact the HKTA.

May/June

○ **Dragon Boat Races** (Tuen Ng Festival). Races of long and narrow boats, gaily painted and powered by oarsmen who row to the beat of drums. It originated in ancient China, where legend held that an imperial adviser drowned himself in a Hunan river to protest government corruption. His faithful followers, wishing to recover his body, supposedly raced out into the river in boats, beating their paddles on the surface of the water and throwing rice to distract sea creatures from his body. There are two different races: first by approximately 500 local Hong Kong teams; the following weekend by teams from around the world.

Where: Stanley, Aberdeen, Chai Wan, Yau Ma Tei, Tai Po, and outlying islands for the local competitions; Tsim Sha Tsui East waterfront for the international races. **When:** Fifth day of the Fifth Moon for local races (June 20, 1996); international races the following weekend (June 29–30, 1996). **How:** The local races can be reached by public transportation. For the international event, there are bleachers set up in Tsim Sha Tsui East, and tour operators run cruises so that visitors can watch the events from a boat. Contact the HKTA for more information.

September/October

○ **Mid-Autumn Festival.** Held in early autumn, this festival (sometimes referred to as the Moon Festival) celebrates the harvest and the brightest moon of the year. In honor of the event, local people light lanterns, gaze at the moon, and eat mooncakes (sweet rolls with sesame seeds, duck eggs, and ground lotus seeds). The mooncakes commemorate the 14th-century uprising against the Mongols, when written messages calling for the revolt were concealed in cakes smuggled to the rebels. Today the Urban Council organizes lantern carnivals in parks on both Hong Kong Island and Kowloon, where you can join the Chinese for strolls among hundreds of lanterns.

Where: Popular places for viewing include Victoria Park in Causeway Bay, Victoria Peak, and Kowloon Park. **When:** The 15th day of the Eighth Moon (Sept 27, 1996). **How:** Take a blanket or walk through the parks.

• Chung Yueng Festival, all Chinese cemeteries. The second time of year when ancestral graves are swept and offerings are made. Ninth Day of the Ninth Moon (Oct 20, 1996).

4 Health & Insurance

STAYING HEALTHY   No shots or inoculations are required for entry to Hong Kong from the United States, but you will need proof of a vaccination against cholera if you have been in an infected area during the 14 days preceding your arrival. Check with your travel agent or call the Hong Kong Tourist Authority if you are traveling through Asia before reaching Hong Kong.

If you need a prescription from a Hong Kong doctor filled, there are plenty of drugstores in the territory. They will not, however, fill prescriptions from elsewhere. See "Fast Facts: Hong Kong" in Chapter 3 for specific addresses.

Generally, you're safe eating anywhere in Hong Kong, even at roadside food stalls. Stay clear of local oysters, however, and remember that many restaurants outside the major hotels and tourist areas include MSG in their dishes as a matter of course. See "Food and Drink" in Chapter 1 for more information.

INSURANCE   Before leaving home, check with your health insurance company about whether you are covered for a trip to Hong Kong. If not, you may want to take out a short-term traveler's medical policy that covers medical costs and emergencies.

You may also want to take extra precautions with your possessions. Is your camera or video equipment insured anywhere in the world through your homeowners insurance? Some insurance companies will not cover loss for homes unoccupied for a specified length of time—is your home insured against theft or loss if you're gone longer than a month? If you are not adequately covered, you may wish to purchase an extra policy to cover losses.

5 Tips for Special Travelers

FOR TRAVELERS WITH DISABILITIES   If you are in a wheelchair, contact the Hong Kong Tourist Association for a free booklet called "Access Guide for Disabled Visitors." It provides information on more than 200 sites, including banks, cinemas, cultural centers, museums, temples, and restaurants, with brief descriptions of accessibility in parking, how many steps there are at the entrance or whether there's a ramp, whether toilets are equipped for the handicapped, and more.

As for transportation, taxis are probably the most convenient mode of transportation, especially since they can load and unload disabled passengers in restricted zones under certain conditions. Otherwise, the MTR (subway) has wheelchair access (elevators) at some stations, and ferries are accessible to wheelchair users on the lower deck. For more information on transportation for travelers with disabilities, contact the Transport Department, Floor 41, Immigration Tower on Gloucester Road in Wan Chai, for a booklet called "A Guide to Public Transport Services in Hong Kong for Disabled Persons."

FOR SENIORS   For the longest time seniors were given no discounts for sightseeing in Hong Kong. Yet those over 56 years of age account for more than 15% of Hong Kong's total visitor arrivals; these percentages are even higher for North American visitors, with seniors making up more than 30% of the visitor total. Hong Kong has finally acknowledged this increasingly important segment of the tourism industry with the introduction in 1994 of a number of discounts for visitors over 60, including reduced rates for hotels (ask your travel agent for details upon booking a hotel), organized sightseeing tours offered by the Hong Kong Tourist Association, and certain restaurants. Most museums have free or half-price admission for those over 60. In addition, seniors over 65 can ride the cross-harbor ferry free of charge and receive reduced fares for ferries to the outlying islands, the trams, and the subway system. For more information on senior discounts, contact the Hong Kong Tourist Association for the booklet "Guide for Travellers Over 60" and the "60 Plus" Privilege Card.

FOR SINGLE TRAVELERS   You shouldn't have any problems as a single traveler to Hong Kong. Almost every time I've come here, I traveled alone. The biggest problem is one of expense, since some hotels charge the same for both double and single occupancy. The other problem is with Chinese food—it's best when enjoyed with a group. Try fixed-price meals when dining alone, or join one of the organized tours where meals are often included.

FOR FAMILIES   Hong Kong is a great place for older kids, because so many of the attractions are geared for them and offer discounts for children, sometimes as much as 50%. In addition, public transportation is half price for children. As for very young children, keep in mind that there are many stairs to climb, particularly in Central with its elevated walkways and at subway stations. Also, young children may not be welcome at the finer restaurants; most hotels offer baby-sitting service.

FOR STUDENTS   If you're a student, the **Hong Kong Student Travel Bureau** can help you with sightseeing tours of the city, visas and trips to China, cheap flights to other destinations, and even rail passes for both Europe and Japan. Even if you're not a student, you can still take advantage of some of the travel bureau's services. Among the half dozen or so offices spread throughout Hong Kong, two are especially conveniently located: on the 10th floor (Room 1021) of Star House in Tsim Sha Tsui, next to the Star Ferry concourse (☎ 852/2730 3269), open Monday through Friday from 10am to 7:30pm, Saturday from 10am to 6:30pm, and Sunday from 10am to 5pm; and in Room 1804 of the Regent Centre, 8 Queen's Rd. Central (☎ 852/2810 7272), open Monday through Friday from 10am to 6:30pm and Saturday from 9am to 2:30pm.

6 Getting There

With more than 30 airlines and half a dozen cruise lines serving Hong Kong, it's certainly not difficult to get there. Your itinerary, the amount of time you have, and your pocketbook will probably dictate how you travel. Below are some pointers to get you headed in the right direction.

BY PLANE

THE MAJOR AIRLINES   Airlines that fly nonstop between North America and Hong Kong include Canadian Airlines International (☎ 800/426-7000), Cathay Pacific Airways (☎ 800/233-2742), Northwest Airlines (☎ 800/225-2525), Singapore Airlines (☎ 800/742-3333), and United Airlines (☎ 800/241-6522). Other airlines flying between North America and Hong Kong with stops en route include China Airlines (☎ 800/227-5118), Japan Airlines (☎ 800/525-3663), Korean Air (☎ 800/438-5000), and Philippine Airlines (☎ 800/435-9725). Contact your travel agent or specific carriers for current information.

To get a head start on your travel adventure, however, it seems only appropriate to fly Hong Kong's own Cathay Pacific Airways, one of Asia's premier airlines. With nonstop flights departing daily from both Los Angeles and Vancouver and offering four flights a week from Toronto, Cathay Pacific is the only airline offering daily, 100%-smoke-free B747-400 service between Los Angeles and Hong Kong. Flight time is 15 hours from Los Angeles to Hong Kong.

Note: When you arrive in Hong Kong, remember that you must confirm your on-going or return flight reservation 72 hours prior to departure or you will lose your seat. Local airline reservation telephone numbers in Hong Kong for some of the major carriers are: British Airways (☎ 852/2868 0303 or 852/368 9255), Canadian Airlines International (☎ 852/2868 3123), Cathay Pacific (☎ 852/2747 1888), China Airlines (☎ 852/2868 2299), Japan Airlines (☎ 852/2523 0081), Korean Air (☎ 852/2368 6221), Northwest Airlines (☎ 852/2810 4288), Philippine Airlines (☎ 852/2369 4521), Qantas Airways (☎ 852/2524 2101), Singapore Airlines (☎ 852/2520 2233), and United Airlines (☎ 852/2810 4888).

REGULAR AIRFARES   Regardless of how you buy your ticket, there are certain regulations you should know about airfare pricing. While first-class, business-class, and regular economy fares (those with no restrictions) are the same year-round to Hong Kong, the cheapest fares (including Advance Purchase Excursion fares, described below), usually vary according to the season. The most expensive time to go is during the peak season (June through August) and the last couple of weeks in December. The lowest fares are available January through March. Fares in between these two extremes, known as the shoulder season, are available in April and May and again from September to the middle of December. To complicate matters, each season also has different rates for both weekday and weekend flights.

Listed below are some of the fare options from Los Angeles to Hong Kong aboard Cathay Pacific at the time of this writing. Be sure to contact the airlines or your travel agent for an update on prices once you've decided on your exact travel plans.

First Class   All airlines provide some luxuries for their first-class passengers. Cathay Pacific's royal treatment, for example, begins as soon as you step up to its special first-class check-in counter, where specially trained staff members are on hand to offer personal assistance and customers receive priority baggage clearance. At major gateways, first-class passengers are also treated to an exclusive first-class lounge, with free alcoholic drinks, coffee, and soda. On board, passengers benefit from upgraded services, including electronically controlled seats upholstered in damask and individual video units offering a choice of in-flight entertainment. Meals are served at times chosen by each passenger, and, according to individual preference, range from full, five-course meals to light refreshments. Lead-free crystal, bone china, Asian lacquerware, silver-plated cutlery, and fine Irish linens round out the dining experience. As we went to press, Cathay's first-class round-trip fare from Los Angeles to Hong Kong was $5,172.

Business Class   Most carriers offer a separate business class, complete with separate check-in counters at the airport and more comfortable seating than in economy class. Cathay Pacific's business class is a notch above the standard offered by most airline business classes, starting with a 50-inch seat pitch on long hauls and comfortable seating that can be adjusted to suit passengers of different heights and builds through such improvements as two footrests, a "winged headrest" to support the neck, and a lumbar airbag that can be inflated or deflated for lower-back comfort. In addition, a personal TV installed in the armrest provides eight channels of entertainment. Meals of both Asian and Western cuisine allow a choice of four main courses and two desserts. Cathay Pacific's business-class round-trip fare from Los Angeles to Hong Kong is $2,882.

Economy Class   Starting in early 1996, Cathay Pacific will begin installing a personal TV into every economy-class seat in the fleet, making it the only major international carrier to offer personal, multichannel television to passengers in all classes. Regular round-trip economy fares—those with no restrictions—are $2,202 from Los Angeles to Hong Kong.

Advance Purchase Excursion Fares (APEX)   You can cut the cost of your flight to Hong Kong by purchasing your ticket in advance and complying with certain restrictions. These are known as APEX (Advance Purchase Excursion) fares and the restrictions may vary with the airline but always require an advance purchase, minimum and maximum stays, and are nonrefundable. Cathay Pacific's APEX fare, for example, must be purchased seven days before departure and requires that you stay at least six days but no longer than six months. Rates vary according to the season, with weekend flights costing more than weekday flights. Cathay Pacific's APEX round-trip fares from Los Angeles to Hong Kong range from $1,497 on a weekend in the summer to $1,082 on a weekday in the winter.

OTHER GOOD-VALUE CHOICES   Since prices can vary according to your gateway, your route, the number of days spent abroad, the days you travel, and whether you travel first class or economy, your best bet is to shop around. Check the travel sections of major newspapers, especially those on the West Coast such as the *Los Angeles Times,* since they often carry advertisements for low fares. Call various travel agencies to inquire about charter flights, APEX fares, or special promotional flights. Many airlines and tour operators offer occasional promotional fares with tight restrictions, as well as package tours; the latter might be the cheapest way to go, since packages include hotels, transfers, and more.

Some companies provide deeply discounted tickets on various airlines (some more than 50% below economy and 30% less than APEX) with some or no restrictions, depending on availability. You can buy your ticket through them either far in advance or at the last moment, if you're lucky. Among the firms that deal with travel to Hong Kong (usually with a stop in Tokyo) are **Nippon Travel** (☎ 202/362-0039), **Japan Associates Travel** (☎ 202/939-8853), and **Japan Express Travel** (☎ 202/ 347-7730). Another large discount firm is **Euro-Asia Express** of Millbrae, California (☎ 415/692-4892 or 800/878-8538). At press time, calls to these discount firms revealed round-trip tickets, with departure from the West Coast, that ranged from approximately $700 to $1,000.

Consolidators like C. L. Thompson Express International in San Francisco and CNH International and Star Tours, Inc., in Los Angeles also sell discounted tickets, but only through travel agents.

If you are a full-time student under 35 years of age with an International Student ID Card or if you are under 25, try **STA Travel** of Los Angeles (☎ 213/934-8722 in Los Angeles, 617/266-6014 in Boston, 212/627-3111 in New York, 215/ 382-2928 in Philadelphia, 415/391-8407 in San Francisco; or 800/777-0112 from anywhere except Los Angeles County, San Francisco, Boston, or New York City).

HONG KONG'S AIRPORT

Hong Kong's **Kai Tak Airport** (☎ 852/2769 7531) is one of the world's few airports right in the middle of a city, located on the densely populated Kowloon Peninsula. Its one runway is among the most spectacular in the world—built right out into the middle of the bay and boasting a takeoff or landing every two minutes. Since it's considered too small to meet future demands, however, a new airport is being constructed on two islands just north of Lantau—check Lap Kok and Lam Chau. Its state-of-the-art facilities will include two runways operating 24 hours a day, four passenger terminals, and a high-speed airport railway that will transport visitors to Tsim Sha Tsui in 18 minutes and to the Central District in 23 minutes. It is expected to be open for business by mid-1998—about a year after Hong Kong reverts to mainland China.

Regardless of which airport is in use when you arrive, visitor services will remain largely the same. One of the first things you should do is stop by the counter of the **Hong Kong Tourist Association (HKTA)** in the arrivals hall, where you can pick up a map of the city, sightseeing brochures, and a wealth of other information. It's open daily from 8am to 10:30pm.

Also in the arrivals hall is the counter of the **Hong Kong Hotel Association,** where you can book a room in one of its 60-some member hotels free of charge; it's open daily, from 7am to midnight. Note, however, that they do not have information on rock-bottom establishments, but they can book rooms in several low-priced lodgings and the YMCAs.

If you plan on traveling to Macau, stop by the **Macau tourist information counter,** also in the arrivals lobby; it's open daily from 9am to 10:30pm.

You can **exchange money** at the airport, but since the exchange rate here is rather unfavorable it's best to exchange only what you need to get into town. About $10 (U.S.) should be enough, and be sure to tell the bank teller that you need small change if you plan to take the airport bus from Kai Tak Airport (described below), since exact change is required.

If you need to leave luggage at the airport, there is a **luggage-storage counter** on the departure floor.

A Note on Departure: The X-ray machines at the security gates in Kai Tak Airport are notoriously bad for film, so all photographers I know always ask for a hand in-spection of film when leaving the country. In addition, keep in mind that when you leave Hong Kong you'll have to pay an airport departure tax of HK$50 ($6.50) for adults (free for children under 12). Also, remember to reconfirm your ongoing or return flight reservation at least 72 hours before departure or you may lose your seat.

GETTING INTO TOWN   Because Kai Tak Airport is so conveniently located, it's only a 20- to 30-minute ride to Tsim Sha Tsui and a 40-minute ride to Central. During rush hours, however (8 to 9:30am and again from 4 to 6:30pm), it can take as long as an hour.

The cheapest and certainly an easy way to travel between Kai Tak and Hong Kong's major hotels is by the **Airbus coach service** (☎ 852/745 4466). There are four different routes serving various hotels, with buses departing every 15 minutes between 7am and midnight. To find the buses, follow the AIRPORT BUS signs from the arrivals lobby or ask at the HKTA counter. Note that the Airbus requires exact fare. Each bus stop generally services a cluster of hotels in the same vicinity, so make sure you know where to exit the bus for your particular hotel (hotel stops are announced on the bus).

Airbus A1 travels through Kowloon and costs HK$12 ($1.55). Take this bus if you're going to the Guangdong Hotel, Holiday Inn Golden Mile, Hyatt Regency, Imperial, International Hotel, Kimberley, Kowloon Hotel, Kowloon Shangri-La, Miramar, New Astor, New World, Omni Hongkong Hotel, Park, Peninsula, Ramada Hotel Kowloon, Hong Kong Renaissance, Regent, Royal Garden, Sheraton, Windsor Hotel, the YMCA on Salisbury Road, or Chungking Mansion.

The other three bus routes service Hong Kong Island and charge HK$17 ($2.20). **Airbus A2** travels through Wan Chai and Central, at or near the Evergreen Plaza Hotel, Furama, Grand Hyatt, Harbour View International House, Mandarin Oriental, Luk Kwok Hotel, Ritz-Carlton, and Wharney Hotel. **Airbus A3** serves hotels in Causeway Bay, including the Excelsior, Park Lane Hotel, New Cathay, and Regal Hong Kong. **Airbus A5** also goes by the Park Lane Hotel before traveling farther east to Tai Koo Shing.

In addition to the Airbus, there are smaller **hotel shuttle vans** that pick up arriving passengers at Kai Tak (near the hotel counter) and deliver them to the front doors of most of the major hotels. Fares vary depending on how far you're going, but it costs HK$60 to HK$100 ($7.80 to $13) to get to Tsim Sha Tsui. These air-conditioned coaches leave every 15 minutes from 7am to 11pm. To return to the airport, ask at your hotel about pickup points and departure times.

The easiest way to travel from Kai Tak, of course, is by **taxi,** which is quite cheap in Hong Kong. Depending on traffic and your final destination, a taxi to Tsim Sha Tsui costs between HK$50 to HK$60 ($6.50 to $7.80), while a taxi to Central

District costs HK$110 to HK$120 ($14.30 to $15.60) because of the extra charge levied for crossing the harbor tunnel. There's also an extra luggage charge of HK$5 (65¢) per piece of baggage.

BY TRAIN

It's unlikely that you'll arrive in Hong Kong by train, unless of course you've been traveling the length of China. Such travel will become easier with the completion of the Beijing-Kowloon Railway some time in 1996, which will provide a direct link between the two cities. What's more likely is that you'll want to take a short trip into China (for which you'll need a visa) once you arrive in Hong Kong. Although the easiest way to spend a couple of days in China is to join an organized tour, you can also travel to and from China on your own via the Kowloon-Canton Railway (KCR). (For more information on traveling to China, see Chapter 10.) In any case, if you're traveling to Hong Kong via train, you'll pass through Customs at Lo Wu, the border station, before continuing on the KCR to Kowloon Station in Hung Hom. The one-way fare between Guangzhou (Canton) and Kowloon Station ranges from HK$215 to HK$265 ($27.90 to $34.40), depending on the train and season, with trips lasting approximately two to three hours.

Kowloon Station is practically right in the middle of the city, though if you have a lot of luggage you might want to take a taxi to your hotel. An alternative is to disembark the KCR at Kowloon Tong Station, changing there to the Mass Transit Railway (Hong Kong's subway system), which will take you straight to Tsim Sha Tsui or Central.

PACKAGE TOURS

Many tours of Asia include stops in Hong Kong or trips exclusively to Hong Kong. Luxury cruise liners are also a common sight in Hong Kong's harbor, anchored conveniently right next to the territory's largest shopping mall at Ocean Terminal on the Kowloon side. Information on package tours and cruises can be obtained from your travel agent.

Getting to Know Hong Kong

3

Hong Kong is an easy city to get to know because it's surprisingly compact and the streets are all clearly marked in English. Public transportation here is not only well organized and a breeze to use, but the Star Ferry and the trams are themselves sightseeing attractions. Mostly, however, walking is the best way to go, particularly in the narrow, fascinating lanes and alleys where vehicles cannot go. This chapter describes the layout of the city, explains how best to get around it, gives practical information and advice, and tells you where to turn for additional information.

1 Orientation

VISITOR INFORMATION

The **Hong Kong Tourist Association (HKTA)** is an excellent source for tourist information, with an office conveniently located in the arrivals lobby of Kai Tak Airport, open daily from 8am to 10:30pm.

There are two other HKTA offices ready to serve you in Hong Kong. On the Kowloon side, there's a convenient office in Tsim Sha Tsui right in the Star Ferry concourse, open Monday through Friday from 8am to 6pm; and on Saturday, Sunday, and public holidays from 9am to 5pm.

On Hong Kong Island you'll find the main HKTA office in the basement, Shop 8, of the Jardine House (formerly the Connaught Centre), in the Central District. That's the tall building with all the round windows that you'll see straight ahead after you exit from the Star Ferry. It's open Monday through Friday from 9am to 6pm and on Saturday from 9am to 1pm (closed Sunday and public holidays).

If you have a question about Hong Kong, you can call the **HKTA telephone information service** (☎ 852/2807 6177), which is available Monday through Friday from 8am to 6pm; and on Saturday, Sunday, and public holidays from 9am to 5pm. After hours, a telephone-answering device will take your call and a member of HKTA will contact you.

The HKTA publishes a large assortment of free literature about Hong Kong. You'd be wise to make the tourist office your first stop, which is easy because the locations are so convenient. "The Official Hong Kong Guide," published monthly, is a booklet available at HKTA offices and in the guest rooms of most upper- and medium-range hotels. It contains a lot of practical information, including a short description of Chinese foods, shopping tips, a rundown of organized sight-seeing tours, an overview of Hong Kong's major attractions, and a listing of festivals, events, and exhibits being held that month.

Be sure to pick up three other nifty free booklets at HKTA: the "Sight-seeing and Culture" guide provides a detailed description of Hong Kong's sights and attractions, along with explanations of how to get there by public transportation; the "Official Dining and Entertainment Guide" highlights Hong Kong's various cuisines, complete with descriptions of major dishes; and the "Official Shopping Guide" gives practical advice on shopping and lists all HKTA member stores.

You can also get a free map of Hong Kong from HKTA, providing close-ups of Tsim Sha Tsui, the Central District, Wan Chai, and Causeway Bay. Invaluable leaflets are available, showing the major bus routes throughout Hong Kong, including Hong Kong Island, Kowloon, and the New Territories. Finally, if you plan to visit any of the outlying islands, be sure to pick up current ferry schedules at HKTA.

To find out what's going on during your stay in Hong Kong, get a copy of *Hong Kong This Week,* a weekly tabloid published by HKTA and distributed free at its offices and major hotels. *HK Magazine,* distributed free at restaurants, bars, and other outlets around town, is a biweekly that lists what's going on at the city's theaters and other venues, including plays, concerts, exhibitions, the cinema, and other events. *Hong Kong,* a tourist tabloid distributed free in hotel lobbies and tourist sites, is filled mostly with advertisements but does give some information on current happenings in Hong Kong, while *Hong Kong Visitor,* published by the *South China Morning Post,* is valuable for information on what's happening in the colony.

CITY LAYOUT

Hong Kong is located at the southeastern tip of the People's Republic of China, some 1,240 miles south of Beijing; it lies just south of the Tropic of Cancer at about the same latitude as Mexico City, the Bahamas, and Hawaii. Most people who have never been to the Orient probably think of Hong Kong as an island—and they'd be right if it were 1841. Not long after the colony was first established on Hong Kong Island, the British felt the need to expand, which they did by acquiring more land across the harbor on the Chinese mainland. Today Hong Kong Island is just a small part of the entire territory, which covers 404 square miles and measures 23^1/$_2$ miles north to south and 31 miles east to west.

Hong Kong can be divided into four distinct parts: Hong Kong Island with the Central District and such major attractions as Victoria Peak, Stanley Market, Middle Kingdom, Ocean Park, and Hong Kong Park; the Kowloon Peninsula with Tsim Sha Tsui at its tip; the New Territories; and 235 outlying islands. The New Territories is by far the largest area, stretching north of Kowloon all the way to the Chinese border. Once a vast area of peaceful little villages, fields, and duck farms, the New Territories in the past couple of decades have witnessed a remarkable mushrooming of satellite towns with huge public-housing projects; approximately half of Hong Kong's population is now housed here. However, much of the New Territories remains open and uninhabited. In fact, 21 country parks and 14 nature reserves throughout the territory account for more than 40% of Hong Kong's land area; another 30% is classified as rural area. The fact that Hong Kong is more than just a city surprises many first-time visitors.

As for Hong Kong's 235 **outlying islands,** most are barren and uninhabited; those that aren't lend themselves to excellent exploration into Hong Kong's past. Lantau,

Lamma, and Cheung Chau are three of the colony's best known and most easily accessible islands, where a gentler, slower, and more peaceful life prevails.

For the visitor, however, most hotels, restaurants, and points of interest are concentrated in four areas: Tsim Sha Tsui on the Kowloon side; and Central District, Wan Chai, and Causeway Bay on Hong Kong Island. Because these areas are so compact, the city must rank as Asia's most accessible and navigable city.

MAIN ARTERIES & STREETS   Hong Kong Island's Central District is larger now than it was originally, thanks to land reclamation. **Queen's Road,** now several blocks inland, used to mark the waterfront, as did **Des Voeux Road** and **Connaught Road** in subsequent years. Today they serve as busy thoroughfares through the Central District, since the steep incline up Victoria Peak follows close on their heels. From the Central District, **Hennessy Road** and **Gloucester Road** lead east through Wan Chai to Causeway Bay.

It wasn't until 1972 that the first **cross-harbor tunnel** was built, connecting Causeway Bay on Hong Kong Island with Tsim Sha Tsui East in Kowloon. In 1989 a second tunnel was completed; a third tunnel is in the works, to be completed in conjunction with Hong Kong's new airport.

On the Kowloon side, the most important artery is **Nathan Road,** which stretches north up the spine of Kowloon Peninsula and is lined with hotels and shops. **Salisbury Road** runs east and west at the tip of Tsim Sha Tsui from the Star Ferry through Tsim Sha Tsui East along the waterfront.

Note: Although it had not been discussed at press time, there is no guarantee that Hong Kong will retain all of its street names after 1997. Most are named after former administrators and personalities, many long forgotten now except in local history books.

FINDING AN ADDRESS   With a good map, you should have no problem finding an address since the system is the same as in North America. The streets are all labeled in English, and building numbers progress consecutively. For the most part, streets that run east to west (such as Des Voeux Road Central, Hennessy Road, Lockhart Road, and Salisbury Road) all have the even-numbered buildings on the north side of the street and the odd-numbered ones on the south. From Central, roads running through Wan Chai all the way west to Causeway Bay start with the lowest numbers near Central, and the highest numbered buildings end at Causeway Bay. On Nathan Road, Kowloon's most important thoroughfare, the lowest numbered buildings are at the southern tip near the harbor; the numbers increase consecutively, with the evens on the east and the odds to the west.

Remember that the floors inside buildings follow the British system of numbering. What we would call the first floor in the United States is called the ground floor in Hong Kong. Our second floor, therefore, is called the first floor in Hong Kong. In addition, if you're trying to find a specific office or factory outlet in a big building, it's useful to know that number 714 means it's on the seventh floor in Room 14, while 2312 means Room 12 on the 23rd floor.

STREET MAPS   You can get a free map of Hong Kong from the HKTA, which shows the major roads and streets of Kowloon and Tsim Sha Tsui, the Central District, Western District, Wan Chai, and Causeway Bay. It should be adequate for locating most hotels, restaurants, shops, and bars mentioned in this book. If you want to explore Hong Kong in more detail, you can purchase an entire book with maps of the city region and areas in the New Territories called *Hong Kong Guide Maps,* but you'll probably need this only if you live here or are writing a guidebook.

NEIGHBORHOODS IN BRIEF
HONG KONG ISLAND

Central District　This is where the story of Hong Kong all began, when a small port and community was established on the north end of the island by the British in the 1840s. Named "Victoria" in honor of the British queen, the community quickly grew into one of Asia's most important financial and business districts. Today the area, known as the Central District but usually referred to simply as "Central," remains Hong Kong's nerve center for banking and business. If there is a heart of Hong Kong, it surely lies here, but there are few traces remaining of its colonial past.

　　The Central District boasts glass and steel high-rises representing some of Hong Kong's most innovative architecture, a couple of the city's poshest hotels, expensive shopping centers filled with designer shops, office buildings, and restaurants and pubs catering to Hong Kong's white-collar workers. Banks are so important to the Central District that their impact is highly visible—the Hongkong and Shanghai Bank and the Bank of China Tower are just two examples of the modern architecture that has dramatically transformed the Central District's skyline in the past decade (the Bank of China Tower, by the way, was designed by I. M. Pei). Yet the neighborhood is also packed with traditional Chinese restaurants, outdoor markets, and the neon signs of family-run businesses. Rickety old trams—certainly one of Hong Kong's most endearing sights—chug their way straight through the district. There are also oases of greenery, at Chater Garden, popular with office workers for a lunchtime break, the Botanical Gardens, and Hong Kong Park with its museum of teaware.

Lan Kwai Fong　A street in Central, which together with D'Aguilar Street make up Central's nightlife district. Lined with restaurants and bars, it's a good place to spend an evening.

Western District　Located next to the bustling Central District, the Western District is a fascinating neighborhood of Chinese shops and enterprises and is one of the most traditional areas on Hong Kong Island. Since it's one of my own personal favorites, I've spent days wandering its narrow streets and inspecting shops selling traditional herbs, ginseng, medicines, dried fish, antiques, and other Chinese products. Unfortunately, modernization has taken its toll, and more of the old Western District seems to have vanished every time I visit, replaced by new high-rises and other projects. One of these projects is an incredibly ambitious people-mover—a series of 20-some escalators and moving sidewalks designed to transport more than 25,000 commuters between Central and the Mid-Levels on Victoria Peak.

Wan Chai　Located on the other side of the Central District, Wan Chai became notorious after World War II for its sleazy bars, easy women, tattoo parlors, and sailors on shore leave looking for a good time. Richard Mason's 1957 novel *The World of Suzie Wong* describes this bygone era of Wan Chai; during the Vietnam War it also served as a popular destination for American servicemen on R&R. Although some of the nightlife remains, Wan Chai has slowly become respectable (and almost unrecognizable) with the addition of new hotels, more high-rises, the Hong Kong Arts Centre, the Academy for Performing Arts, and the Hong Kong Convention and Exhibition Centre (less than a decade old but already expanding onto reclaimed land in a project that will double its size upon completion in mid-1997). Few places have changed as dramatically as Wan Chai.

Hong Kong Orientation

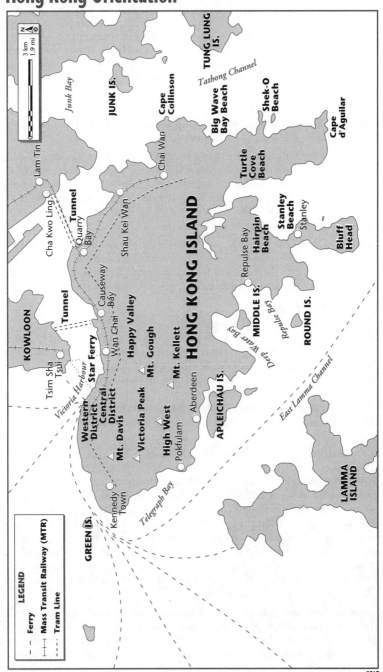

LEGEND

--- Ferry

Mass Transit Railway (MTR)

····· Tram Line

KOWLOON

Tsim Sha Tsui

Victoria Harbour

Star Ferry

Tunnel

Western District

Central District

Mt. Davis

Victoria Peak

High West

Pokfulam

Aberdeen

Kennedy Town

Telegraph Bay

GREEN IS.

APLEICHAU IS.

Mt. Gough

Mt. Kellett

Happy Valley

Wan Chai

Causeway Bay

Tunnel

Quarry Bay

Tunnel

Cha Kwo Ling

Lam Tin

Junk Bay

JUNK IS.

Cape Collinson

Chai Wan

Shau Kei Wan

HONG KONG ISLAND

Repulse Bay

MIDDLE IS.

Deep Water Bay

Repulse Bay

ROUND IS.

Hairpin Beach

Stanley Beach

Stanley

Bluff Head

Turtle Cove Beach

Big Wave Bay Beach

Shek-O Beach

Cape d'Aguilar

TUNG LUNG IS.

Tathong Channel

East Lamma Channel

LAMMA ISLAND

N

3 km

1.9 mi

2156

Causeway Bay   Just east of Wan Chai, Causeway Bay is becoming increasingly popular as a shopping destination, since shops stay open late and there are several department stores. The whole area was once a bay until land reclamation turned the water into soil several decades ago. Now it's a busy area of Japanese department stores; clothing, shoe, and accessory boutiques; street markets; nightclubs; and restaurants. On its eastern perimeter is the large Victoria Park and beyond that the colorful Aw Boon Haw (Tiger Balm) Gardens.

Happy Valley   Once a swampland, Happy Valley's main claim to fame is its racetrack, built in 1846 and the oldest racetrack in Asia outside China.

Aberdeen   On the south side of Hong Kong Island, Aberdeen was once a fishing village but is now studded with high-rises and housing projects. However, it is still known for its hundreds of sampans, junks, boat people, and a couple of huge floating restaurants. Just to the east, in Deep Water Bay, are Ocean Park with its botanical gardens, impressive aquarium, and a re-creation of an old Chinese village called Middle Kingdom; and Ocean World with its pools and water slides open in summer.

Stanley   Once a fishing village, this is now a lively center for discount markets selling everything from designer jeans to rattanware. It's located on the quiet south side of Hong Kong Island and boasts a popular public beach and, most recently, a growing number of trendy restaurants.

KOWLOON PENINSULA

Kowloon   North of Hong Kong Island, across Victoria Harbour, is the Kowloon Peninsula. Kowloon gets its name from Gau Lung, which means "nine dragons." Legend has it that about 800 years ago a boy emperor named Ping counted eight hills here and remarked that there must be eight resident dragons, since dragons were known to inhabit hills. The ninth "dragon" was the emperor himself.

You'd have a hard time finding nine or even eight hills in Kowloon today. Less than $3\frac{1}{2}$ square miles in size, Kowloon, once open countryside, has practically disappeared under the dense spread of hotels, shops, restaurants, and housing and industrial projects.

Tsim Sha Tsui   At the southern tip of Kowloon is Tsim Sha Tsui (also spelled "Tsimshatsui"), which, after Central, rates as Hong Kong's most important area. This is where most tourists stay and spend their money, since it has the greatest concentration of hotels, restaurants, and shops in the colony. In fact, some of my acquaintances living in Hong Kong avoid Tsim Sha Tsui like the plague, calling it the "tourist ghetto." On the other hand, Tsim Sha Tsui does boast the Space Museum, Science Museum, a new cultural center for the performing arts, a great art museum, one of the world's largest shopping malls, a nice selection of international restaurants, a jumping nightlife, and Nathan Road, appropriately nicknamed the "golden mile of shopping." Although you'd be foolish to spend all your time in Tsim Sha Tsui, you'd also be foolish to miss it.

Tsim Sha Tsui East   East of Tsim Sha Tsui is an area called, appropriately enough, Tsim Sha Tsui East. Built entirely on reclaimed land, this area has become increasingly important, with a rash of expensive hotels, entertainment centers, shopping and restaurant complexes, a coliseum, and on its eastern edge, the Kowloon Railway Station, terminus for the Kowloon-Canton Railway that carries passengers through the New Territories and beyond to China.

Yau Ma Tei   If you get on the subway in Tsim Sha Tsui and ride two stations to the north (or walk for about 25 minutes straight up Nathan Road), you'll reach the Yau Ma Tei district (also spelled "Yaumatei"), located on Kowloon Peninsula just north of Tsim Sha Tsui. Like the Western District, Yau Ma Tei is also very Chinese, with an interesting produce market, a jade market, and the fascinating Temple Street Night Market.

Mong Kok   On Kowloon Peninsula north of Yau Ma Tei, Mong Kok is a residential and industrial area, home of the Bird Market, the Ladies' Market on Tung Choi Street, and factory outlets. Its northern border, Boundary Street, marks the beginning of the New Territories.

2 Getting Around

If you've just been to Tokyo or Bangkok, Hong Kong will probably bring a rush of relief. For one thing, English is everywhere—on street signs, on buses, in the subways. In addition, the city of Hong Kong is so compact, and its public transportation system so efficient, that it's no problem at all zipping from Tsim Sha Tsui to Causeway Bay or vice versa for a meal or some shopping. Even the novice traveler should have no problem getting around, so extensive and easy is the public transport. It's also extremely cheap. Just remember that cars drive on the left side of the street, English style, so watch it when stepping off the curb.

BY PUBLIC TRANSPORTATION

Each mode of transportation in Hong Kong—bus, ferry, tram, and train/subway—has its own fare system and therefore requires a new ticket each time you transfer from one mode of transportation to the other. The only exception to this is the subway-train system, which allows transfers throughout the rail network with the purchase of a single ticket. Note, however, that there has been discussion of combining all modes of transportation under one fare system, allowing as many transfers as necessary to reach a final destination.

Until then, however, keep in mind that transportation on buses and trams requires the exact fare. It's therefore imperative to have a lot of loose change with you wherever you go. Even though the ferries and subways will give change, you'll find it more convenient if you have exact change, especially during rush hours. If you plan to do a lot of traveling by public transport, pick up a booklet called "Sight-seeing and Culture," available free at Hong Kong Tourist Association offices.

BY SUBWAY   The Star Ferry and trams are so popular and crowded that it's hard to imagine what they must have been like before Hong Kong's subway system was constructed to relieve the human crunch. Hong Kong's **Mass Transit Railway (MTR)** is modern, efficient, clean, and easy to use, and it's also much faster than the older modes of transportation. The only difficult thing about it is trying to remain seated on the slick, stainless-steel seats (you may laugh now, but wait till you've tried it). Also, take note that there are no public toilets at any of the stations or on the trains, and that smoking, drinking, and eating are prohibited. You'll probably want to avoid rush hours, unless you enjoy feeling like a sardine in a can. The MTR operates daily from 6am to 1am. For general inquiries, telephone 852/2750 0170.

Built primarily to transport commuters in the New Territories to and from work, the MTR runs under the harbor to link Hong Kong Island with Kowloon. There are only three lines on the 24-mile subway system, each color-coded, and the stations are clearly marked in English, so you shouldn't have any problem finding your way around. The most important line for tourists starts in Central on Hong Kong Island, goes underneath Victoria Harbour to Tsim Sha Tsui, and then runs north the length of Nathan Road to Tsuen Wan, with stops at Jordan and Yau Ma Tei stations. This is the orange line. Another line on the Kowloon Peninsula travels north and east to

Kwun Tong. The Island Line, with 14 stations, operates on the north side of Hong Kong Island from Sheung Wan (where you'll find the Macau Ferry Pier) east to Chai Wan, passing through Central, Wan Chai, and Causeway Bay.

Single-ticket, one-way fares range from HK$4 to HK$11 (50¢ to $1.40), depending on the distance, but the most expensive ride is the trip underneath the harbor, which costs HK$7.50 (95¢) from Tsim Sha Tsui to Central (still cheap, but outrageous when compared to the Star Ferry). Fares for senior citizens 65 and older and children ages 3 to 11 range from HK$3 to HK$5 (40¢ to 65¢). Fares are posted in English above each vending machine; unfortunately, these machines do not give change. They accept HK$10, HK$5, HK$2, HK$1, and HK$0.50 coins, and if you put in too much the next person in line benefits (though you can cancel the entire operation and get back the whole amount you've put in). If you don't have the exact change, there are change machines close by for coins; bills can be changed only at ticket offices located at MTR stations.

In any case, your ticket is plastic, the size of a credit card, and you feed it into a slot at the turnstile. It disappears and then shoots up at the other end of the turnstile. *Be sure to save your ticket for the end of your journey,* when you will again insert your ticket into the turnstile (only this time you won't get it back). Since these tickets are used again and again and have a magnetized strip, be careful not to bend or damage them.

If you think you're going to be doing a lot of traveling on the MTR subway and perhaps even the KCR train (which services the New Territories), consider buying the **MTR/KCR Tourist Ticket** for HK$25 ($3.25). It allows HK$20 ($2.60) worth of multiple rides, thus saving you from having to buy another ticket each time you ride. It's used just like a regular subway ticket, and the computerized gate will figure out how much each journey costs and deduct it from the balance left on your card. Remember to collect your ticket from the turnstile after each journey.

Alternatively, if you plan to stay in Hong Kong more than a few days, you might consider purchasing a stored-value ticket, available for HK$70 ($9.10), HK$100 ($13), and HK$200 ($26) worth of travel. Similar to the Tourist Ticket, it saves you the hassle of having to buy a new ticket each time you ride. You can purchase the MTR/KCR Tourist Ticket or a stored-value ticket from any MTR or KCR station booking office (except at Lo Wu Station) and from the Hang Seng minibanks located inside major MTR stations.

BY BUS   Hong Kong buses are a delight—especially the British-style double-deckers. They're good for traveling to places where other forms of public transport don't go, such as to the southern part of Hong Kong Island or up into parts of Kowloon and the New Territories. Depending on the route, buses run from about 6am to midnight, with fares ranging from HK$1 to HK$30.60 (13¢ to $3.95); half fare for children. *You must have the exact fare,* which you deposit into a box as you get on. Drivers often don't speak English, so you may want to have someone at your hotel write down your destination in Chinese, particularly if you're traveling in the New Territories. The two major bus terminals are at both ends of the Star Ferry, in the Central District at Exchange Square on Hong Kong Island and in Tsim Sha Tsui in Kowloon. There is another major bus depot at Admiralty Station.

The HKTA has leaflets that show bus routes to most of the major tourist spots, indicating where you can catch the bus, where to get off, and how long the journey should take. Keep in mind that buses can get very crowded at rush hours and that some buses look pretty ancient—which can make the winding trip to Stanley in a double-decker bus a bone-rattling and exciting experience.

BY TRAM Tramlines are found only on Hong Kong Island. Established in 1904 along what used to be the waterfront, these are old, narrow, double-decker affairs that clank their way in a straight line slowly along the northern edge of the island from Kennedy Town in the west to Shau Kei Wan in the east, with one branch making a detour to Happy Valley. Passing through the Central District, Wan Chai, and Causeway Bay on Des Voeux Road, Queensway Road, and Hennessy Road, they can't be beat for atmosphere and are easy to ride since most of them go only on one line (those branching off to Happy Valley are clearly marked). In the zeal to modernize Central, it's a wonder that these trams have survived at all. Since the advent of the subway there's been talk of getting rid of these ancient trams, but this has raised a storm of protest. Since their future is uncertain, be sure to ride them while you can.

Enter the trams from the back and go immediately up the winding stairs to the top deck. The best seats in the house are those in the front row, where you have an unparalleled view of Hong Kong: laundry hanging from second-story windows, signs swinging over the street, markets twisting down side alleys, food stalls, crowded sidewalks, and people darting in front of the tram who just escape being hit. Riding the tram is one of the cheapest ways of touring Hong Kong Island's northern side, and the fare is the same no matter how far you go. Once you've had enough, simply go downstairs to the front of the tram and deposit the exact fare of HK$1.20 (15¢) into a little tin box next to the bus driver as you exit. Children pay half fare. If you don't have the exact amount, don't panic—no one will arrest you for overpaying a few cents. Trams run daily from 6am to 1am.

BY TRAIN There's only one train line in Hong Kong and it goes from the Kowloon Railway Station in Hung Hom near Tsim Sha Tsui East up to Sheung Shui in the New Territories. That is, Sheung Shui is where you must get off if you don't have a visa to go to China. If you do have a visa, you can continue to the border, change trains, and travel all the way through China—and even Russia and Europe if you want to, ending up in London (but who knows how many years that would take). There are two different kinds of trains: the express to China, which goes to the border station of Lo Wu; and the local commuter service for those going to towns in the New Territories.

Known as the **Kowloon-Canton Railway (KCR),** it passes through Mong Kok, Kowloon Tong, Tai Wai, Sha Tin, Fo Tan, University, Tai Po Market, and Fanling before reaching Sheung Shui. The easiest place to board the KCR is at Kowloon Tong, since it's also a subway stop and transfer is easy. At any rate, the whole trip from Kowloon to Sheung Shui takes only a half hour on Hong Kong's new electric trains, so it's the easiest and fastest way to see part of the New Territories. It's also cheap, costing HK$8 ($1.05) for ordinary (second) class and HK$16 ($2.10) for first class if you go all the way to Sheung Shui. Senior citizens 65 and older and children 3 to 12 pay half fare; those under 3 travel free. On horse-racing days at Sha Tin, there's a flat-fare, round-trip ticket to the Sha Tin Race Course for HK$27 ($3.50). The MTR/KCR Tourist Ticket, which costs HK$25 ($3.25), allows HK$20 ($2.60) worth of travel on both the subway and ordinary class of the KCR (see above). You can also use the stored-value tickets described above. Trains run every 4 to 10 minutes daily from about 6am to midnight.

BY FERRY

THE STAR FERRY A trip across Victoria Harbour on one of the white-and-green ferries of the Star Ferry Company is one of the most celebrated rides in the world. Carrying passengers back and forth between Hong Kong Island and Kowloon ever since 1898, these boats have come to symbolize Hong Kong itself and are almost always featured in travel articles on Hong Kong Island. They all incorporate the word "star" in their names, for example, *Twinkling Star* or *Meridien Star*.

They're very easy to ride. Simply drop your coins into a slot on the ancient-looking turnstile, follow the crowd in front of you down the ramp, walk over the gangway, and find a seat on one of the polished wooden benches. A whistle will blow, a man in a sailor uniform will haul up the gangway, and you're off, dodging fishing boats, tugboats, and barges as you make your way across the harbor. Businesspeople who live in Hong Kong are easy to spot—they're usually buried behind their newspapers; visitors, on the other hand, tend to crowd around the railing, cameras in hand.

The whole trip is much too short, only 7 minutes. But that 7-minute ride is one of the best in the world, and it's also one of the cheapest. It costs only HK$1.40 (18¢) for ordinary (second) class; if you really want to splurge, it's only HK$1.70 (22¢) for first class. First class is located on the upper deck, and it has its own entryway and gangway (follow the signs in the ferry concourse); if it's raining or cold, first class is preferable because there are glass windows surrounding it. Otherwise I find ordinary class much more colorful and entertaining because it's the one the locals use and the view of the harbor is much better.

Star Ferries ply the waters daily from 6:30am to 11:30pm between Hong Kong Island's Central District and the tip of Kowloon's Tsim Sha Tsui. Ferries depart every few minutes, except for early in the morning or late at night, when they leave every 10 minutes.

OTHER FERRIES   Besides the Star Ferry, there are also many ferries to other parts of the city. Ferries from the Central District, for example, also go to Kowloon's Hung Hom, where you can catch the train to China at the Kowloon Railway Station, and to the Yau Ma Tei Ferry Pier, close to Jordan Road. From Tsim Sha Tsui a service operates to the convention center in Wan Chai. From Tsim Sha Tsui East (near the Shangri-La Hotel), there's also hoverferry service to Central District.

In addition to ferries crossing the harbor between Kowloon and Hong Kong Island, there's a large fleet that serves the many outlying islands and the northern part of the mainland. If you want to go to one of the outlying islands, you'll find that most of these ferries depart from newly built piers stretching west of the Star Ferry terminus in Central. Operated by the Hong Kong Ferry Company Ltd. (HKF), these boats vary in size; some even have outdoor deck areas in first class. The latest schedules and fares are available from the Hong Kong Tourist Association (HKTA) or by calling HKF (☎ 852/2542 3081 or 852/2542 3082). One thing to keep in mind is that on the weekend the ferries are unbelievably crowded with locals who want to escape the city. And on weekends the fares are higher, so it's best to travel on a weekday. See Chapter 10, "Easy Excursions from Hong Kong," for more information on ferries to specific islands.

BY TAXI

REGULAR TAXIS   As a rule taxi drivers in Hong Kong are strictly controlled and are fairly honest. If they're free to pick up passengers, a red FOR HIRE flag will be raised in the windshield during the day and a lighted TAXI sign will be on the roof at night. You can hail them from the street, though there are some restricted areas, especially in Central. Probably the easiest place to pick up a taxi is at a taxi stand (located at all bus terminals) or at a hotel. Since many drivers do not speak English, it's a good idea to have your destination written in Chinese. Taxis are generally abundant anytime except when it's raining, during shift change (usually about 4pm), and on horse-racing days from September to May.

Taxis on Hong Kong Island and Kowloon are red; fares start at HK$13 ($1.70), plus HK$1.10 (15¢) for each 200 meters (about 275 yards). Waiting time is HK$1.10 (15¢) for every 60 seconds, and if you go through the harbor tunnel you'll be charged an extra HK$20 ($2.60). The luggage charge is HK$5 (65¢) per piece, and if you call for a taxi it's an extra HK$5 to HK$10 (65¢ to $1.30). Note, too, that there's an additional HK$54 (65¢) per bird or animal you might want to bring with you in the taxi! For a tip, simply round off your bill to the nearest HK$1. Although taxi drivers can service both sides of Victoria Harbour, they tend to stick to a certain neighborhood and often aren't familiar with anything outside their area.

Taxis in the New Territories are green and white, and fares start at HK$11 ($1.45) at flag-fall. They cover only the New Territories.

If you have a complaint about a taxi driver, call the police hotline (☎ 852/ 2527 7177), but make sure you have the taxi's license number.

MAXICABS & MINIBUSES   These small buses are the poor man's taxis; although they are quite useful for the locals, they're a bit confusing for tourists. For one thing, although the destination may be written in both Chinese and English, you almost need a magnifying glass to read the English, and by then the vehicle has probably already whizzed by. Even if you can read the English, you may not know the bus's route or where it's going.

There are two types of vehicles, distinguishable by color, and they both hold up to 14 people. The green-and-yellow ones, called **maxicabs,** follow fixed routes and range in price from HK$1 to HK$8 (13¢ to $1.05), depending on the distance, and require the exact fare as you enter. The most useful ones on Hong Kong Island are probably those that depart from the Star Ferry concourse for Bowen Road and Ocean Park, as well as those that travel from City Hall (opposite the Furama Hotel) to Victoria Peak. In Kowloon, you can ride from the Star Ferry concourse in a maxicab to the Tsim Sha Tsui East shopping district.

The red-and-yellow **minibuses** are a lot more confusing, because they have no fixed route and will stop when you hail them from the street (except for some restricted areas in Central). However, they're useful for traveling along Nathan Road or between Central and Causeway Bay. Fares range from HK$2 to HK$7 (25¢ to 90¢), depending on the distance, but are often higher on rainy days, race days, or cross-harbor trips, and you pay as you exit. Just yell when you want to get off.

BY CAR

Rental cars are not advisable in Hong Kong and hardly anyone uses them, even businesspeople. For one thing, nothing is so far away that you can't get there easily and quickly by taxi or public transport. In addition, there probably won't be any place to park once you get to your destination. If you want a chauffeur-driven car, most major hotels have their own private fleet—you can even rent an air-conditioned limousine (a romantically minded friend of mine picked up her arriving boyfriend at the airport that way). If you're still determined to rent a car or plan to take a driving tour of the New Territories, self-drive firms—Avis, Budget, and Hertz—have branches here, along with a couple of dozen local firms. A valid driver's license is required.

Remember, traffic flows on the left-hand side of the street. Gasoline costs about HK$9 ($1.15) for a liter of unleaded (or about $4.50 a gallon).

BY RICKSHAW

Rickshaws hit the streets of Hong Kong in the 1870s and were once the most common form of transport in the colony. Now, however, they are almost a thing of the past—no new licenses are being issued. A few ancient-looking men hang around the Star Ferry terminal in the Central District, but they're usually either snoozing or reading the paper. I've never once seen them hauling a customer. Rather, they make money by charging HK$20 to HK$50 ($2.60 to $6.50) for tourists who want to take their picture. If you do want to take a ride, they'll charge about HK$50 to HK$100 ($6.50 to $13) to take you around the block, clearly the most expensive form of transportation in Hong Kong, and by their appearance that's probably about as far as they can go. But whether you're just taking a photograph or going for a ride, negotiate the price first.

ON FOOT

One of the great things about Hong Kong is that you can explore virtually the entire city proper on foot. You can walk from the Central District all the way through Wan Chai to Causeway Bay in about an hour or so, while the half-hour walk up Nathan Road to Yau Ma Tei is recommended to all visitors.

In the Central District there are mazes of covered, elevated walkways to separate pedestrians from traffic, connecting office buildings, shopping complexes, and hotels. In fact, some roads have no pedestrians because they're all using overhead passageways. You can, for example, walk from the Mandarin Oriental Hotel to the Prince's Building, Alexandra House, and Landmark all via covered bridges. Likewise, you can walk from the Star Ferry concourse all the way to the Macau Ferry Pier via a walkway.

There's also an interesting "people-mover" between Central Market on Des Voeux Road Central and the Mid-Levels on Victoria Peak—a series of moving walkways and escalators that snake their way through the Central District up the steep slope of the Peak. Constructed in the hope of alleviating traffic congestion for commuters who live in the Mid-Levels (about halfway up the Peak), the "people-mover" has a total length of just less than a mile and transports approximately 27,000 people a day, moving downward in the morning and then uphill during the afternoon and evening rush periods.

FAST FACTS: Hong Kong

Your hotel concierge or guest relations manager is usually a valuable source of information, and the Hong Kong Tourist Association (HKTA) is also well equipped and eager to help visitors and answer their questions.

American Express   American Express offices in Hong Kong are at 16–18 Queen's Rd. Central, Central District (☎ 852/2801 7300); the Mall, Level 2, One Pacific Place, 88 Queensway, Central District (☎ 852/2844 0921); 476–478 Lockhart Rd., Causeway Bay (☎ 852/2832 2916); and just off Nathan Road at 25 Kimberley Rd., Tsim Sha Tsui (☎ 852/2732 7327). All offices are open Monday through Friday from 9am to 5pm and on Saturday from 9am to noon. American Express cardholders can withdraw local currency and traveler's checks 24 hours a day at the Express Cash automated-teller machines at all locations.

Area Code   The international country code for Hong Kong is 852.

Baby-sitters   Most of the expensive and many of the medium-range hotels have baby-sitting services. Check Chapter 4 ("Accommodations") for hotels that provide this service. For a full list of hotels with baby-sitters, contact the Hong Kong Tourist Association.

Bookstores   There are lots of English-language bookstores, particularly in Central and Tsim Sha Tsui. Ask your hotel concierge for the one nearest you. If you're looking for a store with a large selection of worldwide travel guides, try Wanderlust, 30 Hollywood Rd. on the edge of Central (☎ 852/2523 2042), open daily from 10am to 6:30pm.

Business Hours   The usual banking hours are from 9am to about 4:30pm Monday through Friday and 9:30am to 12:30pm on Saturday. Some of the larger branches, however, stay open longer. Both the Hongkong Bank and Standard Chartered Bank, two of Hong Kong's major banks, are open Monday through Friday from 9am to 4:30pm and on Saturday from 9am to 12:30pm. The Hang Seng Bank, which I find often offers good exchange rates, is open Monday through Friday from 9am to 5pm and on Saturday from 9am to 1pm. Keep in mind that some banks stop their transactions an hour before closing time, so the safest hours to visit banks are Monday through Friday from 10am to 3pm and on Saturday from 10am to noon.

Most business offices are open Monday through Friday from 9am to 5pm, with lunch hour from 1 to 2pm; Saturday business hours are generally 9am to 1pm.

Most shops are open 7 days a week. Shops in the Central District are generally open from 10am to 6pm; in Causeway Bay and Wan Chai, from 10am to 9:30pm; in Tsim Sha Tsui, from 10am to 9 or 10pm (and some even later than that); and in Tsim Sha Tsui East, from 10am to 7:30pm.

Car Rentals   See "Getting Around" earlier in this chapter.

Climate   See "When to Go" in Chapter 2.

Currency Exchange   When exchanging money in Hong Kong, you'll get the best rate at banks. The exchange rate can vary among banks, however, so it may pay to shop around if you're exchanging a large amount. Some banks, for example, offer a better exchange rate but charge a commission; others many not charge commission but have lower rates. Most charge a commission on traveler's checks, unless, of course, you're cashing American Express checks at an American Express office.

Hotels give a slightly less favorable exchange rate but are convenient because they're open at night and on weekends. Money changers are found in the tourist areas, especially along Nathan Road in Tsim Sha Tsui. Avoid them if you can. They often charge a commission or a "changing fee," or give a much lower rate. Check exactly how much you'll get in return before handing over your money. If you exchange money at Kai Tak Airport, change only what you need to get into town—$10 (U.S.) should be enough—because the exchange rate here is lower than what you'll get at banks or American Express offices in town.

Customs   Visitors are allowed to bring in free of duty 1 liter of alcohol and 200 cigarettes (or 50 cigars or 250 grams of tobacco).

Dentists and Doctors   Most first-class hotels have in-house doctors or can refer you to a doctor or dentist. See Chapter 4 ("Accommodations") for hotels with in-house physicians. Otherwise, call the U.S. consulate for more information. If it's an emergency, see "Hospitals," below.

Documents Required   See "Visitor Information and Entry Requirements" in Chapter 2.

Drugstores   See "Pharmacies," below.

Electricity   The electricity used in Hong Kong is 200 volts, alternating current (AC), 50 cycles. Most hotels have adapters to fit shavers of different plugs and voltages, but for other gadgets you'll need transformers and plug adapters (Hong Kong outlets take plugs with three rectangular or round prongs). Better yet, buy travel hair dryers or irons that can be used in both the United States and abroad.

Embassies and Consulates   If you need to contact a consulate about applications for a visa, a lost passport, tourist information, or an emergency, telephone first to find out the hours of the various sections. The visa section, for example, may be open only during certain hours of the day.

The American Consulate is at 26 Garden Rd., Central District (☎ 852/2523 9011), open Monday through Friday from 8:30am to 12:30pm and 1:30 to 5:30pm; the passport section is open Monday through Friday from 8:30am to noon and again from 1:30 to 5pm. The Canadian Consulate, Tower One, Exchange Square, 8 Connaught Place, Central District (☎ 852/2810 4321), is open Monday through Friday from 8am to noon and 1:15 to 4pm; closed Wednesday afternoon. The Australian Consulate is on the 23rd and 24th floors of Harbour Centre, 25 Harbour Rd., Wan Chai, on Hong Kong Island (☎ 852/2827 8881), and is open Monday through Friday from 9am to noon and 2 to 4pm. The New Zealand Consulate is in Room 3414, Jardine House, Connaught Place, Central District (☎ 852/2525 5044), and is open Monday through Friday from 8:30am to 1pm and 2 to 5pm. Matters pertaining to the United Kingdom are c/o Overseas Visa Section, Hong Kong Immigration Dept., Second Floor, Immigration Tower, 7 Gloucester Rd., Wan Chai (☎ 852/2824 6111), open Monday through Friday from 8:45am to 4:30pm and on Saturday from 9 to 11:30am.

In case you decide to travel elsewhere in Asia and want to know about visa requirements, other Asian consulates' and commissions' telephone numbers that may help are: India (☎ 852/2528 4028), Indonesia (☎ 852/2890 4421), Japan (☎ 852/2522 1184), Korea (☎ 852/2529 4141), Malaysia (☎ 852/2527 0921), Philippines (☎ 852/2810 0183), Singapore (☎ 852/2527 2212), Sri Lanka (☎ 852/2866 2321), and Thailand (☎ 852/2521 6481).

For information on visa applications to mainland **China,** contact a tour operator such as China Travel Service (☎ 852/2525 2284 or 852/2853 3888).

Emergencies   All emergency calls are free—just dial 999 for police, fire, or ambulance.

Eyeglasses   Hong Kong is a good place for inexpensive frames, and you'll see shops everywhere, particularly along Nathan Road and in the large shopping malls. The Optical Shop is one of the largest chain stores, with about 35 branches throughout Hong Kong, including 8 in the Central District and 10 in Tsim Sha Tsui. The Optical Shop can replace eyeglasses in 24 hours. Ask your hotel for the shop nearest you.

Hairdressers and Barbers   It seems that every luxury and first-class hotel has both a barbershop and beauty salon on its premises, and they're probably your best bet for an English-speaking staff accustomed to an international clientele.

Holidays   See "When to Go" in Chapter 2 for a list of Hong Kong's holidays and festivals. Although there are several bank holidays during the year, the only time the shops close as well is during the Chinese New Year, which falls either in late January or early February. Some restaurants and shops, however, do stay open even then to cater to tourists, especially in Tsim Sha Tsui.

Hospitals The following hospitals can help you around the clock: Queen Mary Hospital, 102 Pokfulam Rd., Hong Kong Island (☎ 852/2855 3838 or 852/ 2855 3111); Hong Kong Adventist Hospital, 40 Stubbs Rd., Hong Kong Island (☎ 852/2574 6211); and Queen Elizabeth Hospital, Wylie Road, Kowloon (☎ 852/2710 2111).

Hotlines The Hong Kong Tourist Association's hotline is ☎ 852/2807 6177, with service available Monday through Friday from 8am to 6pm and on Saturday, Sunday, and holidays from 9am to 5pm. If you need help dealing with depression, call the Samaritans Hotline (☎ 852/2896 0000).

Languages English and Cantonese are Hong Kong's two official languages, though even this, I suppose, could change after 1997. After all, both are foreign languages to officials in Beijing, who speak Mandarin. While Mandarin and Cantonese differ widely, they use the same characters for writing. Therefore, while a Hong Kong Chinese and a mainland Chinese may not be able to communicate orally, they can read each other's newspapers. Chinese characters number in the tens of thousands; knowledge of at least 1,500 characters is necessary to read a newspaper. Chinese is difficult to learn primarily because of the tonal variations. Western ears may find these differences in pronunciation almost impossible to detect, but a slight change in tone changes the whole meaning. One thing you'll notice, however, is that Chinese is spoken loudly—whispering does not seem to be part of the language.

Despite the fact that English is an official language and is understood in hotels and tourist shops, few Chinese outside these areas understand it. Bus drivers, taxi drivers, and waiters in many Chinese restaurants do not speak English and will simply shrug their shoulders to your query. To avoid confusion, have someone in your hotel write out your destination in Chinese so that you can show it to your taxi or bus driver. Most Chinese restaurants—and all those listed in this book—have English menus. If you need assistance, try asking younger Chinese, since it's more likely that they will have studied English in school.

Laundry and Dry Cleaning Most hotels provide same-day laundry service. Otherwise, ask your hotel concierge where the nearest laundry is.

Liquor Laws The drinking age in Hong Kong is 18. The hours for bars vary according to the district, though those around Lan Kwai Fong and Tsim Sha Tsui stay open the longest.

Lost Property If you've lost something in Hong Kong, your best bet is to contact the Hong Kong Police (☎ 999). Items found on the street are generally turned in to that district's closest police station.

Luggage Storage and Lockers The main public place to store luggage is at Kai Tak Airport, which will be replaced by Hong Kong's new airport in 1997. Additional storage is available in Tsim Sha Tsui at Goldside Transportation Ltd. (☎ 852/2302 1181), located in the China Hong Kong Terminal on Canton Road in the departure hall on the first floor (boats depart here for Macau and China). It's open from 6am to 8pm daily. Otherwise, if you're traveling to Macau or China for a few days and plan to return to Hong Kong, ask whether you can leave your luggage at your hotel.

Mail Mailboxes are a bright orange-red in Hong Kong. Airmail letters and postcards to the United States or Europe cost HK$2.60 (35¢) for the first 10 grams; each additional 10 grams is HK$1.20 (15¢). It takes about five to seven days for airmail letters to reach the United States, sometimes longer.

It costs HK$360 ($46.75) to mail a package weighing 10 kilos (22 pounds) to the United States via surface mail. Post offices sell boxes called Postpak that are handy for mailing items home; they come in four sizes ranging from HK$6.50 to HK$18.50 (85¢ to $2.40).

If you don't know where you'll be staying in Hong Kong, you can still receive mail. Have it sent to you "Post Restante" at the General Post Office, 2 Connaught Place, Central District, Hong Kong Island, which is located near the Star Ferry terminus. They'll hold mail for you here for two months; when you come to collect it, be sure to bring along your passport for identification. The counter is on the ground floor.

Newspapers and Magazines   Six English-language newspapers are printed in Hong Kong: the *South China Morning Post,* the *Hong Kong Standard,* the *Asian Wall Street Journal,* the *International Herald Tribune, Eastern Express,* and *USA Today International.*

Pharmacies   There are no 24-hour drugstores in Hong Kong, so if you need something urgently in the middle of the night you should contact one of the hospitals listed below. Otherwise, there are convenience stores such as 7-Eleven that are open 24 hours and sell aspirin.

One of the best-known pharmacies in Hong Kong is Watson's, which first opened in the 1880s. Today there are more than 30 Watson's drugstores in Hong Kong, most of them open from 10am to 7:30 or 9pm. Ask the concierge at your hotel for the location of a Watson's or drugstore nearest you.

Photographic Needs   You're never far from a camera shop, especially in Tsim Sha Tsui. Fotomax is one of the largest film-development chains, with seven shops on Hong Kong Island and three in Tsim Sha Tsui. One of the most convenient Fotomax stores is in the Harbour City shopping complex in Tsim Sha Tsui, not far from the Star Ferry terminal. Open daily from 9am to 6:30pm, it can process slides in one working day and prints in one hour. It also sells film.

Police   You can reach the police for an emergency by dialing ☎ 999, the same number as for a fire or an ambulance. There's a crime hotline (☎ 852/2527 7177), a 24-hour service that also handles complaints against taxis. On the streets, English-speaking policemen are identifiable by a red patch worn under their shoulder number.

Post Offices   All major hotels will mail letters for you. Otherwise, there are plenty of post offices throughout the territory. The major ones are open Monday through Friday from 8am to 6pm and on Saturday from 8am to 2pm. The main post office is on Hong Kong Island at 2 Connaught Place, near the Star Ferry concourse, where you'll find stamps sold on the first floor (what we would call the second floor in the United States). On the Kowloon side, post offices are located at 405 Nathan Rd., between the Jordan and Yau Ma Tei subway stations, and at 10 Middle Rd., which is one block north of Salisbury Road. For more information, call 852/2921 2222.

Radio   There are several English-language radio stations, including Radio 3, broadcasting on 567 kHz (AM); Radio 4, mainly classical music, at 97.6 and 98.9 mHz (FM); and Quote AM 864, at 864 kHz (AM). Metro Broadcast owns three stations: Metro Plus broadcasting on 1044 kHz (AM); Hit Radio on 99.7 mHz (FM); and FM Select on 104 mHz (FM). The BBC World Service is broadcast on 675 kHz (AM) 24 hours a day.

Rest Rooms   The best place to find public facilities in Hong Kong is in its many hotels. Fast-food restaurants and shopping malls are other good bets. There may be an attendant on hand, who will expect a small tip, about HK$2 (25¢). Note that there are no public facilities at any of the MTR subway stations.

Safety   Hong Kong is relatively safe for the visitor, especially if you use common sense and stick to such well-traveled nighttime areas as Tsim Sha Tsui or Causeway Bay. The main thing you must guard against is pickpockets. Although on the decline, they often work in groups to pick men's pockets or slit open a woman's purse, quickly taking the valuables and then relaying them on to accomplices who disappear in the crowd. Favored places are Tsim Sha Tsui, Causeway Bay, and Wan Chai. To be on the safe side, keep your valuables in your hotel's safety-deposit box. If you need to carry your passport or large amounts of money, it's a good idea to conceal everything in a moneybelt. Don't leave your passport in your hotel room unless it's in a safe or safety-deposit box.

Shoe Repair   Shoe-repair chains such as Mister Minit and Mister Louie are found in department stores such as Wing On or Isetan and at MTR stations. You will also see sidewalk vendors who can make quick repairs and polish shoes.

Taxes   Hotels will add a 10% service charge and a 5% government tax to your bill. Restaurants and bars will automatically add a 10% service charge. There's an airport departure tax of HK$50 ($6.50) for adults and children older than 12. If you're taking the boat to Macau, you must pay a Hong Kong departure tax of HK$26 ($3.40).

Taxis   See "Getting Around" earlier in this chapter.

Telephone and Fax   Local calls made from homes, offices, shops, restaurants, and some hotel lobbies are free, so don't feel shy about asking to use the phone. From hotel lobbies and public phone booths, a local call costs HK$1 (15¢); from hotel rooms, about HK$3 to HK$5 (40¢ to 65¢). For directory assistance, dial ☎ 1081 for local numbers, 013 for international inquiries. Two useful telephone directories are the *Business Telephone Directory* and the *Hong Kong Commercial Industrial Guide,* available in most hotel rooms. Note that the prefix digit "2" was added to all Hong Kong telephone and fax numbers in 1995.

Most hotels in Hong Kong will handle faxes and overseas calls and offer direct dialing. Otherwise, long-distance calls can be made from specially marked International Dialing Direct (IDD) public phones and from Hong Kong Telecom Service Centres. The cheapest and most convenient method for making international calls is by using a Cardphone, which comes in denominations ranging from HK$50 to HK$250 ($6.50 to $32.45) and is available at Star Ferry piers, HKTA information offices, the Upper Peak Tower, YMCA Salisbury, and other locations around Hong Kong. Simply insert the card into the slot and dial. You can also charge your telephone call to a major credit card by using one of about 100 credit-card phones in major shopping locations. Otherwise, two Telecom Service Centres open 24 hours are at 11–13 D'Aguilar St. in Central and 10 Middle Road in Tsim Sha Tsui.

The cost of a direct-dial call to the United States, made by dialing 001-1-area code-telephone number, is HK$8.60 ($1.10) per minute. From midnight to 7am, as well as Saturday after 1pm and all day Sunday, the charge is HK$8.60 ($1.10) for the first minute and then drops to HK$6.90 (90¢) per subsequent minute. Country codes include 1 for the United States and Canada, 44 for the United Kingdom, and 61 for Australia.

You can make a collect call from any public or private phone by dialing 010. You can also make cashless international calls from any telephone in Hong Kong by using Home Direct, which gives you immediate and direct access to an operator in the country you're calling. Calls can then be charged collect or charged to an overseas telephone card. Some designated Home Direct telephones in Hong Kong even allow you to talk with an operator in your country with the push of a button. Home Direct numbers from Hong Kong are 800 0061 for Australia, 800 1100 for Canada, 800 0064 for New Zealand, and 800 0044 for the U.K. For the U.S., dial 800 1111 for AT&T, 800 1121 for MCI, and 800 1877 for Sprint. For more information on dial access numbers for Home Direct, phone locations, where Cardphones can be purchased and operated, time zones, or other matters pertaining to international calls, call 013.

Television   There are two English-language television channels, TVB Pearl and ATV World, broadcasting weekday mornings, evenings, and all day weekends and holidays, with a choice of local programs and shows imported from Britain, America, and Australia. In addition, all first-class and most moderate hotels have STAR TV (satellite television) or cable TV, as well as in-house video movies. Many hotels also subscribe to the Hongkong Channel, which features short, 5-minute features on Hong Kong's history, transportation networks, traditional customs and festivals, cultural events, shopping tips, and other information.

Time Zone   Hong Kong is 13 hours ahead of New York, 14 hours ahead of Chicago, and 16 hours ahead of Los Angeles. Since Hong Kong does not have a daylight saving time, subtract one hour from the above times if it's summer. Because Hong Kong is on the other side of the International Date Line, you lose one day when traveling from the United States to Asia. Don't worry—you gain it back when you return to North America, which means that you arrive back home the same day you left Hong Kong.

Tipping   Even though restaurants and bars will automatically add a 10% service charge to your bill, you're still expected to leave small change for the waiter. A general rule of thumb is to leave 5%, but in most Chinese restaurants where meals are usually inexpensive it's acceptable to leave change up to HK$5 (65¢). In the finest restaurants you should leave 10%.

You're also expected to tip taxi drivers, bellboys, barbers, and beauticians. For taxi drivers, simply round up your bill to the nearest HK$1 or add a HK$1 (15¢) tip. Tip people who cut your hair 5% or 10%, and give bellboys HK$10 to HK$20 ($1.30 to $2.60), depending on the number of your bags. If you use a public restroom with an attendant, you may be expected to leave a small gratuity—HK$2 (25¢) should be enough. In addition, chambermaids and room attendants are usually given about 2% of the room charge.

Useful Telephone Numbers   Phone numbers you might need include: emergency services for ambulance, fire, and police (☎ 999); HKTA Tourist Information Service (☎ 852/2807 6177); police hotline and taxi complaints (☎ 852/2527 7177); telephone directory information (☎ 1081); time check and temperature (☎ 18501).

Water   It's perfectly safe to drink Hong Kong's water, though bottled water is widely available.

Weather   If you want to check the day's temperature, dial 18501. Otherwise, if a storm is brewing and you're worried about a typhoon, tune in one of the radio or television stations described above.

Accommodations 4

Except for the cost of getting to Hong Kong, your biggest expenditure is going to be for a place to stay. Hotels are not cheap in Hong Kong, especially when compared with those in many other Asian cities. Rather, prices are similar to what you'd pay in New York. On the brighter side, however, dining and shopping in Hong Kong are still affordable.

For many years hotel managers in Hong Kong were in the enviable position of having too many guests and not enough rooms to accommodate them. Because of this high demand and low supply, hotel prices skyrocketed a few years back, and until recently many hotels raised their room rates a whopping 20% a year (now it's closer to 15% a year). To keep up with the demand, new hotels have mushroomed in the past decade, as though there were no 1997. In December 1985 the Hong Kong Tourist Association reported a total of 18,180 hotel rooms in the colony. By the end of 1997 the number is expected to be an incredible 34,000. Some 20 new hotels opened in 1990 alone. Almost all the older hotels have remodeled in the past few years to keep up with the newer ones, and the new ones keep getting more sophisticated. One disturbing trend has emerged this past year, however—several hotels, including the Hilton, have closed to make way for more lucrative office space.

Luckily for visitors, more hotels mean more competition for the tourist's dollar, and many of the larger hotels offer special packages, including weekend packages, summer incentives, and upgrades. The biggest hotel crunches occur twice a year, from March to early June and again from October to early December, but you'd be wise to reserve a hotel room at least two months in advance no matter when you plan to come. If you're traveling off-season, it doesn't hurt to bargain for a lower rate or at least ask whether you can be upgraded to a better room. In fact, you should always ask about special rates when making reservations; although toll-free numbers in the U.S. and Canada are given for many of the listings below, it's always a good idea to call the hotel directly to inquire about rates and special deals.

The hotels in this chapter are arranged first by price and then by geographical location. Because public transportation is so efficient and easy to use and the city is so compact, no place is really more convenient to stay than any other. However, most visitors do stay in Tsim Sha Tsui, on the Kowloon side, simply because that's where you'll find most of the hotels as well as the greatest concentration of shops and restaurants. Business travelers often prefer the Central District, while those who want to avoid the tourist crowds may like the hotels strung along the waterfront of Wan Chai and Causeway Bay. Mong Kok, situated on the Kowloon Peninsula north of Tsim Sha Tsui, is a great place to stay if you want to be surrounded by Chinese stores and locals, with hardly a souvenir shop in sight.

HOTEL PRICES   Generally speaking, the price of a room in Hong Kong depends upon its view and height rather than upon its size. Not surprisingly, the best and most expensive rooms are those with a sweeping view of Victoria Harbour, as well as those on the higher floors. Keep in mind, however, that the difference in price between a room facing inland and a room facing the harbor can be staggering, with various price categories in between. There are, for example, "partial" or "side" harbor views, which means you can glimpse the harbor looking sideways from your window or between tall buildings. "Deluxe" rooms are generally those on the higher floors. When making your reservation, don't be shy about asking what price categories are available and what the differences among them are. To save money, for example, you might request a "standard" room just below the "deluxe" floors. If deluxe rooms are on floors 8 through 12, for example, ask for a standard room on floor 7. For inexpensive lodging, it's also prudent to inquire whether there's a difference in price between twin and double rooms; some hotels charge more for two beds in a room (more sheets to wash, I guess). On the other hand, if you want a full harbor view, be sure to ask for it when making your reservation, and request the highest floor available. In any case, the wide range of prices listed below for double rooms reflects the various categories available. Single rates are also usually available. Just a few years ago, only a handful of hotels here offered cheaper rates for single travelers; now, however, many offer single rates, so be sure to ask when making your reservation.

Hong Kong's most expensive hotels are certainly among the best in the world, with unparalleled service, state-of-the-art business and health-club facilities, guest rooms equipped with just about everything you might need, and some of the city's best restaurants. Those slightly less expensive, labeled here as "Expensive," also offer a guest-relations desk, 24-hour room service, health clubs, business centers, same-day laundry service, and comfortable rooms, but since these often cater to large tour groups they are also noisier and generally have less personalized service than the deluxe hotels. On the other hand, following a popular trend in Asia, almost all hotels in the very expensive and expensive category have special "executive floors" for business travelers; these floors usually offer express check-in and check-out, use of a private executive lounge, complimentary continental breakfast and cocktails, and an executive-floor concierge or attendant.

Of course, since tour groups are popular in Hong Kong, you're likely to encounter many of them at the moderately and inexpensively priced hotels. As for rooms, you can expect all rooms in the expensive through moderate categories to have air-conditioning (a must in Hong Kong), private bath, color television (usually with satellite or cable programs and in-house movies), telephone with international direct dialing, a stocked refrigerator complete with a minibar offering an assortment of liquor (you can assume that if a room has a minibar, it also has a refrigerator), clock-radio, and usually a hair dryer and room safe. Room service (either 24 hours or until the wee hours of the morning), baby-sitting, same-day laundry service, and complimentary tea and coffee are also standard features of expensive to moderate hotels. Most hotels also offer chauffeured limousine service to Kai Tak Airport, though the prices are much higher than for a taxi. A choice of Western and Asian restaurants and a business center are also standard features for moderate through expensive hotels. Many also offer a health club with swimming pool free for hotel guests, but there has been a recent trend to charge extra for hotel guests wishing to use the club and pool. Some hotels even differentiate among their guests, charging those who book through a travel agent but not those who pay rack rates.

As for inexpensive hotels, they generally offer rooms with a bath and air-conditioning, but they have few services or facilities. Always inquire whether there's a difference in price between rooms with twin beds and those with double beds. If possible, it's best to *see* a room before committing yourself, since some may be better than others in terms of traffic noise, view, condition, and size. For the most part, however, you shouldn't have any problems with the inexpensive hotels recommended here.

The prices listed below are for room rates only—a 10% service charge and 5% government tax will be added to your bill. Since a 15% increase can really add up, be sure to take it into account when checking in. It would also be prudent to check the room rate when making your reservation, since prices in Hong Kong only go up.

All of Hong Kong's expensive and moderately priced hotels and the best of the inexpensive hotels are members of the Hong Kong Hotel Association (HKHA) and the Hong Kong Tourist Association (HKTA). All of the hotels listed here belong to these organizations. The advantage of staying at a member hotel is that if you have a complaint, you can lodge it directly with the Hong Kong Tourist Association. Furthermore, the HKHA maintains a counter at Kai Tak Airport where you can reserve a room at one of its member hotels at no extra charge.

The hotels included here are categorized as follows: for a double room (excluding tax and service) **Very Expensive,** HK$2,500 ($325) and up; **Expensive,** HK$1,800 to HK$2,500 ($235 to $325); **Moderate,** HK$1,100 to 1,800 ($145 to $235); and **Inexpensive,** less than HK$1,100 ($145).

1 Best Bets

Naming a favorite hotel in Hong Kong can be a bit overwhelming, if not impossible, because the choices are so vast. Few cities in the world offer such a large number of first-rate hotels, and few hotels in the world can compete with the service that has made the hotel industry in Hong Kong legendary. Here, however, are my personal favorites.

- **Best Historic Hotel:** This is the only category with no competition, since **The Peninsula,** Salisbury Road, Tsim Sha Tsui (☎ 852/2366 6251), has long been the grand old hotel of Hong Kong. Even its new tower, with hi-tech rooms and trendy rooftop restaurant, only adds to the hotel's aura. The best place to experience Hong Kong's colonial past.
- **Best for Business Travelers:** If you can afford it, spring for a room at **The Ritz-Carlton,** 3 Connaught Road, Central District (☎ 852/2877 6666), conveniently located right in the heart of Central's financial district. Small and intimate and filled with art and antiques, it seems more like an expensive apartment complex than a hotel; it offers rooms with sweeping harbor views, a state-of-the-art business center, and health club with heated outdoor swimming pool.
- **Best for a Romantic Getaway:** Go to Macau! And head straight for the **Hotel Bela Vista,** rua do Comendador Kou Ho Neng, Macau (☎ 853/965333), a renovated 1890s colonial structure with just eight rooms, most with verandas overlooking the sea.
- **Best Lobby for Pretending that You're Rich:** The Peninsula had long been the favorite lobby for people-watching, but now there's nothing to match the extravagance of the **Grand Hyatt,** 1 Harbour Road, Wan Chai (☎ 852/2588 1234), which flaunts space and is decorated like a 1930s art deco ocean liner.

- **Best Moderately Priced Hotel:** The **Evergreen Plaza Hotel,** 33 Hennessy Road, Wan Chai (☎ 852/2866 9111), offers the room amenities, services, and facilities of a more expensive hotel but at moderate prices; guests can enjoy a rooftop heated pool, fitness center, room service, and in-house movies.
- **Best Budget Hotel:** You can't beat the location, view, and facilities of **The Salisbury YMCA,** Salisbury Road, Tsim Sha Tsui (☎ 852/2369 2211). If you want a view of the famous Victoria Harbour and Hong Kong Island, the rooms here are the cheapest available.
- **Best Service:** Other hotels may be just as good, but probably none can match the professional, unobtrusive service offered by **The Peninsula** (see address and telephone above); it has one of the highest staff-to-guest ratios in Hong Kong.
- **Best Location:** The **Mandarin Oriental,** 5 Connaught Road, Central District (☎ 852/2522 0111), a longtime landmark in the heart of Central, is the best place to stay if you want to rub elbows with those who actually live and work in Hong Kong.
- **Best Hotel Pool:** The **Grand Hyatt** (see address and telephone above) and **New World Harbour View,** 1 Harbour Road, Wan Chai (☎ 852/2802 8888), hotels share one of Hong Kong's largest outdoor pools, complete with a landscaped garden and views of the harbor.
- **Best Views:** The best harbor views are from Kowloon, with vistas of Hong Kong Island's stunning architecture and Victoria Peak. And no hotel is as close to the water as **The Regent,** Salisbury Road, Tsim Sha Tsui (☎ 852/2721 1211), built right over the harbor; as many as 70% of its rooms command sweeping views of the water and boast floor-to-ceiling and wall-to-wall windows.

2 Very Expensive

KOWLOON

✪ Kowloon Shangri-La

64 Mody Rd., Tsim Sha Tsui East, Kowloon, Hong Kong. ☎ **852/2721 2111** or 800/942-5050 in the U.S. and Canada. Fax 852/2723 8686. 689 rms, 30 suites. A/C MINIBAR TV TEL. HK$2,500–HK$3,800 ($325–$494) double; HK$2,900–HK$4,000 ($377–$519) Horizon Club executive floor double; from HK$4,400 ($571) suite. Children 18 and under stay free in parents' room. AE, CB, DC, MC, V. MTR: Tsim Sha Tsui.

The 21-story Kowloon Shangri-La, on the waterfront of Tsim Sha Tsui East, is a good choice for business travelers, who make up a large percentage of its clientele. Its two-story lobby is one of the most spacious in Hong Kong, with an expansive white Carrara marble floor, massive Viennese crystal chandeliers, a fountain, and Chinese landscape murals. The hotel, near the hoverferry pier with service to Central, is within walking distance of Tsim Sha Tsui but something of a hike from the nearest MTR station.

Rooms, offering either harbor views or rather mundane "garden views" (a popular euphemism for windows that face inland), are large and luxuriously appointed, with ceiling-to-floor bay windows and either a king-size bed or two double beds. Curtains, TV (with a free 24-hour movie channel as well as in-house pay movies), lights, and other appliances are controlled by bedside panels. Messages are delivered via voice mail and can even be retrieved outside the hotel. The top two floors are the executive

Kowloon Accommodations

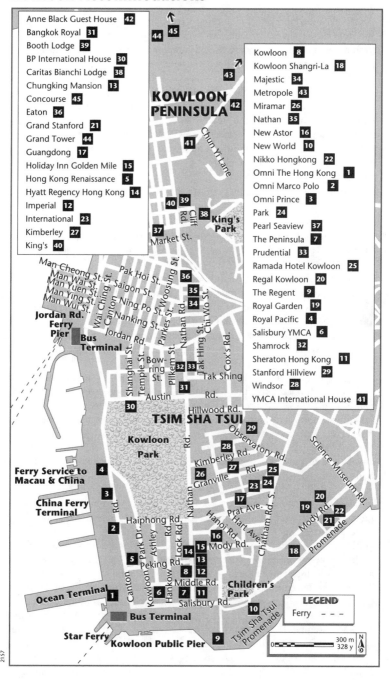

Anne Black Guest House **42**
Bangkok Royal **31**
Booth Lodge **39**
BP International House **30**
Caritas Bianchi Lodge **38**
Chungking Mansion **13**
Concourse **45**
Eaton **36**
Grand Stanford **21**
Grand Tower **44**
Guangdong **17**
Holiday Inn Golden Mile **15**
Hong Kong Renaissance **5**
Hyatt Regency Hong Kong **14**
Imperial **12**
International **23**
Kimberley **27**
King's **40**

Kowloon **8**
Kowloon Shangri-La **18**
Majestic **34**
Metropole **43**
Miramar **26**
Nathan **35**
New Astor **16**
New World **10**
Nikko Hongkong **22**
Omni The Hong Kong **1**
Omni Marco Polo **2**
Omni Prince **3**
Park **24**
Pearl Seaview **37**
The Peninsula **7**
Prudential **33**
Ramada Hotel Kowloon **25**
Regal Kowloon **20**
The Regent **9**
Royal Garden **19**
Royal Pacific **4**
Salisbury YMCA **6**
Shamrock **32**
Sheraton Hong Kong **11**
Stanford Hillview **29**
Windsor **28**
YMCA International House **41**

KOWLOON
PENINSULA

Chun Yi Lane

King's
Park

Cliff Rd.
Market St.

Man Cheong St.
Man Wai St.
Man Yuen St.
Man Ying St.
Man Wui St.

Pak Hoi St.
Saigon St.
Wai Ching St.
Canton Rd.
E Ning Po St.
Nanking St.
Woosung St.
Parkes St.
Nathan Rd.
Chi Wo St.
Tak Hing St.

Jordan Rd.
Ferry
Pier
Bus
Terminal

Jordan Rd.

Shanghai St.
Temple St.
Pilkem St.
Bow-
ring
St.

Cox's Rd.

Tak Shing

Austin Rd.

Hillwood Rd.

TSIM SHA TSUI

Kowloon
Park

Rd.

Observatory Rd.

Science Museum Rd.

Kimberley Rd.
Rd.

Granville Rd.

Nathan Rd.

Hanoi Rd.

Prat Ave.
Hart Ave.

Chatham Rd. S.

Mody Rd.

Promenade

Ferry Service to
Macau & China

China Ferry
Terminal

Haiphong Rd.

Ashley Rd.
Kowloon Park Dr.

Lock Rd.

Peking Rd.

Mody Rd.

Hankow Rd.
Middle Rd.

Children's
Park

Salisbury Rd.

Ocean Terminal

Bus Terminal

Star Ferry
Kowloon Public Pier

Tsim Sha Tsui Promenade

LEGEND
Ferry - - -

0 300 m
   328 y

N

2157

floors; called the Horizon Club, it offers a complimentary chauffeured limousine to and from the airport, an in-room fax, personalized stationery, free laundry and dry cleaning, a 24-hour pressing service, and complimentary breakfast and cocktails.

Dining/Entertainment: The hotel's newest restaurant is **Napa** on the 21st floor, offering Californian cuisine and a stunning view of the harbor. The formal **Margaux** is known throughout Hong Kong for its great French cuisine and views of the harbor. **Shang Palace** is an extravagantly decorated Cantonese restaurant. Other restaurants serve Japanese cuisine and steaks. **The Music Room** is a sophisticated lounge with deep carpets, plush chairs, mellow music, and a small dance floor.

Services: Concierge, 24-hour room service, free newspaper, complimentary welcoming tea, house doctor, limousine, nightly turndown, twice-daily maid service, baby-sitting, same-day laundry.

Facilities: Indoor swimming pool, free health spa with sauna, business center, beauty salon, gift shop, no-smoking floors.

✪ The Peninsula Hotel

Salisbury Rd., Tsim Sha Tsui, Kowloon, Hong Kong. ☎ **852/2366 6251** or 800/262-9467 in the U.S. Fax 852/2722 4170. 246 rms, 54 suites. A/C MINIBAR TV TEL. HK$3,000–HK$4,100 ($390–$532) single or double; from HK$5,400 ($701) suite. AE, CB, DC, MC, V. MTR: Tsim Sha Tsui.

This is Hong Kong's most famous hotel, the place to stay if you are an incurable romantic, have a penchant for the historical, and can afford its high prices. Built in 1928, it exudes elegance from its white-gloved doormen to one of the largest fleets of Rolls-Royces in the world. Priding itself on service, it maintains one of the highest staff-to-guest ratios in Hong Kong. Its lobby, reminiscent of a Parisian palace with high gilded ceilings, pillars, and palms, had been Hong Kong's foremost spot for people-watching.

Although The Peninsula lost its fabled view of the harbor following construction of the unsightly Space Museum on reclaimed land across the street, this problem was remedied in 1993 with the completion of a magnificent 32-story tower that rises just behind the present hotel. Although the tower looks rather unremarkable when viewed from across the harbor, its plain, white exterior is a perfect match, showing unusual restraint in a city known for its splashy architectural boldness. No holds were barred, however, with the tower's interior—its rooftop serves as a helipad, its top-floor restaurant was designed by Philippe Starck, the swimming pool, complete with sun terrace overlooking the harbor, is elegantly modeled on a classical Roman theme, and its guest rooms have amenities and facilities almost beyond belief, creating a new standard of excellence that will surely set off a flurry of renovations as other hotels try to compete.

All rooms are equipped with a silent fax machine (messages are sent to your room via fax), computer hookups, a telephone that shows the time around the world and automatically displays the time in your home country, headphones for both radio and TV, a display panel showing outdoor temperature and humidity, TV with laser-disc CD player, three telephones in the bedroom and two in the bathroom, and a box in the closet where attendants can place your morning newspaper or take your dirty shoes for cleaning. Requests for hotel services, as well as such functions as curtain control, are accomplished with the push of a button. Bathrooms are huge; they are equipped with their own TV, mood lighting, separate bath and shower stall, and two sinks, both with a magnifying mirror. It may be worth the extra money to spring for a harbor view, since the rooms facing the back are a disappointment and those in the older part of the hotel slightly claustrophobic.

Dining/Entertainment: The hotel's premier restaurant is **Gaddi's,** offering French cuisine as well as live music and dancing in the evening. The tower's top-floor restaurant, **Felix,** features an avant-garde interior designed by Philippe Starck, innovative continental cuisine, and dramatic views of Hong Kong. Another good choice is the **Verandah Grill.** Head for the **Chesa** for traditional Swiss food, the **Spring Moon** for Cantonese specialties, or **Imasa** for traditional Japanese food.

Services: Concierge, 24-hour room service, Rolls-Royce limousine service, free newspaper, baby-sitting, same-day laundry, house doctor, complimentary welcoming tea.

Facilities: Shopping arcade, business center, beauty salon, barber, free indoor swimming pool with sun terrace, health club with exercise equipment, Jacuzzis, saunas, steam rooms, solariums, rooftop helipad, a soundproofed music room where guests can practice and rehearse.

⑤ The Regent Hotel

Salisbury Rd., Tsim Sha Tsui, Kowloon, Hong Kong. ☎ **852/2721 1211** or 800/545-4000 in the U.S. and Canada. Fax 852/2739 4546. 508 rms, 94 suites. A/C MINIBAR TV TEL. HK$2,300–HK$3,550 ($299–$461) double; from HK$4,100 ($532) junior suite. Children under 15 stay free in parents' room. AE, CB, DC, MC, V. MTR: Tsim Sha Tsui.

The Regent boasts the best views of the harbor from Tsim Sha Tsui. In fact, you can't get much closer to the water than this—the hotel is located on a projection of reclaimed land and sits on more than 120 pylons sunk into the harbor. Built in 1981 of polished rose granite and rising 17 stories high, it has a bare lobby of polished granite and marble; with the magnificent view of the harbor and Hong Kong Island serving as the lobby's focal point, that's certainly all one needs. The Regent also provides some of Hong Kong's best restaurants, all with great views, an exclusive shopping mall, the world's largest fleet of Daimler limousines outside the U.K., and a spectacular freestanding staircase of white Carrara marble leading to the hotel's ballroom. Even the outdoor pool's sun terrace and whirlpools overlook the harbor.

As many as 70% of its rooms command sweeping views of the harbor, with floor-to-ceiling and wall-to-wall windows. The remaining rooms face the outdoor swimming pool and landscaped sun terrace. All rooms feature remote-control TV with 24-hour CNN and in-house movies, three phones, and facilities for in-room fax machines and personal computers. Unlike most Hong Kong deluxe hotels, there are no designated executive floors; the underlying concept is that all rooms should offer the same degree of efficient and personalized service. There's a butler for every six rooms, on duty 24 hours a day. A notable feature of the Regent is its spacious bathrooms, each fitted in Italian marble with a sunken bathtub and separate shower unit.

Dining/Entertainment: The **Plume** is one of Hong Kong's finest French restaurants, while **Lai Ching Heen** is an elegant Cantonese restaurant. **Yü** is the city's trendiest seafood restaurant, and the **Harbour Side** offers a harbor view along with its inexpensive snacks and meals throughout the day. Steaks and salads are served at the **Steak House.**

Services: Concierge, 24-hour room service, house doctor, baby-sitting, free newspaper, nightly turndown, limousine service, same-day laundry, complimentary welcoming tea, free bottled water.

Facilities: Outdoor swimming pool and whirlpools, business center, health spa, shopping arcade, beauty salon.

CENTRAL DISTRICT

Conrad Hotel

Pacific Place, 88 Queensway, Central, Hong Kong. ☎ **852/2521 3838** or 800/445-8667 in the U.S and Canada. Fax 852/2521 3888. 467 rms, 46 suites. A/C MINIBAR TV TEL. HK$2,700–HK$3,400 ($350–$442) double; HK$3,700–HK$4,000 ($480–$519) executive floor double; from HK$5,000 ($649) suite. Children under 19 stay free in parents' room. AE, DC, MC, V. MTR: Admiralty.

The 61-story Conrad, built in 1990, is one of a trio of exclusive hotels perched on a hillside above Pacific Place, an upscale shopping center located about halfway between the Central District and Wan Chai. The Conrad's facilities appeal to both businesspeople (who make up 70% of the hotel's clientele) and leisure travelers; there is a business center that never closes, an outdoor heated pool, and extra services and amenities designed to answer every need. Although the architecture is modern, the hotel's classic furnishings and interior design soften the modern effect, giving it a cozy atmosphere with wood paneling, polished granite, and comfortable furniture. I especially like the lighthearted touch of the larger-than-life butterflies and wildflowers on the murals of the massive lobby pillars.

Rooms feature large windows that extend the width of the room, offering views of either the Peak or the harbor (harbor-view rooms, of course, are better and cost more). All room TVs have remote control and 19 channels, including eight in-house movie selections; TVs also display messages and can be used for checking out. Other features include three telephones and voice mail, magnifying mirror, an electronic "Do Not Disturb" and "Maid Call" system, two washbasins, and separate shower and bathtub facilities. On a playful note, the bathrooms even feature a floating duck or other toy for a bit of fun in the bathroom, while a stuffed bear is placed on beds at turndown. If you really feel like splurging, four executive floors provide guests with an exclusive lounge open 24 hours a day, as well as complimentary breakfast, cocktails, clothes pressing, personalized stationery, fruit basket, and free local telephone calls. There is even a facsimile machine in each executive room with its own private number.

Dining/Entertainment: **Nicholini's** specializes in authentic northern Italian cuisine, while the **Brasserie** offers traditional French provincial cuisine. The **Golden Leaf** is a classy Cantonese restaurant; the **Garden Café** serves Western and Asian dishes in a casual, tropical setting.

Services: Concierge, free newspaper; 24-hour room service; house doctor; baby-sitting; limousine service; tea- and coffee-making facilities; free bottled water, same-day laundry; welcome basket with tea, fruit, and chocolate; free shuttle bus to Central every half hour.

Facilities: 24-hour business center, health club and sauna, Jacuzzi, heated outdoor swimming pool, shopping arcade, eight no-smoking floors.

✪ Island Shangri-La Hong Kong

Pacific Place, 88 Queensway, Central, Hong Kong. ☎ **852/2877 3838** or 800/942-5050 in the U.S. and Canada. Fax 852/2521 8742. 532 rms, 34 suites. A/C MINIBAR TV TEL. HK$2,900–HK$3,800 ($377–$493) double; from HK$6,300 ($818) suite. Children under 19 stay free in parents' room. AE, DC, MC, V. MTR: Admiralty.

Hong Kong's tallest hotel (measured from sea level) offers the ultimate in extravagance and luxury, rivaling the grand hotels in Paris or London. More than 700 Viennese chandeliers, lush Tai Ping carpets, artistic flower arrangements, and more than 500 paintings and artwork adorn the hotel. The 17-story atrium, which stretches from the 39th floor to the very top of the hotel, features a marvelous 16-story-high Chinese painting, drawn on 250 panels of Chinese paper by 40 artists from Beijing and believed to be the largest landscape painting in the world. Also in the atrium is a private lounge open only to hotel guests and a two-story old world–style library, fitted with leather armchairs and classic lamps and stocked with reference materials, special-interest books, videotapes, and music compact discs. The atrium is surrounded by guest rooms. The hotel is connected to a shopping center and subway station.

Upon arrival, guests are personally escorted to their rooms by a guest relations officer, who also explains features of the room. Rooms here, among the largest in Hong Kong, face either the Peak or Victoria Harbour and feature marble-topped desks, Chinese lacquerware TV cabinets, silk bedspreads, room safe, and oversize bathrooms equipped with two sinks, separate tub and shower areas (harbor-view rooms only), a bidet, bath scales, and even jewelry boxes. A touch of a button turns on the "Do Not Disturb" or "Maid Call" light, and fax machines and personal computers are available on request.

Dining/Entertainment: Petrus is the hotel's signature restaurant, occupying a prime spot on the top floor and serving continental cuisine. Next door is **Cyrano,** a lounge offering jazz entertainment every night and stunning views of the harbor. **Summer Palace** serves Cantonese and Szechuan food; the **Lobster Bar** is an elegant seafood restaurant; the **Island Café,** with a breezy Californian atmosphere, specializes in buffets; and **Nadaman,** a Japanese restaurant, serves kaiseki, teppanyaki, and sushi.

Services: Concierge, free newspaper, 24-hour room service, tea- and coffee-making facilities, free bottled water, same-day laundry, nightly turndown, limousine service, baby-sitting, medical clinic, free shuttle service to Central and the Convention Centre.

Facilities: Outdoor heated swimming pool (covered with see-through dome in cold weather), Jacuzzi, sauna, health club, 24-hour business center, drugstore, barbershop, beauty salon, shopping arcade.

JW Marriott Hotel

Pacific Place, 88 Queensway, Central, Hong Kong. ☎ **852/2841 3000** or 800/228-9290 in the U.S. and Canada. Fax 852/2845 0737. 565 rms, 42 suites. A/C MINIBAR TV TEL. HK$2,600–HK$3,200 ($338–$416) double; HK$3,400–HK$3,800 ($442–$493) executive floor double; from HK$5,700 ($740) suite. AC, DC, MC, V. MTR: Admiralty.

The 27-story Marriott, which was the first hotel to open at Pacific Place in 1989, recently underwent a major renovation, including the redecoration of all its guest rooms. Its lobby, while not as grandiose as others in this category, is nonetheless the only one of Pacific Place's three hotels to offer views of the harbor, though with the expected demise of the Prince of Wales barracks and Naval dockyards on the waterfront, taller buildings that might take their place might block that view. Such is life in Hong Kong.

Rooms are all designed with right-angled "saw-tooth" windows to maximize views of the harbor or Peak and are outfitted with handpainted bedspreads and bedside control panels that also operate the curtains (it's great to wake up in the morning and have the city appear before you with a mere push of a button). On the downside, rooms facing the harbor are subject to the slight din of traffic and a current land reclamation project nearby detracts from the otherwise wonderful view. Some 50 pay movies are available on demand. Large bathrooms have separate bath and shower areas and scales. Four executive floors offer the usual complimentary breakfast and cocktails.

Dining/Entertainment: The **Man Ho** features gourmet Cantonese delicacies. **J.W.'s California** offers the best of the East and West. Light fare for breakfast, lunch, and dinner is served at the **Marriott Café.**

Services: Concierge, free newspaper, 24-hour room service, limousine service, same-day laundry, baby-sitting, welcoming tea, coffee- and tea-making facilities, house doctor.

Facilities: Outdoor heated swimming pool, health center/sauna, shopping mall, beauty salon, business center, six no-smoking floors.

✪ Mandarin Oriental

5 Connaught Rd., Central, Hong Kong. ☎ **852/2522 0111** or 800/526-6666 in the U.S. and Canada. Fax 852/2810 6190. 480 rms, 58 suites. A/C MINIBAR TV TEL. HK$2,800–HK$4,150 ($364–$539) double; from HK$6,000 ($779) suite. AE, CB, DC, MC, V. MTR: Central.

With so many new hotels on Hong Kong Island, the Mandarin, a 25-story landmark built in 1963, seems like a familiar old-timer. Famed for its service and consistently rated as one of the top hotels in the world, the Mandarin Oriental maintains a staff of 1,000 for its 538 rooms and suites; because of its great location in the heart of Hong Kong's business district (not far from Star Ferry), it attracts mostly a business clientele. For tourists, one advantage to staying in Central is that you're surrounded mostly by people who actually live and work in Hong Kong, as opposed to Tsim Sha Tsui, which is crowded largely with other tourists. In addition, the Mandarin's restaurants are among the best in Hong Kong, but its indoor pool is disappointingly small.

Spacious and decorated in an Oriental theme with an understated elegance, most rooms offer balconies (rare in Hong Kong) and face either the harbor or inland. They also feature all the amenities and facilities you could possibly want, including a choice of 60 different movies which can be seen at any time, bathroom scale, magnifying mirror, and room safe; if you are still in need of something, the staff will make every effort to fulfill your wishes.

Dining/Entertainment: Several of the restaurants have a well-deserved reputation for excellent cuisine; there is the **Mandarin Grill** for seafood, the **Man Wah** for Cantonese food, and the **Pierrot** for French specialties, and an adjoining caviar bar. **The Captain's Bar,** just off the hotel lobby, is an intimate, cozy bar popular with Central's executive and professional crowd.

Services: Concierge, complimentary fruit basket and chocolates, free newspaper, 24-hour room service, nightly turndown, same-day laundry, house doctor, limousine service, baby-sitting.

Facilities: Indoor swimming pool, fitness center, sauna, whirlpool, art gallery, business center, shopping arcade, Cuban-style cigar divan, beauty salon, barbershop, flower and gift shop.

✪ The Ritz-Carlton

3 Connaught Rd., Central, Hong Kong. ☎ **852/2877 6666** or 800/241-3333 in the U.S. and Canada. Fax 852/2877 6778. 187 rms, 29 suites. A/C MINIBAR TV TEL. HK$2,750–HK$3,700 ($357–$480) double; HK$4,250 ($552) Ritz-Carlton Club executive floor; from HK$5,700 ($740) suite. Children under 13 stay free in parents' room (maximum: three persons per room). AE, DC, MC, V. MTR: Central.

Opened in 1993, the Ritz-Carlton occupies a smart-looking 25-story art deco building in the heart of the Central District not far from the waterfront and Star Ferry. It follows the Ritz-Carlton tradition of excellent service, an extensive collection of 18th- and 19th-century artwork and antiques, and fine dining. Its lobby is subdued and intimate, resembling more closely a wealthy person's home than a public place, with the reception desk tucked away in an alcove.

The low-key atmosphere prevails upstairs as well; since there are only 11 rooms on each floor, it seems more like an apartment complex than a hotel, which obviously appeals to its overwhelmingly business clientele, many of whom are long-staying guests. The rooms are rather neutral in tone and unexciting, but half of them face the harbor and offer great views; even those that face inland provide a nice view of lush Chater Garden and the Peak. All rooms feature in-house pay movies, marble bathrooms with two sinks, separate toilet areas, scales, and makeup/shaving mirrors. Fax machines are available upon request. The top three floors serve as the Ritz-Carlton Club, where guests enjoy a private lounge as well as special services and amenities.

Dining/Entertainment: The **Toscana** is the premier restaurant, specializing in regional Italian cuisine; other outlets serve Chinese, Japanese, and continental cuisine.

Services: Concierge, 24-hour room service, welcome tea, complimentary fruit basket, same-day laundry, free newspaper, nightly turndown, baby-sitting, limousine service.

Facilities: Heated outdoor swimming pool, steam bath, sauna, whirlpool, fitness room, shopping arcade, business center.

CAUSEWAY BAY/WAN CHAI

Grand Hyatt Hong Kong

1 Harbour Rd., Wan Chai, Hong Kong. ☎ **852/2588 1234** or 800/233-1234 in the U.S. and Canada. Fax 852/2802 0677. 536 rms, 36 suites. A/C MINIBAR TV TEL. HK$3,000–HK$4,000 ($399-$519) double; HK$3,950–HK$4,400 ($513–$571) Regency Club executive floor; from HK$5,850 ($760) suite. Children under 12 stay free in parents' room (maximum: three persons per room). AE, DC, MC, V. MTR: Wan Chai.

In a city with so many first-class hotels and such stiff competition, sooner or later a hotel had to exceed all the others in opulence and grandeur. Walking into the lobby of the Grand Hyatt is like walking into the Bavarian castle of a modern-day King Ludwig, a lobby so palatial in design that the word "understatement" has certainly never crossed its threshold. Decorated to resemble the salon of a 1930s art deco luxury ocean liner, it literally flaunts space, with huge black granite columns, massive flower arrangements, palm trees, bubbling fountains, and furniture and statuettes reminiscent of that era. It appears that no expense was spared in creating Hyatt International's Asian flagship hotel.

Located near the Convention Centre and only a 5-minute walk from the Wan Chai Star Ferry pier that takes people to Tsim Sha Tsui, it offers rooms pleasantly decorated in natural woods, with marble bathrooms complete with 18-karat-gold fixtures, separate bathtub and shower areas, and bathroom scales. Messages are delivered via a voice-mail recording system. Some 70% of the rooms provide a harbor view, while the rest offer a view of the pool (one of Hong Kong's largest) and garden with partial glimpses of the harbor. Extra pampering is offered by the Regency Club's eight floors (serviced by private elevators), where complimentary continental breakfast, cocktails, and hors d'oeuvres are available and guest rooms are outfitted with a laser-disc player and a CD player, complete with a selection of classical and contemporary CDs and access to a laser-disc library with more than 50 popular films.

Dining/Entertainment: The bright and airy **Grissini** serves authentic Milanese cuisine, while **One Harbour Road** is a split-level upscale Cantonese restaurant. **JJ's** is one of the hottest and largest nightspots on the island, featuring live music, a disco, pool, and even a pizza parlor.

Services: Concierge, free newspaper, 24-hour room service, limousine service, baby-sitting, nightly turndown, complimentary transportation to Central and Admiralty MTR station, same-day laundry.

Facilities: Huge outdoor swimming pool (shared with the New World Harbour View Hotel), tennis courts, golf driving range, jogging track, Jacuzzi, fitness club, business center, three no-smoking floors.

Regal Hongkong Hotel

68 Yee Wo St., Causeway Bay, Hong Kong. ☎ **852/2890 6633** or 800/222-8888 in the U.S., 800/233-9188 in Canada. Fax 852/2881 0777. 393 rms, 32 suites. A/C MINIBAR TV TEL. HK$2,600–HK$2,800 ($338–$364) double; HK$3,250–HK$3,500 ($422–$455) Regal Club executive floor double; from HK$4,600 ($597) suite. Children under 12 stay free in parents' room. AE, DC, MC, V. MTR: Causeway Bay.

Causeway Bay's newest deluxe hotel and the Regal Hotel Group's flagship property, the Regal Hongkong opened in 1993; it is a 32-story glass-facade building just a stone's throw from Victoria Park. In an attempt to bring some old-world European grandeur to the Orient, the hotel is decorated in an ornate French style, but for my taste it's a trifle overdone and borders on the gaudy. The lobby literally shimmers with chandeliers, imitation Louis XIV furniture, a marble staircase, and an enormous European-style oil painting commissioned especially for the hotel. In all, 1,700 paintings were commissioned—each guest room features one large painting above the bed, plus three smaller pieces (as my husband pointed out, the paintings are not nailed down). The rooms are comfortable, with bay windows (those facing Victoria Park provide the best view), a sitting area, room safe, hair dryer, and separate tub and shower stall. The alarm clock displays times around the world, and the TV has in-house pay movies. Three floors constitute the Regal Club, where guests can enjoy such extras as a private lounge and complimentary breakfast and evening cocktails.

Dining/Entertainment: The Riviera, located on the 31st floor overlooking Victoria Park, features Mediterranean cuisine with an emphasis on French and Italian fare. There are two Chinese restaurants—one serving Cantonese and the other Chiu Chow—and a cafe and lobby lounge. **The Windsor Arms,** a British-style pub, offers a carvery buffet lunch and evening entertainment, while **Sparkles** is a combination disco and karaoke lounge with live entertainment.

Services: Concierge, 24-hour room service, limousine service, same-day laundry, baby-sitting, free newspaper, nightly turndown, house doctor.

Facilities: Rooftop outdoor swimming pool (closed in winter), fitness room, sauna, steam bath, business center, shopping arcade, no-smoking floors.

3 Expensive

KOWLOON

Grand Stanford (formerly Holiday Inn Crowne Plaza Harbour View)

70 Mody Rd., Tsim Sha Tsui East, Kowloon, Hong Kong. ☎ **852/2721 5161.** Fax 852/2369 5672. 588 rms, 9 suites. A/C MINIBAR TV TEL. HK$2,300–HK$3,250 ($299–$422) double; HK$2,750–HK$3,750 ($357–$487) executive floor double; from HK$5,700 ($740) suite. Children under 19 stay free in parents' room. AE, CB, DC, MC, V. MTR: Tsim Sha Tsui.

Because of its location near Hong Kong's Coliseum in Tsim Sha Tsui East, a number of well-known personalities have stayed here, including David Bowie, Elton John, and John McEnroe. Formerly a Holiday Inn but recently acquired by Stanford Hotels International, this hotel is undergoing a complete renovation that will transform it into the Stanford's flagship property, with completion scheduled for late 1996. About half the rooms offer harbor views; unfortunately, the windows of the least expensive rooms open rather unceremoniously onto a windowless wall. All rooms, nicely renovated, feature double beds (or king-size bed) and bathroom scales; some rooms even come equipped with sofa beds for women executives who might feel uncomfortable hosting a business meeting in a hotel room. The executive floors offer the usual amenities of complimentary newspaper, free breakfast, fruit basket, and

🅐 Family-Friendly Hotels

Conrad Hotel *(see p. 55)* An outdoor heated swimming pool, a television with 19 channels (including 8 in-house movie selections), a floating toy for the bathtub, and a stuffed animal on turned-down beds will keep youngsters of all ages satisfied. Baby-sitting services, a house doctor, a shopping mall, and no extra charge for children under 19 staying in the same room will please parents.

Mandarin Oriental *(see p. 58)* Beginning with check-in, children are invited to participate by entering their name and age into a book reserved for younger guests. Children's menus are available at several of the hotel's restaurants and for room service (jelly beans accompany each room service order). Chinaware features cartoon characters. Room amenities for babies include talcum powder, wet wipes, diapers, a teether, and an educational toy, while older children receive a coloring book with crayons and a reading book or puzzles and games. Items available on loan include cribs, bottle sterilizer units, baby baths, high chairs, board games, and computerized toys.

Salisbury YMCA *(see p. 83)*   The overwhelming choice for families in terms of price, facilities, and location, this Salisbury Road establishment offers large suites suitable for families, an inexpensive cafeteria serving buffet breakfasts and lunches, two swimming pools, a children's pool, and baby-sitting services.

free cocktails, as well as fax machines and coffee- and tea-making facilities. One advantage here is the rooftop swimming pool, heated and open year-round. Probably the biggest drawback to this hotel is that it's about a 10-minute walk to the Tsim Sha Tsui MTR station.

Dining: The **Belvedere** serves continental cuisine, while the **Mistral** specializes in Italian foods. There are also Chinese and Japanese restaurants.

Services: Concierge, 24-hour room service, same-day laundry, baby-sitting, doctor and dentist on call, limousine service, nightly turndown, free shuttle service to Tsim Sha Tsui.

Facilities: Outdoor heated swimming pool, fitness and health center/sauna, business center, shopping arcade, beauty salon.

Holiday Inn Golden Mile

50 Nathan Rd., Tsim Sha Tsui, Kowloon, Hong Kong. ☎ **852/2369 3111** or 800/HOLIDAY in the U.S. and Canada. Fax 852/2369 8016. 586 rms, 8 suites. A/C MINIBAR TV TEL. HK$2,200–HK$2,550 ($286–$331) twin; HK$2,900 ($377) Executive Club twin; from HK$5,500 ($714) suite. Children under 20 stay free in parents' room. AE, CB, DC, MC, V. MTR: Tsim Sha Tsui.

Named after the so-called Golden Mile of shopping on Nathan Road, this Holiday Inn, built in 1975 and recently renovated from top to bottom, has a very good location right in the heart of Tsim Sha Tsui. Maybe that's why its lobby is used as a departure point for a number of sight-seeing tours, which means that it's convenient if you plan to take some organized tours during your stay, but rather noisy and bothersome if you don't, especially if you want to find an empty seat in the lobby. Needless to say, the hotel also caters to tour groups, mainly from Europe and North America. The rooms are very clean and modern, featuring either a king-size bed or two double beds and Chinese-style furniture. Although boasting floor-to-ceiling windows, none of the rooms offers views due to adjacent buildings; some rooms even face the unsightly Chungking Mansion. Four floors of the 18-floor hotel are reserved for

Executive Club rooms, which offer complimentary continental breakfast, discounts on laundry and dry cleaning, free local telephone calls, and free evening cocktails.

Dining/Entertainment: Europe reigns in this Holiday Inn's restaurants, with Austrian and continental foods served in **Café Vienna** and gourmet German cuisine in the **Baron's Table.** There's also a Chinese restaurant and a delicatessen with a take-out counter offering smoked meats, sausages, and baked goods. **The Inn Bar** is popular for its happy hour.

Services: Concierge, 24-hour room service, baby-sitting, same-day laundry, doctor on call.

Facilities: Business center, shopping arcade, heated rooftop swimming pool, fitness room, sauna, beauty salon, four no-smoking floors.

Hong Kong Renaissance Hotel

8 Peking Rd., Tsim Sha Tsui, Kowloon, Hong Kong. ☎ **852/2375 1133** or 800/228-9898 in the U.S. Fax 852/2375 6611. 469 rms, 27 suites. A/C MINIBAR TV TEL. HK$2,240–HK$2,750 ($291–$357) double; HK$2,800–HK$3,200 ($364–$416) Renaissance Club double; from HK$3,700 ($480) suite. Children under 19 stay free in parents' room. AE, CB, DC, MC, V. MTR: Tsim Sha Tsui.

One of Tsim Sha Tsui's newer deluxe hotels, the 16-story Renaissance is just a few minutes' walk from the Star Ferry and bills itself as an "intelligent" hotel. A sophisticated bedside control panel allows guests to operate lights and curtains, adjust air-conditioning levels, select a TV or radio program, call up messages or the hotel bill on the television screen, and switch on a "Do Not Disturb" light which automatically disconnects the door chime. As an added safety precaution, each guest receives an electronic key with a new combination, and staff keys are programmed for specific times only, thereby barring anyone from entering rooms after a shift ends. What's more, a printer records all hotel employee use, indicating when each key was used, where, and by whom. As if that weren't enough, the rooms are also equipped with electronic safes. The most expensive rooms feature harbor views. Tourists account for about half the hotel's guests; the other half are businesspeople, many of whom stay on one of the two floors reserved for the Renaissance Club, which can be reached only by inserting a special key in the elevator. Added amenities here include free limousine transfer from the airport, a private lounge where complimentary breakfast and cocktails are served, facsimile machines in all rooms, free local calls, unlimited free pressing, and personalized stationery and name cards.

Dining/Entertainment: The **Capriccio** may well be Hong Kong's most exclusive Italian restaurant, offering authentic northern Italian cuisine from Tuscany. The **Bostonian** is the talk of the town for its American-style seafood. There's also a Chinese restaurant and a lobby lounge.

Services: Concierge, free newspaper, 24-hour room service, house doctor, welcome tea, baby-sitting, same-day laundry service, limousine service, nightly turndown, welcoming tea.

Facilities: Rooftop outdoor heated swimming pool, squash court, fitness room, sauna, shopping arcade, hairdressing salon, tailor, business center, no-smoking floor.

Hotel Nikko Hongkong

72 Mody Rd., Tsim Sha Tsui East, Kowloon, Hong Kong. ☎ **852/2739 1111** or 800/645-5687 in the U.S. and Canada. Fax 852/2311 3122. 442 rms, 19 suites. A/C MINIBAR TV TEL. HK$2,100–HK$3,000 ($273–$390) double; HK$2,400–HK$3,300 ($312–$429) Nikko executive floor double; from HK$5,300 ($688) suite. Children 14 and under stay free in parents' room. AE, CB, DC, MC, V. MTR: Tsim Sha Tsui.

An affiliate of Japan Airlines and therefore catering heavily to the Japanese, the 15-story Nikko Hongkong is the farthest east of a string of hotels along the waterfront of Tsim Sha Tsui East. Opened in 1988, it's only a 2-minute walk from the Kowloon Railway Station but at least a 15-minute hike to the Star Ferry. Its rooms, more than half of which face the harbor, are decorated with furniture carved from American maple and with either Japanese works of art or Dutch maps of the Far East. An electronic bedside panel enables guests to set the alarm, control the television, and open or shut the curtains. Bathrooms, finished in black-veined white Italian Carrara marble, come equipped with separate bathtubs and showers as well as bathrobes and cotton kimonos. The Nikko executive floors occupy the top two floors of the hotel; amenities include complimentary continental breakfast, a fruit basket, afternoon tea, cocktails, and after-hours champagne.

Dining/Entertainment: Restaurants serve Chinese, Japanese, and French cuisine, while the **Sky Lounge** on the 15th floor offers drinks and a view of Hong Kong's lights.

Services: Concierge, free newspaper, 24-hour room service, house doctor, limousine service, baby-sitting, same-day laundry.

Facilities: Outdoor swimming pool, fitness room, sauna, business center, barbershop.

Hyatt Regency Hong Kong

67 Nathan Rd., Tsim Sha Tsui, Kowloon, Hong Kong. ☎ **852/2311 1234** or 800/233-1234 in the U.S. and Canada. Fax 852/2739 8701. 706 rms, 17 suites. A/C MINIBAR TV TEL. HK$2,200–HK$2,500 ($286–$325) double; HK$2,900 ($325) Regency Club; from HK$5,700 ($740) suite. Children under 18 stay free in parents' room (maximum: three persons per room). AE, DC, MC, V. MTR: Tsim Sha Tsui.

Only a 5-minute walk from the Star Ferry and a 1-minute walk from the Tsim Sha Tsui MTR subway station, the Hyatt Regency was established in 1969 as Hyatt's first property in Asia. It has since undergone extensive renovation—its former red-and-gold lobby was redone in marble and natural teakwood paneling, and its rooms now feature shades of apricot and celadon with natural teakwood furniture. Hints of local culture are represented by the lacquered Chinese chests housing the televisions and Chinese brush paintings on the walls. There are no harbor views here (rates are based on floor height), but all guest rooms are equipped with double-glazed windows and insulated walls to reduce outside noise, telephones in the bathroom and at bedside with an extra plug-in socket at the desk, safe-deposit boxes large enough for a briefcase, and a voice-mail recording system. The hotel's executive floor, the Regency Club, offers the usual complimentary breakfast, cocktails, and personalized stationery, as well as in-room access for fax machines and complimentary pressing of one suit or dress. The Regency Club also has its own fitness room. The hotel is popular with American business and leisure travelers, as well as Japanese and other Asian visitors, including tour groups.

Dining/Entertainment: The hotel boasts five food-and-beverage outlets, including **Hugo's** steakhouse and the trendy, elegant Chinese Restaurant, decorated in modern art deco style. There's nightly entertainment in the very popular **Chin Chin Bar.**

Services: Concierge, free newspaper, 24-hour room service, baby-sitting, 24-hour house nurse, limousine service, same-day laundry, nightly turndown.

Facilities: Business center, shopping arcade, no-smoking rooms.

New World

22 Salisbury Rd., Tsim Sha Tsui, Kowloon, Hong Kong. ☎ **852/2369 4111** or 800/44-UTELL or 800/637-7200 in the U.S and Canada. Fax 852/2369 9387. 501 rms, 42 suites. A/C MINIBAR TV TEL. HK$2,200–HK$2,500 ($286–$325) double; HK$2,700 ($352) executive floors; from HK$3,000 ($399) suite. AE, DC, MC, V. MTR: Tsim Sha Tsui.

This hotel is tucked inside the New World complex, which includes more than 400 shops and boutiques. Modern in both decor and technology, the 17-year-old hotel nevertheless imparts an oriental atmosphere through large flower arrangements, a waterfall with reflecting pool and footbridge, and sleek black furniture, but I find the lobby slightly claustrophobic due to the absence of windows (it was even worse before the ceiling was raised in a major 1991 renovation). Furthermore, despite its prime location right on the waterfront, not one of its rooms faces the harbor. Rather, all rooms face Salisbury Road or the garden; since they're the same price, ask for the garden view. Otherwise, the rooms are comfortable enough, offering the usual room safe, hair dryer, magnifying mirror for applying makeup or shaving, as well as a television with in-house movies. The television screen also displays hotel information, travel news, and individual hotel accounts. Telephone messages are recorded automatically on a voice-mail system. For those who want to splurge, there are four executive floors, some of which do offer partial glimpses of the harbor.

Dining/Entertainment: Five restaurants and bars, including the Western-style **Panorama** with harbor views and a piano bar.

Services: Concierge, free newspaper, 24-hour room service, medical and dental services, limousine service, baby-sitting, same-day laundry, nightly turndown.

Facilities: Shopping arcade, outdoor swimming pool, fitness center, sauna, beauty salon, barbershop, business center, three no-smoking floors.

Omni The Hong Kong Hotel

Harbour City, 3 Canton Rd., Tsim Sha Tsui, Kowloon, Hong Kong. ☎ **852/2736 0088** or 800/ THE-OMNI in the U.S. and Canada. Fax 852/2736 0011. 665 rms, 84 suites. A/C MINIBAR TV TEL. HK$2,200–HK$3,300 ($286–$429) double; HK$3,000–HK$4,000 ($390–$519) Continental Club executive floor; from HK$3,700 ($480) suite. One child under 14 can stay free in parents' room. AE, DC, MC, V. MTR: Tsim Sha Tsui.

A member of the Omni group and the best of three Omni properties lining this street, this hotel is as close as you can get to the Star Ferry and is connected via air-conditioned walkways to the largest shopping complex in Asia. Some of its rooms have unparalleled views of harbor activity, including the ocean liners that dock right next door. The lowest-price rooms face the swimming pool. Its marble lobby is spacious and comfortable, and the guest rooms, all of which have queen- or king-size beds, combine Western and Eastern decor in muted colors and offer pay in-house movies. The rooms on the Continental Club floors feature the usual complimentary breakfast, cocktails, welcome tea, and fruit basket, as well as free pressing service for one suit or dress. Built in the 1960s and well maintained, this 18-story hotel is popular with tour groups, especially from Japan and other Asian countries; it also attracts visitors from Macau due to its close proximity to the China Hong Kong Terminal.

Dining/Entertainment: Among the hotel's seven restaurants and bars, **Tai Pan,** which features international cuisine served to the accompaniment of a piano, is the premier restaurant. Equally good is the **Golden Unicorn,** a Cantonese restaurant that serves an exceptional dim sum lunch.

Services: Concierge, 24-hour room service, baby-sitting, same-day laundry, limousine service, medical and dental clinics, nightly turndown.

Facilities: Beauty salon, barbershop, business center, outdoor heated swimming pool, no-smoking floor.

✪ Royal Garden

69 Mody Rd., Tsim Sha Tsui East, Kowloon, Hong Kong. ☎ **852/2721 5215.** Fax 852/2369 9976. 390 rms, 43 suites. A/C MINIBAR TV TEL. HK$2,000–HK$2,650 ($260–$344) double; HK$2,700–HK$2,900 ($351–$377) Crown Club executive floor double; from HK$3,900 ($506) suite. One child under 12 can stay free in parents' room. AE, CB, DC, MC, V. MTR: Tsim Sha Tsui.

A small hotel with a lot of architectural surprises, the Royal Garden features a 15-story inner atrium, a concept adapted from the traditional Chinese inner garden. Plants hang down from the balconies ringing the soaring space, glass-enclosed elevators glide up the wall, a piano sits on an island in the middle of a pool, and the sound of rushing water adds freshness and coolness to the atmosphere. A wonderful rooftop swimming pool is open overhead in summer, covered and heated in winter. The rooms, the most expensive of which have partial harbor views, are decorated with Chinese furniture and feature in-house movies and a chilled water tap in the bathroom.

Two floors serve as the Crown Club executive floors, which offer their own private lounge, complimentary continental breakfast and evening cocktails, free fruit basket, free shoeshine, free newspaper, personalized stationery, free local telephone calls, and other special privileges.

Dining/Entertainment: The **Falcon** is an exciting venue, offering a roast beef dinner and then transforming itself into a popular and sophisticated disco later at night. **Sabatini** is the hotel's top restaurant, named after three Sabatini brothers who opened their first restaurant in Rome three decades ago, serving Italian food in an authentic Italian setting. There are also Chinese and Japanese restaurants.

Services: Concierge, 24-hour room service, same-day laundry, free newspaper, house doctor, limousine service, baby-sitting, nightly turndown.

Facilities: Heated rooftop swimming pool, fitness room, putting green, tennis court, Jacuzzi, sauna, shopping arcade, business center, beauty salon, barbershop.

Sheraton Hong Kong Hotel & Towers

20 Nathan Rd., Tsim Sha Tsui, Kowloon, Hong Kong. ☎ **852/2369 1111** or 800/325-3535 in the U.S. and Canada. Fax 852/2739 8707. 805 rms and suites. A/C MINIBAR TV TEL. HK$2,400–HK$2,900 ($312–$377) double; Tower rooms HK$3,100–HK$3,700 ($403–$480) double; from HK$3,450 ($448) suite. AE, CB, DC, MC, V. MTR: Tsim Sha Tsui.

The 20-some-year-old Sheraton has one of the most envied locations in Hong Kong—near the waterfront on the corner of Nathan Road and Salisbury Road. In fact, it's such a choice spot that rumors have been buzzing that the Sheraton will close down to make way for a more lucrative office building. There's no official word yet whether or when that might occur, but until then the Sheraton remains an attractive though busy hotel, very popular with Japanese tour groups. Its lobby is often crowded (locals use it as a convenient place to wait for and meet friends), so if you want peace and quiet go somewhere else or splurge on an executive room on the top 16th or 17th floor of the Sheraton Towers, served by private elevator, where you have your own executive lounge and such privileges as complimentary breakfast and evening cocktails, free laundry and pressing, fruit basket, free shoeshine service, and free pressing service for one suit or dress. The guest rooms face either the harbor (great views), an inner courtyard (the cheapest), or surrounding Tsim Sha Tsui. All are comfortable and offer in-house pay movies. The outdoor rooftop swimming pool, heated in winter, offers a spectacular view.

Dining/Entertainment: One of the most popular drinking spots in Tsim Sha Tsui is **Someplace Else,** where it's elbow-to-elbow at the bar during happy hour. For more sophisticated and relaxed drinking, there's the **Sky Lounge** on the 18th floor, which can't be beat for its romantic view of the harbor. **Unkai** offers superb Japanese delicacies, the **Celestial Court** is a Cantonese restaurant, and **Bukhara Tandoori Restaurant** serves tandoori.

Services: Concierge, free newspaper, 24-hour room service, baby-sitting, same-day laundry, limousine service, house doctor, nightly turndown.

Central District Accommodations

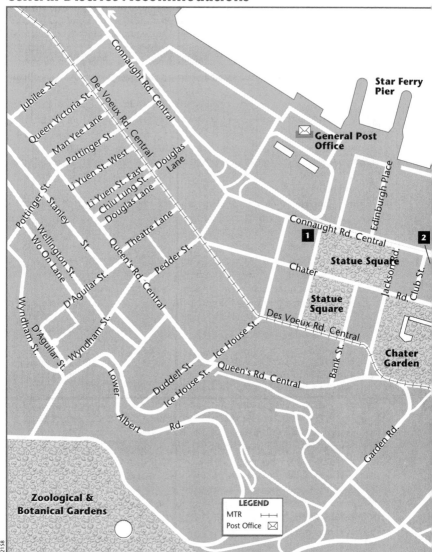

Conrad **6**
Furama Kempinksi **3**
Island Shangri-La **4**
JW Marriott **5**
Mandarin Oriental **1**
Ritz-Carlton **2**

Victoria Harbour

Queen's Pier

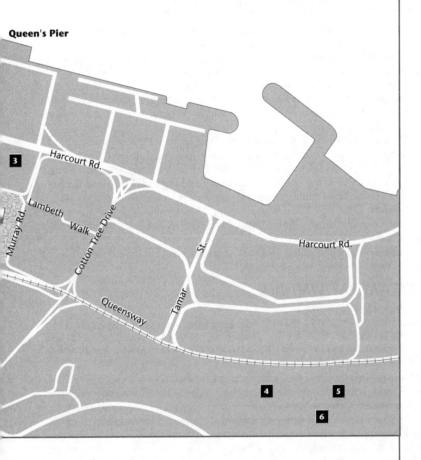

Facilities: Outdoor heated rooftop swimming pool, tennis courts, sauna, fitness room, whirlpools, golf simulator of the world's most famous courses, shopping arcade, business center, beauty salon, barbershop, two no-smoking floors.

CENTRAL DISTRICT

Furama Kempinski Hong Kong

1 Connaught Rd., Central, Hong Kong. ☎ **852/2525 5111** or 800/426-3135 in the U.S. and Canada. Fax 852/2845 9339. 462 rms, 56 suites. A/C MINIBAR TV TEL. HK$1,950–HK$2,700 ($253–$351) double; from HK$3,100 ($403) suite. AE, CB, DC, MC, V. MTR: Central.

Famous for its revolving restaurant on the 30th floor but otherwise fairly middle of the road, the Furama is located in the heart of Central across from Chater Garden; the cozy lobby offers nice views of the garden. Opened some 20 years ago, the hotel provides simple but comfortable guest rooms equipped with the standard hair dryer, safe, and TV with in-house movies; the highest priced rooms feature views of the harbor, followed by views of Victoria Peak; the least expensive rooms look out over the surrounding buildings. The clientele is split 50-50 between business and leisure travelers (including tour groups).

Dining/Entertainment: La Ronda, a revolving restaurant that offers a lunch and dinner buffet of European and Asian cuisine, provides changing vistas of one of the world's most spectacular cityscapes. The Furama's French restaurant, the **Rôtisserie,** features live music in the evenings, as does the **Lau Ling Bar.** The **Island Restaurant** serves Cantonese cuisine, while Japanese specialties are available at **Agehan.**

Services: Concierge, free newspaper, complimentary shoeshine, 24-hour room service, same-day laundry, house doctor, limousine service, baby-sitting, nightly turndown.

Facilities: Shopping arcade, business center, beauty salon, fitness room, sauna, steam room, whirlpool, two no-smoking floors.

CAUSEWAY BAY/WAN CHAI

New World Harbour View

1 Harbour Rd., Wan Chai, Hong Kong. ☎ **852/2802 8888**, 800/538-8882, or 800/44-UTELL in the U.S. Fax 852/2802 8833. 808 rms, 54 suites. A/C MINIBAR TV TEL. HK$2,450–HK$3,800 ($318–$493) double; HK$2,900–HK$3,300 ($377–$429) Dynasty Club double; from HK$4,800 ($623) suite. AE, DC, MC, V. MTR: Wan Chai.

This large hotel sits above the Convention and Exhibition Centre on the Wan Chai waterfront, separated from the Grand Hyatt by an outdoor swimming pool and garden shared by the two hotels. Under the same ownership as the Grand Hyatt, the New World Harbour View provides some of the same facilities and advantages, but at a lower price; it caters mainly to American and Australian business travelers. Its lobby is white and airy with views of the harbor, and more than 65% of the rooms also boast outstanding views of the water. All rooms feature marble bathrooms and the TV doubles as a message center and checkout facility. The top floors comprise the Dynasty Club, where guest rooms are also equipped with a laser/compact disc player and where complimentary breakfast, afternoon tea, and cocktails are available.

Dining/Entertainment: The **Dynasty** serves classic Cantonese food, while **Scala** is the place to go for continental fare. The **Coffee Shop** offers snacks and breakfast and dinner buffets. **Oasis,** under a glass canopy, is the best place for cocktails.

Services: Concierge, free newspaper, free shuttle bus to Central and Admiralty MTR station, coffee- and tea-making facilities, medical and dental consultants, baby-sitting, limousine service, 24-hour room service, same-day laundry.

Facilities: Business center, beauty salon, shopping arcade, outdoor swimming pool, children's pool, jogging track, tennis courts, fitness center, golf driving range, three no-smoking floors.

The Park Lane

310 Gloucester Rd., Causeway Bay, Hong Kong. ☎ **852/2890 3355** or 800/388-1338 in the U.S. Fax 852/2576 7853. 790 rms, 25 suites. A/C MINIBAR TV TEL. HK$2,300–HK$3,200 ($299–$416) double; HK$3,200–HK$3,500 ($416–$454) Premier Club executive rooms; from HK$5,000 ($649) suite. Children under 12 stay free in parents' room. AE, CB, DC, MC, V. MTR: Causeway Bay.

Located across from Victoria Park, this 28-story hotel first opened in 1974 and then underwent extensive renovation in 1994; now its lobby has a more contemporary, brighter look, and the guest rooms on its executive floors have been updated. Attracting primarily business travelers, the hotel offers rooms that vary in price according to floor level and view—the best are those facing Victoria Park with the harbor beyond. All rooms come with a king-size bed or two double beds, marble tabletops, in-house pay movies, and marble bathrooms. Extra perks are available to guests who stay on one of the three Premier Club executive floors, including complimentary breakfast, clothes pressing, fruit basket, and drinks.

Dining/Entertainment: Parc 27, the premier restaurant, provides a view of the harbor along with continental food and a buffet. **The Café** serves sandwiches and Asian dishes, as well as vegetarian and low-calorie meals. Evening diversions include lounges and bars.

Services: Concierge, 24-hour room service, same-day laundry, free newspaper, house clinic, baby-sitting, limousine service, same-day film processing, nightly turndown.

Facilities: Fitness center with exercise room, sauna, massage, steam bath, and Jacuzzi; business center; hair salon; shopping arcade, two no-smoking floors.

4 Moderate

KOWLOON

Grand Tower

627 Nathan Rd., Mong Kok, Kowloon, Hong Kong. ☎ **852/2789 0011.** Fax 852/2789 0945. 512 rms, 12 suites. A/C MINIBAR TV TEL. HK$1,250–HK$2,000 ($162–$260) double; from HK$3,450 ($448) suite. One child under 12 can stay free in parents' room. AE, DC, MC, V. MTR: Mong Kok.

Part of the Grand Plaza shopping center, the Grand Tower is a relatively new hotel in Mong Kok at the northern end of Nathan Road (the only way to reach it from Kai Tak Airport is by taxi, a 15-minute ride). It caters to a largely Asian clientele, split evenly between business and leisure travelers. Its sixth-floor lobby is marble and bright under a skylight, in sharp contrast to the chaos and jumble of the streets below. Its rooms, equipped with hair dryers and coffee- and tea-making facilities, are quite large and pleasant; the cheapest face an interior courtyard, while the most expensive rooms are on upper floors and offer views of the city. You could spend hours just staring out your window at the bustle on Nathan Road. Although it's a bit far from the tip of Tsim Sha Tsui, the hotel is close to both a subway station and bus stops and offers free, hourly shuttle service to Tsim Sha Tsui. Facilities include two Chinese restaurants, a coffee shop offering lunch and dinner buffets, a lobby lounge, a business center, and shopping arcade. Services include a free newspaper, 24-hour room service, limousine service, house doctor, baby-sitting, and same-day laundry.

Guangdong Hotel

18 Prat Ave., Tsim Sha Tsui, Kowloon, Hong Kong. ☎ **852/2739 3311.** Fax 852/2721 1137. 234 rms, 11 suites. A/C MINIBAR TV TEL. HK$1,250–HK$1,600 ($162–$208) double; from HK$1,900 ($247) suite. Children under 12 stay free in parents' room. AE, DC, MC, V. MTR: Tsim Sha Tsui.

The Guangdong, popular with both business and leisure travelers, is a modern hotel located in the heart of Tsim Sha Tsui, about a 10-minute walk from the Star Ferry. Its marble lobby is spacious and bare, reflecting the latest look in Hong Kong's hotels. Two restaurants serve Cantonese and Western food. There's also a business center. The guest rooms are clean and pleasant and offer in-house pay movies, with room rates based primarily on size and amenities. None of the rooms here offer views; most face other buildings. If you want to be away from the din of traffic, ask for a room on a higher floor. Services you can expect include room service (from 6am to 11:30pm), baby-sitting, same-day laundry service, and limousine service.

Hotel Concourse

22 Lai Chi Kok Rd., Mong Kok, Kowloon, Hong Kong. ☎ **852/2397 6683.** Fax 852/2381 3768. 354 rms, 5 suites. A/C MINIBAR TV TEL. HK$1,350–HK$1,800 ($175–$234) double; from HK$2,500 ($325) suite. Children under 13 stay free in parents' room. Long-stay discount available. AE, DC, MC, V. MTR: Prince Edward.

You'll find this hotel with a friendly staff at the northern end of Kowloon Peninsula, in an area known as Mong Kok. Since not many tourists venture this far north, this part of Kowloon has a much more local flavor than that of Tsim Sha Tsui and is popular with mainland Chinese, including many tour groups. For that reason, the lobby can be quite noisy and busy, as is the rest of Hong Kong. The hotel is simple, reminiscent of business hotels in Japan, and offers clean, functional rooms, two-thirds of which are no-smoking rooms. If you are just looking for an inexpensive room without such extras as swimming pool, business center, or shops, this may be the place for you. There are several restaurants, including a casual Western one that serves buffet breakfast, lunch, and dinner, a Cantonese restaurant renowned for its dim sum, and Hong Kong's only Korean restaurant. Guest services include a free newspaper, same-day laundry service, room service from 7am to 1am, baby-sitting, and a house doctor. The easiest way to reach the hotel from Kai Tak Airport is by taxi (a 10-minute drive) or hotel shuttle bus.

Imperial Hotel

30–34 Nathan Rd., Tsim Sha Tsui, Kowloon, Hong Kong. ☎ **852/2366 2201.** Fax 852/2311 2360. 208 rms, 7 suites. A/C MINIBAR TV TEL. HK$1,200–HK$1,400 ($156–$182) double; from HK$2,200 ($286) suite. One child under 12 can stay free in parents' room. AE, CB, DC, MC, V. MTR: Tsim Sha Tsui.

Occupying a great location on Nathan Road between the Sheraton and Holiday Inn, this is a simple, no-frills hotel. Its cheapest rooms face the back of Chungking Mansion, notorious for its cheap and often uninviting rooms. Although the view is not exactly stunning, it is enlightening, with laundry strung everywhere and garbage piled up below, apparently tossed unconcernedly from the windows above. If this view does not appeal to you, ask for a room that faces Nathan Road, although keep in mind that these rooms are subject to the noise of traffic. The rooms on the top floors are high enough to offer glimpses of the harbor. TVs offer in-house movies, and no-smoking rooms are available. Facilities include one Chinese restaurant, a spaghetti restaurant, and, in the basement, one of Tsim Sha Tsui's most popular bars. Room service is available from 7am to 11pm, and there's also same-day laundry service and baby-sitting.

✪ Kimberley Hotel

28 Kimberley Rd., Tsim Sha Tsui, Kowloon, Hong Kong. ☎ **852/2723 3888.** Fax 852/2723 1318. 455 rms, 76 suites. A/C MINIBAR TV TEL. HK$1,550–HK$2,000 ($201–$260) double; from HK$2,300 ($299) suite. AE, DC, MC, V. MTR: Tsim Sha Tsui.

Opened in 1991 and offering more facilities than most hotels in its price range, the 20-story Kimberley Hotel is on the northern edge of Tsim Sha Tsui, about a 15-minute walk from the Star Ferry; it caters to both the tourist and business trade, and attracts primarily Japanese. Guest rooms, constructed with V-shaped windows that let in more sunlight and allow for more panoramic views, are equipped with hair dryers, very firm beds, phone in the bathroom, clothesline, and a complimentary tea- and coffeemaker (however, the plug is inconveniently located in the narrow entryway). The most expensive rooms are on higher floors and are larger, but even these are rather small. The suites represent an especially good deal since they occupy the top three floors and are equipped with kitchenettes and a lounging/dining area, making them ideal for long-term guests. There's a nonsmoking floor. Facilities include two restaurants serving Japanese and Chinese food, a coffee shop offering lunch and dinner buffets, a bar/disco, a cocktail lounge, shopping arcade, business center, sauna, fitness room, putting green, and golf cage. Services include free newspaper, room service (6am to midnight), same-day laundry, house doctor, and baby-sitting.

✪ Kowloon Hotel

19–21 Nathan Rd., Tsim Sha Tsui, Kowloon, Hong Kong. ☎ **852/2369 8698** or 800/262-9467 in the U.S. Fax 852/2739 9811. 709 rms, 26 suites. A/C MINIBAR TV TEL. HK$1,380–HK$2,400 ($179–$312) double; from HK$3,150 ($409) suite. AE, CB, DC, MC, V. MTR: Tsim Sha Tsui.

The Kowloon is a modern glass-walled structure right behind The Peninsula; they are both under the same management. Its location is great, just a few minutes' walk from the Star Ferry, but the rooms are minuscule; although they have V-shaped bay windows, allowing unobstructed views up and down the street, it is no longer possible to see the harbor since The Peninsula's new tower was built. Still, the hotel is popular with American and Japanese business travelers and offers a business center, shopping arcade, free newspaper, limousine service, baby-sitting, same-day laundry service, room service (from 6:30am to 2am), and no-smoking floors, as well as three restaurants, including an excellent pizzeria. Satellite television sets in each room are equipped with a simplified keyboard, allowing access to computerized information files, including location maps, airline telephone numbers, flight information, weather reports, and sightseeing information. Guests can also call up messages and their hotel bills; the television even functions as a word processor, printer, and fax machine and includes video games and video input for guests' video cameras to allow playback. Other room features include voice mail for messages and an outdoor temperature reading. Finally, the hotel lobby has a computerized street directory for consulates, points of interest, and other addresses; its printout is in both English and Chinese to instruct taxi drivers.

Majestic Hotel

348 Nathan Rd., Yau Ma Tei, Kowloon, Hong Kong. ☎ **852/2781 1333** or 800/44-UTELL in the U.S. Fax 852/2781 1773. 378 rms, 9 suites. A/C MINIBAR TV TEL. HK$1,250–HK$1,700 ($162–$221) double; from HK$2,800 ($364) suite. One child under 12 can stay free in parents' room. AE, DC, MC, V. MTR: Jordan.

This modern brick hotel, located in the colorful Yau Ma Tei district with its main entrance on Saigon Street, is just a 2-minute walk from the subway station and a 20-minute taxi ride from the airport. It rises above the Majestic Centre complex, which includes a shopping arcade, food court, children's amusement center, and two small cinemas. The hotel offers good-size rooms, with a desk, sitting area, large windows (but unfortunately no exciting views), satellite television with in-house pay movies, room safe, hair dryer, coffee- and tea-making facilities, and a clothesline in the bathroom. The cheapest rooms occupy the lower floors and face another building. Unlike most hotels in Hong Kong, there are ice machines on every floor. One restaurant serves breakfast, lunch, and buffet dinner, while the hotel bar overlooks Nathan Road and offers live entertainment. There's also a business center. Services include 24-hour room service, baby-sitting, same-day laundry, and house doctor, and there's a no-smoking floor.

Metropole Hotel

75 Waterloo Rd., Yau Ma Tei, Kowloon, Hong Kong. ☎ **852/2761 1711.** Fax 852/2761 0769. 479 rms, 8 suites. A/C MINIBAR TV TEL. HK$1,250–HK$1,500 ($162–$195) double; HK$1, 700–HK$1,800 ($221–$234) executive floor double; from HK$3,100 ($402) suite. One child under 12 can stay free in parents' room. AE, DC, MC, V. MTR: Yau Ma Tei or Mong Kok.

Opened in 1989, this hotel offers a business center, small fitness room, an outdoor rooftop swimming pool, and comfortable rooms, complete with in-house pay movies, hair dryer, tea- and coffee-making facilities, and two no-smoking floors. Guest rooms at the front of the hotel present a slightly better view of the surrounding neighborhood. Guest services include room service (from 6am to 1am), same-day laundry service, baby-sitting, house doctor, and limousine service. Two executive floors offer the following extras: an exclusive lounge, welcome champagne, fruit basket, and nightly turndown service. The hotel's main drawback is its location, about a 10-minute walk from the subway station. To compensate, the hotel offers free hourly shuttle service to Tsim Sha Tsui and the Mong Kok MTR station. Among its several dining facilities, one is unusual in that it offers Portuguese fare.

Miramar

130 Nathan Rd., Tsim Sha Tsui, Kowloon, Hong Kong. ☎ **852/2368 1111** or 800/227-4320, or 800/44-UTELL in the U.S. Fax 852/2369 1788. 482 rms, 18 suites. A/C MINIBAR TV TEL. HK$1,500–HK$2,000 ($195–$260) double; HK$2,650 ($344) Executive Floor double; from HK$4,300 ($558) suite. Children under 15 stay free in parents' room. AE, DC, MC, V. MTR: Tsim Sha Tsui.

Across from Kowloon Park, the Miramar is strategically located in the midst of a shopping area, including the Park Lane shopping arcade. An older family-owned hotel once known for its showy exterior and glitzy gold-colored decor, it toned down its public areas during a major renovation some years back. The lobby is now marble; the last trace of the Miramar's former flashy self can be seen in its stained-glass windows in the atrium ceiling. Its facilities rival those of more expensive hotels, including an indoor swimming pool, fitness room, sauna, beauty salon, business center, and shopping arcade. In addition to the usual hotel restaurants serving Western and Chinese cuisine, the Choice Food Centre in the basement is a cafeteria with various types of Chinese food and snacks.

Since it caters largely to tour groups, all but 22 of the rooms are twins and doubles. Each floor has its own attendant on duty 24 hours (once a feature of most Hong Kong hotels but now increasingly rare). The rooms come equipped with a room safe, clothesline and telephone in the bathroom, hair dryer, and VCR (videos are available for rent from the lobby kiosk). Other amenities include room service (7am to 2am), same-day laundry service, free newspaper, baby-sitting, and limousine service. Some of the higher floor deluxe rooms offer views of Kowloon Park and the harbor in the distance. Executive Floor rooms entitle guests to continental breakfast, a fruit basket, coffee and tea, transportation to and from the airport, personalized stationery, and admission to the health club.

New Astor

11 Carnarvon Rd., Tsim Sha Tsui, Kowloon, Hong Kong. ☎ **852/2366 7261.** Fax 852/2722 7122. 148 rms. A/C MINIBAR TV TEL. HK$1,200–HK$1,700 ($156–$221) double. One child under 12 can stay free in parents' room. AE, DC, MC, V. MTR: Tsim Sha Tsui.

This is an older, small hotel which has been completely remodeled to keep up with more modern competitors. Its facilities are almost nonexistent—just a business center, a cake shop, and one restaurant serving mostly Western fare. Its simple rooms offer just the basics of television with pay movies, stocked refrigerator, hair dryer, and clothesline over the tub. The cheapest rooms face another building, while the best rooms are corner rooms with large windows that face the street. Guest services cover just the minimum—same-day laundry and room service (7am to 11pm). Probably the hotel's best feature is its location, in the heart of Tsim Sha Tsui just off Nathan Road.

Omni Marco Polo Hotel

Harbour City, Canton Rd., Tsim Sha Tsui, Kowloon, Hong Kong. ☎ **852/2736 0888** or 800/ THE-OMNI in the U.S and Canada. Fax 852/2736 0022. 384 rms, 56 suites. A/C MINIBAR TV TEL. HK$1,800–HK$2,000 ($234–$260) double; from HK$3,100 ($402) suite. One child under 14 can stay free in parents' room. AE, DC, MC, V. MTR: Tsim Sha Tsui.

Not far from Omni The Hong Kong Hotel is its lower-priced companion, the Omni Marco Polo, with a rather small and simple lobby. None of its rooms has harbor views; rather, the room prices depend upon the floor (the more expensive rooms are on the upper floors). If noise bothers you, ask for a room away from Canton Road. Otherwise, it's a comfortable hotel in the Harbour City shopping complex; although this Omni hotel has no pool of its own, guests can use the one in Omni The Hong Kong Hotel. The Marco Polo caters mainly to business travelers; its only facilties are a business center and barber shop, but it provides room desks with large work space. Australian and Japanese tour groups also like this hotel. Other amenities include four bars and restaurants, 20-hour room service, same-day laundry service, baby-sitting, house doctor, limousine service, and two no-smoking floors.

Omni Prince Hotel

Harbour City, Canton Rd., Tsim Sha Tsui, Kowloon, Hong Kong. ☎ **852/2736 1888** or 800/ THE-OMNI in the U.S. Fax 852/2736 0066. 350 rms, 51 suites. A/C MINIBAR TV TEL. HK$1,800– HK$2,000 ($234–$260) double; from HK$3,100 ($402) suite. One child under 14 can stay free in parents' room. AE, DC, MC, V. MTR: Tsim Sha Tsui.

The third in a row of Omni hotels on Canton Road (and therefore a slightly longer walk to and from Star Ferry), the Prince Hotel is also situated in the huge Harbour City shopping complex and caters to business travelers and tour groups. It's a small hotel with a gleaming-white marble lobby and rooms that feature either twin or queen-size beds. The lowest-priced rooms are on the lower floors, and none of the rooms has harbor views. Again, guests staying here can use the swimming pool at Omni The Hong Kong Hotel (though it's a hike); facilities within the hotel include a barbershop, business center, and restaurants, including the very good Spice Market, which specializes in Asian buffets. Services include room service (7am to 2:30am), house doctor, limousine service, baby-sitting, and same-day laundry service. There's a no-smoking floor.

✪ Park Hotel

61–65 Chatham Rd. S., Tsim Sha Tsui, Kowloon, Hong Kong. ☎ **852/2366 1371.** Fax 852/ 2739 7259. 399 rms, 21 suites. A/C MINIBAR TV TEL. HK$1,500–HK$1,700 ($195–$221) twin; from HK$2,300 ($299) suite. One child under 12 can stay free in parents' room. AE, DC, MC, V. MTR: Tsim Sha Tsui.

Built in 1961 and kept up-to-date with renovations, the Park Hotel has long been one of the best-known medium-priced hotels in Kowloon. It's a clean and comfortable establishment—you can't go wrong staying here. Especially popular with Australians and Asians, this hotel probably has the largest rooms in the moderate category, a plus if you're tired of cramped quarters. The best rooms are those on the upper floors of the 16-floor property; the lower floors can be noisy. There's a no-smoking floor. Facilities include Western and Cantonese restaurants, a coffee shop, two bars, shopping arcade, and beauty salon. Services include 24-hour medical service, 24-hour room service, baby-sitting, same-day laundry, and limousine service.

Pearl Seaview

262 Shanghai St., Yau Ma Tei, Kowloon. ☎ **852/2782 0882.** Fax 852/2388 1803. 253 rms. A/C MINIBAR TV TEL. HK$1,100–HK$1,380 ($143–$179) double. AE, DC, MC, V. MTR: Yau Ma Tei.

This 19-story brick hotel opened in 1994, looking slightly out of place amidst the hustle and bustle of this Chinese neighborhood and just across the street from a famous Tin Hau Temple. Temple Street's famous night market is just a block away. Catering mainly to tour groups from mainland China and Taiwan, it has a tiny lobby (often packed) and one Western restaurant. Best is the cocktail lounge on the top floor offering views of a harbor (not the famous Victoria Harbour, but a working harbor nonetheless). Narrow corridors lead to small and clean rooms, which lack the convenience of a desk or large closet space. In other words, there's no place to put your luggage. Services include room service (6am to 1am), same-day laundry service, baby-sitting, and house doctor. Basically, it's just a place to sleep.

Prudential Hotel

222 Nathan Rd., Tsim Sha Tsui, Kowloon. ☎ **852/2311 8222.** Fax 852/2311 4760. 414 rms, 20 suites. A/C MINIBAR TV TEL. HK$1,350–HK$1,880 ($175–$244) double; from HK$2,450 ($318) suite. Children under 12 stay free in parents' room. AE, DC, MC, V. MTR: Jordan.

This 1991 hotel, at the northern end of Tsim Sha Tsui, towers 17 stories above a shopping complex and the MTR Jordan station, providing easy and direct access to the rest of Hong Kong. About a 20-minute walk from the Star Ferry and only minutes from the Temple Street Night Market, it is topped by an observation tower 300 feet above street level, providing outstanding views of Kowloon, the harbor, and Hong Kong. Be sure to bring your camera to capture the view from here. Another plus is the 60-foot-long rooftop outdoor swimming pool. The guest rooms have a pleasant modern color scheme of dark red and gray, with modern artwork decorating the walls and Japanese moving panels framing the windows. The rates are based on the view; the cheapest rooms face the back of the hotel. Deluxe rooms feature floor-to-ceiling bay windows, some with a partial glimpse of the harbor. All rooms have facsimile capability (facsimile machines are available for rent from the 24-hour business center), as well as hair dryer, room safe, radio, and TV with in-house movies. The guests are predominantly Southeast Asian and Japanese business people. Although the hotel itself has only a coffee shop and a bar, there are several other restaurants within the shopping complex. Guest services include room service (6am to midnight), same-day laundry service, baby-sitting, house doctor, and limousine service.

Ramada Hotel Kowloon

73–75 Chatham Rd. S., Tsim Sha Tsui, Kowloon, Hong Kong. ☎ **852/2311 1100** or 800/854-7854 in the U.S and Canada. Fax 852/2311 6000. 204 rms. A/C MINIBAR TV TEL. HK$1,100–HK$1,900 ($143–$247) double. One child under 12 can stay free in parents' room. AE, DC, MC, V. MTR: Tsim Sha Tsui.

Popular with the individual business traveler, this no-nonsense hotel offers simple rooms that feature safes (except in the cheapest units, which have glazed windows), satellite TVs with in-house pay movies, and hair dryers in addition to the usual amenities. The electricity in your room is activated when you insert your key into a special slot by the door, which means that your key is easy to find when you leave. The highest priced rooms face Chatham Road. One restaurant serves Western and Asian food, including buffet meals, and there's also one bar and a business center. Services are limited to room service (7am to 1am), limousine service, baby-sitting, and same-day laundry. Its location on Chatham Road is not as convenient as some of the other business hotels in this category, though it is within walking distance of the MTR (about 5 minutes) and Star Ferry (about 15 minutes).

⑤ Regal Kowloon Hotel

71 Mody Rd., Tsim Sha Tsui East, Kowloon, Hong Kong. ☎ 852/2722 1818 or 800/222-8888 in the U.S. Fax 852/2369 6950. 589 rms, 33 suites. A/C MINIBAR TV TEL. HK$1,400–HK$2,500 ($182–$325) double; HK$2,700 ($351) Regal Club executive double; from HK$4,600 ($597) suite. Two children under 12 can stay free in parents' room. AE, CB, DC, MC, V. MTR: Tsim Sha Tsui.

The 15-story Regal Kowloon does a smart job of blending East and West with reproduction 18th-century French antiques and Louis XV–style furniture standing alongside Chinese works of art. The guest rooms, all soundproofed, also feature period furniture and are equipped with room safes, hair dryers, and in-house pay movies. The cheapest rooms face another building and provide no view; the most expensive either face a garden or offer a partial view of the harbor. (In case you're wondering, "partial harbor view" means either that other buildings are obstructing part of your view or that your windows do not squarely face the water). Chefs prepare French haute cuisine at **Le Restaurant de France** and French provincial dishes at **La Brasserie.** There's also a coffee shop, seafood restaurant, one bar, shopping arcade, business center, beauty salon, and health club. Other amenities include 24-hour room service, baby-sitting, house doctor, limousine service, same-day laundry, and a no-smoking floor.

⑤ Royal Pacific Hotel & Towers

33 Canton Rd., Tsim Sha Tsui, Kowloon, Hong Kong. ☎ **852/2736 1188** or 800/44-UTELL in the U.S. Fax 852/2736 1212. 641 rms, 32 suites. A/C MINIBAR TV TEL. HK$1,100–HK$1,480 ($143–$192) double in the hotel, HK$1,800–HK$2,400 ($234–$312) double in the Towers. One child under 14 can stay free in parents' room. AE, CB, DC, MC, V. MTR: Tsim Sha Tsui.

Of the string of accommodations stretching along Canton Road, this one is farthest north; it actually comprises two hotels—each with its own lobby, concept, and room rates. The Royal Pacific Hotel is more moderately priced and attracts tour groups from Germany, Japan, Korea, and Taiwan. Its rooms are rather small but offer all the usual comforts, including three phones (one in the bathroom), a safe, hair dryer, and TV with in-house movies. The Towers is more upscale, catering to individual travelers and businesspeople and offering more personalized services. Only the higher-priced rooms in the Towers provide views of the harbor. The two hotels share two restaurants and a bar, business center, beauty salon, fitness room, sauna, and squash courts; they offer such guest services as room service (6am to 1am), same-day laundry, baby-sitting, limousine service, and house doctor. The only disadvantage is the 10-minute walk from Star Ferry; on the other hand, it's located practically on top of the new China Ferry Terminal, where boats depart for Macau and China.

Windsor Hotel

39–43A Kimberley Rd., Tsim Sha Tsui, Kowloon, Hong Kong. ☎ **852/2739 5665.** Fax 852/2311 5101. 166 rms. A/C MINIBAR TV TEL. HK$1,200–HK$1,600 ($156–$208) twin. One child under 12 can stay free in parents' room. AE, DC, MC, V. MTR: Tsim Sha Tsui.

Although it's about a 15-minute walk from Star Ferry, this relatively new 15-story hotel is pleasant, modern, and simple, with a spotless white interior, small but functional marble lobby, and pastel-colored rooms offering such basics as coffee- and tea-making facilities, hair dryer, and in-room pay movies. Cheaper than the Kimberley down the street, its facilities are minimal—one Cantonese restaurant, a coffee shop, bar, and business center; services include room service (6am to midnight), same-day laundry service, and baby-sitting. Typical of most medium-range hotels throughout Hong Kong, it caters to both groups and individuals; the majority of guests hail from Australia, Japan, and Thailand.

CAUSEWAY BAY/WAN CHAI

Century Hong Kong Hotel

238 Jaffe Rd., Wan Chai, Hong Kong. ☎ **852/2598 8888** or 800/536-7361 in the U.S. Fax 852/2598 8866. 489 rms, 27 suites. A/C MINIBAR TV TEL. HK$1,800–HK$2,200 ($234–$286) double; HK$2,400 ($312) Royal Club executive floor double; from HK$3,400 ($441) suite. AE, DC, MC, V. MTR: Wan Chai.

Opened in 1992, this gleaming white 23-story hotel is a seven-minute walk via covered walkway from the Hong Kong Convention and Exhibition Centre and the Star Ferry terminus, with service to Tsim Sha Tsui. Its airy, two-story lobby has floor-to-ceiling windows overlooking a busy intersection and is plagued by the constant hum of traffic, but since there are very few seats available you probably won't spend much time here anyway. Dull and unimaginative corridors lead to minuscule rooms, which are mercifully equipped with double-paned windows, tea- and coffee-making facilities, in-house pay movies, hair dryers, safes, and "smart" telephones with control panels (for displaying the time worldwide and for operating the TV, radio, lights, and "Do Not Disturb" sign). A few of the most expensive doubles offer a partial harbor view between buildings, as do some of the rooms on the three Royal Club executive floors, which also provide such extras as complimentary continental breakfast, afternoon tea, and cocktails. In addition to an Italian restaurant, coffee shop, and lounge, there's an outdoor pool and wading pool, fitness room, steam room, putting green, business center, and two no-smoking floors. Services include 24-hour room service, same-day laundry service, nightly turndown, baby-sitting, limousine service, and house doctor.

⑤ Evergreen Plaza Hotel

33 Hennessy Rd., Wan Chai, Hong Kong. ☎ **852/2866 9111** or 800/44-UTELL in the U.S. Fax 852/2861 3121. 297 rms, 34 suites. A/C MINIBAR TV TEL. HK$1,150–HK$1,700 ($149–$221) double; from HK$2,200 ($286) suite. AE, DC, MC, V. MTR: Wan Chai.

This business hotel, owned by a Taiwan-based company, offers moderately priced rooms that include many of the same amenities found in higher-priced hotels. It also provides the services and facilities of a bigger hotel on a smaller and more affordable scale, including a rooftop heated swimming pool (large enough for swimming laps), fitness room, sauna, business center, Western and Cantonese restaurants, and a wine bar with live piano music. Opened in 1991, this hotel is nicely situated in the heart of Wan Chai, with room rates based on the size of the room (none provides a view of the harbor). Comfortable and pleasant, the guest rooms are equipped with a safe, clothesline in the bathroom, and other amenities, including the Data View Information System, which allows guests to receive messages on their television sets, check flight schedules, check information (on stocks, finance, or shopping), play video games, order from room service, and view the hotel services directory. There are also in-house pay movies. Services include a free newspaper, room service (6:30am to midnight), same-day laundry service, limousine service, medical and dental services, and baby-sitting.

⑤ Excelsior

281 Gloucester Rd., Causeway Bay, Hong Kong. ☎ **852/2894 8888** or 800/526-6566 in the U.S. and Canada. Fax 852/2895 6459. 903 rms, 22 suites. A/C MINIBAR TV TEL. HK$1,600–HK$2,400 ($208–$312) double; HK$2,600–HK$2,800 ($338–$364) Executive Floor double; from HK$3,200 ($416) suite. AE, DC, MC, V. MTR: Causeway Bay.

Located on the waterfront near a lively shopping area, the Excelsior, built in 1973, belongs to the Mandarin Oriental group of hotels. This is a good place to stay if you like to jog, since it's close to 50-acre Victoria Park, Hong Kong's largest city park. However, because it's popular with tour groups, the lobby is usually overcrowded and buzzing with activity, sometimes making it difficult to get front-desk service or find an empty seat. The elevators are also crowded. All rooms are the same size with the same decor, and include in-house pay movies, but those that command a view of the harbor, the Hong Kong Yacht Club, and Kowloon are more expensive. The guest rooms on the three Executive Floors offer use of a private lounge, complimentary continental buffet breakfast, complimentary fruit basket, a traditional afternoon tea, and cocktails. There are two no-smoking floors. Among several restaurants and bars that serve Western and Cantonese food, the **Dickens Bar,** an English-style pub, is well-known for its Sunday jazz concerts. A top-floor lounge offers spectacular harbor views. Other facilities include covered and air-conditioned rooftop tennis courts, fitness room, sauna, steam room, Jacuzzi, business center, beauty salon, and shopping arcade, but unfortunately no swimming pool. Services include free newspaper, 24-hour room service, house doctor, limousine service, baby-sitting, and same-day laundry.

Luk Kwok Hotel

72 Gloucester Rd., Wan Chai, Hong Kong. ☎ **852/2866 2166.** Fax 852/2866 2622. 198 rms. A/C MINIBAR TV TEL. HK$1,700–HK$1,900 ($221–$247) double. AE, DC, MC, V. MTR: Wan Chai.

The Luk Kwok was originally built in the 1930s on what was then the waterfront; seven stories in height, it was the tallest building in Wan Chai. It achieved its greatest fame, however, for its role in Richard Mason's fictional *The World of Suzie Wong,* when Wan Chai was the domain of prostitutes and sailors. How things have changed since then! After a complete demolition, the Luk Kwok reopened in 1990 as a totally new and remodeled larger hotel, slightly antiseptic and appealing mainly to business travelers, probably because its only facility is a business center. Now located some two blocks inland (because of land reclamation), the new hotel is high-tech and modern, with a granite-and-marble lobby and updated rooms. The hotel's two restaurants serving Western and Cantonese food are on the first floor, while the next 17 floors are used for a parking garage and offices. A small cocktail lounge is available for hotel guests only. Guest rooms are located on the 19th to 29th floors; the most expensive rooms are those on the higher floors since they offer glimpses of the harbor. There's one no-smoking floor. Rooms, decorated in celadon green and peach, come with remote-control TV and in-house pay movies, tea- and coffee-making facilities, a large counter space in the bathroom, and a clothesline. Services include free newspaper, 24-hour room service, same-day laundry, same-day photo processing, baby-sitting, limousine service, and house doctor.

Causeway Bay/Wan Chai Accommodations

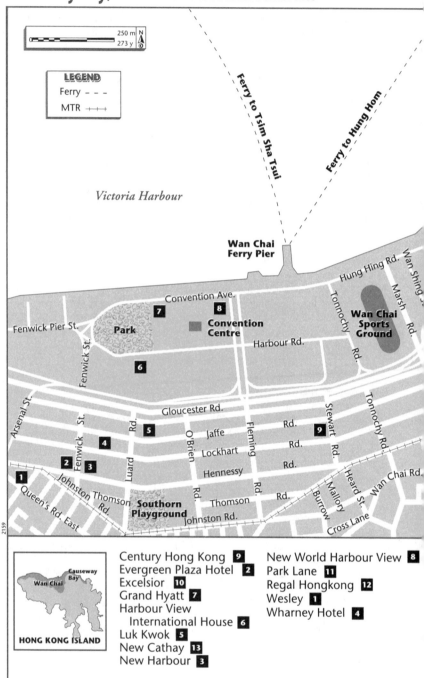

Century Hong Kong **9**
Evergreen Plaza Hotel **2**
Excelsior **10**
Grand Hyatt **7**
Harbour View
  International House **6**
Luk Kwok **5**
New Cathay **13**
New Harbour **3**

New World Harbour View **8**
Park Lane **11**
Regal Hongkong **12**
Wesley **1**
Wharney Hotel **4**

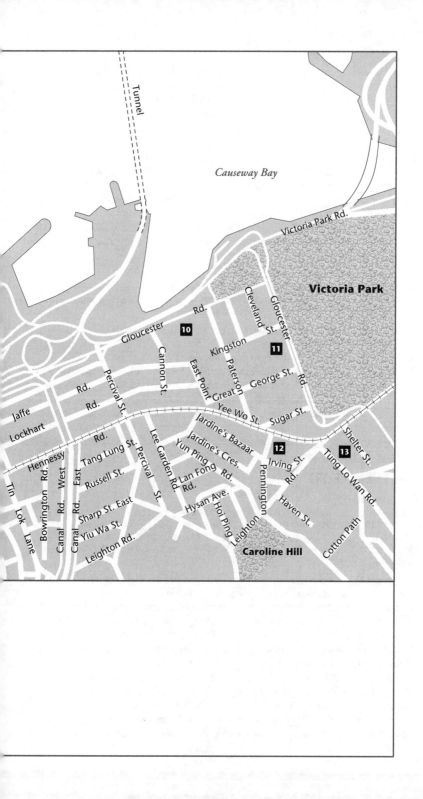

Wesley

22 Hennessy Rd., Wan Chai, Hong Kong. ☎ **852/2866 6688.** Fax 852/2866 6633. 251 rms. A/C MINIBAR TV TEL. HK$1,100–HK$2,500 ($143–$325) double. Monthly rates available. One child under 12 can stay free in parents' room. AE, DC, MC, V. MTR: Admiralty.

This simple business hotel opened in 1992 on the former site of the famous Soldiers' & Sailors' Home, a Hong Kong landmark for more than a century. In keeping with Hong Kong's unofficial preferred decorating style, its small lobby is sparsely furnished, and the only hotel facility is a business center. There's also a coffee shop and Chinese restaurant. All rooms are equally small, with V-shaped windows, and provide coffee- and tea-making facilities; the rates are based on bed configurations (the cheapest rooms are furnished with single or twin beds; the most expensive have king-size beds with a small sitting area). Rooms facing the front of the hotel are noisier. The bathrooms are only large enough for one person, and the closets aren't tall enough to hang dresses. Services are limited to room service (7am to 11pm), same-day laundry, baby-sitting, and house doctor.

Wharney Hotel

57–73 Lockhart Rd., Wan Chai, Hong Kong. ☎ **852/2861 1000.** Fax 852/2529 5133. 335 rms. A/C MINIBAR TV TEL. HK$1,650–HK$2,000 ($214–$260) double. One child under 12 can stay free in parents' room. AE, DC, MC, V. MTR: Wan Chai.

This pleasant business hotel is conveniently situated in the heart of Wan Chai, offering small but adequate rooms that feature hair dryers, tea- and coffee-making facilities, and satellite TV with pay in-house movies. There are three types of rooms: The two lower-priced categories base their rates on room decor and the floor where the room is situated; the best rooms are located in a newer addition. There's one no-smoking floor. Facilities include a coffee shop that serves Asian and Western selections, a Cantonese restaurant, a bar with live evening entertainment, rooftop swimming pool, whirlpool, fitness room, sauna, and business center. Services include baby-sitting, same-day laundry, complimentary newspaper, limousine service, and room service (6am to 1am).

NEAR THE AIRPORT

Regal Airport Hotel

30–38 San Po Rd., Kowloon, Hong Kong. ☎ **852/2718 0333** or 800/222-8888 in the U.S., 800/233-9188 in Canada. Fax 852/2718 4111. 368 rms, 21 suites. A/C MINIBAR TV TEL. HK$1,800–HK$2,200 ($234–$286) double; from HK$3,200 ($415) suite. Two children under 12 can stay free in parents' room. AE, CB, DC, MC, V. Connected to Kai Tak Airport via a walkway.

The Regal is a good choice if you have only one or two nights in Hong Kong and you want to stay near Kai Tak Airport. Linked directly to the airport by an air-conditioned walkway with a conveyor belt for your luggage, this hotel caters to business travelers, layovers, and air personnel; it features rooms with soundproof windows and TV screens with flight information, as well as in-house pay movies. A free shuttle-bus service transports guests to the Star Ferry about every half hour.

An insider's tip is that this is a good place to hang out if you have a couple hours to kill or your flight is delayed; there are flight screens throughout the hotel, which offers the best dining and wining in the vicinity, including a bar that overlooks the runway that extends out into the harbor. Facilities include a shopping arcade, business center, medical clinic, and beauty salon, while services run the gamut from 24-hour room service and same-day laundry service to baby-sitting and limousine service.

IN TSUEN WAN

⑤ Kowloon Panda Hotel

3 Tsuen Wan St., Tsuen Wan, New Territories, Hong Kong. ☎ **852/2409 1111** or 800/
344-1212 in the U.S. and Canada. Fax 852/2409 1818. 974 rms, 52 suites. A/C MINIBAR
TV TEL. HK$1,200–HK$1,600 ($156–$208) double; HK$1,800 ($234) Mega Club executive
floors. Children under 13 stay free in parents' room. AE, DC, MC, V. MTR: Tsuen Wan.

One of Hong Kong's largest hotels, the Kowloon Panda was the topic of much
speculation when it opened in 1992, due to its location way out in Tsuen Wan,
a satellite town full of housing projects and the last stop on the subway line. Aggres-
sive marketing, reasonable rates, free shuttle service to Tsim Sha Tsui, a friendly staff,
and a convenient location to Hong Kong's new airport, however, have assured
the hotel a niche in the colony's competitive market, and its Cantonese and Italian
restaurants are popular among those who live in the area. A 30-story building easily
recognizable by its facade of painted pandas and just five minutes from the subway
station, it offers comfortable rooms with all the usual amenities, including TV with
in-house pay movies and tea- and coffee-making facilities. Two executive floors
offer the following extras: hair dryer, bathroom scales, complimentary fruit basket,
daily newspaper, continental breakfast, and cocktails. Diversions include an outdoor
swimming pool, fitness room, sauna, business center, department store, and top-floor
lounge with nightly live entertainment. Hotel guests also enjoy 24-hour room
service, same-day laundry, baby-sitting, and limousine service.

5 Inexpensive

KOWLOON

Anne Black Guest House (YWCA)

5 Man Fuk Rd., Kowloon, Hong Kong. ☎ **852/2713 9211.** Fax 852/2761 1269. 169 rms,
127 with bath. A/C TV TEL. HK$480 ($62) twin without bath, HK$580–HK$750 ($75–$97) twin
with bath. Discounts available for long-term stays. AE, MC, V. MTR: Yau Ma Tei.

This 20-story YWCA, built in 1972 and located atop a hill about a 10-minute walk
from the nearest MTR station, welcomes both men and women in its spotless rooms,
most of which are twins with unstocked refrigerator and private toilet and shower.
Six twin rooms have sinks but no baths, so if you're on a budget be sure to book these
rooms far in advance. The rooms are fairly plain in a no-nonsense dormitory kind
of way; those that face the front offer slightly better views of the surrounding neighborhood. Ask for a room on a higher floor. There's one coffee shop that offers simple
Western and Cantonese food, including dim sum and a set lunch that costs less than
HK$30 ($3.90). There are also laundry facilities. The staff is friendly, making this
a good choice despite its out-of-the-way location.

Bangkok Royal

2–12 Pilkem St., Kowloon, Hong Kong. ☎ **852/2735 9181.** Fax 852/2730 2209. 70 rms
(all with bath). A/C MINIBAR TV TEL. HK$600–HK$800 ($78–$104) double. AE, DC, MC, V.
MTR: Jordan.

Located off Nathan Road just north of Kowloon Park, the Bangkok Royal has one
of the best locations in its price range; it's within a 15-minute walk of Star Ferry.
Although an older hotel (and still looks it despite renovation), it enjoys a reputation
for offering good and reasonable Thai food in its popular restaurant. There is also a
Western restaurant, room service from 7:30am to 11:30pm, and laundry service.
Rooms come with unstocked refrigerators (which is best for those on a budget, since

you can then fill them with less expensive beverages from the nearest convenience store); note that the cheapest rooms are windowless.

Booth Lodge

11 Wing Sing Lane, Yau Ma Tei, Kowloon, Hong Kong. ☎ 852/2771 9266. Fax 852/2385 1140. 53 rms (all with bath). A/C MINIBAR TV TEL. HK$550–HK$900 ($71–$117) double. AE, MC, V. MTR: Yau Ma Tei.

About a 30-minute walk to the Star Ferry but close to the Jade Market and the Temple Street Night Market, Booth Lodge is located on the seventh floor of the Salvation Army building. Its rooms are all doubles and twins, and though they have as much personality as a college dormitory, they're perfectly adequate. There's one restaurant, laundry service, and a gift shop.

✪ BP International House

8 Austin Rd., Tsim Sha Tsui, Kowloon, Hong Kong. ☎ 852/2376 1111. Fax 852/2376 1333. 536 rms (all with bath). A/C TV TEL. HK$1,100–HK$1,600 ($143–$208) double. AE, DC, MC, V. MTR: Jordan.

This is the first inexpensive lodging to open in the heart of Tsim Sha Tsui in a long time. Built in 1993 and rising 25 stories above the north end of Kowloon Park, it's a modern and well-managed property; the word "House" in its name is slightly misleading. This is actually a hotel, and a fairly nice one at that, with a spacious marbled lobby, bustling bellboys (a rarity for inexpensive accommodations), Chinese restaurant, and coffee shop. There are even vending machines that dispense beverages on each floor and a coin-operated laundry (though laundry service is available). Within the same building is a full-line health club (for which guests pay extra), and the indoor and outdoor public swimming pools in Kowloon Park are just a stone's throw away. The guest rooms are clean, pleasant, and modern, and although located inland, the best and priciest rooms offer views of the harbor. Little wonder this hotel attracts travelers of all ages and nationalities.

Caritas Bianchi Lodge

4 Cliff Rd., Yau Ma Tei, Kowloon, Hong Kong. ☎ 852/2388 1111. Fax 852/2770 6669. 90 rms (all with bath). A/C MINIBAR TV TEL. HK$790 ($103) double. Rates include continental or Oriental breakfast. Off-season discount available. AE, DC, MC, V. MTR: Yau Ma Tei.

Just down the street from Booth Lodge, this HKTA member is another good choice in this price category. Most of its rooms face toward the back of the hotel offering a view of a cliff and a small park, certainly a nicer vista than most hotels can boast. Try to get a room on a higher floor. This establishment has one restaurant on the sixth floor and offers such services as laundry service and room service (7:30am to 9pm).

✪ Eaton Hotel

380 Nathan Rd., Yau Ma Tei, Kowloon, Hong Kong. ☎ 852/2782 1818. Fax 852/2782 5563. 392 rms (all with bath). A/C MINIBAR TV TEL. HK$880–HK$1,450 ($114–$188) double; HK$1,600–HK$2,150 ($208–$279) executive floor double. AE, DC, MC, V. MTR: Jordan.

This handsome, brick 21-story hotel, located above a shopping complex, features one of the longest hotel escalators I've ever seen—it takes guests straight up to the fourth-floor lobby. The lobby lounge is bright and cheerful, with a four-story glass-enclosed atrium that overlooks a garden terrace with a water cascade. The guest rooms are small, but come with such comforts as a feather duvet, coffee- and tea-making facilities, clothesline in the bathroom, clock, radio, hair dryer, safe, and a "Do Not Disturb" button that lights up a signal outside the door. The top 10 floors (comprising executive rooms) offer special amenities. There are also no-smoking floors. The best views are of Nathan Road. Facilities include a Cantonese restaurant, coffee shop, cozy bar with a "colonial" atmosphere, and business center. Guest services include complimentary newspaper, room service (7am to 2am), and same-day laundry service. In all, this accommodation offers more than most in the inexpensive group, and has the feel of a moderately priced hotel.

International Hotel

33 Cameron Rd., Tsim Sha Tsui, Kowloon, Hong Kong. ☎ **852/2366 3381.** Fax 852/2369 5381. 89 rms (all with bath). A/C TV TEL. HK$740–HK$1,090 ($96–$142) double. One child under 10 can stay free in parents' room. MC, V. MTR: Tsim Sha Tsui.

A member of HKHA, this hotel is more than 40 years old and looks it, with a tired-looking lobby and dreary rooms. However, for an inexpensive hotel, it has one of the best locations—right in the heart of Tsim Sha Tsui, about a 12-minute walk from Star Ferry. The hotel accepts only international guests (Hong Kong residents are not permitted). Some of the double rooms offer balconies, although the view is nothing to write home about; the rooms that face toward the back of the hotel have glazed windows. The one restaurant serves Swatow Chinese dishes and Western fare. Laundry and baby-sitting service are available.

King's Hotel

473 Nathan Rd., Yau Ma Tei, Kowloon, Hong Kong. ☎ **852/2780 1281.** Fax 852/2782 1833. 72 rms (all with bath). A/C MINIBAR TV TEL. HK$600–HK$630 ($78–$82) twin. No credit cards. MTR: Yau Ma Tei.

Just a basic hotel with no frills, this establishment caters primarily to Asians, including mainland Chinese. It has a good Thai restaurant and offers such luxuries as bellboys, laundry service, and room service from 8am to 10pm. The rooms are old and worn, with peeling and stained wallpaper; the one elevator cannot adequately serve all hotel guests; and the traffic on Nathan Road is noisy. However, the rooms are clean and the location is good.

Nathan Hotel

378 Nathan Rd., Yau Ma Tei, Kowloon, Hong Kong. ☎ **852/2388 5141.** Fax 852/2770 4262. 173 rms, 13 suites. A/C MINIBAR TV TEL. HK$1,090–HK$1,200 ($142–$156) twin; from HK$1,380 ($179) suite. AE, DC, MC, V. MTR: Jordan.

More than 30 years old, the Nathan Hotel has been completely renovated but still resembles an older, tired hotel, due, in part, to the persistence of a brown color scheme in its rooms (long ago most hotels chose the brighter look of white walls and pastel fabrics). One advantage, however, is that since the hotel dates from an earlier era when land was less expensive, its rooms and bathrooms are quite large compared with those in most Hong Kong hotels; also, as in earlier days, there are attendants on duty on each floor around the clock (as had previously been the custom at all Hong Kong hotels). The rooms are simple and clean with just the basics; the hotel attracts business travelers from China, Thailand, and other Asian countries. Facilities include three restaurants serving Cantonese and Western food and a business center. Services include complimentary newspaper (on request), room service (7am to midnight), same-day laundry service, baby-sitting, and limousine service. It's located north of Tsim Sha Tsui, about a 15- to 20-minute walk from the Star Ferry.

✪ The Salisbury YMCA

Salisbury Rd., Tsim Sha Tsui, Kowloon, Hong Kong. ☎ **852/2369 2211.** Fax 852/2739 9315. 304 rms, 62 suites (all with bath). A/C MINIBAR TV TEL. HK$1,000–HK$1,200 ($130–$156) double; HK$1,650–HK$1,950 ($214–$253) suite. Dormitory bed HK$190 ($25). AE, DC, MC, V. MTR: Tsim Sha Tsui.

The overwhelming number-one choice among low-cost accommodations has always been the YMCA on Salisbury Road, which has the good fortune to be right next to The Peninsula Hotel on the waterfront, just a two-minute walk from both the Star

Ferry and subway station. For years there was a fear that it might be torn down in the face of land-hungry developers, but instead the YMCA was completely rebuilt, with a spacious and cheerful lobby, additional rooms, and a sports facility added in 1991. Welcoming families as well as individual men and women, it offers 19 single rooms (none with harbor view) and more than 280 twins (the most expensive twins provide great harbor views), as well as suites with and without harbor views. There are also 56 dormitory-style bunk beds, available on a first-come, first-served basis for a maximum of seven nights. There are three food and beverage outlets, including the **Salisbury Restaurant** serving a buffet breakfast and fixed-price lunch and dinner menu. The sports facility (which costs extra) boasts two indoor swimming pools (including a children's pool), four squash courts, and a fitness gym. Same-day laundry service is available, as well as baby-sitting from 3:30 to 11:30pm and room service from 7am to 11pm. Needless to say, the Salisbury is so popular that you should make reservations at least three months in advance. Although the Salisbury may seem expensive for a YMCA, the location and facilities are worth the price; here you have Tsim Sha Tsui's cheapest rooms with harbor views. Highly recommended.

Shamrock Hotel

223 Nathan Rd., Yau Ma Tei, Kowloon, Hong Kong. ☎ 852/2735 2271. Fax 852/2736 7354. 148 rms (all with bath). A/C MINIBAR TV TEL. HK$920–HK$1,200 ($119–$156) double. AE, DC, MC, V. MTR: Jordan.

A pioneer member of HKHA, the Shamrock, built in the early 1950s, caters mainly to visitors from Southeast Asia. The guest rooms, equipped with empty refrigerators, are rather small, but high ceilings give the rooms something of a spacious feeling. A restaurant on the 10th floor serves Western, Chinese, and Malaysian dishes. The most remarkable thing about this hotel is its lobby—although small, the ceiling is covered with about a dozen chandeliers and lights of different designs. I don't think this place has changed much in the past 30 years, despite recent lobby renovations that added marble floors and walls and artwork from Beijing. There is 24-hour room service as well as laundry service. It's about a 15-minute walk from the Star Ferry.

✪ Stanford Hillview Hotel

13–17 Observatory Rd., Tsim Sha Tsui, Kowloon, Hong Kong. ☎ **852/2722 7822** or 800/44-UTELL in the U.S. Fax 852/2723 3718. 163 rms. A/C MINIBAR TV TEL. HK$900–HK$1,800 ($117–$234) double. AE, DC, MC, V. MTR: Tsim Sha Tsui.

This small, intimate hotel, built in 1991, is in the heart of Tsim Sha Tsui and yet it's a world away from it too, located on top of a hill in the shade of some huge banyan trees next to the Royal Observatory with its colonial building and greenery. Its lobby is quiet and subdued (quite a contrast to most Hong Kong hotels); the hotel has a business center, as well as a restaurant that serves Western and Asian dishes. Its cheapest ("economy") rooms are smaller and are located on the second floor facing the back of the hotel; since there are only four of these rooms, they should be booked well in advance. The most expensive rooms are on higher floors; ask for one that faces the Observatory. Room service is available from 6:30am to 11:30pm; there's also same-day laundry service and baby-sitting. All in all, a very civilized place.

YMCA International House

23 Waterloo Rd., Yau Ma Tei, Kowloon, Hong Kong. ☎ 852/2771 9111. Fax 852/2388 5926; reservation fax 852/2771 5238. 277 rms (255 with bath). A/C. HK$820–HK$1,070 ($106–$129) twin with bath; from HK$1,200 ($156) suite. Children under 12 stay free in parents' room. AE, DC, MC, V. MTR: Yau Ma Tei.

This modern facility accepts both men and women, though only men are accepted for its single rooms, which come without a bathroom. All other rooms have a private bathroom, minibar, TV, and telephone, though are simple enough to remind one of dormitory accommodations. Laundry service is available. The Y has a fitness center and sauna, as well as one restaurant and a bar. An addition is being built (expected completion in 1996) that will provide an indoor swimming pool, sauna, squash and tennis courts, and 100 more rooms.

CAUSEWAY BAY/WAN CHAI

✪ Harbour View International House

4 Harbour Rd., Wan Chai, Hong Kong. ☎ **852/2802 0111.** Fax 852/2802 9063. 320 rms (all with bath). A/C MINIBAR TV TEL. HK$980–HK$1,450 ($127–$188) twin/double. Children under 12 stay free in parents' room. AE, DC, MC, V. MTR: Wan Chai.

Opened in 1986, this modern YMCA occupies a prime spot on the Wan Chai waterfront, right next to the Hong Kong Arts Centre. Rooms, all twins or doubles, are simple but functional; facilities and services include a coffee shop, one restaurant with a view of the harbor, room service (7am to 11:30pm), laundry service, and free shuttle-bus service to the Star Ferry and Causeway Bay. Best yet, more than half the rooms face the harbor, making this one of the least expensive places in the colony with great views. Rooms that face inland are even cheaper.

New Cathay Hotel

17 Tung Lo Wan Rd., Causeway Bay, Hong Kong. ☎ **852/2577 8211.** Fax 852/2576 9365. 223 rms. A/C MINIBAR TV TEL. HK$980–HK$1,250 ($127–$162) double and twin. One child under 12 can stay free in parents' room. AE, DC, MC, V. MTR: Causeway Bay.

Built in 1967, the New Cathay finally underwent a much-needed renovation in 1989, but unfortunately the workmanship was a bit shoddy and the materials used were cheap. Still, the hotel offers large, bright rooms, modestly furnished with the basics. The guest rooms that face the back have a rather uninspiring view; it is better to request a room that faces the front. By far the best rooms are the deluxe twins on the 10th floor—they come with large balconies. Facilities include one Chinese restaurant and one coffee shop. Room service (7:30am to 11:30pm) and laundry service are available. The New Cathay caters largely to tour groups.

ROCK-BOTTOM ACCOMMODATIONS

Hong Kong's cheapest accommodations are not hotels, nor are they recommended for visitors who expect cleanliness and comfort. Rather, these accommodations attract a young backpacking crowd, many of whom are traveling through Asia and are interested only in a bed at the lowest cost. Some offer rooms with a private bathroom; others are nothing more than rooms filled with bunk beds. Of Hong Kong's rock-bottom establishments, none is more notorious than **Chungking Mansion.** Although it occupies a prime spot at 40 Nathan Road, between the Holiday Inn Golden Mile and the Sheraton in Tsim Sha Tsui, Chungking Mansion is easy to overlook; there's no big sign heralding its existence. In fact, its ground floor is one huge maze of inexpensive shops, many of them owned by Indians living in Hong Kong.

But above all those shops are five towering concrete blocks, each served by its own tiny elevator and known collectively as Chungking Mansion. Inside are hundreds of little businesses, apartments, guest houses, eateries, and sweatshops. Some of the guest houses are passable; many are not.

I stayed at Chungking Mansion on my first trip to Hong Kong in 1983, living in a neon-colored cell that was furnished with two sagging beds, a night table, and closet. In the shared bathroom down the hall lived the biggest spider I have ever seen, a hairy thing that nevertheless behaved itself whenever I was there—it never moved an inch the whole time I took a shower, and when I returned each evening it was always motionless in another part of the room. I figured that it survived only by being unobtrusive, and I wouldn't be surprised if it's still there. I shared my room with another woman and we paid $5 (U.S.) each.

Chungking Mansion has changed a lot since then. Ten years ago there wasn't much choice among the guest houses within Chungking Mansion; most of them were on the borderline of squalor. Today there are literally dozens of new ones, and many of the older ones have cleaned up their act in their bid for the tourist's dollar. I myself counted about 70 guest houses here, though a security guard estimated that there were as many as 200 spread throughout the complex; many are very small with only a handful of rooms. The new ones are spanking clean, and during my last visit I noticed something I had never seen there before—respectable-looking middle-aged tourists, no doubt forced to seek accommodations at Chungking Mansion because of the extravagant hotel rates elsewhere in Hong Kong.

Still, Chungking is not the kind of place you'd want to recommend to your grandmother or to anyone uninitiated in the seamier side of travel. The views from many room windows are more insightful than some guests might like—the backside of the building and mountains of trash down below. Even worse are the ancient-looking elevators filled to capacity with human cargo; you might want to stick to the stairs. In any case, sometimes the elevators don't work at all, making it a long hike up the dozen flights of stairs to the top floors. Still, for the budget traveler, Chungking Mansion is a viable alternative to Hong Kong's high-priced hotels. And you can't beat it for location.

Chungking Mansion is divided into five separate blocks, from A Block to E Block. For the less daring, A Block is the best, since its elevator is closest to the front entrance to the building. The other elevators are farther back in the shopping arcade, which can be a little disconcerting at night when the shops are all closed and the corridors are deserted. I recommend that you begin your search in Block A. If these are full or you want to save money, check the guest houses toward the back of the building in the other blocks. At Chungking Mansion, no matter what the block, never leave any valuables in your room.

Chungking House

A Block, 4th and 5th floors, Chungking Mansion, 40 Nathan Rd., Tsim Sha Tsui, Kowloon, Hong Kong. ☎ **852/2366 5362.** 82 rms (all with bath). A/C TV TEL. HK$420–HK$460 ($55–$60) double/twin. No credit cards. MTR: Tsim Sha Tsui.

This is the best-known guest house in Chungking Mansion—due primarily to the remarkable fact that it's a member of the Hong Kong Tourist Association (remarkable in that it's far shabbier than the other accommodations that belong to the association). It also has the best location at Chungking, in the A Block on a lower floor. With its front desk and lobby, it's more like a hotel than a guest house. The rooms are larger too, though wood paneling makes the place a bit dreary and the staff tends to be unconcerned and gruff. Even so, it's often fully booked. Still, you might want to try this place first before tackling the elevator or stairs to check out the guest houses on the upper floors.

YOUTH HOSTELS/CAMPSITES

There are a number of youth hostels and camping sites in Hong Kong, including its islands and territories, and they offer the cheapest rates around.

If you don't have a youth hostel card, you can still stay at a youth hostel by paying an extra HK$25 ($3.25) per night. After six nights, nonmembers are eligible for member status and subsequently pay overnight charges at members' rates.

The most conveniently located youth hostel is **Ma Wui Hall**, on the top of Mount Davis on Hong Kong Island (☎ **852/2817 5715**). It charges HK$25 ($3.25) per night for members under 18; HK$50 ($6.50) for those aged 18 and over. To reach it, take bus no. 5B from Des Voeux Road in front of the Hongkong Bank Monday through Friday from 6:50am to 10:14am or 4:50pm to 8:20pm. Otherwise, take bus no. 47 from Exchange Square and get off on Victoria Road. Follow the hostel sign and walk 30 minutes up Mount Davis Path (do not confuse Mt. Davis Path with Mt. Davis Road).

There are six other youth hostels on some of the outlying islands and in the New Territories; most charge HK$15 ($1.95) per night for members under 18 and HK$25 ($3.25) for those 18 and older. They also permit camping, which costs HK$13 ($1.70) per hostel member and HK$25 ($3.25) for each nonmember. Since these hostels are not easily accessible, they are recommended only for the adventurous traveler. For more information on Hong Kong's youth hostels, contact the **Hong Kong Youth Hostels Association,** Room 225-226, Block 19, Shek Kip Mei Estate, Sham Shui Po, Kowloon (☎ 852/2788 1638).

There are also camping facilities on some of the outlying islands, ranging in price from free to about HK$40 ($5.20). You must bring your own tent, but some of the camps provide sheets and blankets. The more primitive campsites lack water or latrine facilities—but they're free. For more information on campsites, contact the HKTA.

5 Dining

Dining is one of *the* things to do in Hong Kong. Not only is the food excellent, but the prices are reasonable and the range of culinary possibilities is nothing short of staggering. With an estimated 7,000 restaurants, Hong Kong has probably the greatest concentration of Chinese restaurants in the world, as well as a wide range of Japanese, Indian, Thai, Vietnamese, Italian, French, and other international establishments. I'm convinced that you can eat just as well in Hong Kong as in any other city in the world. And no matter where you eat or how much you spend, it's sure to be an adventure of the senses.

It is little wonder that a common greeting among Chinese in Hong Kong translates literally as "Have you eaten?" In Hong Kong, eating is the most important order of the day. See "Food and Drink" (Chapter 1) for information on dining customs and a brief rundown on Chinese cuisine.

Chinese restaurants often have very long menus, sometimes listing more than 100 dishes. The most expensive dishes will invariably be such delicacies as bird's nest, shark's fin, or abalone, for which the sky's the limit on how much you could spend. In specifying price ranges for "Main Dishes" under each Chinese establishment below, therefore, I excluded both these delicacies and the inexpensive rice and noodle dishes. In most cases, "Main Dishes" refers to meat and vegetable combinations. Remember, since the price range is large, you can eat cheaply even at moderately priced restaurants by choosing wisely. Remember, too, that it's customary to order one main dish for each diner, plus one more, and to share.

By far Hong Kong's best and most exclusive restaurants, both Chinese and Western, are in the hotels. That's not surprising when you realize that first-class hotels are accustomed to catering to well-traveled visitors who demand high quality in service, cuisine, and decor.

Keep in mind, however, that Western restaurants tend to be more expensive than Chinese ones, and that wine is especially expensive. The estimated meal prices for the restaurants presented here do not include wine, since you could easily spend a fortune on drinks alone. To keep costs down, stick with beer: The two most popular brands are San Miguel (Filipino) and Tsingtao (Chinese). And speaking of beer, many bars and pubs mentioned in Chapter 9, "Hong Kong After Dark," also serve food. In any case, remember that a 10% service charge will be added to your food and beverage bill. There is no tax, however.

One good way to save money is to eat your big meal at lunch. Many Asian and Western restaurants offer special fixed-price lunches that are much cheaper than evening meals; their menus often include an appetizer, main course, and side dishes. If you feel like splurging in an expensive restaurant, lunch may be the way to go. Don't neglect these restaurants just because you assume they're out of your price range. For example, you can eat lunch at Gaddi's (one of Hong Kong's most famous restaurants) for less than $34 per person.

Buffet spreads are another great Hong Kong tradition; they have become so popular that more and more restaurants are jumping on the buffet bandwagon. Almost all hotels nowadays offer buffets, often for breakfast, lunch, and dinner; independent restaurants are more likely to feature buffets at lunch. Some include a variety of both Asian and continental dishes, a real bonus for lone diners who want to sample a variety of cuisines at a reasonable cost. If you have a hearty appetite, buffets are one of the best bargains in town.

Dim sum, served mainly in Cantonese restaurants, are another way to economize on breakfast or lunch. Dim sum are usually served four to a basket or plate; two or three baskets are usually filling enough for me, which means I can have breakfast or lunch for less than HK$80 ($10.40).

The restaurants listed below are grouped first according to location (the most popular areas are Kowloon, the Central District, and Causeway Bay/Wan Chai) and then according to price. Those in the **Very Expensive** category will cost more than HK$500 ($65) for a meal without drinks (some restaurants average HK$800 ($104) or more per person). In the **Expensive** category, meals average HK$250 to HK$500 ($32.50 to $65). **Moderate** restaurants serve meals ranging from HK$125 to HK$250 ($16.25 to $32.50), while **Inexpensive** restaurants offer meals for less than HK$120 ($15.60). Keep in mind, however, that these guidelines are approximations only.

The usual lunch hour in Hong Kong is 1 to 2pm, when thousands of office workers pour into the city's more popular restaurants. Try to eat before or after the lunch rush hour unless you plan on an expensive restaurant and have a reservation.

Unless stated otherwise, the open hours given below are exactly that—the hours a restaurant remains physically open but not necessarily the hours it serves food. The last orders are almost always taken at least a half hour before closing. Restaurants that are open for lunch from noon to 3pm, for example, will probably stop taking orders at 2:30pm. To avoid disappointment, call beforehand to make a reservation or arrive well ahead of closing time.

1 Best Bets

I'm convinced Hong Kong has some of the best restaurants in the world—which makes it extremely difficult to choose the best of the best. With apologies to all of the other greats, these are my own personal favorites.

- **Best Spot for a Romantic Dinner: The Plume,** The Regent Hotel, Salisbury Road, Tsim Sha Tsui (☎ 852/2721 1211), has all the makings of a special evening à deux: great harbor view, excellent service, and some of the best cuisine in Hong Kong—original creations that use Asian foods to enhance classical European dishes. You'll want to linger for some time here, savoring the food, the ambience, the view, and each other.
- **Best Spot for a Business Lunch:** Business travelers have long favored the **Mandarin Grill,** Mandarin Oriental Hotel, 5 Connaught Road, Central (☎ 852/2522 0111). It offers drawing-room comfort and high-powered food, a winning combination for clinching those business deals.

- **Best Spot for a Celebration:** An elegant, colonial-age setting, attentive service, dependably good food, and an extensive wine list make **Gaddi's,** The Peninsula Hotel, Salisbury Road, Tsim Sha Tsui (☎ 852/2366 6251), a natural for a splurge or special celebration.
- **Best Decor: Felix,** The Peninsula Hotel, Salisbury Road, Tsim Sha Tsui (☎ 852/2366 6251), was designed by Philippe Starck; in addition to providing Hong Kong's most unusual setting, the restaurant offers stunning views, one of the world's smallest discos, and exhibitionist bathrooms.
- **Best View:** In a town famous for its views, you might as well go to the very top, where the curved facade of **Cafe Deco,** Peak Galleria, Victoria Peak (☎ 852/2849 5111), offers Hong Kong's best panorama, along with live jazz in the evening and moderately priced international cuisine.
- **Best Wine List:** Not only does **Petrus,** Island Shangri-La Hotel, Supreme Court Road, Central (☎ 852/2877 3838), a French restaurant, offer what is probably the most definitive wine list in Hong Kong, but it provides great views, an intriguing menu, and a lavish, elegant setting.
- **Best Cantonese Cuisine:** With some of the world's best Cantonese restaurants located in Hong Kong, this is obviously a tough call, but you can't go wrong at **Lai Ching Heen,** The Regent Hotel, Salisbury Road, Tsim Sha Tsui (☎ 852/2721 1211), where the emphasis is on stark simplicity, a view of the harbor, and traditional and creative dishes that border on Chinese nouvelle cuisine.
- **Best French Cuisine:** The **Pierrot,** Mandarin Oriental Hotel, 5 Connaught Road, Central (☎ 852/2522 0111), with views of the harbor, was Hong Kong's first hotel restaurant to introduce French nouvelle cuisine and it has remained one of the city's favorites ever since. It's also the best spot in town to indulge in caviar, imported from the Petrossian purveyors of Russian caviar.
- **Best Italian Cuisine:** There are a lot of contenders in this category, but the harbor views, airy palatial setting, and traditional northern Italian home-style cooking combine to make **Grissini,** Grand Hyatt Hong Kong Hotel, 1 Harbour Road, Wan Chai (☎ 852/2588 1234), a favorite choice for lunch or dinner.
- **Best Buffet Spread:** Lots of hotels offer buffets, but none can match the view from the 30th-floor revolving **La Ronda,** Furama Kempinski Hotel, 1 Connaught Road, Central (☎ 852/2525 5111), which offers a wide selection of Asian and Western dishes for both lunch and dinner.
- **Best Dim Sum Experience:** First opened in 1925, **Luk Yu Tea House,** 24–26 Stanley Street, Central (☎ 852/2523 5464), is one of Hong Kong's oldest restaurants, famous for its dim sum and filled daily with regular customers. It's hard to find an empty seat here, but it's worth the effort, since this restaurant offers a truly unique dining experience.
- **Best Burgers and Beer: Dan Ryan's Chicago Grill,** 88 Queensway, Central (☎ 852/2845 4600), with two locations (one on each side of the harbor), offers casual dining, good burgers, and drinks throughout the day; its Kowloon branch even provides a view of the busy harbor.
- **Best Pizza: The Pizzeria,** Kowloon Hotel, 19–21 Nathan Road, Tsim Sha Tsui (☎ 852/2369 8698), a casual upbeat restaurant, offers eight unusual pizza combinations, as well as pasta selections, salads, and meat dishes, all at very reasonable prices. This is a great place to eat when you don't feel like getting dressed up but still want good food and good service.

- **Best Outdoor Dining:** Atop Victoria Peak, away from the constant drone of Hong Kong's traffic, is the delightful **Peak Cafe,** 121 Peak Road, Victoria Peak (☎ 852/2849 7868), with its outdoor terrace and lush foliage, where you can actually hear the birds sing. Some tables provide views of Hong Kong Island's southern coast.
- **Best Afternoon Tea:** For that most British institution, no place is more famous than the golden-age **Peninsula Hotel Lobby,** Salisbury Road, Tsim Sha Tsui, (☎ 852/2366 6251), where you can nibble on delicate finger sandwiches and scones, watch the parade of people, and listen to live classical music.
- **Best Breakfast:** You'll be spoiled forever, or at least for the rest of the day, if you begin your morning at **The Verandah,** The Peninsula Hotel, Salisbury Road, Tsim Sha Tsui (☎ 852/2366 6251); it is wonderfully reminiscent of the colonial era and serves delicious breakfasts. If ever there were a place that inspired champagne for breakfast, this is it.

2 Restaurants by Cuisine

AMERICAN

Al's Diner (Central, *I*)
The Bostonian (Kowloon, *E*)
Dan Ryan's Chicago Grill (Kowloon, Central, *M*)
Hard Rock Cafe (Kowloon, *M*)
L.A. Cafe (Central, *M*)

ASIAN

Felix (Kowloon, *E*)
Food Fare (Causeway Bay, *I*)
The Spice Market (Kowloon, *M*)
Stanley's Oriental Restaurant (Stanley, *M*)

CANTONESE

Broadway Seafood Restaurant (Wan Chai, *I*)
The Chinese (Kowloon, *E*)
City Hall Chinese Restaurant (Central, *I*)
Fook Lam Moon (Kowloon, Wan Chai, *E*)
Golden Unicorn Restaurant (Kowloon, *E*)
Greenwood Restaurant (Kowloon, *I*)
Jade Garden Restaurant (Kowloon, *M*)
Jumbo Floating Restaurant (Aberdeen Harbour, *M*)

Lai Ching Heen (Kowloon, *VE*)
Luk Yu Tea House (Central, *M*)
Man Wah (Central, *VE*)
Mythical China (Western District, *E*)
One Harbour Road (Wan Chai, *E*)
Shang Palace (Kowloon, *E*)
Spring Moon (Kowloon, *E*)
Super Star Seafood Restaurant (Kowloon, *M*)
Tai Pak Seafood Restaurant (Aberdeen Harbour, *M*)
Tin Tin Seafood Harbour (Causeway Bay, *M*)
Tsui Hang Village Restaurant (Kowloon, *M*)
Yung Kee (Central, *E*)
Zen Chinese (Central, *E*)

CHIU CHOW

Chiuchow Garden (Central, *M*)
City Chiuchow Restaurant (Kowloon, *M*)
Golden Island Bird's Nest (Kowloon, *M*)
Harbour City Chiuchow Restaurant (Causeway Bay, *M*)

Key to abbreviations: *E*=Expensive; *I*=Inexpensive; *M*=Moderate; *VE*=Very Expensive

CONTINENTAL

Harbourside (Kowloon, *M*)
Hugo's (Kowloon, *VE*)
Jimmy's Kitchen (Kowloon,
  Central, *M*)
Landau's (Wan Chai, *M*)
Mandarin Grill (Central, *VE*)
Parc 27 (Causeway Bay, *E*)
The Plume (Kowloon, *VE*)
Quo Quo (Central, *E*)
Sammy's Kitchen (Western
  District, *I*)
Tables 88 (Stanley, *E*)
The Verandah (Kowloon, *E*)

FRENCH

Cafe de Paris (Central, *E*)
Gaddi's (Kowloon, *VE*)
Petrus (Central, *VE*)
Pierrot (Central, *VE*)
Stanley's French Restaurant
  (Stanley, *E*)

HUNANESE

Hunan Garden (Central, *M*)

INDIAN

The Ashoka (Central, *I*)
Gaylord (Kowloon, *M*)
Koh-I-Noor (Kowloon, *I*)
The Viceroy (Wan Chai, *M*)

INTERNATIONAL

Cafe Deco (Victoria Peak, *M*)
La Ronda (Central, *E*)
Peak Cafe (Victoria Peak, *M*)
Portico (Central, *M*)
Rick's Cafe (Wan Chai, *I*)
The Salisbury (Kowloon, *I*)
Wah Yuen Restaurant
  (IKowloon, *I*)

ITALIAN

Capriccio (Kowloon, *VE*)
Grappa's (Central, *M*)
Grissini (Wan Chai, *VE*)
La Taverna (Central, *M*)
Nicholini's (Central, *VE*)
The Pizzeria (Kowloon, *M*)
Rigoletto (Wan Chai, *M*)

Sabatini (Kowloon, *E*)
Spaghetti House (Kowloon,
  Causeway Bay, Central, *I*)
Va Bene (Central, *E*)

JAPANESE

Benkay Japanese Restaurant
  (Central, *VE*)
Kansai (Kowloon, *I*)
Unkai (Kowloon, *VE*)
Yorohachi (Central, *M*)

KOREAN

Arirang Korean Restaurant
  (Kowloon, *M*)

MALAYSIAN/SINGAPOREAN

Banana Leaf Curry House
  (Kowloon, *I*)

MEXICAN

Zona Rosa (Central, *M*)

PEKINESE

American Restaurant (Wan Chai, *I*)
Spring Deer Restaurant
  (Kowloon, *M*)

SEAFOOD

Bentley's (Central, *E*)
Lobster Bar (Central, *VE*)
Yü (Kowloon, *VE*)

SHANGHAINESE

Great Shanghai (Kowloon, *M*)
Shanghai Garden (Central, *M*)
Wu Kong (Kowloon, *M*)

SZECHUAN

Cleveland Szechuan Restaurant
  (Causeway Bay, *M*)
Fung Lum Restaurant (Kowloon, *M*)
Red Pepper (Causeway Bay, *M*)
Sichuan Garden (Central, *M*)
Sze Chuen Lau Restaurant
  (Wan Chai, *M*)

TEAS/CAKES

Clipper Lounge (Central, *E*)
Peninsula Hotel Lobby
  (Kowloon, *E*)

THAI

Bangkok Royal Thai Restaurant
(Kowloon, *I*)
Chili Club (Wan Chai, *I*)
Golden Elephant Thai Restaurant
(Kowloon, Central, *M*)
Sawadee (Kowloon, *M*)
Supatra's (Central, *M*)

VEGETARIAN

Bodhi Vegetarian Restaurant
(Kowloon, *I*)
Vegi Food Kitchen
(Causeway Bay, *I*)

VIETNAMESE

Golden Bull (Kowloon, *M*)

3 Kowloon

VERY EXPENSIVE

Capriccio

In the Hong Kong Renaissance Hotel, 8 Peking Rd., Tsim Sha Tsui. ☎ **852/2375 3311**, ext.
2260. Reservations recommended. Jacket and tie required. Main courses HK$240–HK$460
($31.15–$59.75); fixed-price lunch HK$215–HK$250 ($27.90–$32.45); fixed-price dinner
HK$460 ($59.75). AE, DC, MC, V. Mon–Sat noon–3pm and 6–11pm. MTR: Tsim Sha Tsui.
ITALIAN.

Whereas most hotels feature French or continental cuisine in their top restaurant, the
Hong Kong Renaissance highlights northern Italian cuisine from Tuscany. This is
easily the most exclusive Italian restaurant in Hong Kong, elegant with exquisite
flower arrangements, innovative yet with soft lighting and a low-key interior design
of soothing pale yellows and grays. All pasta is homemade, there's a wide range of
Italian wine, and though the menu changes monthly, one popular staple is lobster
with tomato and pesto; the meat antipasto misto of Italian hams and sausages is probably the best in Hong Kong. Three- and four-course fixed-price lunches are available;
the four-course meal includes an appetizer buffet spread, a pasta, a fish or meat dish
(from half a dozen choices), and dessert. Cellular phones are forbidden (hurray!).

✪ Gaddi's

In The Peninsula Hotel, Salisbury Rd., Tsim Sha Tsui. ☎ **852/2366 6251**, ext. 3989.
Reservations recommended at lunch, required at dinner. Jacket and tie required at dinner.
Main courses HK$300–HK$410 ($39.85–$51.95); fixed-price lunch HK$280–HK$350
($36.35–$45.45); fixed-price dinner HK$970 ($125.95). AE, CB, DC, MC, V. Daily noon–2:30pm
and 7–10:30pm. MTR: Tsim Sha Tsui. FRENCH.

Named after a former general manager of The Peninsula, Gaddi's has had a reputation as the best European restaurant in town ever since it opened in 1953. Although
that reputation is now being challenged by other hotels, the service is still excellent,
the waiters are all professionals, the food is always beyond reproof, and it's still a
legend in the Orient.

The atmosphere, intended to evoke the hotel's original 1928 neoclassical architecture, is that of an elegant European dining room blended with the best of Asia; there
are two crystal-and-silver chandeliers from Paris, a pure wool Tai Ping carpet in royal
blue and gold, a Chinese coromandel screen dating from 1670, and Biedermeier-style
chairs. As for the food, it's French haute cuisine at its finest—the soufflés are
sublime. The menu changes every six months, but it always includes steak and
seafood and sometimes a fixed-price dinner with wines to complement the various
dishes. The wine cellar is among the best and largest in Hong Kong, with a collection of rare vintages—but who could blame you if you get carried away and splurge
on champagne? Dinner is likely to cost at least HK$800 ($103.90), but it'll be much

more if you order caviar followed by lobster. There's live music at night and a small dance floor. Lunch, especially the fixed-price two-course menu which includes a glass of wine, is quite affordable, making this the top splurge for the money-conscious.

Hugo's

In the Hyatt Regency, 67 Nathan Rd., Tsim Sha Tsui. ☎ **852/2311 1234,** ext. 877. Reservations recommended. Jacket and tie required. Main courses HK$280–HK$350 ($36.35–$45.45); fixed-price lunch HK$220–HK$240 ($28.55–$31.15); fixed-price dinner HK$640–HK$930 ($83.10–$120.75). AE, DC, MC, V. Daily noon–2:30pm (last order) and 7–10:45pm (last order). MTR: Tsim Sha Tsui. CONTINENTAL.

This was the first Hugo's opened by Hyatt in Asia; now there's a Hugo's in all their deluxe hotels. The rather masculine and slightly grim decor features swords on the walls, booths with heavy wooden partitions, leather-bound menus, and big green water glasses. Popular with the locals and visiting businesspeople, it's a good choice for power lunches and a lively place for dinner, with Filipino musicians serenading evening diners. The specialty is U.S. prime rib of beef, with seafood flown in from around the world. The menu changes twice a year, but if lobster bisque or baked artichoke hearts topped with lobster (the house special) are on the menu, I would recommend them. The desserts are always spectacular, and the wine list is extensive.

✪ Lai Ching Heen

In The Regent Hotel, Salisbury Rd., Tsim Sha Tsui. ☎ **852/2721 1211.** Reservations recommended (request a window seat). Main dishes HK$130–HK$500 ($16.90–$64.95). AE, DC, MC, V. Daily noon–2:30pm and 6–11:30pm. MTR: Tsim Sha Tsui. CANTONESE.

One of Hong Kong's top Cantonese restaurants, Lai Ching Heen emphasizes the beauty of stark simplicity. Bonsai trees, flower arrangements, and a color scheme of rose and pale gray offset beautiful jade table settings and ivory and silver chopsticks; large windows treat diners to a view of famous Victoria Harbour. Dishes are traditional Cantonese, as well as imaginative creations of the executive chef that border on Chinese nouvelle cuisine. The menu changes with each lunar month but always includes seafood, seasonal vegetables, and a wide selection of desserts. Examples include crabmeat and golden mushrooms with Portuguese sauce wrapped in rice paper, and sautéed sliced pigeon with fresh pineapple and mixed bell peppers. Since most diners follow the Chinese example of ordering several dishes and then sharing, the average dinner bill without wine here begins at HK$850 ($110.40) for two. For lunch an additional menu is offered that includes three or four main dishes averaging about HK$110 ($14.30) in price, as well as dim sum.

✪ The Plume

In The Regent Hotel, Salisbury Rd., Tsim Sha Tsui. ☎ **852/2721 1211.** Reservations required (request a window seat). Jacket and tie required. Main courses HK$330–HK$480 ($42.85–$62.35); fixed-price meal HK$750–HK$1,000 ($97.40–$129.85). AE, DC, MC, V. Daily 7–11pm. MTR: Tsim Sha Tsui. CONTINENTAL.

Giving Gaddi's a run for its money is The Plume in The Regent Hotel. In fact, some people consider The Plume the best European restaurant in Hong Kong. Certainly it feels like a great restaurant, sitting right over the water with a grand view of Hong Kong Island and offering very interesting nouvelle cuisine served by an excellently trained staff.

It's open only for dinner, which begins with a complimentary glass of Mir (champagne with a hint of blackberry liqueur), Indian bread, and goose-liver pâté. The menu, which features only original creations that mix the best of the East and the West, changes every day but always includes the house specialty: a delicate cream of artichoke soup with beluga. In any case, the food is so imaginative and full of

Kowloon Dining

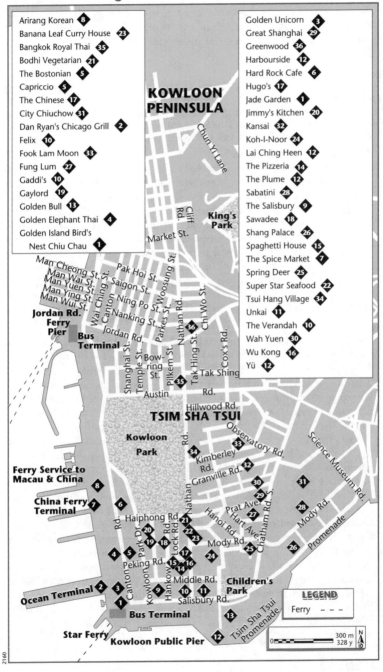

Arirang Korean 8
Banana Leaf Curry House 23
Bangkok Royal Thai 35
Bodhi Vegetarian 21
The Bostonian 5
Capriccio 5
The Chinese 17
City Chiuchow 31
Dan Ryan's Chicago Grill 2
Felix 10
Fook Lam Moon 33
Fung Lum 27
Gaddi's 10
Gaylord 19
Golden Bull 13
Golden Elephant Thai 4
Golden Island Bird's
    Nest Chiu Chau 1

Golden Unicorn 3
Great Shanghai 29
Greenwood 36
Harbourside 12
Hard Rock Cafe 6
Hugo's 17
Jade Garden 1
Jimmy's Kitchen 20
Kansai 32
Koh-I-Noor 24
Lai Ching Heen 12
The Pizzeria 14
The Plume 12
Sabatini 28
The Salisbury 9
Sawadee 18
Shang Palace 26
Spaghetti House 15
The Spice Market 7
Spring Deer 25
Super Star Seafood 22
Tsui Hang Village 34
Unkai 11
The Verandah 10
Wah Yuen 30
Wu Kong 16
Yü 12

KOWLOON PENINSULA

Chuin Yi Lane

Cliff Rd.

King's Park

Market St.

Man Cheong St.
Man Wai St.
Man Yuen St.
Man Ying St.
Man Wui St.

Pak Hoi St.
Saigon St.
Ning Po St.
Woosung St.
Parkes St.

Wai Ching St.
Canton
Nanking St.

Jordan Rd.
Ferry Pier

Bus Terminal

Shanghai St.
Temple St.

Jordan Rd.

Bow-ring St.
Pilkem St.

Nathan Rd.
Chi Wo St.
Cox's Rd.

Tak Hing St.

Tak Shing Rd.

Austin

Hillwood Rd.

TSIM SHA TSUI

Kowloon Park

Kimberley Rd.

Observatory Rd.

Science Museum Rd.

Granville Rd.

Ferry Service to Macau & China

China Ferry Terminal

Haiphong Rd.

Hanoi Rd.

Prat Ave.
Hart Ave.

Chatham Rd. S.

Mody Rd.

Peking Rd.

Hankow Rd.
Lock Rd.
Kowloon Park Dr.
Canton Rd.

Middle Rd.

Children's Park

Ocean Terminal

Salisbury Rd.

Bus Terminal

Star Ferry

Kowloon Public Pier

Tsim Sha Tsui Promenade

Promenade

LEGEND
Ferry - - -

0   300 m
         328 y

N

2160

surprises that epicures will want to set up camp—assuming, of course, that they remembered to pack a coat and tie or cocktail dress, the required uniform here. If you order à la carte, expect to spend at least HK$800 ($103.90) per person, without wine.

Unkai

In the Sheraton Hong Kong Hotel and Towers, 20 Nathan Rd., Tsim Sha Tsui. ☎ **852/2369 1111,** ext. 2. Reservations recommended. Kaiseki HK$700–HK$900 ($90.90–$116.90); tempura courses HK$300–HK$470 ($38.95–$61.05); shabu-shabu or sukiyaki HK$530 ($68.85); fixed-price lunch HK$145–HK$280 ($18.85–$36.35). AE, CB, DC, MC, V. Daily noon–2:30pm and 6:30–10:30pm. MTR: Tsim Sha Tsui. JAPANESE.

The Hong Kong branch of a well-known group of restaurants in Japan, Unkai might be the best Japanese restaurant in town. True to Japanese form, the elegance of the restaurant is subtly understated, an aesthetic that is also carried into the food presentation. Foremost, of course, are the kaiseki courses, artfully arranged dishes that change according to the seasons. These are the most expensive fixed-price meals on the menu, but are so huge that two of you can share. There's also tempura (meat and vegetables coated in batter and then deep-fried), shabu-shabu (thinly sliced beef cooked in a broth with vegetables at your table), and sushi (raw fish). Since ordering à la carte can be expensive, order a fixed-price meal (called a "course" on the menu) or come for lunch, when you have a choice of several fixed-price menus, including sushi courses, a tempura course, and an obento lunch box. The obento is especially charming, a small lacquered chest with dishes of food in each of the drawers.

Yü

In The Regent Hotel, Salisbury Rd., Tsim Sha Tsui. ☎ **852/2721 1211.** Reservations necessary (request a window seat). Main courses HK$190–HK$325 ($24.65–$42.20); fixed-price lunch $300 ($38.95). AE, DC, MC, V. Daily noon–2pm and 6–11pm. MTR: Tsim Sha Tsui. SEAFOOD.

There's no mistaking what this restaurant serves—it's all right there in front of you, swimming blissfully in a 40-foot "bubble wall," unaware that the days are numbered. On the other side of the restaurant spreads Victoria Harbour. Located in the swank Regent Hotel but trendily low-key (the dress can be described as "smart casual"), the Yü offers a nice concept—fresh seafood for cautious diners reluctant to tempt fate by ordering locally caught fish in Hong Kong's cheaper, noisier, and more colorful seaside restaurants favored by Hong Kong Chinese. Of course, you also pay a mountain more to eat here, but from the looks of things there are plenty of takers. All the seafood, including a variety of garoupa, trout, and other fish, lobsters, crabs, prawns, abalone, mussels, and oysters, are kept alive in tanks until the moment they're ordered; sometimes they have even been quarantined after being flown in to ensure quality. Colorful cards of fish are presented to diners to show the day's catch, which can be prepared in a variety of ways. However, most diners stick to the imported oysters or begin their meal with the seafood platter—fresh seafood laid on a mountain of ice, including oysters, shrimp, prawns, mussels, and lobster, served with different sauces. Another good choice is the lobster bisque or seafood basket, a variety of bamboo-steamed seafood. The wine list is limited, consisting understandably mostly of whites, but a wider selection is available from The Plume's wine cellar.

EXPENSIVE

The Bostonian

In the Hong Kong Renaissance Hotel, 8 Peking Rd., Tsim Sha Tsui. ☎ **852/2375 1133,** ext. 2070. Reservations recommended at dinner. Main courses HK$185–HK$390 ($24–$50.65);

lunch buffet HK$185–HK$205 ($24–$26.60). AE, DC, MC, V. Daily noon–2:30 and 6–11pm. MTR: Tsim Sha Tsui. AMERICAN.

It's hard to think of a more fun-oriented restaurant than The Bostonian. All of its tables feature paper tablecloths and lots of crayons so you can scribble to your heart's content. The menu includes wisecracks along with the selections—for the Cajun seafood pot, for example, it says, "It's real hard to get the Cajuns into the pot." There's also a "Jane Fonda Diet Corner (for all who wanna be Ann O. Rexias)." Needless to say, the atmosphere is laid-back and casual, and the restaurant looks as though it had been imported intact from the U.S. East Coast.

The Bostonian has an eclectic menu; despite its name it features mainly California and New Orleans cuisine, with seafood and steaks comprising most of the dishes. Selections include New Orleans seafood boil, barbecue shrimp, salmon with Creole hollandaise, Kansas prime rib, baby back ribs, spring chicken with avocado mousse and sweet corn salsa. Lunch features a create-your-own sandwich bar, as well as a buffet that includes appetizers, salads, desserts, and a choice of about a half dozen main courses, including a vegetarian dish. A huge selection of American wines is offered (more than 300 vintages). Clearly, you could spend a small fortune here.

✪ The Chinese

In the Hyatt Regency, 67 Nathan Rd., Tsim Sha Tsui. ☎ 852/2311 1234, ext. 881. Reservations recommended at dinner. Main dishes HK$110–HK$200 ($14.30–$25.95); fixed-price lunch HK$290 ($37.65). AE, DC, MC, V. Daily 11:30am–3pm and 6:30–11:30pm. MTR: Tsim Sha Tsui. CANTONESE.

Decorated in stark black and white with a blend of art deco and modern Chinese, this was Hong Kong's first Chinese restaurant to ignore the traditional red and gold. This trend-setting restaurant remains one of Hong Kong's most refined Cantonese restaurants, with a small and intimate dining room reminiscent of Chinese teahouses of the 1920s. The innovative menu combining Chinese ingredients with Western presentation changes with the seasons, but if available, the shark's fin served in papaya, deep-fried crispy chicken, minced pigeon with butter lettuce, drunken shrimp, and fried lobster balls are all equally delicious. Another great deal is the special dim sum available for lunch.

✪ Felix

In the Peninsula Hotel, Salisbury Rd., Tsim Sha Tsui. ☎ 852/2366 6251. Reservations recommended. Main courses: HK$165–HK$250 ($21.40–$32.45). AE, DC, MC,V. Daily 6–11pm. MTR: Tsim Sha Tsui. ASIAN

Located on the top floor of the Peninsula's new tower addition, this strikingly avant-garde restaurant comes as something of a shock in the otherwise staid and traditionally conservative hotel. But what else can you expect from a restaurant designed by Philippe Starck? He was given free rein to create one of Hong Kong's most unusual settings. Your first hint that Felix is not your ordinary dining experience begins with the elevator's wavy walls, which suggest a voyage to the world beyond. The wave pattern continues inside the restaurant—a huge aluminum wavy wall and two glass facades curve seductively to reveal stunning views of Kowloon. Off to the sides of the high-ceilinged dining area, done mostly in mahogany, are two eye-catching zinc cylinders, which vaguely resemble gigantic snails and contain cocoon-cozy bars and what may be one of the world's tiniest discos, complete with a heat-sensitive floor that illuminates dancers' movements. Be sure to check out the rest room for the thrill of its slightly exhibitionist setting. The dining area itself is rather—what can I say— stark, with various styles of tables in marble, glass, and wood, all devoid of such "superfluous" decorations as table linen or flowers. The chair backs, also designed by Starck, are embellished with portraits of himself and his friends, but such details may be overlooked when the restaurant is full. Indeed, even the view from the windows tends to take second place in this self-conscious, people-watching setting. The food, featuring Western cuisine enhanced by Pacific rim ingredients, is quite good but also secondary to the setting. Dishes have ranged from Asian grilled rack of lamb with a coconut basil sauce to roasted chicken with a Tex-Mex risotto and chili sauce. Clearly, the main reason for dining here is for the experience—something else to describe to the folks back home.

Fook Lam Moon

53–59 Kimberley Rd., Tsim Sha Tsui. ☎ **852/2366 0286.** Main dishes HK$100–HK$170 ($13–$22.10). AE, DC, MC, V. Daily 11:30am–11:30pm. MTR: Tsim Sha Tsui. CANTONESE.

Upon entering this restaurant (look for the shrine to the kitchen god at the entrance), you immediately feel as if you've stepped back a couple of decades to a Hong Kong that has all but vanished. In years past there were a large number of indifferent, slow, and seemingly bored Chinese waiters standing around. However, on my most recent visit, I noticed that they have been replaced by an army of younger and more atten- tive employees. (Many Chinese restaurants are now hiring ambitious youths in an attempt to transform their image into that of a trendy establishment). Some custom- ers may find the service too attentive. In any case, Fook Lam Moon specializes in exotic dishes, including shark's fin, bird's nest, and abalone, served in a variety of ways, as well as more down-to-earth dishes such as fried crispy chicken. Shark's fin, however, is the obvious number-one choice, with 19 different renditions listed on the menu. If you feel like splurging, prices for half a bowl of shark's fin begin at HK$240 ($31.15). If you are not careful, you could end up spending a small fortune, but whatever you order it's apt to be memorable. Indeed, some Hong Kong old-timers swear this restaurant serves the best Cantonese food in the world. Unlike many Chinese restaurants, this establishment provides both small (for two to four diners) and large tables.

There's another branch in Wan Chai at 35–45 Johnston Rd. (☎ 852/866 0663), with the same hours.

Golden Unicorn Restaurant

In Omni the Hong Kong Hotel, 3 Canton Rd., Tsim Sha Tsui. ☎ **852/2730 6565.** Reserva- tions recommended. Main dishes HK$90–HK$190 ($11.70–$24.65); fixed-price menu HK$300 ($38.95). AE, DC, MC, V. Daily noon–midnight. MTR: Tsim Sha Tsui. CANTONESE.

Opened in 1986, this sixth-floor restaurant was one of the pioneers in the trend to serve Chinese food in a more modern and formal setting. This restaurant features white tablecloths and flowers on each table and uses Wedgwood china and Christofle silverware. Its Cantonese food with a Western flair includes drunken prawns; deep- fried chicken; and duck, pork, and seafood selections. If you're by yourself you'll probably want to order the fixed-price menu, which changes monthly and allows you to sample several dishes. Otherwise, most dishes are in the HK$90 to HK$140 ($11.70–$18.20) range.

✪ Sabatini

In the Royal Garden, 69 Mody Rd., Tsim Sha Tsui East. ☎ **852/2733 2000.** Reservations recommended. Pasta HK$120–HK$150 ($15.60–$19.50); main courses HK$200–HK$250 ($25.95–$32.45); fixed-price lunch HK$135 ($17.55); fixed-price dinner HK$490 ($63.65). AE, DC, MC, V. Daily noon–2:30pm and 7–11pm. MTR: Tsim Sha Tsui. ITALIAN.

In 1954, three Sabatini brothers opened their first restaurant in Rome; their success led them to open branches in Japan and, in 1992, Hong Kong. The dining hall is rustic and cozy yet refined, with a brick and terra-cotta tile floor, wooden ceiling, and traditional Roman murals, giving it a more casual and relaxed ambiance than most hotel Italian restaurants in the same price range. Its menu is an exact replica of the original Roman fare; with a liberal dose of olive oil, garlic, and peppers, it features such popular dishes as baked snapper with olives; veal escallops with white wine, tomatoes, and mushrooms; grilled lamb chops; and linguine with clams and shrimp. All of the pasta is handmade, and though only Italian wine is available, the list is seemingly endless. Evenings feature guitar music; lunch is popular for its reasonably fixed-price menu.

Shang Palace

In the Shangri-La Hotel, 64 Mody Rd., Tsim Sha Tsui East. ☎ **852/2721 2111.** Reservations required. Main dishes HK$90–HK$190 ($11.70–$24.65); fixed-price lunch for two HK$280 ($36.35). AE, CB, DC, MC, V. Mon–Sat 12:30–3pm; Sun and holidays noon–3pm; daily 6:30–11pm. MTR: Tsim Sha Tsui. CANTONESE.

This is one of the most elaborately decorated Chinese restaurants in Hong Kong. The entryway, with its rows of red columns, is cleverly set with mirrors to give the illusion of a long corridor, as though entering a royal palace. The walls of the restaurant itself are of carved red lacquerware, and Chinese lanterns hang from the ceiling. All in all, it fits every expectation of how an authentic Chinese restaurant should look.

The dinner menu is quite extensive, with a large variety of seafood, chicken, duck, pigeon, beef, and pork, cooked Cantonese-style. Specialties include shark's-fin soup, barbecued pork, Peking duck, steamed shrimp in lotus leaf, braised vegetables, and pan-fried minced pigeon with lettuce. If cost is no object, you might consider bird's nest with bamboo fungus, which runs HK$300 ($38.95) or more. Lunch is more economical. Although the lunch menu changes every two weeks, it always includes more than a dozen varieties of dim sum, as well as a great fixed-price menu for two people.

✪ The Verandah

In The Peninsula Hotel, Salisbury Rd., Tsim Sha Tsui. ☎ **852/2366 6251,** ext. 3166. Reservations highly recommended at lunch or dinner. Main courses HK$130–HK$270 ($16.90–$35.05); fixed-price lunch HK$215 ($27.35); fixed-price dinner HK$380 ($49.35). AE, CB, DC, MC, V. Daily 7–11am, noon–2:30pm, and 6:30–11pm. MTR: Tsim Sha Tsui. CONTINENTAL.

If you find Gaddi's too stuffy and Felix too pretentious, this restaurant, reminiscent of the colonial era, may be more to your liking. Its light blue-and-green canopy visible from Salisbury Road, the Verandah is an airy, bright, and cheerful place that gives the illusion of being a verandah. Ceiling fans whirl noiselessly overhead; graceful palms placed strategically between tables and cushioned rattan chairs give an air of privacy. The big windows wrap themselves around the U-shaped front of the hotel, offering a view which unfortunately has been spoiled somewhat by a monstrosity across the street (the Space Museum). However, the food is so good and the service so attentive that you'll soon forget to look any farther than your own table.

The specialties here are traditional home-cooked dishes and healthy, light cuisine, including imaginative salads and pastas. The menu changes often, but might include penne with braised duck ragout, sun-dried tomatoes, and fresh basil; grilled prawns with spicy pepper, chili, and tomato sauce; beef mignons of foie gras and madeira sauce; and roast lamb loin on spinach gratin with grilled baby potatoes. Fixed-price lunches, which include salad bar, soup of the day, choice of entrée, and dessert, are a bargain; on Saturday there is also a curry buffet. I love to start the day by coming here for breakfast; the attentive service makes me feel deliciously pampered. A Sunday brunch is served for HK$300 ($38.95).

MODERATE

Arirang Korean Restaurant

Shop 210, The Gateway, 25 Canton Rd., Tsim Sha Tsui. ☎ **852/2956 3288.** Main courses HK$105–HK$120 ($13.65–$15.60). AE, DC, MC, V. Daily noon–3pm and 6–11pm. MTR: Tsim Sha Tsui. KOREAN.

This simple Korean restaurant is located in the Gateway shopping complex on Canton Road, not far from the Omni Prince Hotel. The waiters and waitresses are not likely to speak much English, but the English menu presents photographs of more than a dozen choices of Korean barbecues, which come with side orders of kimchee (cabbage spiced with red chilies) and noodles. My own personal favorites are the beef strips of bulgogi or the kalbi. The dishes tend to be small, so if there are two of you you'll probably want to order three different platters (or order two and then see if you want to add a third). You'll do your own barbecuing at smokeless grills at your table, which can be great fun, somewhat like an indoor cookout.

City Chiuchow Restaurant

East Ocean Centre, 98 Granville Rd., Tsim Sha Tsui East. ☎ **852/2723 6226.** Main dishes HK$80–HK$120 ($10.40–$15.60). AE, DC, MC, V. Mon–Thurs 11am–3pm and 5pm–midnight, Fri–Sun 11am–midnight. MTR: Tsim Sha Tsui. CHIU CHOW.

Riding the crest of the wave of a newfound popularity for Chiu Chow food, this spacious restaurant overlooks gardens leading down to a major promenade in Tsim Sha Tsui East. Decorated in the colors the Chinese adore—gold and orange—it seats 500 and features a big tank with fish swimming about, soon to end up on the chopping block.

Famous dishes here include Chiu Chow shark's-fin soup, much thicker and stronger tasting than the Cantonese version; double-boiled shark's-fin-and-chicken soup, not as strong but equally popular; sliced soy goose; fried chicken with a black spicy sauce; and seafood dishes, including lobster. I particularly recommend the cold sliced lobster in a special honey sauce—it's not on the menu but it's available year-round. Dim sum is also served. And don't forget to try the Iron Buddha tea, a specialty of Chiuchow's, a tea that is so strong it will knock your socks off—and may keep you awake all night. Complete meals here average HK$130 to HK$200 ($16.90 to $25.95).

Dan Ryan's Chicago Grill

200 Ocean Terminal, Harbour City, Tsim Sha Tsui. ☎ **852/2735 6111.** Main courses HK$60–HK$240 ($7.80–$31.15) before 6pm, HK$85–HK$240 ($11.05–$31.15) after 6pm. AE, DC, MC, V. Mon–Fri 11am–11:30pm; Sat–Sun 9am–11:30pm. MTR: Tsim Sha Tsui. AMERICAN.

At last, a restaurant in Hong Kong that serves real American food, with portions big enough to satisfy a hungry cowboy. The decor is Anywhere, U.S.A., but with a difference—since it's located right by the Star Ferry, the Chicago Grill offers views of the famous harbor. The lunch menu is substantial, including such classic American favorites as buffalo chicken wings, potato skins, nachos, New England clam chowder, barbecued ribs, spaghetti, lasagne, chili, great hamburgers, and large deli sandwiches. The dinner menu is more limited, mainly confined to barbecued steaks, chops, fish, and pasta. Admittedly, most dishes here are a bit pricey, but if you're hungering for the real thing you might consider it a lifesaver.

Fung Lum Restaurant

21–23 Prat Ave., Tsim Sha Tsui. ☎ **852/2367 8686.** Small dishes HK$55–HK$110 ($7.15–$14.30); large dishes HK$80–HK$180 ($10.40–$23.40). AE, MC, V. Daily 11am–10:30pm. MTR: Tsim Sha Tsui. SZECHUAN.

Rather bare-looking but very popular, the first-floor Fung Lum has been open more than a quarter of a century, surviving so far the onslaught of clothing stores that have slowly transformed this area from one of dining to one of shopping. Specialties include Szechuan chicken, shrimp with chili-and-garlic sauce, sliced pork in garlic-and-chili sauce, beef fillet with pepper and hot garlic sauce, scallops in garlic-and-onion sauce, and frogs' legs with chili. Spicy dishes are indicated on the menu, and since all dishes come in two sizes (small dishes are suitable for two people and large dishes for four or more), it's a good place to dine no matter how many are in your party.

✪ Gaylord

23–25 Ashley Rd., Tsim Sha Tsui. ☎ **852/2376 1001.** Main courses HK$50–HK$140 ($6.50–$18.20); lunch buffet HK$95 ($12.35). AE, DC, MC, V. Daily 11:30am–3pm and 6–11pm. MTR: Tsim Sha Tsui. INDIAN.

This long-established restaurant in the heart of Tsim Sha Tsui is classy and comfortable, with private booths and overstuffed sofas. Singers perform in the evenings. It is popular for its authentic North Indian classics, including tandoori, lamb curry cooked in North Indian spices and herbs, chicken cooked in hot fiery vindaloo curry, prawns cooked with green pepper and spices, and fish in potato, coriander, and tomato. There are a dozen vegetarian dishes, and the lunchtime buffet, served every day except public holidays until 2:30pm, is a winner. Otherwise, expect to spend about HK$200 ($25.95) per person for dinner.

Golden Bull

In the New World Centre, 20 Salisbury Rd., ☎ **852/2369 4617;** and in Ocean Centre, Harbour City, ☎ **852/2730 4866;** both in Tsim Sha Tsui. Main courses HK$60–HK$125 ($7.80–$16.25). AE, DC, MC, V. Daily noon–11pm. MTR: Tsim Sha Tsui. VIETNAMESE.

The two Golden Bull restaurants are both in shopping arcades; they have the same open hours and menu. If you're not familiar with Vietnamese cuisine, you might want to try the Golden Bull Platter for HK$125 ($16.25) which is actually an appetizer plate with a variety of dishes, including spring rolls, fish balls, and satay. Otherwise, typical Vietnamese items include crisp spring rolls wrapped in lettuce and dipped in a tangy sauce, hot-and-sour prawns, roast pig, various noodle dishes, barbecued fish Vietnamese style, grilled jumbo prawns in garlic butter, barbecued chicken, and seafood. The lunch menu offers Vietnamese snacks such as various rolls of steamed pork or beef, cellophane noodles, vermicelli, and congee, most in the HK$35–HK$40 ($4.55–$5.20) price range.

Golden Elephant Thai Restaurant

17 Canton Rd., Tsim Sha Tsui. ☎ **852/2735 0733.** Main dishes HK$85–HK$200 ($11.05–$25.95); lunch buffet HK$118 ($15.30); dinner buffet HK$240 ($31.15). AE, DC, MC, V. Daily noon–2:30pm and 6:30–10pm. MTR: Tsim Sha Tsui. THAI.

Thai food is quite popular in Hong Kong these days, and one of the first Thai restaurants to open was this place, recently ensconced in a new location not far from the Star Ferry. Affiliated with Thai Airways, it serves both spicy and mild foods that have been toned down for the Chinese tongue, so if you want something authentically hot, be sure to tell the waitress. The lunch buffet is a great bargain, as is the dinner buffet; both attract hordes of the hungry. If you opt for an à la carte meal, you might want to start with Thai crispy rice served with minced pork and shrimp sauce, Thai shrimp crackers, or the spicy beef salad. Main courses include such delectables as boiled beef with satay sauce, fried diced chicken with red chili and hot basil leaf, Thai fish cake, steamed fish with plum sauce and ginger, and grilled chicken. Most dishes cost less than HK$100 ($13).

Golden Island Bird's Nest Chiu Chau Restaurant

Star House (2nd floor), 3 Salisbury Rd., Tsim Sha Tsui. ☎ **852/2736 6228.** Main dishes HK$55–HK$130 ($7.15–$16.90). AE, MC, V. Daily 11am–3pm and 6–11:30pm. MTR: Tsim Sha Tsui. CHIU CHOW.

This Chiu Chow restaurant is conveniently located—right in front of the Star Ferry terminus. As the prices above indicate, you can eat quite cheaply here if you order only one dish per person, but you'll pay more if you choose the house specialty—bird's nest, prepared 14 different ways and available as a soup, entrée, and even dessert. This was Hong Kong's first restaurant to offer bird's nest as a specialty; although the prices for this dish have risen dramatically the past few years, here it costs around HK$240 ($31.15)—expensive, but less than what you'd pay elsewhere. Anyway, I would suggest that you try at least one of the bird's-nest dishes, along with such Chiu Chow preparations as oyster omelets, prawn balls, or roast soy goose, topping it off with a thimble-size cup of Chiu Chow tea, which is believed to aid digestion.

✪ Great Shanghai

26 Prat Ave., Tsim Sha Tsui. ☎ **852/2366 8158.** Main dishes HK$70–HK$200 ($9.10–$25.95). AE, DC, MC, V. Daily 11am–3pm and 6:30–11pm. MTR: Tsim Sha Tsui. SHANGHAINESE.

Established in 1958, this well-known spot in Tsim Sha Tsui is a big old-fashioned dining hall up on the first floor (not to be confused with the much humbler Shanghai Restaurant next door). In addition to its bright lights, white tablecloths, and army of waiters in white shirts, it has a gigantic menu with more than 300 items, most in the HK$85–HK$140 ($11.05–$18.20) range. Since the area of Shanghai has no cuisine of its own, it has borrowed heavily from neighboring provinces, including Szechuan; however, this restaurant is about as close as you can get to food the way Mom used to cook, assuming, of course, you're from Shanghai. Try the Shanghainese dumplings, prawns in chili sauce, vegetarian imitation goose, diced chicken with cashews, cold chicken in wine sauce, Szechuan soup, or Peking duck. The house specialty is beggar's chicken for HK$270 ($35.05), but it's available only at night and you must call in your order by mid-afternoon. My own particular favorite is braised shredded eel, which is cooked in an oily garlic sauce, but all eel dishes here are good. I've also left the ordering entirely up to the waiter and ended up with a well-rounded good sampling of Shanghainese food.

Harbour Side

In The Regent Hotel, Salisbury Rd., Tsim Sha Tsui. ☎ **852/2721 1211.** Main courses HK$70–HK$170 ($9.10–$22.10). AE, DC, MC, V. Daily 6am–midnight. MTR: Tsim Sha Tsui. CONTINENTAL.

Although located in the elegant Regent Hotel, this is an informal dining hall, rather plain and bare with a brick floor and wooden chairs, but bright and airy because of its three-story-high wall of glass facing the harbor, offering water-level views and nonstop all-day dining. Its open kitchen emphasizes light continental dishes such as pasta and salads, but sandwiches, hamburgers, seafood, and steak are included on a menu that changes daily. If you want to come just for the view, a cup of coffee is HK$42 ($5.45) and cocktails average HK$75 ($9.75).

Hard Rock Cafe

100 Canton Rd., Tsim Sha Tsui. ☎ **852/2377 8118.** Main courses HK$70–HK$170 ($9.10–$22.10). AE, DC, MC, V. Sun–Thurs 11:30am–3am, Fri–Sat 11:30am–4pm. MTR: Tsim Sha Tsui. AMERICAN.

It had to happen sooner or later—Hard Rock Cafes seem to be springing up all over the world these days. Opened in 1995, this one is betting on success with a total of four floors of dining and memorabilia, with one floor even devoted to live bands and a DJ. In an attempt to weed out the young ones, no one under 21 years of age is allowed to enter the premises after 10:30pm. Otherwise, it's the usual Hard Rock formula of T-shirts and burgers, as well as salads, sandwiches, fish and chips, steaks, and barbecue. Be forewarned that the music tends to be loud, so you might just want to put on your T-shirt and run.

Jade Garden Restaurant
Star House (4th floor), 3 Salisbury Rd., Tsim Sha Tsui. ☎ **852/2730 6888.** Main dishes HK$65–HK$140 ($8.45–$18.20). AE, DC, MC, V. Mon–Sat 10am–3pm and 5:30–11:30pm; Sun and holidays 8am–11:30pm. MTR: Tsim Sha Tsui. CANTONESE.

Jade Garden is part of a chain of restaurants owned by the Maxim's Group, a company that has been wildly successful throughout Hong Kong (other establishments in the group include Peking Garden, Sichuan Garden, Shanghai Garden, and Chiu Chow Garden). Jade Garden is geared toward the Chinese-food novice. Thus if you don't know much about Chinese food, feel that you should try it, but still aren't very keen on the idea, Jade Garden may be for you. As in most Cantonese restaurants, lunch is dim sum served from trolleys pushed through the aisles. If you'd rather order from the menu or come for dinner, you might consider deep-fried crispy chicken with soy sauce or fried prawns with lemon peel and orange, or, if you feel like splurging, barbecued Peking duck, which costs HK$320 ($41.55).

In Tsim Sha Tsui Jade Garden has another branch at 25–31 Carnarvon Rd. (☎ 852/2369 8311), open daily from 7:30am to midnight.

On the Hong Kong side, there are Jade Garden restaurants in the Swire House at 11 Chater Rd. in Central (☎ 852/2526 3031), open Monday to Saturday from 11:30am to 11pm and Sunday from 10am to midnight; in the Jardine House at 1 Connaught Place in Central (☎ 852/2524 5098), open daily from 11am to 3pm and 5:30 to 11:30pm; and in Causeway Bay at 500 Hennessy Rd. (☎ 852/2895 2200), open daily from 8am to midnight.

Jimmy's Kitchen
29 Ashley Rd., Tsim Sha Tsui. ☎ **852/2376 0327.** Main courses HK$90–HK$190 ($11.70–$24.65). AE, DC, MC, V. Daily noon–11pm. MTR: Tsim Sha Tsui. CONTINENTAL.

This is the Kowloon version of Central District's Jimmy's Kitchen, which originated in Shanghai and opened in Central more than 60 years ago. It serves dependably good continental food from an extensive menu that has hardly changed over the decades, including seafood, steaks, chicken, imported oysters, and curries. And don't forget to check the blackboards for the daily specials. A good old standby.

✪ The Pizzeria
In the Kowloon Hotel, 19–21 Nathan Rd., Tsim Sha Tsui. ☎ **852/2369 8698.** Pasta and pizza HK$79–HK$100 ($10.25–$13); main courses HK$90–HK$175 ($11.70–$22.75); fixed-price lunch HK$135 ($17.55); fixed-price dinner HK$260 ($33.75). AE, CB, DC, MC, V. Daily noon–2:30pm, and 6–11pm. MTR: Tsim Sha Tsui. ITALIAN.

Located on the second floor of the Kowloon Hotel (just behind The Peninsula), this casual and bustling dining hall with large windows is one of my favorite places in Tsim Sha Tsui for a relaxed meal and good prices, especially when I want great pizza or pasta and don't feel like getting dressed up. Despite its name, this restaurant specializes in pasta, with an à la carte menu that changes often but has included such mouth-watering choices as green lasagne with Bel Paese cheese, tortellini with mushrooms and truffles in an herb-cream sauce, and beef-and-pork ravioli on spinach. There are also eight different kinds of pizza, and main courses have included grilled king prawns; baked salmon with herbs, olive oil, and garlic on a bed of spinach; lamb dishes; and chicken in red sauce, stewed with peppers, onions, tomato, and mushrooms. Save room for dessert—they're all delicious. For the budget-conscious, lunch is a great time to come, when a trip through the antipasto and salad bar, choice of main dish (meat, pasta, or pizza), and dessert and coffee, are available at a great price; if your appetite is small, you can choose just the antipasto and salad bar for HK$70 ($9.10).

Sawadee

6 Ichang St., Tsim Sha Tsui. ☎ **852/2376 3299.** Main dishes HK$50–HK$130 ($6.50–$16.90). MC, V. Daily 11am–11pm. MTR: Tsim Sha Tsui. THAI.

Easily overlooked on a tiny side street just north of Peking Road and between Hankow and Ashley Roads, this is one of Hong Kong's longest standing Thai restaurants, first opened years ago by Thai stewardesses who wanted to introduce their native cuisine to the people of Hong Kong. It is modestly decorated with a simple and cafeterialike atmosphere; although the tables are too close together and the lighting is too bright, the restaurant's saving grace is that it offers great Thai food, including spicy soups, beef salad, seafood, and noodle dishes. There are more than 100 items on the menu, most in the HK$65 to HK$100 ($8.45 to $13) price range; since all of it looks good, you'll probably end up spending at least HK$150 to HK$200 per person ($19.50–$25.95), including a few rounds of Singha beer.

☻ The Spice Market

In the Omni Prince Hotel, 23 Canton Rd., Tsim Sha Tsui. ☎ **852/2377 6046.** Lunch buffet HK$118 ($15.30); dinner buffet HK$215 ($27.90). AE, DC, MC, V. Daily noon–2:30pm and 6:30–10pm. MTR: Tsim Sha Tsui. ASIAN.

Accessible from both the Omni Prince Hotel and the third floor of the Gateway shopping mall, this dark and cozy restaurant specializes in buffets serving a variety of Asian dishes, thereby offering diners a culinary adventure throughout the Orient. There's Japanese sushi and noodles, Indian curries, Chinese, Thai, and Philippine favorites, steamed fish, satays, soups, salads, appetizers, and desserts. True to its name, many of the foods are spicy. While none of the dishes is outstanding, most of them are good; with so many choices, you'll probably end up eating more than you should.

♻ Spring Deer Restaurant

42 Mody Rd., Tsim Sha Tsui. ☎ **852/2723 3673.** Small dishes HK$39–HK$90 ($5.05–$11.70); medium dishes HK$59–HK$175 ($7.65–$22.75). AE, MC, V. Daily noon–3pm and 6–11pm. MTR: Tsim Sha Tsui. PEKINESE.

An old favorite in Hong Kong, this long-established restaurant offers excellent Pekinese food at reasonable prices. Spring Deer is cheerful and very accessible to foreigners, but don't expect anything fancy; in fact, your tablecloth is likely to have holes in it, but it will be clean—and the place is often packed with loyal fans. This is one of the best places to come if you want to try its specialty—Peking duck, which costs HK$250 ($32.45). Since you'll probably have to wait 40 minutes for the duck if you order it during peak time (7:30 to 9:30pm), it's best to arrive either before or after the rush. Chicken dishes are also well liked, including the deep-fried chicken in soy sauce, and the handmade noodles are excellent. Most dishes come in small, medium, and large sizes; the small dishes are suitable for two people. Remember, you'll want to order one dish apiece, plus a third to share.

Super Star Seafood Restaurant

91–93 Nathan Rd., Tsim Sha Tsui. ☎ **852/2366 0878.** Main dishes HK$75–HK$270 ($9.10–$35.05); fixed-price menu HK$260–HK$300 ($33.75–$38.95). AE, DC, MC, V. Daily 7am–midnight. MTR: Tsim Sha Tsui. CANTONESE SEAFOOD.

Walk past the tanks filled with fish, lobsters, prawns, and crabs, up to this lively Cantonese restaurant on the first floor. Its menu includes pictures of major dishes;

as its name implies, the restaurant specializes in seafood. Recommended are the deep-fried stuffed crab claws, sliced sole with spice and chili, baked lobster with minced spinach, and fish in season. Prices for seafood vary with the season and depend on the size of the creature you desire. If you want a specific fish or something else in the tank, simply point, but be sure to ask the price first. Stone fish is popular with the Chinese. It's a rather ugly fish and poisonous to boot, if not prepared correctly. If this is what you want, you'll have to wait an hour for it to cook. Dim sum, served until 5pm, starts at HK$27 ($3.50) per plate.

Tsui Hang Village Restaurant

Park Lane Square, 1 Kimberley Rd., Tsim Sha Tsui. ☎ 852/2368 6363. Main dishes HK$55–HK$170 ($7.15–$22.10). AE, MC, V. Mon–Sat 11:30am–midnight, Sun 10am–midnight. MTR: Tsim Sha Tsui. CANTONESE.

Located across the street from the Miramar Hotel on the ground floor of a new shopping complex called Park Lane Square, this restaurant is named after the home village of Dr. Sun Yat-sen. Bright, clean and modern, with a white jade statue of the goddess of mercy at its entrance, this restaurant specializes in its own Cantonese original creations but also serves traditional, home-style Chinese cooking. Its award-winning dish is shark's fin with bamboo pitch, asparagus, and crab claw, which is priced at HK$300 ($39). Other dishes you might want to try include fresh lobster, deep-fried minced shrimp balls with crisp almond, sautéed minced pigeon with lettuce, barbecued Peking duck, roast goose, or fried milk fritters. Dim sum, served during lunch and afternoon teatime Monday through Saturday from 11:30am to 5:30pm and on Sunday from 10am to 5pm, is priced from HK$16 to HK$34 ($2.10 to $4.40) per plate.

⑤ Wu Kong

27 Nathan Rd. (entrance on Peking Rd.), Tsim Sha Tsui. ☎ 852/2366 7244. Menu items HK$50–HK$180 ($6.50–$23.40). AE, DC, MC, V. Daily 11:30am–midnight. MTR: Tsim Sha Tsui. SHANGHAINESE.

This basement restaurant in the heart of Tsim Sha Tsui just off Nathan Road, is often packed during mealtimes with locals who come for the good food at excellent prices. More upscale than most Shanghainese restaurants with its soothing peach-and-white color scheme and pond with goldfish in the foyer, it serves a variety of shark's-fin dishes, as well as the usual sautéed fresh prawns, braised shredded eels, braised eggplant with hot garlic sauce, stuffed bean curd, and other dishes common to Shanghai. Other selections include Peking duck, crispy duck, and sautéed sliced duck. If you've had your fill of the more readily available and popular Cantonese and Szechuan food and are ready to experiment with other types of Chinese cuisine, this is an excellent place to start.

INEXPENSIVE

Banana Leaf Curry House

Golden Crown Court, 68 Nathan Rd., Tsim Sha Tsui. ☎ 852/2721 4821. Main dishes HK$50–HK$100 ($6.50–$13). AE, DC, MC, V. Daily noon–2:30pm and 6–11:30pm. MTR: Tsim Sha Tsui. MALAYSIAN/SINGAPOREAN.

This fast-growing local chain has a good idea—more than 100 dishes, including chicken, mutton, beef, seafood, and vegetables, cooked in several varieties of curry; and a gimmick—meals are served on banana leaves. Add to that the brisk, efficient service and reasonable prices, and you've got the makings of a winner for cheap Malaysian, Singaporean, and North Indian food. You might want to start with chicken satay and peanut sauce or samosas which come with a mint chutney. Main dishes run the gamut, from Hainan chicken to vegetarian selections; the dilemma is in making a choice.

Bangkok Royal Thai Restaurant

In the Bangkok Royal Hotel, 2–12 Pilkem St., Yau Ma Tei. ☎ **852/2735 9181.** Main courses HK$37–HK$130 ($4.80–$16.90); fixed-price lunch HK$35–HK$45 ($4.55–$5.85). AE, DC, MC, V. Daily noon–11pm. MTR: Jordan. THAI.

Just off the lobby of the Bangkok Royal Hotel, located north of Kowloon Park, is this Thai restaurant known for low prices and fairly good food. The fixed-price lunch, served until 2:30pm, offers a couple of choices for a soup and main dish. The à la carte menu lists typical Thai curries with coconut milk and chilies. My favorites are sour-and-spicy Thai soup with prawns or fish, Thai-style fried rice noodles, and chicken curry with coconut milk.

⊗ Bodhi Vegetarian Restaurant

81 Nathan Rd., Tsim Sha Tsui. ☎ **852/2366 8232.** Main dishes HK$50–HK$75 ($6.50–$9.75). AE, DC, MC, V. Daily 11:30am–2:30pm and 6–10:30pm. MTR: Tsim Sha Tsui. VEGETARIAN.

Head upstairs to this simple establishment, which serves vegetarian dishes so artfully crafted that you'd swear some of them contained meat. The gluten platter, for example, is an appetizer of wheat flour looking all the world like cold cuts. Other ingredients include bean curd, fungi, and bamboo shoots, which are used in such dishes as diced vegetables in a deep-fried-potato basket, fried vegetable steak with chili in a sweet-and-sour sauce, and deep-fried mashed taro stuffed with vegetables and sweet-and-sour sauce. Flavorful sauces accompany many of the dishes, while nuts, crunchy vegetables, and other textured foods add variety. Lunch buffets, offered Monday, Saturday, and Sunday, as well as Sunday dinner buffets, represent great value. All in all, a good place to indulge in a mild feeding frenzy, and even feel good about yourself afterward.

⊗ Greenwood Restaurant

12 Nanking St., Yau Ma Tei. ☎ **852/2771 6719.** Main dishes HK$16–HK$35 ($2.10–$4.55). No credit cards. Daily noon–10:30pm. MTR: Yau Ma Tei. CANTONESE.

If you've passed all those hole-in-the-wall Chinese restaurants, knowing that they're often much cheaper than establishments catering to tourists, but you've hesitated to enter because no one speaks English and there are no English menus, this is the place for you. Small, clean, and boasting an English menu with photos of each dish, this Cantonese restaurant with the improbable English name bills itself as the "Best Noodle Stall in Town." It serves a variety of tasty noodle dishes, especially wonton, available as a soup or main dish. You might also want to try *juuk* (rice porridge). In any case, this unassuming place is sure to please even the most frugal of diners.

Kansai

29 Granville Rd., Tsim Sha Tsui. ☎ **852/2311 0709.** Main dishes HK$13–HK$65 ($1.70–$8.40); fixed-price lunch HK$38 ($4.95); fixed-price dinner HK$70–HK$145 ($9.10–$18.85). No credit cards. Daily 11:30am–2am. MTR: Tsim Sha Tsui. JAPANESE.

Taking its cue from Japan, this Chinese-owned establishment offers plates of sushi, as well as noodle and rice dishes, which circle around the counter via a conveyor belt. Customers, seated at the counter, simply reach out and take whatever they want. Conveyor-belt sushi restaurants have long been popular in Japan; maybe it's yet another Japanese "product" destined to be an import success. The plates vary in price, so if you don't know the price, be sure to ask. Probably the best deals are the *teishoku*, which are fixed-price complete meals. Tempura, noodles, beef, grilled fish, and sashimi teishoku are available, which come with rice, soup, and pickled vegetables.

Purists will find the food too oriented to Chinese taste, but these prices make it a good and fast bet for a Japanese food fix.

⊛ Koh-I-Noor

Peninsula Apartments, 16C Mody Rd., Tsim Sha Tsui. ☎ **852/2368 3065.** Curries HK$46–HK$150 ($5.95–$19.50); Tandoori HK$70–HK$140 ($9.10–$18.20). AE, DC, MC, V. Daily 11:30am–3pm and 6–11pm. MTR: Tsim Sha Tsui. INDIAN.

Don't let the dinginess of the Peninsula Apartments deter you from trying this restaurant. Located up on the first floor, it's modern and clean, with spotless tablecloths and a pleasant purple color scheme. What's more, service is prompt and courteous and the food is great and reasonably priced; the specialties here are North Indian tandoori and fresh seafood. Taking its name from a renowned diamond mined in central India years ago, the restaurant is especially proud of its king prawns, barbecued and then flambéed at your table. Of course, there are also chicken, lamb, and vegetable curries; my favorites include the crab with coconut and the Gosht vindaloo—a spicy mix of lamb and potatoes. There's also mashed eggplant with onions and tomatoes, palak paneer (Indian cottage cheese with spinach), garlic-flavored nan (Indian flat bread) or nan stuffed with cheese, potatoes, or meat, and—well, all of it's good and recommendable. The dishes can be ordered mild, medium, or fiery hot, according to taste.

The Salisbury

In the YMCA, 41 Salisbury Rd., Tsim Sha Tsui. ☎ **852/2369 2211.** Main courses HK$50–HK$120 ($6.50–$15.60); fixed-price lunch HK$90 ($11.70); fixed-price dinner HK$205 ($26.62). AE, MC, V. Mon–Sat noon–2:30pm, daily 6:30–9:30pm. MTR: Tsim Sha Tsui. INTERNATIONAL.

One of the cheapest places for a filling meal in Tsim Sha Tsui is the YMCA's main restaurant, a bright and cheerful dining hall located on the fourth floor of the south tower. It serves both Western and Asian food, with an à la carte menu offering sandwiches, pasta, and Asian dishes. Best, however, are the lunch and dinner buffets. The lunch buffet includes a roast beef wagon, as well as other meat dishes, soups, salads, and desserts, while the dinner buffet includes many more entrées plus unlimited soda or beer. If these prices are too high, there's a ground-floor cafeteria called Mall Cafe which offers sandwiches and daily specials, as well as a fixed-price lunch for HK$55 ($7.15) and a fixed-price dinner for HK$70 ($9.10).

Spaghetti House

57 Peking Rd., Tsim Sha Tsui. ☎ **852/2367 1683.** Individual-size pizza HK$60–HK$85 ($7.80–$11.05); spaghetti HK$55–HK$75 ($7.15–$9.75). AE, MC, V. Daily 11am–11pm. MTR: Tsim Sha Tsui. ITALIAN.

The Spaghetti House chain has a total of 18 branches throughout the colony—and there will probably be more by the time you read this. They're popular with families, young Chinese couples on dates, and foreigners who have had their fill of Chinese food and crave something familiar but cheap. Spaghetti and pizza cooked American-style are the specialties here, and the decor and atmosphere resemble American pizza parlors. There are 14 varieties of spaghetti, as well as pizzas (in all sizes), lasagne, sandwiches, chili con carne, and fried chicken. Although the food is only average in quality, the quantity more than makes up for it; most orders can be taken out.

Other branches in Tsim Sha Tsui are located in the Imperial Hotel, 30–34 Nathan Rd. (☎ 852/2721 2082); 38 Haiphong Rd. (☎ 852/2376 1015); and 16 Cameron Rd. (☎ 852/2721 8628). All Spaghetti Houses have the same hours.

Wah Yuen Restaurant

37 Cameron Rd., Tsim Sha Tsui. ☎ **852/2721 6132.** Main dishes HK$26–HK$40 ($3.40–$5.20). No credit cards. Daily 7am–midnight. MTR: Tsim Sha Tsui. INTERNATIONAL.

Nothing fancy about this place. In fact, it looks like an American diner or truck stop, except that here both tables and customers are sometimes so packed in there's hardly room to walk. More than likely you'll share your table with other diners and you'll be expected to clear out as soon as you've finished eating. People come here to chow down, not to socialize. Popular with both locals and tourists, this restaurant strives to please both palates with an extensive menu that includes everything from sand-wiches and spaghetti to curry dishes served with rice, fried noodle selections, and Chinese-style rice plates. However, while many Chinese would label some of the dishes Western, most Westerners will find them decidedly Chinese, or at least definitely not Western. There's ox-tongue spaghetti, tomato and egg sandwich, and many other unusual combinations. Other items are less exotic—pork chop and sweet corn, for example, or barbecued pork spaghetti. The Chinese dishes are less likely to be a surprise, with such common fare as sliced beef and vegetable with rice, and roasted pork with bean curd. Noodle dishes are another good bet, ranging from Singapore fried vermicelli to braised E-Fu noodles. None of the dishes here will win any culinary awards, but they won't break your budget, either.

4 Central District

VERY EXPENSIVE

Benkay Japanese Restaurant
First basement of the Landmark, Des Voeux Rd., Central. ☎ 852/2521 3344. Reservations rec-ommended, especially for lunch. Fixed-price meals HK$180–HK$770 ($23.40–$100). AE, CB, DC, MC, V. Mon–Sat 11:30am–3pm, Sun and holidays noon–3pm; daily 6–9:45pm (last order). MTR: Central. JAPANESE.

Affiliated with Japan Airlines and located among the expensive boutiques of the classy Landmark shopping complex, Benkay uses screens and lighting to create a traditional atmosphere, complete with Japanese instrumental music in the background. If you are new to Japanese cuisine, the menu might be somewhat confusing; therefore, it might be advisable to order one of the fixed-price meals. Cream of the crop are the kaiseki meals, which begin at HK$650 ($84.40). Changed each season, they consist of many individual dishes, each artfully arranged. Other temptations include a sukiyaki or shabu-shabu (thin slices of beef cooked with vegetables) meal for HK$460 ($59.75), or a platter of assorted sushi (raw fish) for HK$330 ($42.85). Other items on the menu include sushi, sashimi, tempura (deep-fried meats and vegetables), Kobe beef, teppanyaki, and soba (noodles). Most diners end up spending about HK$800 ($103.90) for dinner, without drinks.

Lobster Bar
In the Island Shangri-La, Pacific Place, 88 Queensway, Central. ☎ 852/2820 8560. Reserva-tions recommended, especially for lunch. Pasta HK$155–HK$180 ($20.15–$23.40); fixed-price lunch HK$230–HK$260 ($29.85–$33.75); fixed-price dinner HK$640 ($83.10). AE, DC, MC, V. Daily noon–2:30pm and 6:30–10:30pm. MTR: Admiralty. SEAFOOD.

If you love lobster, this upscale restaurant will almost certainly be on your agenda. The entrance features a beautiful aquarium, while the interior has elegant overtones of mahogany, leather, and imported French fabrics covering deep comfortable chairs, making the setting seem more like a lounge than a restaurant. The crustacean is king here, so you might want to start with lobster bisque or lobster chowder, followed by one of the seasonal dishes, possibly morels and asparagus with lobster or grilled lobster with a shallot-herb sauce. Another good choice is the traditional seafood platter, which comes in three sizes, or one of the fixed-price meals. The limited menu

🅐 Family-Friendly Restaurants

Al's Diner *(see p. 120)*   This may be the perfect antidote for restless teenagers who are threatening mutiny if they don't see any "real food" soon. It's located in Central's nightlife district (which might perk your teenager's interest) and offers burgers, hot dogs, sandwiches, sundaes, ice-cream floats, and banana splits. The jukebox is a good diversion, too.

The Bostonian *(see p. 96)*   Prices are high, but the paper tablecloths and crayons on each table may keep the youngsters occupied while you enjoy New Orleans and Californian cuisine. The lunch menu includes a limited choice of sandwiches and pizza.

Dan Ryan's Chicago Grill *(see pp. 100 and 115)*   These two restaurant/bars serve the best burgers in town, as well as huge deli sandwiches. There are plenty of other American dishes as well, and the setting looks just like home.

Hard Rock Cafe *(see p. 102)*   You can dine on American food and pick up that famous T-shirt, too, at Hong Kong's tribute to modern music and musicians.

Mandarin Grill *(see below)*   For little ones who expect only the best, treat them to Sunday brunch at the Mandarin Grill, which boasts a children's table filled with standby favorites as well as exotic choices.

The Pizzeria *(see p. 103)*   A great place for pasta and pizza, especially the lunch-time pasta buffet.

Portico *(see p. 118)*   Saturdays at this Central restaurant are likely to please the whole family with special children's meals and even make-it-yourself pizzas, created in the kitchen under the supervision of a chef wearing bunny ears.

Spaghetti House *(see p. 107)*   Locations all over town and low prices make this family chain a winner. There are 14 different kinds of spaghetti, as well as a wide range of pizza. Just like pizza parlors back home.

features a few nonlobster dishes, such as fresh seafood, a handful of pasta selections prepared with seafood, and a daily carving that might include prime rib or veal loin.

Mandarin Grill

In the Mandarin Oriental Hotel, 5 Connaught Rd., Central. ☎ **852/2522 0111**, ext 4020. Reservations required. Jacket required for dinner. Main courses HK$280–HK$380 ($36.35–$49.35). AE, DC, MC, V. Daily 7–11am, noon–3pm, and 6:30–11pm. MTR: Central. CONTINENTAL.

Decorated in dark green with details of gold, this is the Mandarin's most popular all-purpose restaurant, offering everything from breakfast (the Sunday brunch includes a special table for children) to steaks and seafood. But since this is the Mandarin, it caters to a well-heeled clientele, and men are expected to wear jackets for dinner (except in summer). Both U.S. and Kobe beef are featured, as well as veal, Welsh lamb, and a wide selection of seafood. Lobster is available prepared in a variety of styles. Especially recommended is the spinach salad tossed with bay scallops, mushrooms, shallots, and quail eggs in a balsamic vinegar dressing; the U.S. Black Angus prime rib beef; and the rack of lamb. The wine list is extensive, with more than 400 varieties available.

✪ Man Wah

In the Mandarin Oriental Hotel, 5 Connaught Rd., Central. ☎ **852/2522 0111**, ext. 4025. Reservations required. Main dishes HK$105–HK$308 ($13.65–$40); fixed-price meal HK$530 ($68.85). AE, DC, MC, V. Daily noon–3pm and 6:30–11pm. MTR: Central. CANTONESE.

Central District Dining

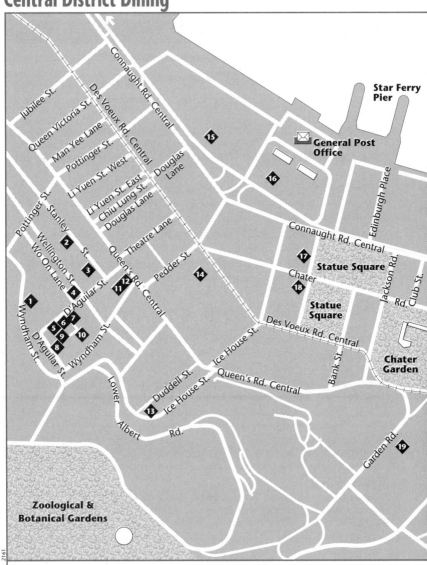

Al's Diner ◆9
The Ashoka ◆1
Benkay Japanese ◆14
Bentley's ◆18
Cafe de Paris ◆6
Chiuchow Garden ◆16
City Hall Chinese ◆20

Dan Ryan's Chicago
  Grill ◆24
Golden Elephant Thai ◆24
Grappa's ◆24
Hunan Garden ◆15
Jimmy's Kitchen ◆11
L.A. Cafe ◆23

La Ronda ◆21
La Taverna ◆13
Lobster Bar ◆25
Luk Yu Tea House ◆2
Man Wah ◆17
Mandarin Grill ◆17
Nicholini's ◆26

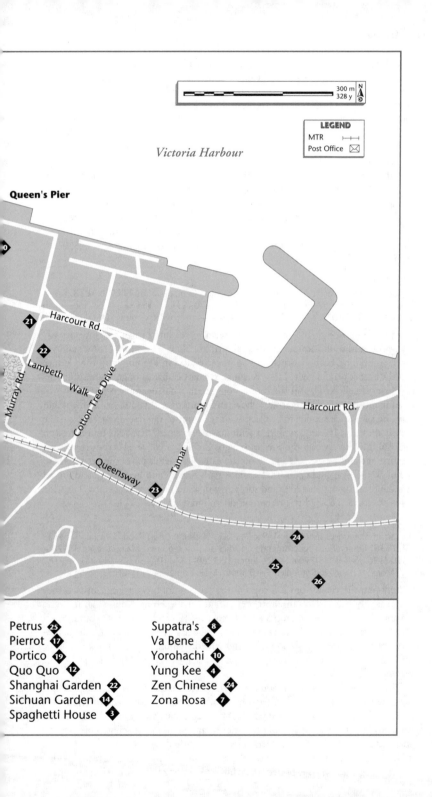

Victoria Harbour

Queen's Pier

Man Wah has long been one of the most elegant Chinese restaurants in Hong Kong. Traditionally decorated with local rosewood, wood carvings, lanterns that resemble birdcages, and painted silk portraits of Mandarins; and featuring gold tablecloths, exquisite Naruma bone chinaware, fresh flowers, and candles on every table—it's about as romantic as you can get. Unfortunately, although it's located on the 25th floor, only a few tables offer good views of the harbor, so be sure to request a harborside seat when making your reservation. And with a seating capacity of only 62, reservations here are a must.

Although the Cantonese menu changes seasonally, signature dishes usually available include the sautéed fillet of sole with green vegetables in a black bean sauce (complete with a wonderful carving of a dragon fashioned from carrots), deep-fried chicken with walnuts and honey-glazed ham, anything with shark's fin, and beggar's chicken (order in advance). Also, if available, the spicy-and-sour soup is divine—piquant and full of noodles, tofu, and mushrooms. Meals here average HK$500 to HK$700 ($64.95–$90.90).

Nicholini's

In the Conrad Hotel, Pacific Place, 88 Queensway Rd., Central. ☎ **852/2521 3838.** Reservations recommended. Main courses HK$240–HK$420 ($31.15–$54.55); fixed-price lunch HK$215 ($27.90). AE, DC, MC, V. Daily noon–3pm, 7–11pm. MTR: Central. ITALIAN.

Most of Hong Kong's Italian restaurants seem to fall into one of two categories—high-brow and sophisticated, or rustic and trattorialike. This one is neither and yet both, combining both elegance and lightheartedness in keeping with the Conrad Hotel's overall playful style. Dress is casual to smart casual (though no jeans or tennis shoes are allowed), and the dining room bathes patrons in soothing colors of celadon green, pink, aquamarine, yellow, and plum rose. If you're a fan of Murano glass, be sure to check out the collection at the front of the restaurant. The cuisine here is northern Italian, combined with an inventiveness that adds uniqueness to many of the daily specials. Lobster with herbs and Tuscan olive oil is the overwhelming first and most expensive entrée on the extensive menu; other courses kinder to the pocketbook include pan-fried scallops with brandy and herb sauce and grilled chicken breast with goose liver and spinach with a sun-dried tomato sauce. The wine list is extensive. Too bad this restaurant doesn't have a view.

Petrus

In the Island Shangri-La (56th floor), Pacific Place, Supreme Court Road, Central. ☎ **852/ 2877 3838.** Reservations recommended. Jacket and tie required. Main courses HK$280–HK$390 ($36.35–$50.65). Fixed-price lunch HK$280–HK$310 ($36.35–$40.25). AE, DC, MC, V. Mon–Sat noon–2:30pm, daily 7–10:30pm. MTR: Admiralty. FRENCH.

Simply put, the views from this top-floor restaurant are breathtaking. In fact, they are probably the best of any hotel restaurant on the Hong Kong side; the only place with a better view is atop Victoria Peak. If you can bear to take your eyes off the windows, you'll find the restaurant decorated like a French castle, with the obligatory crystal chandeliers, black marble and gilded columns, statues, thick draperies, impressionist paintings, murals gracing dome-shaped ceilings, and classical music playing softly in the background.

The cuisine emphasizes contemporary French creations, with a menu that changes often but has included such intriguing combinations as roast rack of lamb with cinnamon and red curry, accompanied by an eggplant gratin; and seared salmon fillet served with candied onion, garlic cloves, and potato mousseline. Foie gras is a specialty, available in several variations, from stuffed with raisin and walnut in a Gewürztraminer jelly to sautéed with sesame and poppy seeds and served with a sherry vinegar gravy. As expected, the wine list is among the best in Hong Kong. In any case, with the impressive blend of great views, refined ambience, and excellent cuisine, this restaurant is a top choice for a splurge, romantic dinner, or special celebration.

✪ Pierrot

In the Mandarin Oriental Hotel (25th floor), 5 Connaught Rd., Central. ☎ **852/2522 0111,** ext. 4028. Reservations required. Jacket and tie required. Main courses HK$200–HK$350 ($25.95–$45.45). fixed-price lunch HK$440 ($57.15). AE, DC, MC, V. Mon–Fri noon–3pm; daily 7–11pm. MTR: Central. FRENCH.

The Pierrot, its name inspired by Picasso's painting of his son in a Pierrot costume, broke ground as the first hotel restaurant to introduce Hong Kong gourmets to a year-round menu of French nouvelle cuisine and has remained one of the city's favorites ever since. To remain on top of the cutting edge, the Pierrot recently became Asia's first caviar restaurant, offering beluga, ossetra, sevruga, and pressed caviar from the Petrossian purveyors of Russian caviar. In addition to individual portions of caviar, beginning at HK$190 ($24.65) for 30 grams (about 1 ounce), many main courses include caviar in the preparation, such as shark's fin with sevruga caviar in a vodka cream, or Norwegian salmon flavored with crayfish reduction and sevruga caviar.

As for its classic French cuisine, the restaurant's menu changes twice a year, with most à la carte meals, excluding wine, costing upward of HK$800 ($104). Specialties include pressed duck, prepared tableside for at least two diners, and roast rack of lamb. The wine list is superb, including some rare, old French vintages, and the food excellent, representing French haute cuisine at its best. You can't go wrong dining here, unless you forget your jacket and tie. After dinner, you might enjoy retiring to the Harlequin Bar for a cocktail. In any case, both the bar and the restaurant offer a great view of the harbor, making for romantic dining day and night.

EXPENSIVE

Bentley's

Prince's Building, 10 Chater Rd., Statue Sq., Central. ☎ **852/2868 0881.** Reservations required at lunch, recommended at dinner. Main courses HK$130–HK$265 ($16.90–$34.40). AE, DC, MC, V. Mon–Sat noon–2:30pm and 6–10:30pm. MTR: Central. SEAFOOD.

Part of London's famous chain of seafood restaurants, Hong Kong's own Bentley's hit the scene in 1987 as a faithful rendition of the original Bentley's in Piccadilly. The atmosphere is cozy and chummy, and the establishment has quickly become a favorite of business-suited expatriates working in Central. The specialty is oysters, flown in from Scotland and Australia, served either on the half shell or on a bed of spinach, or dressed with such delicious sauces as tomato and curry or tomato, chili, and bacon. If you don't like oysters (heaven forbid!), then start your meal with lobster bisque, salmon tartare, or smoked salmon served with avocado and dressed with cream. As a main course, I highly recommend the Dover sole (poached in Mornay sauce and served with lobster, shrimps, oysters, and mushrooms), baked crab, or lobster. For dessert, try one of the traditional English puddings. Dinners here average about HK$400 ($51.95), excluding wine.

✪ Cafe de Paris

30–32 D'Aguilar St., Central. ☎ **852/2524 7521.** Reservations required. Main courses HK$175 ($22.70). AE, DC, MC, V. Mon–Fri noon–3pm; Mon–Sat 7–11pm. MTR: Central. FRENCH.

Located in the heart of Central's nightlife district (Lan Kwai Fong), this small and intimate restaurant is cheerfully decorated like a Parisian bistro with white tablecloths, candles, and fresh flowers. Its owner, Michel Bezardin, acquired the restaurant only recently, but he has kept the original staff and kitchen and is always on hand to describe, in detail, the traditional French cuisine. Although the menu changes every three months, there are several perennial favorites, including a hearty French onion soup, pâté, salad niçoise, sole Florentine, and beef in a black pepper sauce, all of which can be complemented with selections of French wine. To simplify bookkeeping, all main courses cost the same; adding an appetizer and a dessert comes at a fixed price of HK$295 ($38.30). Considering how expensive most French restaurants are, this unassuming establishment offers good value for the money.

La Ronda

In the Furama Kempinski Hotel (30th floor), 1 Connaught Rd., Central. ☎ **852/2525 5111.** Reservations required at dinner. Lunch buffet HK$230 ($29.85) Mon–Sat, HK$255 ($33.10) Sun; dinner buffet HK$355 ($46.10). AE, CB, DC, MC, V. Daily noon–2:30pm and 6:30–10:30pm. MTR: Tsim Sha Tsui. INTERNATIONAL.

A revolving restaurant with stunning views! The buffets are quite a spread too, offering salads, desserts, appetizers, and international cuisine ranging from sashimi and sushi to roast beef and Chinese dishes. Monthly specials feature additional dishes from a particular country, such as Thailand or Malaysia. The food, while mediocre, is more than compensated for by the view. Come for lunch, which is less expensive.

✪ Quo Quo

Entertainment Building (3rd and 4th floors), 30 Queen's Rd., Central. ☎ **852/2843 3988.** Reservations required. Main courses HK$160–HK$250 ($20.80–$32.45); lunch buffet HK$230–HK$250 ($29.85–$32.45). AE, DC, MC, V. Daily 11am–2:30pm, 7pm–12:30am. MTR: Central. CONTINENTAL.

You've never been in a restaurant that looks like this before—unless you're Alice in Wonderland and have spent some time in a jewelry box. Giant beads, made of wood but lacquered to resemble gleaming ivory, are strung ceiling to floor around massive columns, giving humans the appearance of thimble size. It sounds weird, I know, but the effect is actually quite sophisticated, with subdued lighting and live jazz adding a sparkle every evening except Sunday. There's even a small terrace for outdoor dining, about as common in Central as the rickshaw. The food, in keeping with its hip decor, is a veritable playground of possibilities, making choices difficult and dining a delight. Dungeness crabcakes, served with lettuce, leeks, and tarragon remoulade? Spaghetti with truffles? How about wok-fried Maine lobster médaillons with spicy black beans and scallions, or sautéed tiger prawns with bell peppers, saffron, and fennel sauce? And that's just dinner. Lunch offers a whole new sensation of tastes, including more pasta and even sandwiches, but the best solution for the undecided is the lunch buffet spread. This restaurant opened in 1993, and from the looks of things, is a winner.

⑤ Va Bene

58–62 D'Aguilar St., Central. ☎ **852/2845 5577.** Reservations required. Pasta HK$125–HK$135 ($16.25–$17.55); main courses HK$158–HK$170 ($20.50–$22.10); fixed-price lunch HK$150 ($19.50). AE, DC, MC, V. Mon–Fri noon–3pm and daily 7pm–midnight (last order 10:30pm). MTR: Central. ITALIAN.

This upscale Italian restaurant, in the middle of Central's nightlife district, strives for the simplicity of a rustic Italian villa with its sponged walls in hues of terra-cotta and sky blue and with rows of terra-cotta pots serving as the main decorations. It's extremely popular with Hong Kong's well-heeled expat community, making it a lively, boisterous place, and diners don't even seem to mind that seating is a bit cramped and that dinner is served in two seatings, the first at 7 to 7:30pm and the second between 9 and 9:30pm. Perhaps it's the prices that have everyone smiling. Perhaps you'll want to start your meal with carpaccio, artichokes cooked in olive oil and garlic, or the capellini primavera or linguine with clams. As a main course, you can choose from a number of veal, beef, and seafood offerings, including veal scaloppine, cornish game hen with sun-dried tomato and fresh herb stuffing served with a light red wine sauce, or beef tenderloin pan-roasted with porcini mushrooms and Barolo wine. Good Italian wines, great desserts, and attentive service round out the evening.

✪ Zen Chinese

The Mall, Pacific Place, 88 Queensway, Central. ☎ 852/2845 4555. Reservations recommended. Main dishes HK$80–HK$200 ($10.40–$25.95). AE, DC, MC, V. Mon–Sat 11:30am– 2:30pm, Sun 10:30am–4:30pm; daily 6–11pm. MTR: Admiralty. CANTONESE.

Both its name and its appearance leave no doubt that this is not an ordinary Cantonese restaurant. You won't find any reds and golds here, or any glittering chandeliers. Rather, the restaurant is somewhat austere in the Zen Buddhist style, with a concrete ceiling, double-layered white tablecloths, fresh flowers on each table, and an open dining hall that allows customers to see and be seen. To offset the simplicity and starkness of the room, a succession of large glass bowls running the length of the restaurant are suspended from the ceiling, filled with water in a never-ending cascade as water trickles from one bowl to the next.

As for the food, there is a wide variety of Cantonese specialties that border on the nouvelle. Try the shark's-fin soup with shredded chicken, sautéed prawns with sweet nuts and dried chili, deep-fried boneless duck stuffed with shrimp and almonds, minced partridge, or one of the seasonal special dishes. Unlike most Chinese restaurants, the wine list is rather extensive. With most dishes averaging HK$90 to HK$130 ($11.70 to $16.90), you can easily dine here for around HK$240 ($31.15), not including drinks. For lunch you can even eat more cheaply, with dim sum available for HK$26 to HK$33 ($3.40 to $4.30) a plate.

MODERATE

Chiuchow Garden

Jardine House, 1 Connaught Place, Central. ☎ 852/2525 8246. Main dishes HK$85–HK$150 ($11.05–$19.50). AE, DC, MC, V. Daily 11:30am–3pm and 5:30–11pm. MTR: Central. CHIU CHOW.

The popular Chiuchow Garden, part of the Maxim's Group, is large and functional in a brisk, militarylike fashion, consistent in both its good service and its food. Conveniently located in the same building as the Hong Kong Tourist Association (in the basement), it specializes in shark's-fin dishes, bird's nest, soya-sauce goose, baked chicken with onion sauce, fried sliced pigeon with chinjew sauce, or fried pomfret. Try to avoid the lunchtime crunch, since this place is popular with the building's office workers and can be quite noisy and frenetic, though the staff manages rather well under the circumstances.

Dan Ryan's Chicago Grill

The Mall, Pacific Place, 88 Queensway, Central. ☎ 852/2845 4600. Main courses HK$85– HK$240 ($11.05–$31.15). AE, DC, MC, V. Mon–Fri 11am–midnight, Sat–Sun 9am–midnight. MTR: Admiralty. AMERICAN.

This is the Hong-Kong-side branch of Dan Ryan's Chicago Grill (described above in the "Kowloon" section). A casual bar and grill, complete with English-language newspapers for leisure perusal, it offers all the American classics for lunch, including hamburgers, barbecued ribs, lasagne, potato skins, chicken wings, and huge deli sandwiches, while its dinner menu focuses on barbecued steaks, chops, fish, and pasta. There's also a children's menu and a weekend breakfast selection.

Golden Elephant Thai Restaurant

Pacific Place, 88 Queensway, Central. ☎ **852/2522 8696.** Reservations recommended. Main courses HK$85–HK$200 ($11.05–$25.95); buffet lunch HK$118 ($15.30); buffet dinner HK$240 ($31.15). AE, DC, MC, V. Daily noon–2:30, 6–10pm. MTR: Admiralty. THAI.

Similar to its Kowloon counterpart, this popular restaurant offers a very popular and tasty buffet filled with Thai favorites, making it a great place to chow down if you don't mind battling the crowds to get to the food. There's also an à la carte menu, and you can wash it all down with Thai beer.

Grappa's

Pacific Place, 88 Queensway, Central. ☎ **852/2868 0086.** Reservations recommended. Pizza and pasta HK$85–HK$135 ($11.05–$17.55); main dishes HK$125–HK$190 ($16.25–$24.65). AE, DC, MC, V. Daily noon–3pm, 6–10:30pm. MTR: Admiralty. ITALIAN.

If you like to eat pizza or pasta to the accompaniment of noise, commotion, and lots of people parading past, this is the place for you. Grappa's is decorated like a trattoria, but with big glass windows overlooking the shops of Pacific Place, there's no escaping the fact that this is not a sidewalk cafe but a mall. The open kitchen, while providing some diversion, adds to the noise. Still, this is certainly the best place for Italian food anywhere in the area, even though it is strictly standard fare. Bread, served with olive oil and fresh Parmesan, is brought swiftly to every table (and replenished if desired);it is so delicious that you may be tempted to eat your fill before the meal arrives, especially if the place is full and service is slow. The salads are good here, as are the dozen or so authentic Italian pizzas and the even larger selection of pastas. The entrées lean toward the tried and true, from saltimbocca to roasted lamb chops with rosemary. The Italian wines are affordable. Too bad this place is in a mall.

✪ Hunan Garden

The Forum (3rd floor), Exchange Sq., Central. ☎ **852/2868 2880.** Reservations recommended. Main dishes HK$90–HK$160 ($11.70–$20.80). AE, DC, MC, V. Daily 11:30am–3pm and 5:30–11pm. MTR: Central. HUNANESE.

Although Hunanese food is quite popular in Taiwan, this is one of the few Hunan restaurants in Hong Kong. It's puzzling, because Hunanese food is very spicy, and one would think that with the booming popularity of Thai and Szechuan food in the colony, Hunanese food would catch on. In any case, this is a great restaurant, both in decor and food. It's decorated in hot pink and green, and the motif is clearly lotus (Hunan province is famous for its lotus). The dining area is spacious, with tables spread luxuriously far apart, and there's even a view of the harbor.

But the real treat is the food. The chefs were trained in both Hunan province and Taiwan and they don't tone down the spiciness of their authentic dishes. Start your meal with one of the soups, served in a length of bamboo. I tried the Hunan mashed-chicken soup, a clear soup base with ginger and mousse of chicken, served piping hot. If you like hot-and-spicy foods, you'll love the braised bean curd with shredded meat and chili, developed by one of Hunan province's most famous chefs. The best-known Hunanese dish, however, is probably Viceroy chicken, stir-fried with chili and garlic and named after its creator, Viceroy Tso, trainer of the Hunanese army. Other good dishes include Hunan-style ham served in pancakes and duck tongue with a mustard sauce. As a special treat, try one of the Hunanese wines.

Jimmy's Kitchen

1 Wyndham St., Central. ☎ **852/2526 5293.** Main courses HK$90–HK$190 ($11.70–$24.65). AE, DC, MC, V. Daily noon–11pm. MTR: Central. CONTINENTAL.

First opened in 1928 and one of Hong Kong's oldest Western restaurants, Jimmy's Kitchen had several homes before moving in the 1960s to its present site. The atmosphere reminds me of an American steakhouse, with white tablecloths, dark-wood paneling, and elevator music, but it's a favorite with foreigners living in Hong Kong and serves dependably good European food. The daily specials are written on a blackboard, and an extensive à la carte menu offers seafood, steaks, salads and soups, chicken, spaghetti, and curries. You can have oysters imported from the United States, New Zealand, or Australia, and there's a large selection of seafood, including sole, scallops, and the local garoupa. It's a good place also for corned beef and cabbage, pork sausages, beef Stroganoff, and hearty German fare.

L.A. Cafe
Tamar and Queensway, Central. ☎ **852/2526 6863.** Main courses HK$100–HK$200 ($13–$25.95); lunch buffet HK$125–HK$175 ($16.25–$22.75). AE, DC, MC, V. Daily 11am–11pm. MTR: Admiralty. AMERICAN.

Located across from the Admiralty bus depot, this California-style restaurant/bar is decorated with the predictable movie posters, California memorabilia, and palm trees. Its menu features a little of everything, from soups and salads to burgers, Mexican fare, pasta, chicken, and seafood; the dinner menu also includes steaks. Weekdays there's a lunch buffet from 11am to 3pm, and Sundays there's a breakfast brunch. TVs everywhere feature satellite sports programs from the United States, the staff wear baseball caps, and about once a week (beginning at 11pm) a live band is showcased with free admission. Fridays from 11pm to 3am the place is transformed into a disco, with a HK$55 ($7.15) cover charge.

La Taverna
24–30 Ice House St., Central. ☎ **852/2522 8904.** Pasta and pizza HK$90–HK$115 ($11.70–$134.9); main courses HK$130–HK$180 ($16.90–$23.40); fixed-price lunch HK$115 ($154.95). AE, DC, MC, V. Mon–Sat noon–2:30pm; daily 6:30–11pm. MTR: Central. ITALIAN.

First opened more than two decades ago but ensconced in its present home a few years back, La Taverna is Italian-owned and employs an Italian chef to prepare its daily specials, as well as such favorites as homemade pasta, thinly sliced beef tenderloin in olive oil and rosemary dressing, veal, chicken, seafood, and pizza. On weekdays, the fixed-price lunch is a bargain. A guitarist serenades in the evenings, while candles on all the tables bathe the restaurant in a warm, soft glow. Chianti bottles hang from the ceiling, but the wine list is actually much more extensive, with a large selection of Italian wines. The desserts are a sinful must. Since La Taverna opened, a number of trendier Italian restaurants have made their debut, but this remains a reliable standby.

There's another branch in Tsim Sha Tsui at 36–38 Ashley Rd. (☎ 852/376 1945) with the same hours.

✪ Luk Yu Tea House
24–26 Stanley St., Central. ☎ **852/2523 5464.** Main dishes HK$55–HK$160 ($7.15–$20.80); dim sum HK$25–HK$45 ($3.25–$5.85). No credit cards. Daily 7am–9:30pm. MTR: Central. CANTONESE.

Luk Yu, first opened in 1925, is the most famous teahouse remaining in Hong Kong. In fact, unless you have a time machine, you can't get any closer to old Hong Kong than this wonderful Cantonese restaurant, with its ceiling fans, spittoons, individual wooden booths for couples, marble tabletops, wood paneling, and stained-glass windows. It's one of the best places to try a few Chinese teas, including bo lai, jasmine, lung ching (a green tea), and sui sin (narcissus or daffodil).

But Luk Yu is most famous for its dim sum, served from 7am to 5pm. The problem for foreigners, however, is that the place is always packed with regulars who have their own special places to sit, and the staff is sometimes surly to newcomers. In addition, if you come after 11am, dim sum is no longer served by trolley but from a menu written only in Chinese. If you want to come during the day (certainly when Luk Yu is most colorful), try to bring along a Chinese friend. Otherwise, consider going for dinner when it's not nearly so hectic. Also, at dinner there is an English menu listing more than 200 items, including all the Cantonese favorites. Dinner will average HK$200 ($25.95) a person.

Portico
Citibank Plaza, 3 Garden Rd., Central. ☎ **852/2523 8893.** Pasta and Pizza HK$95–HK$135 ($12.35–$17.55); main courses HK$95–HK$160 ($12.35–$20.80). AE, DC, MC, V. Mon–Sat 11:30am–2:30pm, 6:30–10:30pm. MTR: Central. INTERNATIONAL.

Located just a short walk from Hong Kong Park and the Victoria Peak tram terminus, this restaurant/bar was in a state of flux at the time of my last visit so it's hard to predict what the state of affairs will be by the time you get there. It opened a few years ago with much fanfare under the artful direction of chef Franz Kranzfelder, who had directed a team of international chefs at the former Hilton across the street. Franz and the Hilton are now gone, but taking up the reins is Franz's sous chef, who had also worked under Kranzfelder at the Hilton. At any rate, the management has vowed to keep to the same innovative menu begun by Franz, and the restaurant has even managed to obtain a mural that once graced a Hilton restaurant. The food includes both Asian and Western selections, with preference for Italian ingredients, as well as combinations of both, such as Singapore-style fried rice vermicelli with barbecue pork, baby shrimp, and bean sprouts; spicy Thai chicken pizza with spring onions, broccoli, and bean sprouts; penne pasta with tomato, basil, garlic, and red chilies; and roasted salmon with crispy skin with a potato cake, greens, and tomato salsa. On Saturday, American breakfasts are offered, along with a children's buffet for HK$65 ($8.40) which includes such favorites as spaghetti and barbecue chicken but also such exotics as Japanese sushi and deep-fried quail eggs in tomato sauce. More appealing, perhaps, is the opportunity every Saturday from 11:30am to 2:30pm for children ages 3 to 11 to create their own pizza in the kitchen under the supervision of a bunny-eared chef.

Shanghai Garden
Hutchinson House (1st floor), Murray Rd., Central. ☎ **852/2524 8181.** Reservations recommended. Main dishes HK$75–HK$300 ($9.75–$38.95). AE, CB, DC, MC, V. Daily 11:30am–3pm and 5:30–11pm. MTR: Central. SHANGHAINESE.

Located next to the Furama Hotel, the Shanghai Garden (part of the Maxim's Group of restaurants) does a good job in presentation and cuisine. Since Shanghai does not have its own cuisine, the dishes served here are from Peking, Nanking, Sichuan, Hangchow, and Wuxi, as well as a few from Shanghai. The menu is extensive, including hot-and-sour shredded-meat-and-fish soup or shark's-fin soup, such cold dishes as spiced duck or chicken in wine sauce, and such main courses as sautéed prawns, beggar's chicken, quick-fried beef with green pepper, braised pig with vegetables, and fried noodles with pork and cabbage. This place, pleasantly and brightly decorated, does a roaring business, especially for lunch. With most dishes priced around HK$95 to HK$145 ($12.35 to $18.85), you can expect your dinner here to cost about HK$200 to HK$250 ($25.95–$32.45) excluding drinks.

Sichuan Garden
Gloucester Tower (3rd floor), Landmark Building, Des Voeux Rd., Central. ☎ **852/2521 4433.** Reservations recommended, especially at lunch. Main dishes HK$80–HK$180 ($10.40–$23.40). AE, DC, MC, V. Daily 11:30am–3pm and 5:30–11pm. MTR: Central. SZECHUAN.

Another Maxim's restaurant, the Sichuan Garden is in the chic Landmark Building, which explains its high prices (someone has to pay the rent). The atmosphere is bright, spotless, and elegantly simple, the food excellent, and the service attentive. It's quite popular and almost always crowded, especially at lunch. The hot-and-spicy dishes are clearly marked on the 150-item menu to help the uninitiated, though those who appreciate fiery food will find that the dishes here are only mildly hot. Recommended are the hot-and-sour soup, fried prawns with chili sauce, shredded pork in hot garlic sauce, bean curd with minced beef in a pungent sauce, smoked duck, and pigeon smoked in camphor wood and tea leaves. I ordered the pigeon and found it quite good, but I was not prepared to have the head brought out as well—perhaps as a decoration (at least, I assume it wasn't for consumption).

Supatra's

50 D'Aguilar St., Central. ☎ **852/2522 5073.** Main dishes HK$75–HK$210 ($9.75–$27.25); buffet lunch HK$108 ($14). AE, DC, MC, V. Daily noon–11pm. MTR: Central. THAI.

Supatra's declares rather boldly that its food "is like great sex—the more you have the more you want." Certainly variety is the spice of life here, with more than 50 items listed on the menu. In addition to traditional Thai dishes, specialties include fresh prawns simmered in coconut milk with chili and shallots flavored with lime juice; and fish cake mixed with red curry paste, kaffir lime leaves, and string beans. The restaurant, located in Central's nightlife district (up on a first floor), is simple but pleasant and has a loyal clientele. On the ground floor is a bar, which serves light fare and snacks at cheaper prices; most items are priced at less than HK$60 ($7.80). On weekdays, the buffet lunch is a bargain.

Yorohachi

5–6 Lan Kwai Fong, Central. ☎ **852/2524 1251,** or 852/2845 2041. Sushi and sashimi HK$50–HK$190 ($6.50–$24.65); fixed-price teppanyaki meals HK$290–HK$600 ($37.65–$77.90). AE, DC, MC, V. Mon–Sat 11am–3pm; daily 6–11pm. MTR: Central. JAPANESE.

Yorohachi is actually two Japanese restaurants, both tiny affairs, located side by side in Central's nightlife district and readily recognizable by the customary short curtains that hang above the front doors of all Japanese restaurants. One serves sashimi (raw fish) and sushi (raw fish on vinegared rice), as well as tempura priced at HK$65 to HK$110 ($8.40 to $14.30), obento lunch boxes for HK$70 to HK$180 ($9.10 to $23.40), and soba and udon noodles for HK$55 to HK$75 ($7.15 to $9.75). There's also a raw fish dish served with soup, pickles, and rice for HK$105 ($13.65). The other restaurant specializes in teppanyaki (Japanese-style steak), with higher prices.

Zona Rosa

1 Lan Kwai Fong, Central. ☎ **852/2801 5885.** Reservations recommended weekends. Main courses HK$110–HK$169 ($14.30–$21.95); lunch buffet HK$135 ($17.55). AE, DC, MC, V. Mon–Fri noon–2:30pm; Mon–Sat 7–11pm. MTR: Central. MEXICAN.

If you can't go long without a Mexican food fix, and Asian spicy cuisines such as Szechuan and Thai don't fit the bill, this is the place for you. Although Hong Kong has had its share of boisterous Mexican restaurants during the past decade, this is the first to offer authentic Mexican fare (as opposed to Chinese-Mexican or Tex Mex) and a convenient location in the heart of Central's nightlife district. Located up on the first floor of a modern building but cozily decorated in hacienda style with adobelike whitewashed walls and items brought from Mexico, it has a Mexican head chef to direct operations in the kitchen. Tortillas are made fresh daily, and the menu runs the gamut from chilapas and shrimp tostadas to Yucatan lime soup, chili rellenos, vegetable enchiladas, chicken mole, and fish wrapped and steamed in banana leaf with shrimp, scallops, onions, garlic, green tomato, and spices. Both spicy and vegetarian selections are marked on the menu, and Mexican music played over the sound system sets a lively tone. ¡Caramba!

INEXPENSIVE

Several restaurants in the moderate category above offer lunches that even the budget-conscious can afford. In addition, check the section on "Dim Sum" later in this chapter. For fast food, head to Pacific Place, 88 Queensway (near the Admiralty MTR station), where you'll find Food Fare, with outlets for KFC, Pizza Hut, and McDonald's, as well as counters serving Singaporean, Thai, and Chinese food. You can eat for less than HK$50 ($6.50) here, and the outlets are open daily from 11am to 8pm.

Al's Diner

39 D'Aguilar St., Central. ☎ **852/2521 8714** or 852/2869 1869. Main courses HK$55–HK$120 ($7.15–$15.60). AE, DC, MC, V. Mon–Thurs noon–1am, Fri–Sat noon–3am. MTR: Central. AMERICAN.

This is one of the cheapest places for a late-night meal if you're carousing Central's small nightlife district around Lan Kwai Fong. Although it may not win any culinary awards, this informal diner hits the spot with burgers, hot dogs, sandwiches, chili, milk shakes, ice-cream floats, and banana splits. It serves breakfast anytime.

✿ The Ashoka

57–59 Wyndham St., Central. ☎ **852/2524 9623** or 852/2525 5719. Reservations recommended. Main courses HK$44–HK$135 ($5.70–$17.55); fixed-price meals HK$55 ($7.15) at lunch, HK$100–HK$105 ($13–$13.65) at dinner. AE, DC, MC, V. Daily noon–2:30pm and 6–10:30pm. MTR: Central. INDIAN.

Within walking distance of Central up on winding Wyndham Hill, the Ashoka is just one of several Indian restaurants in the area but is probably the best known and most popular. Opened in 1973, it claims to be the oldest Indian restaurant on Hong Kong Island. In any case, it's extremely tiny and crowded (only 60 seats), so be prepared to sit practically in your neighbor's lap. It's worth it, for the food, mainly northern Indian, is great, the service is enthusiastic, and the prices are even better, with ridiculously cheap fixed-price lunches—there are two menus available, a vegetarian and a tandoori, both costing HK$55 ($7.15) and available Monday through Friday (except public holidays). In addition to the usual fixed-price dinners, there's an early-bird menu served Monday through Thursday (except public holidays) from 6 to 7:30pm for just HK$65 ($8.40). If you order à la carte, you will find such house specialties as fish or chicken tikka, chicken bhurtha, stuffed tomato, beef bhuna, and vegetarian selections.

✿ City Hall Chinese Restaurant

City Hall (2nd floor), Low Block, Central. ☎ **852/2521 1303.** Reservations recommended, especially at lunch. Main dishes HK$65–HK$160 ($8.40–$20.80); dim sum HK$17–HK$27 ($2.20–$3.50). AE, V. Mon–Fri 10am–3pm and 5:30–11:30pm, Sat 10am–11:30pm, Sun and holidays 8am–11:30pm. MTR: Central. CANTONESE.

Decorated in Chinese red, this large restaurant on the second floor of city hall offers a view of the harbor and is so popular at lunchtime that you'll probably have to wait if you haven't made a reservation (report immediately to the woman at the desk near the door to get on the waiting list). The clientele is almost exclusively Chinese, and the food is Cantonese, with the usual shark's-fin, bird's-nest, abalone, pigeon, duck, vegetable, beef, and seafood dishes, most priced in the range of HK$75 to HK$110

($9.75–$14.30). The food is fast and average; better, in my opinion, is the dim sum, served from trolleys until 3pm. Ask for the dim sum menu in English.

Spaghetti House

Malahon Centre, 10 Stanley St., Central. ☎ **852/2523 1372.** Individual-size pizza HK$60–HK$85 ($7.80–$11.05); spaghetti HK$55–HK$75 ($7.15–$9.75). AE, DC, MC, V. Daily 11am–11pm. MTR: Central. ITALIAN.

Part of a Hong Kong chain specializing in spaghetti and pizza cooked American-style, this family-style restaurant serves 14 different kinds of spaghetti and pizzas ranging from individual to large sizes, as well as lasagne, sandwiches, chili con carne, and fried chicken. Items can be prepared for take-out.

Yung Kee

32–40 Wellington St., Central. ☎ **852/2522 1624.** Main dishes HK$50–HK$120 ($6.50–$15.60); dim sum HK$11–HK$24 ($1.45–$3.10). AE, MC, V. Daily 11am–11:30pm. MTR: Central. CANTONESE.

Popular for decades, Yung Kee started out in 1942 as a small shop selling roast goose, which it did so well that it soon expanded into a very successful Cantonese enterprise. Its specialty is still roast goose with plum sauce, cooked to perfection with tender meat on the inside and crispy skin on the outside. Other specialties include bean curd combined with prawns, shredded chicken, or delicacies; fillet of garoupa sauté; sautéed fillet of pomfret with chili and black bean sauce; and hundred-year-old eggs (which are included with each meal). Dining is up on the first floor in a red-and-gold room, but if all you want is a bowl of congee or some other rice dish, join the office workers who pour in for a quick meal on the ground floor. This place is very Chinese.

5 Causeway Bay/Wan Chai

VERY EXPENSIVE

✪ Grissini

In the Grand Hyatt Hong Kong Hotel, 1 Harbour Rd., Wan Chai. ☎ **852/2588 1234.** Reservations required. Pasta and risotto HK$130–HK$180 ($16.90–$23.40); main courses HK$250–HK$275 ($32.45–$35.70). AE, CB, DC, MC, V. Daily noon–2:30pm and 7–11pm. MTR: Wan Chai. ITALIAN.

This stylish, airy Italian restaurant echoes the palatial setting of the Grand Hyatt Hotel, with a tall ceiling, parquet floors, slick black furniture, and ceiling-to-floor windows offering a spectacular view of the harbor. Dining is on two levels, giving everyone a ringside seat. The menu offers some of the best Italian fare in town. Although the menu changes often, it might include such appetizers as a chicken-and-pistachio salad with fragrant white truffle oil, or thinly sliced salmon marinated in lemon and oregano. For a second course, you might choose pumpkin ravioli with thyme and butter, or ricotta and spinach dumplings on Fontina cheese and leek sauce. Main courses might include baked garoupa with white wine, black olives, capers, and parsley; poached fillet of sole with basil and pine-nut sauce; sliced beef tenderloin with virgin olive oil, herbs, and tomatoes; baked lamb chops with thyme and garlic; and veal médaillon with lemon-and-parsley sauce. At lunch there is lighter fare and more choices of pasta and risotto; Monday through Friday a fixed-price lunch is available for HK$230 ($29.85) and on Saturday for HK$215 ($27.90). Sundays and holidays feature a lavish lunch antipasto buffet, choice of entrée, and dessert for HK$325 ($42.20). Whether lunch or dinner, you can't go wrong dining here.

Causeway Bay/Wan Chai Dining

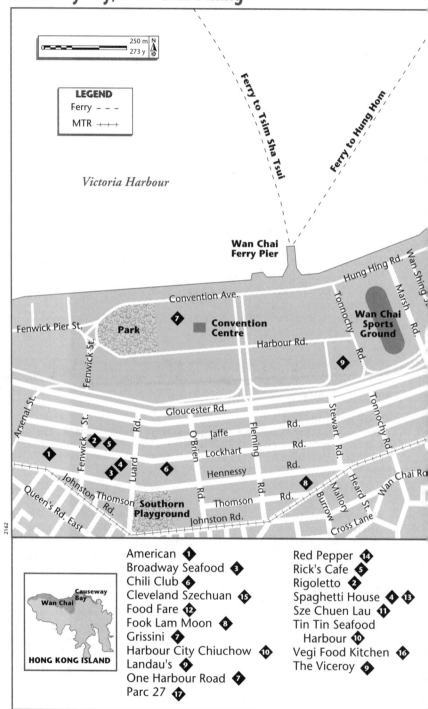

250 m
273 y

LEGEND
Ferry - - -
MTR +++

Victoria Harbour

Ferry to Tsim Sha Tsui

Ferry to Hung Hom

Wan Chai Ferry Pier

Hung Hing Rd.

Wan Shing

Convention Ave.

Fenwick Pier St.

Park

Convention Centre

Harbour Rd.

Tonnochy

Marsh Rd.

Wan Chai Sports Ground

Fenwick St.

Gloucester Rd.

Arsenal St.

Fenwick St.

Rd.

O'Brien

Jaffe

Lockhart

Fleming

Rd.

Rd.

Rd.

Hennessy

Stewart Rd.

Tonnochy Rd.

Luard

Rd.

Rd.

Rd.

Thomson

Wan Chai Rd

Queen's Rd. East

Johnston

Thomson Rd.

Southorn Playground

Thomson

Rd.

Rd.

Burrow

Mallory

Heard St.

Johnston Rd.

Cross Lane

American ❶
Broadway Seafood ❸
Chili Club ❻
Cleveland Szechuan ❶❺
Food Fare ❶❷
Fook Lam Moon ❽
Grissini ❼
Harbour City Chiuchow ❿
Landau's ❾
One Harbour Road ❼
Parc 27 ❶❼

Red Pepper ❶❹
Rick's Cafe ❺
Rigoletto ❷
Spaghetti House ❹ ❶❸
Sze Chuen Lau ❶❶
Tin Tin Seafood
Harbour ❿
Vegi Food Kitchen ❶❻
The Viceroy ❾

HONG KONG ISLAND

Causeway Bay

Wan Chai

2162

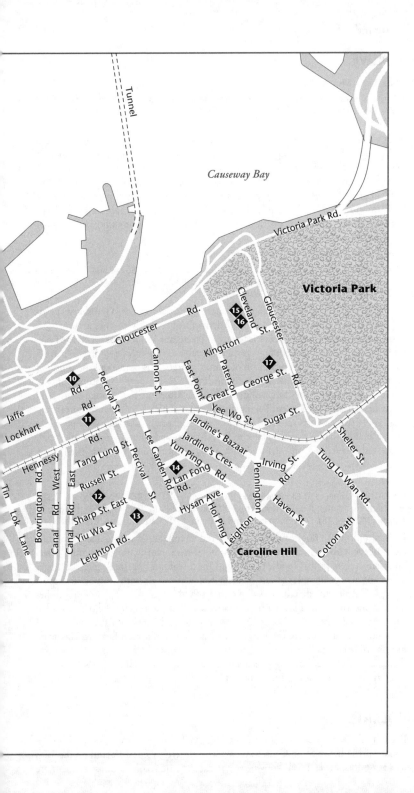

EXPENSIVE

✪ Fook Lam Moon
335–45 Johnston Rd., Wan Chai. ☎ **852/2866 0663.** Reservations required. Main dishes HK$100–HK$185 ($13–$24). AE, DC, MC, V. Daily noon–2:30pm, 6–11pm. MTR: Wan Chai. CANTONESE.

After passing the shrine to the kitchen god, head upstairs to the sophisticated dining room, famed in Hong Kong for serving some of the best Cantonese food in town, if not the world. It specializes in exotic fare, including bird's nest and shark's fin (a half bowl of shark's fin with shredded chicken starts at HK$240, or $31.15), original creations, and home-style Chinese cooking, making it a good place for both the novice and Cantonese food aficionado. Pan-fried lobster bars, deep-fried crispy chicken, and, for dessert, bird's nest in coconut milk, come highly recommended.

✪ One Harbour Road
In the Grand Hyatt Hong Kong Hotel, 1 Harbour Rd., Wan Chai. ☎ **852/2588 1234.** Reservations required. Main dishes HK$110–HK$200 ($14.30–$25.95). AE, CB, DC, MC, V. Daily noon–2:30pm and 6:30–10pm. MTR: Wan Chai. CANTONESE.

For elegant Chinese dining in Wan Chai, head to the lobby of the Grand Hyatt Hotel, where a glass bubble elevator will deliver you directly to this eighth-floor restaurant. Designed to resemble the terrace of an elegant 1930s mansion on the Peak, it's bright and airy, with fresh flowers on every table and split-level dining, which offers views of the harbor. A profusion of plants, a large lotus pond, and the sound of running water give the illusion of outdoor dining. The extensive Cantonese menu, adapted to Western tastes but wonderful just the same, offers the usual shark's-fin specialties, abalone, bird's nest, Peking duck, beggar's chicken (order in advance), and roast goose (which costs substantially more than the prices given above). Specialties include braised shark's fin with crab roe, baked crabmeat, bamboo fungus stuffed with bird's nest, roasted pigeon enhanced with preserved bean curd, and deep-fried crispy chicken skin.

Parc 27
In the Park Lane Hotel, 310 Gloucester Rd., Causeway Bay. ☎ **852/2890 3355,** ext. 3344. Reservations recommended. Main courses HK$200–HK$275 ($25.95–$35.70); fixed-price dinner HK$340 ($44.15). Daily noon–3pm and 6–11pm. MTR: Causeway Bay. CONTINENTAL.

Located on the top floor of the Park Lane and commanding spectacular panoramic views of the harbor and North Point, this hotel restaurant (with live evening entertainment) offers grilled foods, roasts, and fresh seafood; the small menu changes often but always includes about three or four choices in both seafood and meat entrées. Actually, the descriptions don't do the food justice—examples of past dishes include braised sole and lobster in an orange vegetable sauce, chicken breast stuffed with leeks and served with Asian mushroom stew, and lamb with feta and sautéed bok choy. For dessert, try the house specialty, Grand Marnier–flavored chocolate mousse with berries in filo. The set dinner is a steal, and from Monday to Friday there's a lunch buffet featuring Asian and Western dishes for HK$195 ($25.30). On Sunday, an international lunch buffet costs HK$215 ($27.90) for adults and HK$109 ($14.15) for children.

MODERATE

If you're not sure what you want to eat and have time to browse, head to Times Square, 1 Matheson St. in Causeway Bay, where there's a **Food Forum** on the 10th to 13th floors. Several well-known restaurants have outlets here; most of them are open daily from 11:30am to 3pm and 6:30 to 11pm. Prices vary, but you can eat lunch at most places for less than HK$170 ($22.10).

Cleveland Szechuan Restaurant

6 Cleveland St., Causeway Bay. ☎ **852/2576 3876.** Small dishes HK$70–HK$180 ($9.10–$23.40); medium dishes HK$110–HK$265 ($14.30–$34.40). AE, DC, MC, V. Daily 11:30am–2:30pm and 5:30pm–11:15pm. MTR: Causeway Bay. SZECHUAN.

This Szechuan restaurant is popular with local Chinese, especially families with children. Its decor is rather plain, but the prices are good and most dishes come in two sizes. The small size is suitable for two people, while the medium is enough for four (remember, if there are two of you, you'll want to order at least two small-size dishes and then share). The specialty of the house is its smoked duck with camphor tea. Other highly recommended dishes are fried king prawn on a sizzling plate, fried diced chicken with black beans and pepper, deep-fried fish with sweet-and-sour sauce, cold sliced pork with garlic sauce, and beef fillet with hot garlic sauce. A good choice if you want to rub elbows with the locals rather than other tourists.

Harbour City Chiuchow Restaurant

Elizabeth House (2nd floor), 250 Gloucester Rd., Causeway Bay. ☎ **852/2833 6678** or 852/2893 6788. Main dishes HK$60–HK$130 ($7.80–$16.90). AE, DC, MC, V. Daily 11am–3pm and 5pm–midnight. MTR: Causeway Bay. CHIU CHOW.

About a 3-minute walk west of the Excelsior Hotel, this modern, pink-and-black restaurant is one of the many Chiu Chow establishments to hit the Hong Kong scene in the past decade. There are almost 200 selections on the menu, including lobster, crab, scallops, squid, goose, duck, abalone, whelk, and chicken dishes. Specialties include fresh fish, sliced soya goose, and shark's-fin soup, though the least expensive shark's-fin dish is a soup mixture with chicken for HK$160 ($20.80).

Landau's

Sun Hung Kai Centre (2nd floor), 30 Harbour Rd., Wan Chai. ☎ **852/2827 7901.** Reservations recommended, especially Fri–Sat. Main courses HK$105–HK$190 ($13.65–$24.65). AE, DC, MC, V. Daily noon–2:30pm and 7–10:30pm. MTR: Wan Chai. CONTINENTAL.

Owned by the same company as Jimmy's Kitchen, Landau's is popular among Hong Kong's expatriates for its hearty and dependable European fare. The dining area itself is nothing spectacular, but the atmosphere is convivial and the service attentive. The regular menu hasn't changed in years; main dishes include black-pepper steak, duck marinated in port wine, New Zealand lamb chops, Wienerschnitzel, beef Stroganoff, Australian rock oysters, paprika veal goulash, corned beef and cabbage, fresh Tasmanian sole, poached Norwegian salmon, and vegetarian fare. Don't forget to check the blackboards for daily specials; there are also frequent promotionals featuring regional Australian and New Zealand cuisine. On weekends and public holidays, an à la carte fixed-price brunch is available for HK$165 ($21.40) for adults and HK$88 ($11.45) for children.

✪ Red Pepper

7 Lan Fong Rd., Causeway Bay. ☎ **852/2576 8046.** Reservations recommended, especially at dinner. Small dishes HK$70–HK$120 ($9.10–$15.60); medium dishes HK$100–HK$170 ($13–$22.10). AE, DC, MC, V. Daily noon–11:15pm (last order). MTR: Causeway Bay. SZECHUAN.

Open since 1970, the Red Pepper has a large following among the colony's expatriates, many of whom seem to come so often that they know everyone in the place. It's a very relaxing, small restaurant, with a rather quaint decor. Specialties include fried prawns with chili sauce on a sizzling platter, sour-pepper soup, smoked duck marinated with oranges, and shredded chicken with hot garlic sauce and dry-fried string beans. Most dishes are available in two sizes, with the small dishes suitable for two people and the medium dishes recommended for four to six.

Rigoletto

14–16 Fenwick St., Wan Chai. ☎ **852/2527 7144.** Main courses HK$140–HK$175 ($18.20–$22.75); pizzas and pastas HK$85–HK$105 ($11.05–$13.65). AE, DC, MC, V. Mon–Sat noon–3pm and 6pm–midnight. MTR: Wan Chai. ITALIAN.

This moderately priced Italian eatery in Wan Chai has been around for about as long as anyone can remember, and now seems somewhat neglected with the advent of trendier and more smartly decorated Italian restaurants. Still, this is a good choice if you're in the vicinity, especially for lunch, with its dark and subdued lighting and large front windows offering an interesting perspective on the doings of Wan Chai. The fixed-price lunch, available Monday through Friday, is a good bargain at HK$115 ($14.95). The pizza and homemade pasta are also good. Main courses consist mainly of northern Italian seafood and veal dishes.

Sze Chuen Lau Restaurant

466 Lockhart Rd., Wan Chai. ☎ **852/2891 9027.** Reservations required. Small dishes HK$70–HK$175 ($9.10–$22.75); medium dishes HK$110–HK$260 ($14.30–$33.75). AE, MC, V. Daily 11:30am–10:30pm. MTR: Causeway Bay. SZECHUAN.

This is a small, rather nondescript restaurant, similar to many family-run neighborhood eateries all over Hong Kong and very popular with local Chinese. It serves the usual Szechuan specialties, including chili prawns on a sizzling plate, smoked duck (excellent), sliced pork with hot garlic dressing, and cold chicken with chili-sesame sauce. Dishes come in three different sizes, which is nice for the lone diner. Try to get a table downstairs, but keep in mind that this place caters to the Chinese, not to foreign visitors, and the staff is not keen about explaining anything on the menu—assuming, of course, they understand English, which they may not. If you're already familiar with Szechuan food and know what you want, you'll find this place rewarding both price-wise and tongue-wise.

Tin Tin Seafood Harbour

Elizabeth House (4th floor), 250 Gloucester Rd., Causeway Bay. ☎ **852/2833 6683.** Reservations required. Most meals HK$250 ($32.45) per person. AE, MC, V. Daily 11am–3:30pm, 6–11pm. MTR: Causeway Bay. CANTONESE SEAFOOD.

Although located on the fourth floor of a rather nondescript office building, the entrance to this restaurant resembles a local market, with tank after tank of huge lobsters, crabs, prawns, and fish, all representing the menu of the day. Prices, which change daily, are written on a blackboard; the best strategy is to point to what looks good and ask how much it will cost. There's also a Cantonese menu with the usual seafood, chicken, pigeon, and duck selections, but why order these when fresh seafood is so close at hand, unless they're eaten as accompanying side dishes? The no-smoking section has window seats with good views of the harbor; if you want one of these seats, try to have someone from your hotel make a reservation for you. Prices for meals will vary, of course, according to what you order, but most meals average HK$250 to HK$300 ($32.45–$38.95) per person.

The Viceroy

Sun Hung Kai Centre (2nd floor), 30 Harbour Rd., Wan Chai. ☎ **852/2827 7777.** Main dishes HK$55–HK$140 ($7.15–$18.20); lunch buffet HK$108 ($14). AE, DC, MC, V. MTR: Wan Chai. INDIAN.

Under the same management as the long-popular Gaylord in Tsim Sha Tsui, this restaurant has something its sister establishment doesn't—outdoor seating on a terrace with great views of the harbor, Wan Chai waterfront, and Kowloon. In the evening, the experience is almost magical. On days when the weather doesn't cooperate (too cold, too hot, rainy), indoor dining is a good second choice, with large windows offering the same views. Despite its name, the restaurant offers a choice of various Asian cuisines, primarily Indian, Thai, and Indonesian. You might want to start your meal with satays, mulligatawny soup, or the delicious Tom Kha Kai (chicken soup with coconut milk, lemongrass, kaffir leaves, and spices). Tandooris and curries ranging from prawns with a Balinese chili sauce to chicken breast cooked with almonds, cashews, saffron sauce, and finished with morels round out the menu. A lunch buffet is offered weekdays only.

INEXPENSIVE

In addition to the recommendations below, be sure to go through the moderate section above for inexpensive buffet and fixed-price lunches; also see the "Dim Sum" section later in this chapter.

⑤ American Restaurant

20 Lockhart Rd., Wan Chai. ☎ 852/2527 1000 or 852/2527 7277. Small dishes HK$40–HK$90 ($5.20–$11.70); medium dishes HK$60–HK$130 ($7.80–$16.90). No credit cards. Daily 11:30am–11pm (last order). MTR: Wan Chai. PEKINESE.

Despite its name, the American Restaurant serves hearty Pekinese food and has been doing so since it opened right after World War II. In fact, not much has changed here in the past five decades, including the bright green-and-red facade, paneled interior, and old-school Chinese waiters (one friend told me that it's not unusual for the waiters here to actually throw the plates onto the table). Still, the restaurant continues to attract a faithful clientele of both Chinese and Western residents. The English menu lists almost 200 dishes, but the perennial specialties have always been barbecued Peking duck, beggar's chicken (which must be ordered a day in advance), and the sizzling beef hot plate. Of these, Peking duck remains the favorite and should be shared by two or more people.

Broadway Seafood Restaurant

73–85B Hennessy Rd., Wan Chai. ☎ 852/2529 9233. Main dishes HK$60–HK$130 ($7.80–$16.90); dim sum HK$13–HK$26 ($1.70–$3.40). AE, DC, MC, V. Daily 11am–midnight. MTR: Wan Chai. CANTONESE.

This first-floor establishment is just like a Cantonese restaurant should be—noisy, lively, and crowded with families, particularly on weekends. Fresh seafood and chicken dishes, especially crispy chicken, are the most popular fare. The menu includes fresh scallops, prawns, snapper, garoupa, sole, crab, barbecued pork, barbecued goose, Peking duck, fried chicken with lemon sauce, and sliced beef with satay sauce. A fixed-price five-course meal for one, great for lone diners, is available for HK$175 ($22.75); a six-course meal for two costs HK$ 300 ($38.95). Peking duck costs HK$220 ($28.60). Dim sum is served daily from 11am to 4pm.

Chili Club

88 Lockhart Rd., Wan Chai. ☎ 852/2527 2872. Main dishes HK$40–HK$120 ($5.20–$15.60). AE, DC, MC, V. Daily noon–3pm, 6–10:30pm. MTR: Wan Chai. THAI.

This simple upstairs restaurant wastes no money on decor. In fact, the only hint that you're in Asia comes from the rattan chairs. But the food, which includes all the Thai favorites, is as spicy as this national cuisine should be. What's more, the price is right, making this one of Hong Kong's best dining values. Try to get a seat near the window where you can watch the action on the street below and, if possible, avoid the lunchtime rush.

Food Fare

Shop B222-223 of the Market, basement of Times Square, 1 Matheson St., Causeway Bay. ☎ 852/2506 1411. Main dishes HK$26–HK$46 ($3.40–$5.95). No credit cards. Daily 11am–10:30pm. MTR: Causeway Bay. ASIAN.

This no-nonsense cafeteria offers rushed diners what they want—fast food at very low prices. The offerings change daily. Pay first at the cashier, then hand your ticket over when you go through the food line. Dishes offered here have included chicken fillet in pandamus leaf packet, fish cakes, and Thai fried rice. Vegetable dishes, noodles, and soup are always available. A sign reads, NO GUEST IN INDECENT DRESS CAN BE ENTERTAINED, but at these prices, no one expects to be entertained beyond saving a few dollars to be spent elsewhere.

Rick's Cafe

78–82 Jaffe Rd., Wan Chai. ☎ **852/2528 1812.** Main courses HK$75–HK$130 ($9.75–$16.90); fixed-price lunch HK$93 ($12.10). AE, DC, MC, V. Mon–Fri 11:30am–3am, Sat–Sun 11:30am–5am. MTR: Wan Chai. INTERNATIONAL.

Rick has gone native in this Casablanca-themed restaurant with its tentlike roof, orange claylike walls, rattan chairs, and starry lights. The ambience, however, is casual sophistication—a place where Bogart himself might have felt at home. A branch of the long-established Rick's Cafe in Tsim Sha Tsui, this is actually a restaurant/bar, featuring half-price drinks at lunchtime and one of the longest happy hours in Hong Kong, when you can get two drinks for the price of one from 3 to 10pm. The menu has a bit of everything, from satays and a spicy Thai salad to Cajun rib eye, spaghetti, burgers, barbecue ribs, Sri Lankan chicken curry, and even a vegetarian platter of grilled vegetables. The fixed-price lunch includes unlimited tea or coffee, a real boon to caffeine freaks.

Spaghetti House

5 Sharp St., Causeway Bay. ☎ **852/2895 2245.** Individual-size pizza HK$60–HK$85 ($7.80–$11.05); spaghetti HK$55–HK$75 ($7.15–$9.75). AE, MC, V. Daily 11am–11pm. MTR: Causeway Bay. ITALIAN.

This chain of spaghetti houses offers cheap pizza and pasta, including takeout. There's another branch nearby at Hennessy and Luard Roads, Wan Chai (☎ 852/529 0901; take the MTR to Wan Chai).

Vegi Food Kitchen

13–15 Cleveland St., Causeway Bay. ☎ **852/2890 6660** or 852/2890 6603. Reservations recommended. Main dishes HK$55–HK$100 ($7.15–$13). AE, DC, MC, V. Daily 11am–11pm. MTR: Causeway Bay. VEGETARIAN.

This small and ornate restaurant with black furniture and red lanterns serves only vegetarian food, offering combinations of mushrooms, fungus, nuts, bean curd, and seasonal vegetables. No alcohol is allowed on the premises. It's famous for its Buddhist Carnival, a plate of assorted vegetables, as well as its vegetarian "shark's-fin" soup, made with vermicelli and shredded mushrooms. Another popular soup is its white fungus with either sweet corn or asparagus. Fixed-price meals for two persons range from HK$260 to HK$430 ($33.75 to $55.85). You'll find it on Vogue Alley, a pedestrian lane lined with smart clothing boutiques.

6 Around Hong Kong Island

WESTERN DISTRICT

Mythical China

Western Market, 323 Des Voeux Rd. Central, Sheung Wan. ☎ **852/2815 3212.** Main dishes HK$70–HK$160 ($9.10–$20.80). AE, DC, MC, V. Daily 11am–3pm, 6–11pm. MTR: Sheung Wan. CANTONESE.

The food here is typical Cantonese food, including such delicacies as shark's fin, bird's nest, and abalone, and such ordinary dishes as duck and pigeon. Dim sum is served until 3pm. What makes this place special is its setting—on the upper level of the restored Western Market, an attractive 1906 brick building once serving as a public market and now home to specialty shops, souvenir stands, and retailers selling bolts of cloth. The restaurant itself is quite spacious, with two tiers of dining under a tall ceiling with exposed beams, Chinese lanterns, and traditional Chinese music, all reminiscent of a 1920s teahouse setting. With its English menu, this is a good choice if you're exploring the very Chinese Western District.

Sammy's Kitchen
204–206 Queen's Rd. West, Sheung Wan. ☎ **852/2548 8400.** Main courses HK$65–HK$100 ($8.40–$13). AE, DC, MC, V. Daily 11:30am–11:30pm. MTR: Sheung Wan. CONTINENTAL.

There's no better place for Western food in the Western District than Sammy's Kitchen, recognizable by the sign in the shape of a cow outside its door. A simple and unpretentious place, it offers reasonably priced meals, but best yet is the presence of owner/chef Sammy Yip, who has been cooking professionally for almost 50 years and opened this restaurant of his own two decades ago. The menu includes fresh seafood, steaks from the United States and New Zealand, and such specialties as veal with Parmesan and marsala, chicken with special pepper sauce flaming with cognac, filet mignon, beef Wellington, and chateaubriand for two. If you opt for seafood, you may wish to try garoupa dipped in egg and flour and then wrapped in paper with onion, garlic, shallots, tomato, parsley, mushrooms, hollandaise, and lemon and baked in the oven. Simpler fare such as spaghetti is also available, as well as Chinese food.

VICTORIA PEAK

✪ Cafe Deco
Peak Galleria, Victoria Peak. ☎ **852/2849 5111.** Reservations required. Pizzas and pastas HK$100–HK$130 ($13–$16.90); main courses HK$90–HK$190 ($11.70–$24.65). AE, DC, MC, V. Daily 10am–10:45pm (last order). Peak tram. INTERNATIONAL.

No expense was spared, it seems, in designing this chic restaurant with its wood inlaid floor, art deco trimmings, and open kitchen; ever since it opened in 1994, a nattily dressed crowd has been clamoring to get in. In the evening, diners are treated to live jazz. All this is secondary, however, to the restaurant's real attraction—the best view in town of Hong Kong. That alone is enough reason for dining here, so be sure to reserve a ringside window seat well in advance. The food is as trendy as the restaurant, with an eclectic mix of international dishes and ingredients from around the world, including Mexican snapper cooked in banana leaves with chili paste; free-range spring chicken with lemongrass, chili, coriander, and honey; grilled steaks; pastas; roast rack of lamb; and tandoori. Some of the entrées fall short of expectations; the pizzas, however, are great and may be the best items on the menu. The Szechuan pizza is my own favorite, made with roasted duck, black beans, chilies, peppers, bean sprouts, and shitake. The salads are generous enough for two to share.

✪ Peak Cafe
121 Peak Rd., Victoria Peak. ☎ **852/2849 7868.** Reservations required for dinner and weekends. Main courses HK$95–HK$200 ($12.35–$25.95). AE, DC, MC, V. Daily 11am–10:45pm (last order). Peak tram. INTERNATIONAL.

Across the street from the Peak tram terminus and Peak Galleria is the small Peak Cafe. Formerly a rickshaw station, it's a delightful place for a meal, with exposed granite walls, a tall timber-trussed ceiling, open fireplace, wooden floor, Chinese antiques, and a greenhouselike room that extends into the garden. You can also sit outdoors amid the lush growth where you can actually hear birds singing—one of the best outdoor dining opportunities in Hong Kong (be sure to request a table outdoors if that's what you want). The menu is eclectic, offering soups, sandwiches, and a combination of American, Chinese, Indian, Southeast Asian, and vegetarian dishes, including spinach and feta cheese lasagne, rib-eye steak, tandoori, curries, grilled satay, quesadillas, samosas with sweet peas and cilantro, and Thai smoked duck curry.

STANLEY

✪ Stanley's French Restaurant
86–88 Stanley Main St., Stanley. ☎ 852/2813 8873. Reservations required. Main courses HK$170–HK$220 ($22.10–$28.55). AE, DC, MC, V. Daily 9am–3pm; tea 3–5pm; 7–10:30pm. Bus: no. 6 or 260. FRENCH.

Whatever you save by bargain-shopping at Stanley Market may well go toward a meal at Stanley's Restaurant, and I can't think of a better place to spend it. This is an absolutely charming spot, refined, cozy, and romantic. There are several floors of dining, all in small rooms that look as if they're part of someone's home. There are flowers on the tables, pictures on the walls, and even an upstairs outdoor patio.

For starters you might try Caesar salad, considered a house specialty, or smoked salmon pâté or foie gras. For soup there's the zucchini-and-dill soup. Although the menu changes every two months, examples of what's been offered in the past include sautéed Tasmanian scallops and calamari in lemon-garlic butter, blackened fillet of pomfret, roast whole spring chicken, chicken-and-yogurt curry, blackened prime rib eye of beef with Cajun hollandaise, rack of lamb provençal, and Macau sole. There are also daily specials, written on a blackboard that will be brought to your table. Fixed-price vegetarian and meat lunches are available for HK$115 ($14.95) and HK$170 ($22.10), except on Saturday and Sunday when lunch costs HK$210 ($27.25). Fixed-price dinners range from HK$315 to HK$440 ($40.90 to $57.20). This restaurant is tucked away in a corner of the market, beside Stanley Beach.

Stanley's Oriental Restaurant
90B Stanley Main St., Stanley. ☎ 852/2813 9988. Reservations required. Main courses HK$105–HK$185 ($13.65–$24); fixed-price dinner HK$300 ($38.95); fixed-price lunch HK$150–HK$260 ($19.50–$33.75). AE, DC, MC, V. Daily noon–3pm; tea 3–5pm; 7–10:30pm. Bus: no. 6 or 260. ASIAN.

Under the same ownership as Stanley's French Restaurant and just around the corner facing the sea is an attractive eatery decorated in cool colonial style, with several floors of dining on open-fronted verandas cooled by ceiling fans. Its menu offers a bit of everything and changes often, with dishes from Sri Lanka, India, Thailand, and China. Featured dishes have included grilled blackened Macau sole, Thai hot-and-sour prawn soup, hot-and-spicy chicken curry, and tandoori. Vegetarian dishes are also available. Fixed-price meals are available daily for lunch and dinner. All in all, a civilized and relaxing place to unwind after a hectic day of shopping.

Tables 88
88 Stanley Village Rd., Stanley. ☎ 852/2813 6262. Reservations required on weekends. Main courses HK$140–HK$320 ($18.20–$41.55); fixed-price lunch HK$165–HK$185 ($21.45–$24); fixed-price dinner HK$395–HK$470 ($51.30–$61.05). AE, DC, MC, V. Daily noon–2:30pm, 6:30–10:30pm. Bus: no. 6 or 260. CONTINENTAL.

This restaurant, together with Cafe Deco on the Peak, was the hottest place in town when it opened in 1994. Now, of course, there are newer and probably hotter places that have garnered the spotlight in this scene-crazed town. Any competitor would have to be pretty outlandish to topple Tables 88's ranking as the most weirdly decorated restaurant in Hong Kong. From the outside, Tables 88 looks positively historic—a rather quaint-looking, century-old former police station. Inside, however, it's a different world—the decorating style might be called funky aboriginal, urban native, or upscale primitive. The management prefers to call it "rustic and raw." In any case, because the structure itself is historic, none of the walls could be knocked down (thank goodness), but that seems to have been the only restriction in decorating the warren of tiny rooms on two levels. Wooden floors, stone walls, exposed wooden beams, a tin roof, soft sofas, African wall prints, and modern artwork seem all the more mysterious by dim candlelight. You'll either love it or hate it. The menu has more superlatives on one page than a tourist brochure: "exceptional Boston lobster," "superior peppered Norwegian salmon steak," "fabulous gratinated artichokes decked with luscious crabmeat and fresh herbs." Surprisingly, however, the food *is* superlative, and no matter what you order on the changing menu (which the management calls "mondo cuisine"), you're apt to be pleased.

7 Floating Restaurants

No doubt you've heard about Hong Kong's floating restaurants in Aberdeen. Although they are often included in Hong Kong's organized nighttime tours, they're no longer touted by the tourist office as something every visitor must see—there are simply too many other restaurants that are more authentic, more affordable, and have better food. However, if you've always wanted to eat in a floating restaurant, try one of the two listed below, located side by side in the Aberdeen Harbour and under the same management. Simply take the bus to Aberdeen and board the restaurant's own free shuttle boat to either restaurant.

Jumbo Floating Restaurant
Aberdeen Harbour, Hong Kong Island. ☎ **852/2553 9111.** Main dishes HK$60–HK$160 ($7.80–$20.80); dim sum HK$13–HK$24 ($1.70–$3.10). AE, DC, MC, V. Daily 7:30am–11pm. Bus: no. 70 from Central to Aberdeen, then the restaurant's private boat. CANTONESE/DIM SUM.

Probably the largest and most garish of the floating restaurants, this Cantonese one has more reds, golds, and dragon motifs than you've ever seen in one place. The best views are from the large roof patio, designed like a traditional Chinese garden with a pagoda and pavilions. Be sure to stop by the "Seafood Exhibition" on the lower deck, where you'll see tanks of live creatures swimming about. Many diners like to make their seafood selections here. Dishes include everything from noodles and rice combinations to garoupa balls and fresh seafood (prawns are a particular favorite). From 7:30am to 4pm, dim sum is served from trolleys—certainly the least expensive way to enjoy the floating restaurant experience.

Tai Pak Seafood Restaurant
Aberdeen Harbour, Hong Kong Island. ☎ **852/2552 5953.** Main dishes HK$60–HK$160 ($7.80–$20.80). AE, DC, MC, V. Daily 11:30am–11pm. Bus: no. 70 from Central to Aberdeen, then the restaurant's private boat. CANTONESE.

Connected via a walkway to Jumbo Floating Restaurant, this is a smaller boat, with an even more ornate dining hall featuring a tall pagodalike ceiling and stained glass. The portions are large and the Cantonese menu is diverse; you will find the usual shark's-fin soup, braised garoupa (a local fish), sautéed scallops, sliced beef in oyster sauce, and steamed chicken with vegetables.

8 Dim Sum

Everyone should try a dim sum meal at least once, as much for the atmosphere as the food. Prices are low and you order only as much as you want. Simply look over the steaming baskets being pushed around by trolley and choose what appeals to you.

Fancier restaurants, particularly those in hotels, offer dim sum from an English menu rather than carts; they claim that since the food is cooked to order it is fresher, but the prices are also higher. In most restaurants that offer dim sum, one pays by the basket and each basket usually contains two to four items of dim sum; the average price is about HK$20 to HK$25 ($2.60 to $3.25). Most Chinese eat dim sum for breakfast or lunch. The prices given below, unless otherwise specified, are per basket; expect to spend HK$50 to HK$100 ($6.50 to $13) per person for a light meal.

KOWLOON

The Chinese

In the Hyatt Regency Hotel, 67 Nathan Rd., Tsim Sha Tsui. ☎ **852/2311 1234**, ext. 881. Dim sum HK$24–HK$36 ($2.85–$4.30). AE, DC, MC, V. Daily 11:30am–2:45pm for dim sum. MTR: Tsim Sha Tsui. CANTONESE.

A refined, modern, and fancy setting for dim sum, with correspondingly high prices. There are no trolleys here, but there's a great dim sum lunch for HK$100 ($13) or HK$150 ($19.50), which gives you several different varieties. Individual dim sum, costing HK$24 to HK$36 each ($2.85–$4.30), are also available.

City Chiuchow Restaurant

East Ocean Centre, 98 Granville Rd., Tsim Sha Tsui East. ☎ **852/2723 6226**. Dim sum HK$19–HK$26 ($2.45–$3.40). AE, DC, MC, V. Mon–Sat 11am–3pm, Sun 11am–5pm for dim sum. MTR: Tsim Sha Tsui. CHIU CHOW.

Although it's a Chiu Chow restaurant, it serves its own dim sum, which is not too surprising if you consider that Chiu Chow food has been greatly influenced by Cantonese food.

Fook Lam Moon

53–59 Kimberley Rd., Tsim Sha Tsui. ☎ **852/2366 0286**. Dim sum HK$25–HK$50 ($3.25–$6.50). AE, DC, MC, V. Daily 11:30am–3pm. MTR: Tsim Sha Tsui. CANTONESE.

Another Hong Kong old-timer, with an atmosphere that is reminiscent of an earlier era. There aren't any trolleys here, however—just a Chinese menu. Ask an English-speaking waiter for translations.

Jade Garden Chinese Restaurant

Star House (4th floor), 3 Salisbury Rd., Tsim Sha Tsui. ☎ **852/2730 6888**. Dim sum HK$16–HK$37 ($2.10–$4.80). AE, DC, MC, V. Mon–Sat 10am–3pm, Sun and hols 8am–3pm. MTR: Tsim Sha Tsui. CANTONESE.

An easy place for the uninitiated, this Cantonese chain is tourist-friendly and conveniently situated across from the Star Ferry terminus. There's an English dim sum menu, and the prices are reasonable as well.

Lai Ching Heen

In The Regent Hotel, Salisbury Rd., Tsim Sha Tsui. ☎ **852/2721 1211**. Dim sum HK$33–HK$37 ($4.30–$4.80). AE, DC, MC, V. Daily noon–2:30pm. MTR: Tsim Sha Tsui. CANTONESE.

One of Hong Kong's top Cantonese eateries, this elegant restaurant with large windows treats diners to views of the harbor. A daily changing menu offers about seven varieties of dim sum.

Shang Palace

In the Shangri-La Hotel, 64 Mody Rd., Tsim Sha Tsui East. ☎ **852/2721 2111**. Dim sum HK$22–HK$35 ($2.60–$4.40). AE, CB, DC, MC, V. Mon–Sat 12:30–3pm, Sun and holidays noon–3pm. MTR: Tsim Sha Tsui. CANTONESE.

One of Kowloon's most elaborate Chinese restaurants comes complete with red-lacquered walls and Chinese lanterns hanging from the ceiling. Because it provides a menu in English, this is a great place to try dim sum for the first time, not to mention the fact that its dim sum is among the best in town—a bit more expensive, but worth it. Choose your dim sum from the menu, which changes every two weeks and always includes more than a dozen varieties.

Spring Moon
In The Peninsula Hotel, Salisbury Road, Tsim Sha Tsui. ☎ **852/2739 2332.** Dim sum HK$35–HK$39 ($4.55–$5.05). AE, DC, MC, V. Daily 11:30am–3pm. MTR: Tsim Sha Tsui. CANTONESE.

As you'd expect from a restaurant in the venerable Peninsula Hotel, this is a very refined and civilized place for the humble dim sum, with an English menu.

Super Star Seafood Restaurant
83–97 Nathan Rd., Tsim Sha Tsui. ☎ **852/2366 0878.** Dim sum HK$25–30 ($3.25–$3.90). AE, DC, MC, V. Daily 9:30am–5pm. MTR: Tsim Sha Tsui. CANTONESE.

This lively and popular seafood restaurant is one of Tsim Sha Tsui's best places for trying authentic dim sum in a typical Chinese setting. There's no English menu, so you'll just have to look at the offerings of the various trolleys.

Tsui Hang Village Restaurant
Park Lane Square, 1 Kimberley Rd., Tsim Sha Tsui. ☎ **852/2368 6363.** Dim sum HK$16–HK$30 ($2.10–$3.90). AE, MC, V. Mon–Sat 11:30am–5:30pm, Sun 10am–5pm. MTR: Tsim Sha Tsui. CANTONESE.

Tsui Hang Village, a modern restaurant located in a shopping complex near the Miramar Hotel, offers inexpensive plates of dim sum.

CENTRAL

City Hall Chinese Restaurant
City Hall (2nd floor), Low Block, Connaught Rd., Central. ☎ **852/2521 1303.** Dim sum HK$17–HK$27 ($2.20–$3.50). AE, V. Mon–Sat 10am–3pm, Sun and holidays 8am–3pm. MTR: Central. CANTONESE.

A popular place, City Hall Chinese Restaurant is often crowded, filled with shoppers and office workers. There's an English dim sum menu, trolleys deliver food, and there are even views of the harbor.

Luk Yu Tea House
24–26 Stanley St., Central. ☎ **852/2523 5464.** Dim sum HK$25–HK$45 ($3.25–$5.85). No credit cards. Daily 7am–5pm. MTR: Central. CANTONESE.

The most authentic dim sum teahouse in Hong Kong is often so packed with regulars that mere tourists can't get a seat. Furthermore, trolleys with dim sum are pushed through the place only until 11am, after which there's only a Chinese menu. Try to bring along a Chinese friend to help you with your selections.

Yung Kee
32–40 Wellington St., Central. ☎ **852/2522 1624.** Dim sum HK$11–HK$24 ($1.45–$3.10). AE, MC, V. Mon–Fri 2–4:30pm, Sat–Sun 11am–4:30pm. MTR: Central. CANTONESE.

Famous for its roast goose, Yung Kee also offers dim sum weekday afternoons and throughout most of the day on the weekend, with an English dim sum menu.

Zen Chinese
The Mall, Pacific Place, 88 Queensway, Central. ☎ **852/2845 4555.** Dim sum HK$26–HK$33 ($3.40–$4.30). AE, DC, MC, V. Mon–Sat 11:30am–3pm, Sun 10:30am–4:30pm. MTR: Admiralty. CANTONESE.

Starkly modern and hip, this Cantonese restaurant offers dim sum daily, with more varieties available on the weekend.

CAUSEWAY BAY/WAN CHAI

Broadway Seafood Restaurant

73–85B Hennessy Rd., Wan Chai. ☎ **852/2529 9233**. Dim sum HK$13–HK$26 ($1.70–$3.40). AE, DC, MC, V. Daily 11am–4pm. MTR: Wan Chai. CANTONESE.

Noisy, lively, and crowded, the Broadway Seafood Restaurant offers dim sum typical of a Cantonese restaurant, with trolleys.

Fook Lam Moon

35–45 Johnston Rd., Wan Chai. ☎ **852/2866 0663**. Dim sum HK$25–HK$45 ($3.25–$5.85). AE, DC, MC, V. Daily 11:30am–3pm. MTR: Wan Chai. CANTONESE.

This well-known, expensive Cantonese restaurant offers dim sum from a Chinese menu only (no trolleys). Ask an English-speaking waiter for translations.

9 Afternoon Tea

Clipper Lounge

In the Mandarin Oriental Hotel, 5 Connaught Rd., Central. ☎ **852/2522 0111**. Fixed-price afternoon tea HK$150 ($19.50) for one person, HK$260 ($33.75) for two. AE, DC, MC, V. Daily 3–6pm. MTR: Central. TEAS/CAKES.

If you're in Central in the afternoon, stop by the Clipper Lounge for one of England's finest traditions—afternoon tea. Besides 15 varieties of tea (or, if you must, coffee), you'll have a choice of English tea sandwiches, "savoury puffs," homemade scones with Devonshire clotted cream and jam, brownies, fruit tartlets, Windsor cakes, and other goodies to sample. À la carte items are also available, but if there are two of you, you're better off getting the tea-for-two special. At any rate, you'll probably want to skip lunch or dinner if you indulge here.

Peninsula Hotel Lobby

In The Peninsula Hotel, Salisbury Rd., Tsim Sha Tsui. ☎ **852/2366 6251**. Fixed-price afternoon tea HK$135 ($17.55). AE, DC, MC, V. Daily 3–6:30pm. MTR: Tsim Sha Tsui. TEAS/CAKES.

The ornate lobby of The Peninsula Hotel, built in 1928, is the most famous lobby in Hong Kong. A popular place to see and be seen, the lobby features soaring columns topped with elaborate gilded ceilings and sculpted figures of gods and angels, palm trees, a Tai Ping carpet, and classically styled furniture. As late as the 1950s, the lobby was divided into east and west wings—one for the British and one for everyone else, including, as one pamphlet put it, women "seeking dalliance." The fixed-price tea includes finger sandwiches, French pastries, and scones with clotted cream. No reservations are accepted, so you may have to wait for a table. Classical music emanates from an upstairs balcony.

What to See & Do in Hong Kong

Most people think of Hong Kong as an exotic shopping destination. In the past decade, however, Hong Kong has revved up its sight-seeing potential, opening new city parks and revamping older ones, constructing community art centers, expanding museums or developing new ones, and redesigning organized sight-seeing tours to reflect the territory's changing demographics. And if all you want to do is hike or lie on the beach, you can do that in Hong Kong, too.

To help you get the most out of your stay here, this chapter will suggest sight-seeing strategies; introduce you to the top sights; and discuss places of interest to children, organized tours, and sports.

If you want to do Hong Kong justice, you should plan to stay at least a week. Barring that, if you're on the go from dawn until past dusk, you can see quite a bit of the city and its outlying attractions in 3 to 5 days, simply because the colony is so compact and transportation is so efficient. To help you get the most out of your stay, the following suggested itineraries will guide you to the most important attractions.

SUGGESTED ITINERARIES

If You Have 1 Day

If you have only 1 day to spend here, I feel sorry for you. I think I'd have a coronary racing around in a panic trying to see everything, growing more anxious by the minute as I realized that there were so many more things I wouldn't have time for. The best thing to do if you have only 1 day is to devote the morning to a half-day organized sight-seeing tour, which should include a trip up to Victoria Peak and a tour of either Aw Boon Haw Tiger Balm Gardens or Stanley Market, and perhaps a drive to the southern end of the island to Aberdeen.

The afternoon should be structured according to your own interests, but ought to include a ride on the famous Star Ferry across Victoria Harbour. To get a feel for Hong Kong, you might want to board the double-decker tram on Hong Kong Island or follow part of the walking tour for either the Central and Western District or Kowloon (see Chapter 7). For one-stop shopping, try one of the large stores specializing in Chinese products such as Chinese Arts & Crafts Ltd., China Products Co., or Yue Hwa (see Chapter 8).

With only one evening, think about joining one of the organized evening tours. If you haven't yet visited Aberdeen, you might want to take a sunset cruise that includes a meal at one of the floating restaurants there. Tours can be booked through most tourist hotels in Hong Kong (for more information on evening tours, see Chapter 9, "Hong Kong After Dark").

If You Have 2 Days

Spend your first morning on a half-day tour of Hong Kong Island, as outlined above. Spend the rest of the afternoon on Hong Kong Island according to your interests—Stanley for bargain shopping, a tram ride to Causeway Bay, a visit to Hong Kong Park, a do-it-yourself tour of the Central and Western Districts for insight into traditional Chinese life, or a stop at Ocean Park and the Middle Kingdom. In the evening, take an organized evening tour, perhaps a sunset harbor cruise. If you'd rather be on your own, head back up to the top of Victoria Peak, where the view of Hong Kong takes on a whole new shimmering and romantic aspect after nightfall. Eat dinner at one of the Peak's restaurants, followed by the 1-hour circular walk around the Peak.

Start the next morning with dim sum at a Chinese restaurant. If you haven't yet ridden the Star Ferry, do so, or take a 1-hour cruise of the harbor. Spend the rest of the day exploring Kowloon, with visits to the Space Museum, the Hong Kong Science Museum, Museum of History, the many shops along Nathan Road, and the Jade Market. Begin the evening with a cocktail at one of Hong Kong's many lounges that offer a view of the harbor, followed by dinner at a Chinese or Western restaurant. Afterward, visit Temple Street Night Market with its festive atmosphere and outdoor stalls where clothing and accessories are sold. If you still have energy to spare after 11pm, head to one of Hong Kong's discos, where the action is just beginning.

If You Have 3 Days

Start your first day with a dim sum breakfast at a Chinese restaurant. Then, for your first breathtaking view of Hong Kong, ride the famous Star Ferry across Victoria Harbour. Afterward, for an even better perspective, take the tram to the top of Victoria Peak, where you'll be rewarded with a spectacular view of the city—that is, if the weather is clear. Take an hour's walk along the circular path around Victoria Peak, where you'll have changing vistas of Central, Kowloon, Aberdeen, and even Cheung Chau and other islands.

Have lunch at one of Central's many restaurants or at one of its English-style pubs, followed by a do-it-yourself walking tour of the Central and Western Districts, where you can observe traditional Chinese life firsthand, shop for antiques, and visit the Man Mo Temple. If you have time, see Aw Boon Haw Gardens or Hong Kong Park. For your first evening, try one of Hong Kong's organized evening tours, such as a sunset cruise. Alternatives include a nighttime visit to Victoria Peak or a tram ride to Causeway Bay.

Devote your second day to Kowloon. Start with a tour of Tsim Sha Tsui and Yau Ma Tei, where you can visit the Space Museum, Science Museum, Museum of History, and the Jade Market. Reserve time later in the day for shopping, including the many shops along Nathan Road and the huge shopping complexes, such as Harbour City. Visit the factory outlets in Tsim Sha Tsui or Hung Hom in Kowloon. When evening comes, head for a cocktail lounge that offers a view of the harbor, followed by dinner and then entertainment in a pub or disco.

For your last morning in Hong Kong, get up early and head for one of the outlying islands. Cheung Chau is good for a short excursion; Lamma is recommended if you want to do some hiking. (See Chapter 10 for descriptions of the outlying islands.) Spend the afternoon following your own inclinations: Stanley for shopping; Aberdeen for a sampan ride; a tram ride to Causeway Bay for more shopping;

What's Special About Hong Kong

Museums
- Hong Kong Museum of Art, with a wonderful collection of Chinese antiquities, paintings, and art.
- Hong Kong Museum of History, which presents the history of Hong Kong with vivid representations of daily life through the ages.
- Hong Kong Space Museum, with displays relating to space science and astronomy and the Space Theatre with thrilling Omnimax and Skyshow presentations.
- Hong Kong Science Museum, with sections devoted to science, life science, technology, and more, with plenty of action for the entire family.

Parks
- Hong Kong Park, with its dancing fountain, Southeast Asia's largest greenhouse, a wonderful aviary, and the Flagstaff House Museum of Tea Ware.
- Kowloon Park, with its outdoor swimming pools, open-air sculpture garden, children's playground, and Hong Kong Museum of History.

Especially For Kids
- Ocean Park, with performances by whales and dolphins, a shark aquarium, a bird aviary, playground, and the Middle Kingdom, a re-creation of an ancient Chinese village.
- Water World, with diving platforms, and even a pool with a sandy beach and waves.
- Zoological and Botanical Gardens, housing lions, jaguars, monkeys, and birds.
- The Space Museum and the newly opened Science Museum, with hands-on exhibits designed especially for children.

Transportation
- The Star Ferries, in use since 1898, offering one of the cheapest and yet most thrilling rides in the world.
- The Peak Tram, which carries passengers up Victoria Peak for a magnificent view of Hong Kong.
- Double-decker trams, providing an unparalleled view of Hong Kong Island.
- Ferries to outlying islands, with great views of Hong Kong along the way.

Outlying Islands
- Cheung Chau, a bustling island community with narrow streets and cottage industries, but no motorized vehicles.
- Lantau, home of the famous Po Lin Monastery and an interesting village called Tai O.
- Lamma, famous for its hiking trails and fresh seafood.

Events/Festivals
- The Hong Kong Arts Festival, with performances in pop, jazz, dance, and theater (Jan or Feb).
- Rugby Sevens, the most popular annual sporting event (March).
- Tin Hau Festival, in honor of the goddess of the sea (Apr or May).
- Cheung Chau Festival, held on the island of Cheung Chau and featuring a street parade (May).
- Dragon Boat Races, an international affair with hundreds of teams racing in long, narrow wooden boats (May or June).

Ocean Park and the Middle Kingdom; or Aw Boon Haw Gardens. After dinner at a traditional Chinese restaurant, take a stroll through Temple Street Night Market in Kowloon.

If You Have 5 Days or More

Consider yourself lucky! Spend the first 3 days as outlined above. Note, however, that if you're having an article of clothing custom-made, you should visit the tailor on your first day to discuss needs and fittings. On the fourth day, take a trip to the New Territories (see Chapter 10 for more information). The easiest way to see this vast area is by joining the 6-hour "Land Between" Tour, but you may prefer to explore the New Territories on your own via the Kowloon-Canton Railway. If you're interested in historical settings, one alternative might be to visit Sam Tung Uk Museum in Tsuen Wan, a restored Hakka walled village, followed by a bus trip to Kam Tin, a walled village still inhabited by the Hakka. If you have children or enjoy organized tours, you might want to join a tour of Sung Dynasty Village, a re-creation of the way a Chinese village may have looked 1,000 years ago. If you're not too tired by evening, take the tram to Victoria Peak (if you haven't done so already) for a romantic, spectacular nighttime view of Hong Kong, ablaze with glittering lights, or stroll the promenade along the Tsim Sha Tsui waterfront.

On the fifth day, spend the morning visiting another island. Devote the afternoon to all those things you haven't had time for—whether more shopping, sight-seeing, or unstructured exploration. If you haven't yet been to Stanley, Ocean Park, or Causeway Bay, for example, this is your last chance. If it's horse-racing season, try to get in on the action. If you've had something custom-made, don't forget to pick it up. For a memorable last evening in Hong Kong, splurge at one of Hong Kong's fine Chinese or Western restaurants.

If you still have time to spare, cross the Pearl River Estuary by jetfoil to the old Portuguese city of Macau, the first European settlement in the Far East (see Chapter 11 on Macau). You will find many great restaurants there, as well as expensive and moderately priced accommodations and more shopping opportunities. Or, if you wish, cross the border in the New Territories for a trip to China.

1 The Top Attractions

The four basic activities I would recommend to every visitor to Hong Kong are: ride the Star Ferry across the harbor, ride the peak tram to the top of Victoria Peak, ride one of the rickety old trams on Hong Kong Island, and take one of the ferries to the outlying islands (see Chapter 10, "Easy Excursions from Hong Kong," for information on the various islands, the ferries, and the fares). Nothing can beat the thrill of these four experiences, nor give you a better insight into the essence of Hong Kong and its people. What's more, they're all inexpensive.

✪ The Star Ferries

The stars of the show, of course, are the Star Ferries, green-and-white vessels that have been carrying passengers back and forth between Kowloon and Hong Kong Island since 1898. At only HK$1.40 (18¢) for the regular, lower-deck fare, it's one of the cheapest—and yet most dramatic—7-minute rides in the world. (For tips on using the Star Ferry, see "Getting Around" in Chapter 3.)

Since a 7-minute ride isn't nearly enough time to soak up the ambience of Victoria Harbour, you may want to board a special Star Ferry for a 1-hour harbor cruise. These cruises depart five times daily from both the Kowloon and Hong Kong sides. (For more information on this and other cruises, read "Organized Tours," below, or call 852/ 2366 7024.)

Hong Kong Attractions

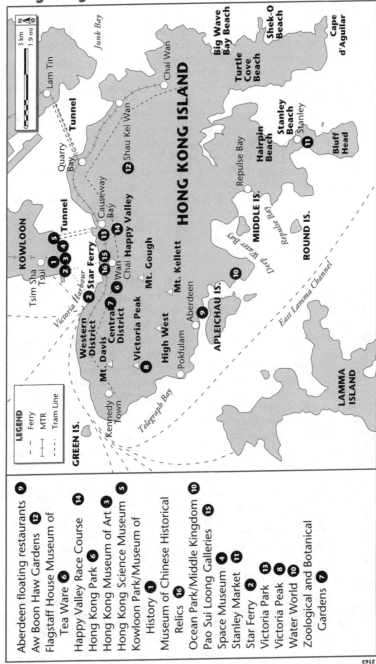

LEGEND
- - - Ferry
+--+ MTR
- · · - Tram Line

GREEN IS.

Junk Bay

Lam Tin

Quarry Bay

Tunnel

Chai Wan

Shau Kei Wan 12

Causeway Bay 13

Wan 14 Chai Happy Valley

HONG KONG ISLAND

Tsim Sha Tsui

KOWLOON

Tunnel

1
5
2 3 4
2 Star Ferry
16 15
6

Western District
Central District

Mt. Davis
Victoria Harbour

Mt. Gough

Mt. Kellett

2 7
Victoria Peak

High West
8

Aberdeen 9

Kennedy Town

Pokfulam

Telegraph Bay

APLEICHAU IS.

10

Repulse Bay

MIDDLE IS.

ROUND IS.

Deep Water Bay

Repulse Bay

East Lamma Channel

LAMMA ISLAND

Turtle Cove Beach

Big Wave Bay Beach

Shek-O Beach

Cape d'Aguilar

Stanley Beach

Hairpin Beach

Stanley 11

Bluff Head

Aberdeen floating restaurants 9
Aw Boon Haw Gardens 12
Flagstaff House Museum of Tea Ware 6
Happy Valley Race Course 14
Hong Kong Park 6
Hong Kong Museum of Art 3
Hong Kong Science Museum 5
Kowloon Park/Museum of History 1
Museum of Chinese Historical Relics 16
Ocean Park/Middle Kingdom 10
Pao Sui Loong Galleries 15
Space Museum 4
Stanley Market 11
Star Ferry 2
Victoria Park 13
Victoria Peak 8
Water World 10
Zoological and Botanical Gardens 7

✪ Victoria Peak

At 1,308 feet, Victoria Peak is Hong Kong Island's tallest hill and offers spectacular views of the city and surrounding area. It's always been one of the colony's most exclusive places to live, since the peak is typically cooler than the sweltering city below. A hundred years ago, the rich reached the peak after a 3-hour trip in sedan chairs, transported to the top by coolies. Then, in 1888, the **peak tram** began operations, cutting the journey from a grueling 3 hours to a mere 8 minutes.

In 1989 the original, cast-iron green funicular cars with mahogany seats were replaced by new, modern cars imported from Switzerland, which increased the passenger load from 72 to 120 people. I was sorry to see the old cars go, but I guess it will make life easier for the residents. After all, the peak tram is used by residents and tourists alike. Making several stops along the way, the tram takes children to and from school and commuters to and from work.

The easiest way to reach the peak tram station, located on Garden Road, is to take one of the free, open-top shuttle buses that operate between the tram terminal and the Star Ferry in Central (after you exit from the Star Ferry, turn left; shuttle buses depart from a traffic island located between the parking garage and City Hall). Shuttle buses run every 20 minutes from 10am to 8pm. Otherwise, it's about a 10-minute walk from Chater Garden.

One-way tickets for the peak tram cost HK$12 ($1.55) for adults and HK$4 (50¢) for children. Round-trip tickets cost HK$19 ($2.45) and HK$7 (90¢), respectively. Trams depart every 10 to 15 minutes and operate Sunday through Thursday from 7am to midnight and Friday and Saturday from 7am to 1:30am. The tram climbs almost vertically to the top of the peak—don't worry, there's never been an accident in its entire 100-odd years of operation. At the top there's the **Peak Galleria,** a three-story complex with shops, restaurants, children's playground, and a viewing terrace. Don't miss the wonderfully playful fountain in front of the Galleria, which seems to have a life of its own as it spouts water in mesmerizing rhythm combinations and sounds rather like a whale coming up for air.

But the best thing to do atop Victoria Peak is to take a walk. If you're feeling particularly energetic, you might want to hike up Mount Austin Road to the former site of the governor's summer lodge—usually shrouded in mist. Only the formal gardens remain, carefully tended and offering a pleasant respite from the congestion of the city below.

My favorite walk on Victoria Peak is the hour-long circular hike on Lugard Road and Harlech Road, both located just a stone's throw from the peak tram terminus. Mainly a footpath, it snakes along the side of the cliff, offering great views of the Central District below, the harbor, Kowloon, and then Aberdeen and the outlying islands on the other side. This is one of the best walks in Hong Kong; at night, it offers one of world's most romantic views. Don't miss it.

✪ A Tram Ride

Just as the Star Ferry is the best way to see the harbor, the tram is the most colorful and cheapest way to see the northern end of Hong Kong Island, including the Central District, Western District, Wan Chai, and Causeway Bay. In fact, the tram is so much a part of Hong Kong life that it was chosen for Hong Kong's exhibit at the Vancouver '86 Expo. Dating from 1904, the tram line follows what used to be the waterfront (before the days of land reclamation). Old, narrow, double-decker affairs, the trams cut through the heart of the city, from Kennedy Town in the west to Shau Kei Wan in the east. There's only one detour—off to Happy Valley—so it's impossible to get lost.

In any case, if you're in Central, you can board the tram on Des Voeux Road Central. Climb to the upper deck and try to get a seat in the front row. (For more information on the fare and how to ride the tram, see "Getting Around" in Chapter 3.) I especially like to ride the tram at night, when neon signs are ablaze and the outdoor markets of Causeway Bay are in full swing. If you're a tram nut, you may even want to take an organized tram tour that includes drinks (see "Organized Tours," below).

Ferries to the Outlying Islands
While most of Hong Kong's 235 outlying islands are uninhabited, ferry trips to the most interesting ones are described in Chapter 10, "Easy Excursions from Hong Kong." These ferries, which depart from the Central District, are the cheapest way to see Hong Kong harbor, with most trips lasting an hour or less. Some even offer an outside deck, where you can sit with a coffee or beer and watch Hong Kong float past.

2 More Attractions

Although Hong Kong is compact and easy to navigate, it makes sense to divide the city into sections when planning your sight-seeing. The following information on various attractions, therefore, is presented according to area. Don't forget to read over the suggested walking tours in Chapter 7, since they include stops at several of Hong Kong's top attractions.

For sight-seeing on the outlying islands and the New Territories, see Chapter 10.

If you plan to visit Hong Kong's four major museums—and I would strongly encourage you to do so if you have time—you'll want to take advantage of the special "Monthly Pass" for HK$50 ($6.50), which allows unlimited admissions for one month to the Hong Kong Museum of Art, Hong Kong Museum of History, Hong Kong Space Museum, and Hong Kong Science Museum and entitles you to a 10% discount on all purchases at the museums' shops. Otherwise, a regular single admission to each museum is HK$55 ($7.15).

HONG KONG ISLAND SIGHTS
With its 30 square miles, Hong Kong Island has the largest number of attractions for the visitor. This is where the colony's history began, and everything is here—from museums to gardens to beaches and amusement parks.

CENTRAL DISTRICT & VICINITY

Hong Kong Park
Supreme Court Rd. and Cotton Tree Dr., Central. ☎ 852/2521 5041. Free admission. Daily 6:30am–11pm (aviary open daily 9am–5pm in summer, 9am to 4:30pm in winter). MTR: Admiralty; then follow the signs through Pacific Place to escalators going up to Hong Kong Park.

Opened in 1991, Hong Kong's newest park features a dancing fountain at its entrance, Southeast Asia's largest greenhouse with more than 2,000 rare plant species, an aviary housing 500 exotic birds in a tropical setting with an elevated walkway, various gardens, a children's playground, and a viewing platform reached by climbing 105 stairs. The most famous building on the park grounds is the Flagstaff House Museum of Tea Ware (described below). Since the marriage registry is located at the edge of the park, the gardens are a favorite place for wedding photographs, especially on weekends and auspicious days of the Chinese calendar.

Flagstaff House Museum of Tea Ware

Hong Kong Park, Cotton Tree Dr., Central. ☎ **852/2869 0690.** Free admission. Thurs–Tues 10am–5pm. Closed Jan 1, first 3 days of the Chinese New Year, and Dec 25–26. MTR: Admiralty; then follow the signs through Pacific Place to Hong Kong Park.

Flagstaff House, located in Hong Kong Park, is the oldest colonial building in Hong Kong—the best place to go if you want to see typical Hong Kong architecture of 150 years ago. The house was built in 1844 in Greek Revival style for the commander of the British forces. Now a museum devoted to the subject of tea culture in China, its collection includes about 500 pieces of tea ware ranging from earthenware to porcelain, primarily of Chinese origin, dating from the 7th century to the present day. With explanations in both English and Chinese, the exhibits also describe methods of making the various kinds of tea favored by the major dynasties. Don't miss the museum shop, which sells beautifully crafted teapots and tea.

Zoological and Botanical Gardens

Upper Albert Rd., Central. ☎ **852/2530 0152** or 852/2530 0153. Free admission. Zoo daily 6am–7pm; botanical garden daily 6am–10pm. MTR: Central; then a 15-minute walk on Garden Road. Bus: no. 3 or no. 12 to Caritas Centre stop.

Established in 1864, these gardens on the slope of Victoria Peak are a popular respite for Hong Kong residents. Come here early, around 8am, and you'll see Chinese residents going through the slow motions of tai chi (shadowboxing), a disciplined physical routine of more than 200 individual movements, designed to exercise every muscle of the body and bring a sense of peace and balance to its practitioners. In the gardens themselves, flowers are almost always in bloom, from azaleas in the spring to wisteria and bauhinea in the summer and fall; plants in the botanical gardens include Burmese rosewood trees, Indian rubber trees, camphor trees, and the Hong Kong orchid. The small zoo houses mountain lions, jaguars, orangutans, and monkeys, and there's an aviary with about 1,400 birds representing 350 species, including Palawan peacocks, birds of paradise from Papua New Guinea, cranes, and Mandarin ducks. The zoo is well known for its success in breeding birds on the verge of extinction and for supplying zoos around the world with new stock. If you're tired of Central and its traffic, this is a pleasant place to regain your perspective.

Tsui Museum of Art

11th floor, Bank of China Building, 2A Des Voeux Rd., Central. ☎ **852/2868 2688.** Admission HK$20 ($2.60) adults, HK$10 ($1.30) children. Mon–Fri 10am–6pm, Sat 10am–2pm. Closed public holidays. MTR: Central.

This privately owned museum houses some 3,000 Chinese antiquities, including bronzes, bamboo, wood and ivory carvings, jade, enameled ware, glass, and furniture, which are displayed on a rotating basis. Its most prominent collection, however, is that of Chinese ceramics, which span 5,000 years from the Neolithic period to the Qing dynasty. Look for the museum's most prized possession—a Ming dynasty blue-and-white porcelain dish with a bird perched on a lychee branch. Nearby is a doughnut-shaped blue-and-white porcelain container; used to store the jade belt of a major official, it is one of only three such pieces in the world. Two rooms of the museum are outfitted in Qing period furniture, representing an imperial official's office and a scholar's study. Small and pleasant, the museum also features temporary displays.

WESTERN DISTRICT

Fung Ping Shan Museum

94 Bonham Rd., University of Hong Kong, Sai Ying Pun. ☎ **852/2859 2114.** Free admission. Mon–Sat 9:30am–6pm. Closed public holidays, Chinese New Year's Eve, Mar 16, Christmas Eve,

and New Year's Eve. Bus: no. 3 from Edinburgh Place (outside City Hall); get off at the Bonham Road stop opposite St. Paul's College.

This university museum, west of Central, has collections of Chinese art, primarily ceramics and bronzes. The bronze collection includes Shang and Zhou ritual vessels, decorative mirrors, and 967 Nestorian crosses of the Yuan dynasty, the world's largest collection.

The ceramics collection includes painted pottery of the third millennium B.C., tomb pottery of the Han dynasty, three-color glazes of the T'ang dynasty, wares of the Song dynasty kilns, blue-and-white wares, monochromes and polychromes of the Ming and Qing dynasties, and recent works by Jingdezhen and Shiwan potters.

CAUSEWAY BAY/WAN CHAI

Hong Kong Arts Centre Pao Galleries

Fourth and 5th floors, Hong Kong Arts Centre, 2 Harbour Rd., Wan Chai. ☎ **852/2582 0256.** Free admission. Daily 10am–8pm. Closed during exhibition changes. MTR: Wan Chai.

Changing exhibitions of contemporary international and local art include paintings, graphic art, sculpture, photography, crafts, and calligraphy.

Museum of Chinese Historical Relics

Causeway Centre, 28 Harcourt Rd., Wan Chai. ☎ **852/2827 4692.** Admission usually free to special exhibits; HK$5 (65¢) to museum. Mon–Sat 10am–6pm, Sun 1–6pm (subject to change). MTR: Wan Chai.

China, its products and handcrafts, as well as its art are the subject of the changing displays here. One exhibition, for example, showcased products made in Shanghai from machinery to clothing. Another displayed works of contemporary mainland Chinese craftsmen, with jewelry, teapots, and other items offered for sale. To the side of the large exhibition space is the small, one-room Museum of Chinese Historical Relics, with displays of archaeological finds from the Neolithic Age (7,000 years ago) to the Ching dynasty of the early 20th century. Before making a special trip here, be sure to call in advance for information on current exhibits, admission price, and opening times.

Police Museum

27 Coombe Rd., Wan Chai. ☎ **852/2849 7019.** Free admission. Tues 2–5pm, Wed–Sun 9am–5pm. Closed public holidays. Bus: no. 15 from Exchange Square in Central; get off at Stubbs Road and Peak Road.

Located on the site of the former Wan Chai Gap Police Station, this museum highlights the history of the Royal Hong Kong Police Force from its inception in 1844 to the present day. In addition to uniforms, historic documents, and descriptions of the development of the force, there are displays relating to the triad societies and narcotics (remember, Hong Kong was founded on the narcotics trade).

Noon Day Gun

Gloucester Rd., Causeway Bay. MTR: Causeway Bay.

This may not be worth going out of your way to see, but if you're near the Excelsior Hotel, look for a small garden opposite the hotel near the harbor (accessible via a tunnel under Gloucester Road, with an entrance west of the Excelsior in front of the World Trade Center). There you'll find a gun, a well-known historical landmark associated with Jardine, Matheson & Co., Hong Kong's oldest trading house. Pointing out over the Royal Hong Kong Yacht Club, the gun is fired every day at noon, an act immortalized in Noël Coward's *Mad Dogs and Englishmen*: "In Hong Kong they strike a gong and fire off the noon day gun, to reprimand each inmate who's in late." The tradition, so they say, started in the last century when the Jardine trading company fired off a double-gun salute to welcome its returning bosses. The salute, usually reserved for the military, so incensed a senior British naval officer that he ordered the Jardines to fire the gun every day at noon as punishment. Now, of course, it's a tradition.

Victoria Park

Causeway and Gloucester Rds., Causeway Bay. Free admission. Daily 24 hours. MTR: Causeway Bay.

This 19-acre park is one of Hong Kong's largest, serving as the green lungs of the city. Constructed on land formerly used for a typhoon shelter, it has tennis and squash courts, a 50-meter swimming pool, soccer fields, basketball courts, playgrounds, a skating rink, and a jogging track. The Mid-Autumn Festival is held here, as well as a flower market a few days before Chinese New Year.

Aw Boon Haw Gardens

Tai Hang Rd., Causeway Bay. Free admission. Daily 9:30am–4pm. Bus: no. 11 from the Exchange Square Bus Terminal in Central or the Causeway Bay MTR station; get off after passing the Lai Tak Tsuen public housing project when you see a white pagoda ahead of you.

Formerly known as the Tiger Balm Gardens, these are probably the most bizarre gardens you'll ever see. They were created in 1935 by Chinese millionaire and philanthropist Aw Boon Haw, who made his fortune with a cure-all ointment called Tiger Balm. The 7½-acre gardens feature grottoes and colorfully painted statues from Chinese mythology, some of which are rather grotesque, especially those depicting unfortunate souls being tortured in hell. The message here is quite clear: behave yourself, or else! Because the gardens are so colorful, you can get some great photographs to show the folks back home.

ABERDEEN

Situated on the south side of Hong Kong Island, Aberdeen is nestled around a naturally protected harbor. Famous for its colorful floating seafood restaurants and boat people who live on junks in Aberdeen Harbour, the town has undergone massive changes in recent years. Originally a typhoon shelter and land base for seafarers, it used to be a charming fishing village and boatbuilding port, supported primarily by several thousand junks and boat people. Many of the boat people, however, have been moved to massive housing projects, and the waterfront surrounding Aberdeen is now crowded with high-rises.

Still, Aberdeen continues to be popular with the tourist crowd because of its remaining boat population and floating restaurants. Women operating sampans will vie for your dollars to tour you around the harbor, which is definitely worth the price since it's about the only thing to do here and is the best way to see the junks. Although the boat population is shrinking, you'll pass huge boats that house extended families; you'll see men repairing fishing nets, women hanging out their laundry, dogs barking and children playing, and families eating. There was a time when a boat person could be born, live, marry, and die on board without ever setting a foot on shore. Nowadays, however, young people are moving to shore to seek more stable employment.

A 20-minute tour from a licensed operator such as Watertours will cost approximately HK$50 ($6.50) per person and is offered daily between 9am and 5pm. There are also old women with wide-brimmed straw hats who will try to persuade you to board their sampan, with the price open to bargaining and dependent on the tourist trade. On one particularly slow day, for example, I was offered, and took, a sampan tour for HK$40 ($5.20), and I was the only one in the boat.

Other Aberdeen attractions include its floating restaurants—Jumbo and Tai Pak (see Chapter 5, "Dining") and a Tin Hau temple. Built in 1851, the temple is dedicated to Tin Hau, protectress of fishing folk, and is located at the junction of Aberdeen Main Road and Aberdeen Reservoir Road.

To get to Aberdeen, take bus no. 7 or 70 from the Exchange Square Bus Terminal in the Central District or bus no. 72 from Causeway Bay.

DEEP WATER BAY

☼ Ocean Park and Middle Kingdom

☎ **852/2552 0291** or 852/2555 3554. Admission HK$130 ($16.90) adults, HK$65 ($8.40) children ages 3–11. One adult may bring one child under the age of 12 into the park free. Daily 10am–6pm. Bus: Ocean Park Citybus from the Admiralty MTR station every half hour (buy round-trip tickets, which include park admission, for HK$146, or $18.96, for adults and HK$73, or $9.50, for children, at major MTR stations); or no. 70 from Exchange Square in Central or no. 72 from Causeway Bay (get off at the first stop after the tunnel). Minibus: no. 6 from Star Ferry in Central except Sunday.

If you're a kid or a kid at heart, you'll love Ocean Park, a combination marine park and amusement center, which also includes a replica of an old Chinese village. Situated along a dramatic rocky coastline on the island's southern shore, the park is divided into two areas, a "lowland" and a "headland."

The lowland boasts greenhouses with cacti, foliage, orchids, and other flowering plants; a butterfly house (shaped, interestingly enough, like a caterpillar) with 1,000 free-flying butterflies; and the Golden Pagoda, with more varieties of goldfish than you ever imagined possible, most of them from China. The Pompomed Bull goldfish, for example, has large pompomlike growths on its head, while the Dragon Eyes goldfish has huge buglike eyes. And then there's the Lamp Dragon Eyes, too bizarre for words. For children, there's the Dinosaur Discovery Trail, with 17 lifelike models of dinosaurs, and Kids' World, with kiddie rides, trains, playgrounds, a games arcade, and shows geared to children.

From the lowland, visitors board cable cars for a spectacular 10-minute ride over a hill to the headland, while being treated to great views along the way. The headland area, situated on a peninsula that juts into the sea, has an artificial wave cove that is home to seals, sea lions, and penguins; it also offers various thrill rides, including a Ferris wheel and a roller coaster that turns upside down three times. Ocean Theatre features shows by talented dolphins, sea lions, and a killer whale. Other exhibits include a Japanese Garden; a 230-foot-high Ocean Park Tower offering panoramic views of southern Hong Kong Island; the Shark Aquarium, with 40 species of sharks; and the Aviary, with 2,000 birds. But my favorite is the Atoll Reef, one of the world's largest aquariums, with 5,000 fish of 500 different species. The observation passageway circles three stories outside the aquarium, enabling you to see from different angles everything from giant turtles to schools of tropical fish.

After touring the headland, take the long escalator down to the Middle Kingdom. Opened in 1989, this is a small, re-created village from China's past with full-size temples, shrines, pavilions, pagodas, street scenes, and public squares. Its streets lead visitors past 13 dynasties of Chinese history, each represented by a building, statue, or object. Representing the Ming dynasty (A.D. 1368–1644), for example, is a replica of a boat used by Admiral Cheng Ho, who traveled as far west as the Red Sea; from the third century B.C. are replica terra-cotta figures—soldiers, horses, and a chariot—unearthed near Xian. Throughout the Middle Kingdom are various craftspeople at work making paper, silk weavings, iron castings, pottery, and glass.

Shops sell a variety of Chinese products, from writing instruments to tea, engravings, and incense. There are also performances by Chinese acrobats and magicians.

Water World

☎ **852/2555 6055.** Admission HK$60 ($7.80) adults, HK$30 ($3.90) children; after 5pm HK$40 ($5.20) adults, HK$20 ($2.60) children. July–Aug daily 9am–9pm; June and mid-Sept daily 10am–6pm. Closed Oct–May. Bus: Ocean Park Citybus from Admiralty MTR station (HK$10, $1.30, one way); or minibus no. 6 from Star Ferry on Hong Kong Island daily except Sun.

Located next to Ocean Park's lowland entrance and under the same management, Water World is a good place to cool off on a hot summer's day. It contains several pools with various slides and diving platforms, a rapids ride, and even a pool with a sandy beach and waves. Don't forget your bathing suit.

STANLEY

When Hong Kong Island was ceded to the British in the 1840s, Stanley was one of the largest fishing villages on the island, with a population of 2,000. Today it's a residential area of about 6,000 and has become a rather fashionable address.

The best-known attraction in Stanley is its daily **market,** a mecca for those in search of inexpensive jeans, silk, and sportswear. Other attractions include a **Tin Hau temple,** built in 1767; a **Kwun Yum temple**, with a 20-foot statue of Kwun Yum, the goddess of mercy; and **Stanley Main Beach,** popular in the summer for swimming.

To get there, take bus no. 6 or no. 260 from Exchange Square in Central. If you're coming from Aberdeen, take bus no. 73 from Aberdeen Main Road.

KOWLOON SIGHTS

In addition to its myriad hotels, restaurants, and shops, southern Kowloon has a number of attractions that are worth visiting. More information on Kowloon, especially at its northern end near the border of the New Territories, is presented in Chapter 10, under "The New Territories."

✪ Space Museum

10 Salisbury Rd., Tsim Sha Tsui. ☎ **852/2734 2722.** Admission to museum HK$10 ($1.30) adults, HK$5 (65¢) children, students, and senior citizens; Space Theatre HK$26 ($3.40) adults, HK$13 ($1.70) children, students, and senior citizens. Mon and Wed–Fri 1–9pm, Sat–Sun and holidays 10am–9pm. MTR: Tsim Sha Tsui.

Located in front of The Peninsula Hotel on the Tsim Sha Tsui waterfront, the Space Museum is easy to spot with its white-domed planetarium. It's divided into three parts: the Hall of Space Science, the Hall of Astronomy, and the Space Theatre. The Hall of Space Science includes exhibits on ancient astronomical history, science fiction, early rockets, manned spaceflights, and future space programs. The Hall of Astronomy presents information on the solar system, solar science, the stars, and the universe, including a small theater for relevant presentations.

The Space Theatre, a planetarium with a 75-foot domed roof, has a Zeiss star projector that can project up to about 9,000 stars and an Omnimax projection system that produces an almost 360° panorama. Hour-long shows, which range from celestial phenomena like the Milky Way to such wonders of the world as the Great Barrier Reef, are given throughout the afternoon and evening every day except Tuesday; on Sundays and holidays the shows begin at 11:30am. Only a few shows are narrated in English; in the case of those that are not, free headsets are available with simultaneous English translations. Buy your ticket at least a day in advance, either at the museum or any URBTIX outlet. Call 852/2734 2722 for show schedules.

Hong Kong Museum of Art

Hong Kong Cultural Centre, Salisbury Rd., Tsim Sha Tsui. ☎ **852/2734 2167.** Admission HK$10 ($1.30) adults, HK$5 (65¢) students and senior citizens. Fri–Sat and Mon–Wed 10am–6pm, Sun and holidays 1–6pm. Closed Jan 1, first 3 days of Chinese New Year, and Dec 25–26. MTR: Tsim Sha Tsui.

If you visit only one museum in Hong Kong, this should be it. Located on the Tsim Sha Tsui waterfront between the Cultural Centre and Space Museum and just a 2-minute walk from the Star Ferry terminus, this museum has a vast collection of Chinese antiquities, including ceramics, bronzes, jade, cloisonné, lacquerware, bamboo carvings, and textiles, as well as paintings and calligraphy dating from the 16th century to the present. The works are arranged in five permanent galleries on three floors of exhibit space, plus one gallery devoted to changing exhibits. The Historical Pictures Gallery is especially insightful, with 1,000 works in oils, watercolors, pencil drawings, and prints that provide a visual account of life in Hong Kong, Macau, and Guangzhou in the late 18th and 19th centuries.

Hong Kong Science Museum

2 Science Museum Rd., Tsim Sha Tsui East. ☎ **852/2732 3232.** Admission HK$25 ($3.25) adults, HK$12.50 ($1.60) children, students, and senior citizens. Tues–Fri 1–9pm, Sat–Sun 10am–9pm. MTR: Tsim Sha Tsui.

Opened in 1991, this is a "living" museum, with plenty of hands-on exhibits relating to science that are sure to appeal to children and adults alike. Exhibits cover four floors, with sections devoted to science, life science, technology, and an area specially designed for children between the ages of 3 and 7. Visitors can play with different optical illusions, enter a rotating room to learn physics in a noninertial frame, and pick up remote voices with a large parabolic disc. There are exhibits designed to test a visitor's fitness, such as lung capacity, endurance, and blood pressure. In the computer section are more than 30 personal computers, where guests can learn about computer software ranging from word processing for children to learning how to type and how to produce graphics.

Hong Kong Museum of History

Kowloon Park, Haiphong Rd. or Nathan Rd., Tsim Sha Tsui. ☎ **852/2367 1124.** Admission HK$10 adults ($1.30), HK$5 (65¢) children, students, and senior citizens. Mon–Thurs and Sat 10am–6pm, Sun and holidays 1–6pm. Closed Jan 1, first 3 days of the Chinese New Year, and Dec 25–26. MTR: Tsim Sha Tsui.

Housed in two former barracks dating from the late 19th century, this museum outlines the history of Hong Kong from its beginnings as a Neolithic settlement to its development as a fishing village and then to a modern metropolis. Through displays that include replicas of fishing boats, furniture, clothing, and items from daily life, the museum introduces Hong Kong's ethnic groups and their traditional means of livelihood, customs, and beliefs. My favorite part of the museum is a re-created street in old Hong Kong, complete with a Chinese herbal medicine shop originally located in Central 100 years ago and reconstructed here. There are also 19th- and early 20th-century photographs, poignantly showing how much Hong Kong has changed through the decades. My only complaint is that the museum seems too small for its intended purpose; it barely scratches the surface of a fascinating and complex history.

Kowloon Park

Nathan and Austin Rds., Tsim Sha Tsui. Admission to Kowloon Park free; swimming pools HK$17 ($2.20) adults, HK$8 ($1.05) children. Kowloon Park daily 6am–midnight; children's playground daily 6:30am–9pm; aviary daily 7am–7pm; swimming pools daily 6:30am–9pm. MTR: Tsim Sha Tsui.

Occupying the site of an old military encampment first established in the 1860s, Kowloon Park boasts an indoor heated Olympic-size swimming pool, three outdoor leisure pools linked by a series of waterfalls, an open-air sculpture garden featuring works by local and overseas sculptors, a Chinese garden, a fitness trail, an aviary, a maze formed by hedges, a children's playground, and a bird lake with flamingos and other waterfowl. The Hong Kong Museum of History (described above) is also in Kowloon Park.

Jade Market

Kansu St., Yau Ma Tei. Free admission. Daily 10am–3pm. MTR: Yau Ma Tei or Jordan.

More than 400 vendors sell jade and freshwater pearls here, laying out their wares on everything from cloths spread out on the sidewalk to satin-lined display cases. Morning is the best time to visit. Unless you're an expert, don't buy anything here, other than perhaps a small souvenir (jade represents eternal life).

Bird Market

Hong Lok St. (between Argyle and Nelson Streets), Mong Kok. Free admission. Daily 10am–5pm. Closed Chinese New Year. MTR: Mong Kok (take the Nelson Street western exit).

Two blocks west of Nathan Road (off Argyle Street), there's a fascinating lane filled with shop after shop selling songbirds, beautifully crafted wood and bamboo cages, live crickets and mealy worms, and tiny porcelain food bowls. Nothing, it seems, is too expensive for these tiny creatures. The lane is also crowded with scores of people buying and selling birds, or perhaps just taking their birds for an outing. This lane is very Chinese and a lot of fun to see. Incidentally, birds are favorite pets in Chinese households and the price of a bird is determined not by its plumage but by its singing talents. *Note:* The Bird Market is scheduled to move to another site, the Yuen Po Street Mongkok Complex, by the end of 1996; inquire at HKTA.

---

❷ Did You Know?

- Hong Kong has the largest American Chamber of Commerce outside the United States.
- Hong Kong is the world's third-largest financial market (after New York and London).
- Hong Kong is the world's second busiest container port.
- Hong Kong is the world's largest exporter of watches and radios, second-largest of toys and clothing.
- The world's largest neon sign is in Hong Kong: it is an advertisement for Marlboro cigarettes that measures 210 by 55 feet, contains 35,000 feet of tubing, and weighs 126 tons.
- The world's largest wall of glass is in Hong Kong: at the Hong Kong Convention and Exhibition Centre.
- Hong Kong has the world's highest per capita consumption of cognac and per capita ownership of cellular phones and Rolls-Royces.
- About 98% of Hong Kong households have television, and about 66% have a VCR.
- The Hong Kong Housing Authority is the world's largest public landlord; more than half the population lives in public housing; and the world's largest public housing project is in Hong Kong.

Sung Dynasty Village

Mei Lai Rd., Kowloon. ☎ **852/2741 5111.** Admission HK$120 ($15.60) adults, HK$85 ($11.05) children; Sat–Sun and holidays noon–5pm, HK$80 ($10.40) adults, HK$35 ($4.55) children. Daily 10am–8pm. Bus: no. 6A from Star Ferry; then a 4-minute walk. MTR: Mei Foo Station; then a 20-minute walk north along Lai Wan Road and Mei Lai Road.

This small replica of the way a Chinese village may have looked 1,000 years ago during the Sung dynasty took 5 years to construct and cost the equivalent of $2 million U.S. Re-created with close attention to architectural detail, the village consists of open-fronted wooden shops, stalls, and buildings grouped around a willow-lined stream. Staffed by villagers dressed in Sung dynasty costumes, each shop is based on a different theme and offers a different product, from almond cookies and Chinese tea to hand-painted fans and incense. There's a rice wine shop, an herbal medicine shop, a Chinese restaurant, and a replica of a rich man's house. There's also entertainment, from a monkey show to Chinese acrobatics and opera.

3 Especially for Kids

Several attractions listed above would especially appeal to children.

On the Kowloon side, the **Space Museum** is very much oriented to children, with buttons to push, telescopes to look through, and computer quizzes to test what they've learned, not to mention the films featured in the Space Theatre. The **Science Museum** also has lots of hands-on exhibits, including a special play area for children between the ages of 3 and 7.

Sung Dynasty, a replica of a Chinese village, is a fantasy-filled experience for children, who love the monkey and acrobatic shows. Next door is **Lai Chi Kok** (☎ 852/2741 4281), a small, rather old-fashioned amusement park popular with Chinese families for its rides, shooting galleries, and Chinese opera performances. It's open Monday through Friday from 11am to 9:30pm, on Saturday from 11am to 10:30pm and on Sunday and holidays from 10am to 9pm. Admission is HK$15 ($1.95) for adults and HK$10 ($1.30) for children. And don't forget **Kowloon Park** right on Nathan Road, which has a playground for children, a pond with flamingos and other waterfowl, an aviary, swimming pools, and lots of space to run.

On Hong Kong Island, the biggest draw for kids of all ages is **Ocean Park,** which boasts a wide mix of things to do and see, including thrill rides; a shark aquarium; animal performances; life-size dinosaurs; and a children's section with rides, a playground, a games arcade, and lots more. Of all the things to do in Hong Kong, this is probably the one kids enjoy most. Next door is **Water World**, with its swimming pools, water rides, and slides. For free entertainment, visit the **Zoological and Botanical Gardens** with the monkeys, birds, and other animals; **Aw Boon Haw Gardens** with its macabre statues (sure to intrigue teenagers); and **Hong Kong Park** with its greenhouse, aviary, and children's playground.

4 Organized Tours

Hong Kong offers lots of organized tours, so if you're pressed for time this may be the best way to go.

CITY TOURS

For general sight-seeing, the Hong Kong Island Tour is a 4- to 5-hour trip offered both morning and afternoon and may include stops at Victoria Peak, Aberdeen, Stanley, and Aw Boon Haw Gardens. On the Kowloon side, there's the 4- to 5-hour

Kowloon and New Territories Tour, with takes in the industrial area of Kowloon and the rural regions and satellite towns of the New Territories, with stops that may include a 200-year-old walled village now serving as a museum, a Buddhist or Taoist temple, a rural market, and the walled village of Kam Tin. Prices for both tours depend on the routes taken; they range from HK$185 to HK$220 ($24 to $28.55) for adults and HK$100 to HK$160 ($13 to $20.80) for children.

There are also organized tours to Ocean Park, Cheung Chau Island, Lantau Island, and Sung Dynasty Village, but I personally think you're much better off exploring these areas on your own. All tours can be booked through your hotel, a travel agent, or the HKTA.

For information about organized evening tours, see Chapter 9, "Hong Kong After Dark."

SPECIAL-INTEREST TOURS

These tours, all organized and offered by the Hong Kong Tourist Authority, are highly recommended. Some, such as the Family Insight Tour or Heritage Tour, would be very difficult, if not impossible, to do on your own. Others, such as the "Land Between" Tour and the "Come Horse Racing" Tour, make life easier because they leave the driving to HKTA.

THE "LAND BETWEEN" TOUR   This is a 6-hour excursion, with departures every day except Sundays and public holidays; visitors are taken through the New Territories via air-conditioned motorcoach, enabling them to see the development of this part of Hong Kong and how it contrasts with the older section. Passing satellite towns with high-rise apartment buildings, farms, and villages, the bus stops at: a Buddhist monastery, a lookout point on Hong Kong's tallest mountain, the traditional rural market at Luen Wo, a bird sanctuary, a fishing village, and a Cantonese restaurant for lunch. The price of this tour is HK$335 ($43.50) for adults and HK$285 ($37.10) for children under 16 and seniors 60 and over.

FAMILY INSIGHT TOUR   This is my favorite HKTA-sponsored tour because it gives participants the chance to learn about the daily life of ordinary Hong Kong residents; it focuses on the large proportion (more than half) of Hong Kong's population who now lives in government housing estates. Each of these publicly funded estates is like a self-contained city, with approximately six to eight 30-story apartment blocks and its own shopping, recreational, and educational facilities. Each apartment block contains about 1,000 flats—tiny, one-room units (about 250 square feet in size) usually shared by two parents and two children. This tour lets you see such a home and visit with the family that lives there; it also takes you to a children's day-care center, a "dry" market that sells ordinary household goods, and the Wong Tai Sin Temple. Very educational. Tours, lasting approximately 4 hours, are scheduled once a week on Thursday (unless it's a public holiday) and cost HK$240 ($31.15) for adults and HK$200 ($25.95) for senior citizens and children.

HERITAGE TOUR   This tour explores Hong Kong's past by taking visitors to sites in the New Territories that even Hong Kong residents seldom see; it is a *must* for those who are interested in local historical architecture. Two options are available, one lasting approximately 5 hours and the other 8¹/₂ hours. The half-day tour departs every Wednesday, Friday, and Saturday (except public holidays) and costs HK$295 ($38.30) for adults and HK$245 ($31.20) for senior citizens. Stops include Sam Tung Uk Museum, a 200-year-old walled village and now a museum; Tai Fu Tai, a Chinese-style ornate mansion built in 1865; Man Shek Tong, an ancestral hall; and a temple and marketplace in Tai Po.

The 8¹/₂-hour tour, departing every Monday (except public holidays) and costing HK$480 ($62.35) for adults and HK$430 ($55.85) for senior citizens, covers the same highlights as the half-day tour, and then continues with lunch and visits to the Kun Ting Study Hall, built in 1870 for education and ancestor worship; the Tang Ancestral Hall, one of the biggest such halls in the New Territories and an excellent example of traditional Chinese architecture; Sheung Cheung Wai, a walled village; and the Tsui Shing Lau Pagoda, Hong Kong's only authentic, ancient pagoda.

"COME HORSE RACING" TOUR   Yet another HKTA-sponsored tour, this one allows visitors to experience the excitement of the races, at either Happy Valley or Sha Tin, an excitement that grows proportionately according to how much you bet. Tours are only scheduled during the horse-racing season—September through May—on Wednesday evenings and on Saturday and/or Sunday afternoons. Included in the tour price is a prerace Western-style buffet lunch or dinner, personal entry badge to the luxurious Visitors' Box in the Members' Enclosure, transportation, guide services, and even hints to help you place your bets. Tours are limited to individuals over 18 years of age who have been in Hong Kong fewer than 21 days (be sure to bring your passport with you when booking and participating in this tour). More information on the horse races is presented in "Spectator Sports," below. The price of the tour is HK$490 ($63.65).

SPORTS AND RECREATION TOUR   Sports enthusiasts may want to take advantage of the Sports and Recreation Tour, which takes participants to the Clearwater Bay Golf and Country Club on Sai Kung Peninsula for an entire day. At the club there is a golf course, outdoor tennis courts, squash and badminton courts, an outdoor swimming pool, saunas, and a Jacuzzi. Tours are offered only on Tuesday and Friday (except public holidays) and last approximately 8 hours, including travel time. Costing HK$380 ($49.35) for adults and HK$330 ($42.85) for seniors, the tour price includes only transportation to and from the club, lunch, and admission to the club. Use of the facilities costs extra. Greens fees are an additional HK$1,000 ($129.85) for 18 holes; tennis costs HK$70 ($9.10) per hour. Both clubs and racquets are available for rent. Use of the swimming pool, open April to November, is HK$45 ($5.85).

BOAT TOURS

Since so many of Hong Kong's attractions are on the water, there is a large variety of boat tours. The most popular and frequent one is the harbor cruise; others that last from 1 to 7¹/₂ hours range from the harbor itself to Aberdeen and the outlying islands, including lunch, sunset, and evening cruises, as well as combination water-and-land tours. For complete information, consult the sight-seeing desk at your hotel, a travel agent, or the HKTA; hotels and travel agents can help you with bookings.

One of the most popular cruises is the 1-hour trip aboard a **Star Ferry.** Departing from the Star Ferry piers in both Central and Tsim Sha Tsui, the cruise takes passengers past the Macau Ferry Terminal, the Central District, Causeway Bay Typhoon Shelter, North Point, the airport runway, and Tsim Sha Tsui East. There are seven departures daily: 11am and 12:30, 2, 3:15, 6:45, 8, and 9:15pm (it would be wise to verify these times). The cruises, which include complimentary drinks, cost HK$130 ($16.90) for adults and HK$90 ($11.70) for children and can be booked at the Star Ferry terminals.

Watertours (☎ 852/2525 4808 or 852/2526 3538), Hong Kong's largest tour operator of boat and junk cruises, also offers a 1-hour cruise costing HK$130

($16.90) for adults and HK$100 ($13) for children, including unlimited soft drinks and beer. They also schedule about 20 other longer boat trips, including Chinese junk cruises to Aberdeen, and sunset and evening cruises. Particularly interesting is the nightly 3-hour Lei Yue Mun Dinner Cruise, which includes a seafood dinner and a tour through Lei Yue Mun, famous for its endless stalls where live fish, lobsters, and other seafood are sold.

TRAM TOURS   Two of Hong Kong's original trams from the early part of this century have been refurbished for the **Open Top Tram Tour,** which lasts 2 hours. Costing HK$125 ($16.25) for adults and HK$90 ($11.70) for children, the price includes drinks for participants to enjoy while they rumble through colorful neighborhoods on Hong Kong Island. At last check, there were four tours a day: at 10:15am, noon, 1:45pm, and 3:30pm, with departure from the Central ferry pier. For more information, call 852/2366 7024 or 852/2845 2324. Tickets are available at both the Tsim Sha Tsui and Central Star Ferry terminals.

5 Outdoor Activities

Despite the fact that Hong Kong is densely populated, there's enough open space to pursue everything from golf to hiking to windsurfing. For the hardworking Chinese and expatriates, recreation and leisure are essential for relaxing and winding down. With that in mind, try to schedule your golfing, swimming, or hiking trips on week-days unless you enjoy jostling elbows with the crowds.

GOLF   It's not as cheap to play golf as it used to be. Greens fees have tripled in the past decade, driven up no doubt by the flocks of golfing enthusiasts from Japan, where the cost of a game is through the roof. But compared with playing golf in Japan, Hong Kong is a giveaway.

The **Royal Hong Kong Golf Club** maintains courses in both Fanling (☎ 852/2670 1211) and Deep Water Bay (☎ 852/2812 7070) and welcomes visitors Monday through Friday only (except public holidays). No advance reservations are taken, so visitors should arrive early. There are three 18-hole courses in Fanling, in the New Territories, with greens fees at HK$1,400 ($182.80); you should begin playing between 7:30 and 11:30am. Deep Water Bay, on Hong Kong Island, is a 9-hole course, with greens fees at HK$400 ($51.95) for 18 holes. Club rentals are extra.

The **Discovery Bay Golf Club,** on Lantau Island (☎ 852/2987 7271), has a beautiful 18-hole course developed by Robert Trent Jones Jr., offering great views of Hong Kong and the harbor. Visitors are allowed to play here Monday through Friday (except public holidays), and greens fees range from HK$800 ($103.90) if you play between 4 and 6:30pm to HK$900 ($116.90) for day and night golfing. Clubs and carts cost extra.

Another scenic 18-hole course, operated by the **Clearwater Bay Golf and Country Club** (☎ 852/2719 5936), is located near Sai Kung. Visitors' greens fees are HK$1,200 ($143). On weekends, guests must be signed in by a member, but greens fees remain the same. If you're interested in playing golf here but want to let someone else arrange for transportation, contact the HKTA for its Sports and Recreation Tour, described in "Organized Tours," above.

HIKING   With 21 country parks—amounting to more than 40% of Hong Kong's space—there are many trails of varying levels of difficulty throughout Hong Kong. Serious hikers, for example, may want to consider the **MacLehose Trail** in Sai Kung, which stretches about 60 miles through eight county parks in the New

Territories, or the **Lantau Trail,** a 43-mile circular trail on Lantau Island. The Lantau Trail begins and ends at Mui Wo (also called Silvermine Bay), passing several popular scenic spots and campsites along the way and including a $2^1/_2$-hour trek to the top of Lantau Peak. Both the MacLehose and Lantau Trails are divided into smaller sections of varying difficulty, which means that you can tailor your hike to suit your own abilities and time constraints. The Hong Kong Government Publications Office, located on the ground floor of the main post office in Central (right next to the Star Ferry concourse), has leaflets on county parks and maps, including the excellent "Countryside Series."

The HKTA also offers a comprehensive self-guided walking tour of Sai Kung, called the *Sai Kung Explorer's Guide;* it is available for HK$28 ($3.65). The guide takes hikers to the most important sights and vistas in Sai Kung, located in the New Territories; this is Hong Kong's second-largest and least-populated district. Included are walks that cover Sai Kung Town, a public market, temples, a folk museum, nature trails, an island, and a Chinese herbal garden.

JOGGING   The best places to jog on Hong Kong Island without dodging traffic are **Victoria Park's jogging track** in Causeway Bay and **Bowen Road,** which stretches from Stubbs Road to Magazine Gap Road and offers great views over the harbor. In addition, an inside track at the Happy Valley racecourse is open for runners when the horses aren't using the field. On the other side of the harbor, there's **Kowloon Park,** as well as the waterfront promenade along Tsim Sha Tsui and Tsim Sha Tsui East.

Remember that it can be quite hot and humid during the summer months, so try to jog in the early morning or in the evening.

ROLLER & ICE SKATING   Two easily accessible roller-skating rinks are the **Sportsworld Association,** located inside the Telford Gardens adjacent to the Kowloon Bay MTR station in Kowloon (☎ 852/2757 2211); and **Rollerworld,** in Cityplaza at the Taikoo Shing MTR station on Hong Kong Island (☎ 852/2567 0391).

Cityplaza Phase II, at Taikoo Shing (☎ 852/2885 4697), has an ice-skating rink.

SWIMMING   In addition to the many outdoor and indoor swimming pools at Hong Kong's hotels that are available for hotel guests, there are numerous public swimming pools, including those at **Kowloon Park** and **Victoria Park.** Prices range from HK$13 to HK$17 ($1.70-$2.20) for adults and HK$7 to HK$8 (90¢-$1.05) for children and senior citizens. Avoid hot weekends, when the pools can become quite crowded. For serious water recreation, there's **Water World,** an aquatic playground with a wave pool, splash pool, water slides, a rapids ride, and the Lazy River.

There are also about 40 **beaches** in Hong Kong that are free for public use; most of them have lifeguards on duty in the summer, changing rooms, and snack stands or restaurants. Even on Hong Kong Island itself you can find a number of beaches, including Big Wave Bay and Shek O on the east coast, and Stanley, Deep Water Bay, and Repulse Bay on the southern coast. Repulse Bay, by far the most popular beach in Hong Kong, becomes unbelievably crowded on summer weekends. There are prettier beaches on the outlying islands, including Hung Shing Ye on Lamma, Tung Wan on Cheung Chau, and Cheung Sha on Lantau. It is, however, advisable to check on water pollution before plunging in, especially on the islands. Furthermore, I wouldn't recommend the waters around Sai Kung peninsula. There seem to be fatal shark attacks here every couple of years; somehow they always seem to occur in June, exactly when I am visiting Hong Kong. I was beginning to feel guilty until I learned that the attacks were due to fish migration, not my presence, but I certainly wouldn't want to tempt fate.

TENNIS   Public courts in Hong Kong are very much in demand simply because there are not enough of them. Prices average about HK$34 ($4.40) an hour during the day and HK$46 ($5.95) in the evening. For information, inquire at **Victoria Park,** in Causeway Bay (☎ 852/2570 6186); **King's Park,** in Yau Ma Tei, Kowloon (☎ 852/2385 8985); or the **Tennis Centre,** on Wong Nai Chong Gap Road in Happy Valley, Hong Kong (☎ 852/2574 9122).

6 Spectator Sports

A popular sporting event is the **Cathay Pacific/Hongkong Bank Invitation Seven-A-Side Rugby Tournament** (called the Sevens), held in March or April. During the cooler winter months, a number of marathons are held, of which the best known is the **International Marathon,** held in the spring. There are also tennis tournaments, including the **Super Tennis Classic** and the **Marlboro Championship.** If you enjoy watching golf, the highlight of the year is the **Hong Kong Open Golf Championships,** held in February at the Royal Hong Kong Golf Club in Fanling (the New Territories).

If you're here anytime from September through May, join the rest of Hong Kong at the **horse races.** Horse racing got its start in the colony in Happy Valley more than 100 years ago, making the Happy Valley track the oldest racecourse in Asia outside China. There is also a newer, modern track in Sha Tin (the New Territories).

Without a doubt, horse racing is by far the most popular sporting event in Hong Kong. It's not, perhaps, the sport itself that draws so much enthusiasm, but rather the fact that, aside from the local lottery, racing is the only legal form of gambling in Hong Kong. The Chinese love to gamble, and there are even off-course betting centers throughout the colony for those who can't get to the races in person.

Races are held at Happy Valley Wednesday evenings and at either Sha Tin or Happy Valley most Saturday afternoons and some Sunday afternoons. Both tracks feature giant color screens that show close-ups of the race. It's fun and easy to get in on the betting action, and you don't have to bet much—HK$10 ($1.30) per race is enough.

The lowest admission price is HK$10 ($1.30), which is for the general public and is standing room only. If you want to watch from the Hong Kong Royal Jockey Club members' stand, are older than 18, and have been in Hong Kong fewer than 21 days, you can purchase a temporary member's badge for HK$50 ($6.50). It's available upon showing your passport at either the Badge Enquiry Office at the main entrance to the members' private enclosure (at either track) or at the off-course betting center near the Star Ferry concourse in Central. Tickets are sold on a first-come, first-served basis.

If you don't want to go to the races but would still like to bet on the winning horses, you can place your bets at one of the off-course betting centers. There's a convenient one near the Star Ferry concourse in the Central District and another one at 2–4 Prat Avenue in Tsim Sha Tsui.

On the other hand, an easy way to see the races is to take an HKTA-sponsored tour to the tracks, described in "Organized Tours," above. For information on current sporting events and future dates, contact the Hong Kong Tourist Association.

Hong Kong Strolls

Surprisingly compact, Hong Kong is an easy city to explore on foot. If it weren't for the harbor, you could walk everywhere—Tsim Sha Tsui, Yau Ma Tei, the Central District, Wan Chai, and Causeway Bay. Walking affords a more intimate relationship with your surroundings, permits chance encounters with the unexpected, and lets you discover that vegetable market, temple, or shop you would have otherwise missed.

If, for example, you're in the Central District and want to have dinner in Causeway Bay, you can walk there in less than an hour, passing through colorful Wan Chai on the way. Causeway Bay is good for exploring since it's full of little sidewalk markets, street vendors, restaurants, and shops patronized by the locals. Another great place for walking is the Western District, fascinating because it encompasses a wide spectrum of traditional Chinese shops, from chop makers to ginseng wholesalers. If you like panoramic views, nothing can beat the hour-long circular walk on Victoria Peak.

On the other side of the harbor, a walk up Nathan Road from the harbor to the Yau Ma Tei subway station takes less than 30 minutes, although you might want to browse in some of the shops and department stores along the way. And Yau Ma Tei itself is another good place for wandering about since it, too, offers insight into the Chinese way of life with its markets and traditional shops.

What follows are three recommended strolls: one through the Central financial district with a few colonial-era buildings sprinkled in among the modern skyscrapers; another through the Western District with its Chinese shops and antique stores; the third along Nathan Road in Kowloon, from Tsim Sha Tsui to Yau Ma Tei. If you want detailed maps of these three areas, you may want to purchase two nifty booklets issued by the Hong Kong Tourist Association and available at its offices. The first, *Central and Western District Walking Tour,* describes a 4-hour walk through the Central and the Western Districts. The second, *Yau Ma Tei Walking Tour*, details visits to the Jade Market, traditional shops, and the Temple Street Night Market. Each costs HK$28 ($3.65) and comes with a map and lots of information on the various sights and shops you'll see along the way. If you really enjoy self-guided tours, there are four other HKTA guides in this series: *Central and Western District Heritage Trail, Cheung Chau Walking Tour, Lantau Island Explorer's Guide,* and *Sai Kung Explorer's Guide.*

WALKING TOUR 1
The Central District

Start: Star Ferry terminus, Central District.
Finish: Pacific Place, 88 Queensway, Central.
Time: About 4 hours.
Best Times: Weekdays, when the shops and restaurants are in full swing.
Worst Times: Wednesday, when the Flagstaff House Museum of Tea Ware is closed; Saturday afternoon, Sunday, and public holidays, when the Tsui Museum of Art and some stores and restaurants in the Central District are closed.

The birthplace of modern Hong Kong, the Central District used to be called "Victoria"; it boasted elegant colonial-style buildings with sweeping verandas and narrow streets filled with pigtailed men pulling rickshaws. That's hard to imagine nowadays. With Central's gleaming glass-and-steel skyscrapers, there's little left of its colonial beginnings. Still, this is the logical starting place for a tour of Hong Kong. The handful of historic buildings scattered among towering monoliths symbolize both the past and the future of this ever changing city.

If you're arriving from Tsim Sha Tsui, board the Star Ferry for an exhilarating ride across the world-famous harbor. You'll disembark in the heart of Central. Ahead of you—just outside the terminus—are all that remain of Hong Kong's once mighty fleet of:

1. **Rickshaw drivers.** First appearing in Japan (the name is derived from the Japanese *jinriksha,* which translates as "people-powered vehicle") and brought to Hong Kong in the 1870s, rickshaw drivers are now tourist attractions rather than providers of transportation. In all my days in Hong Kong, I've never once seen a driver plying the streets of Central, and since no new licenses are being issued, the tradition will end when the last of these ancient-looking men give up their trade. Rather than riding a rickshaw, most tourists prefer to have their photos taken sitting in one, but even that is likely to cost HK$50 ($6.50). Negotiate the price beforehand.

To your right, just outside the ferry wickets, is the General Post Office, in front of which is the:

2. **Jardine House,** easily recognizable by its many round windows. If you haven't yet been to the Hong Kong Tourist Association, head to the building's basement, where you'll find a branch of this great organization. You'll find a wealth of free pamphlets, booklets, and maps here.

Otherwise, if you continue walking inland from the Star Ferry terminus (with the post office to your right), you'll find an underground pedestrian passage leading straight to:

3. **Statue Square.** A statue of Queen Victoria used to stand here, but it has been moved to Victoria Park. Perhaps appropriately for a town that was established to make money, the only statue remaining in the square is of a banker, Sir Thomas Jackson, former manager of the Hongkong and Shanghai Bank. Also in the square is a cenotaph commemorating "The Glorious Dead" of both world wars. On the weekend, Statue Square and surrounding Central become the domain of Filipino housemaids and nannies, thousands of whom work in Hong Kong and send most of what they earn back home to their families. On their day off, they meet friends here, sitting on blankets spread on the concrete and sharing food, photographs, and laughter, infusing the staid business district with a certain vitality and festivity.

Walking Tour—The Central District

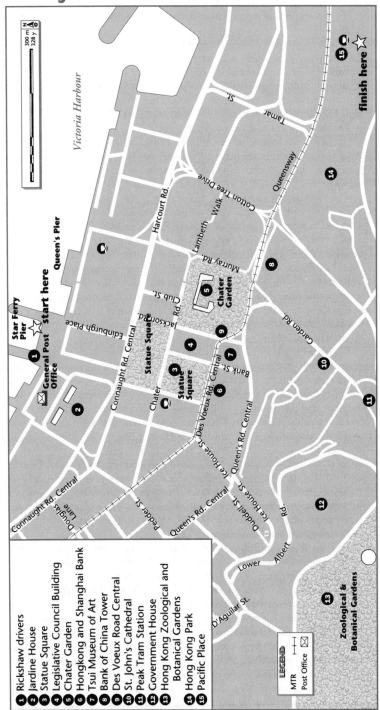

300 m
328 y

Victoria Harbour

Queen's Pier

Star Ferry Pier

start here

General Post Office

Edinburgh Place

Connaught Rd. Central

Connaught Rd. Central

Douglas Lane

Pedder St.

Chater Rd.

Statue Square

Statue Square

Jackson Rd.

Club St.

Chater Garden

Harcourt Rd.

Murray Rd.

Lambeth Walk

Cotton Tree Drive

Tamar St.

Queensway

Garden Rd.

Bank St.

Des Voeux Rd. Central

Ice House St.

Queen's Rd. Central

Queen's Rd. Central

Duddell St.

Ice House St.

Albert Rd.

Lower Albert Rd.

D'Aguilar St.

finish here

Zoological & Botanical Gardens

LEGEND
MTR
⊠ Post Office

1. Rickshaw drivers
2. Jardine House
3. Statue Square
4. Legislative Council Building
5. Chater Garden
6. Hongkong and Shanghai Bank
7. Tsui Museum of Art
8. Bank of China Tower
9. Des Voeux Road Central
10. St. John's Cathedral
11. Peak Tram Station
12. Government House
13. Hong Kong Zoological and Botanical Gardens
14. Hong Kong Park
15. Pacific Place

2164

To the left (east) of Statue Square is a historic building that looks curiously out of place, the

4. **Legislative Council Building** (formerly the Supreme Court). It was built in 1912 by architect Aston Webb, who later redesigned Buckingham Palace, and now houses Hong Kong's lawmaking body, popularly known as "Legco." With its local pink-and-gray granite, Ionic columns, and Chinese roof, the neoclassical structure is typical of late-Victorian colonial architecture and boasts a carved stone figure above the main portico of the Goddess of Justice holding scales.

On the other side of the Legco building is:

5. **Chater Garden,** former site of the Hong Kong Cricket Club. Today this is the only spot of green in the heart of Central and is popular among those who practice tai chi (shadowboxing) in the early morning and among office workers on lunch break.

The most conspicuous building visible from Statue Square, however, is the:

6. **Hongkong and Shanghai Bank** straight ahead on Des Voeux Road Central, designed in the mid-1980s by Sir Norman Foster; it attracts visiting architects the world over for its innovative external structure. Hong Kong's first city hall once stood on this site; the Hongkong and Shanghai Bank, located here since 1865, issued the colony's first bank notes in 1881. The two bronze lions you see at the entrance have been "guarding" the bank since 1935. Walk underneath the bank's open ground plaza for a look up into this unique structure, or, if you choose, take the escalator up to the first floor. Much care was given to the angle of these escalators, as well as to many other aspects of construction, in order not to disturb the spirits who reside here.

Beside the bank to the east is another bank building (there are lots of them around here)—the older and attractive Bank of China, also "guarded" by stone lions. Here, up on the 11th floor, is the:

7. **Tsui Museum of Art,** a private collection of Chinese antiquities ranging from furniture and jade to an impressive display of Chinese ceramics. The museum is small, but well worth an extra 30 minutes or so to walk through the several rooms.

To the east of the Bank of China is Hong Kong's other impressive bank structure, the:

8. **Bank of China Tower,** rising like a glass finger pointing into the sky. Designed by I. M. Pei, this futuristic building also observes the principles of *fung shui* (Chinese geomancy), as do all modern structures in Hong Kong in an effort to maintain harmony with their natural environment. Otherwise, disaster would surely strike—something no builder in Hong Kong wants to risk.

Running in front of these three banks is:

9. **Des Voeux Road Central,** easily recognizable by the tramlines snaking along it. What a contrast these quaint-looking trams make when viewed against the high-rise banks. Established in 1904 and now the colony's oldest form of transportation, trams are the most colorful way to travel from the Western and Central Districts to Causeway Bay, especially at night when Hong Kong is ablaze in neon. Des Voeux Road itself was constructed as part of an early 1800s land reclamation project; before that the waterfront was situated farther inland—at Queen's Road. Land reclamation has been proceeding continuously throughout Hong Kong's history, slowly encroaching on the harbor itself. One Hong Kong resident I met joked that so much land was being reclaimed it wouldn't be long before you could walk across the harbor. With Central's most recent reclamation project—which extended the ferry piers far into the water—the joke no longer seems quite so funny.

☕ **TAKE A BREAK**   If it's before 3pm, consider having a typical Chinese snack of dim sum at **City Hall Chinese Restaurant**, a casual Cantonese restaurant on the second floor of the Low Block, located just a stone's throw from the Star Ferry terminus and Statue Square. For a restaurant that will remind you of Hong Kong's British connections, have lunch at **Bentley's**, located in the basement of the Prince's Building right on Statue Square.

Between the Hongkong and Shanghai Bank and the Bank of China Tower is a major thoroughfare leading uphill, **Garden Road.** At its lower end, on the corner, stands the building that once housed the former Hilton Hotel but now has a more lucrative life as an office building. Behind the Hilton, on your right, is the gothic-style:

10. St. John's Cathedral, inaugurated in 1849 and the oldest Anglican church in the Far East. Farther up Garden Road, on the left, is the:

11. Peak Tram Station, which opened in 1888, reducing the travel time to the top of Victoria Peak from 3 hours (by sedan chair) to 8 minutes. Today the tram is the steepest funicular railway in the world, and the view from the peak is the best in Hong Kong. I suggest you visit the peak twice during your stay: during the day for the great panoramic view of the city, and again at night for its romantic atmosphere.

A short trek farther uphill on Garden Road will bring you to Upper Albert Road, where you'll see:

12. Government House on your right; it was completed in 1855 and serves as the official residence of all Hong Kong's governors. During the World War II Japanese occupation, it served as the headquarters of Lt. Gen. Isogai, who ordered some extensive building renovations that today appear to be a curious mix of Asian and Western architecture.

Across the street, on Upper Albert Road, is a staircase leading up to the main entrance of the:

13. Hong Kong Zoological and Botanical Gardens, a wonderful oasis of plants and animals that was established in 1864. There is free entrance, and the grounds are not too extensive, so it's worth taking the time to wander through.

Retrace your steps back down Garden Road, turning right after the Peak Tram Station. On the other side of the station is Cotton Tree Drive; cross this and go downhill toward Central. On your right side, look for the entrance to:

14. Hong Kong Park, once the grounds of Victoria Barracks which opened as a park in 1991. To your right after you enter the park is the pink Rawlinson House, formerly the private residence of the Deputy General and now serving as a marriage registry. If it's a weekend or an auspicious day in the Chinese calendar, you'll find many newlyweds posing for pictures in the park. You'll also find a greenhouse and an aviary. Signs will direct you to the park's most important building and Hong Kong's oldest surviving colonial-style structure—the Flagstaff House Museum of Tea Ware, built in 1846. It houses a small collection of tea utensils, with descriptions of tea-making through the various Chinese dynasties. From here, walk past the fountain (a favorite backdrop for picture-taking) to the escalators that will take you downhill to:

15. Pacific Place, a large complex filled with department stores, clothing boutiques, restaurants, and hotels. The nearest subway station from here is Admiralty Station.

☕ **TAKE A BREAK**   There are many eating and drinking establishments in Pacific Place. **Dan Ryan's Chicago Grill** is a casual bar and grill that remains open throughout the day for drinks, burgers, and other American favorites. **Zen Chinese** is the ultimate in Chinese hip dining, with a Zenlike decor and specialties that border on Cantonese nouvelle. **Grappa's** is a moderately priced trattoria with an open kitchen and good food.

WALKING TOUR 2
The Western District

Start: Star Ferry terminus, Central District.
Finish: Lan Kwai Fong, Central.
Time: About 4 hours.
Best Times: Weekday mornings, Monday to Friday, when markets are in full swing.
Worst Time: Sunday, when some shops are closed.

While the Central District seems to be Western in style, with its banks, high-rises, and smart department stores, the Western District is very Chinese—a fascinating neighborhood of family-owned shops and businesses. Traditional herbs, ginseng, antiques, preserved fish, name chops, coffins, funeral items, and Hong Kong's oldest temple are just some of the things you'll see in the Western District, my favorite area on Hong Kong Island.

As you exit from the Star Ferry terminus, take the first stairs you see (by the post office) up to the elevated covered walkway that leads past the post office and Jardine House. If you haven't yet been to the Hong Kong Tourist Association, it has an office in the basement of Jardine House. Incidentally, there are elevated walkways throughout Central, an efficient way of separating foot traffic from automobiles. Follow the signs a couple of minutes until you reach our first destination, the:

1. **Landmark,** on the corner of Des Voeux Road Central and Pedder Street. This is an ultrachic shopping complex with the boutiques of Gucci, Tiffany, Louis Vuitton, and Wedgwood.

    Return to Des Voeux Road Central, cross Pedder Street, and then turn left. Just up the street on your right is the:

2. **Pedder Building,** a shopping center since 1926. It is now famous for its dozens of factory outlets and clothing boutiques; look for the elevator that services the first through seventh floors. Be aware, however, that just a handful of shops here are true factory outlets. The rest are simply taking advantage of the location to set up boutiques to sell their usual goods at regular prices. If you have the time, you might want to hunt for some bargains here. I usually take the elevator up to the seventh floor and then work my way down.

    Behind the Pedder Building, reached by taking the small alley that runs just in front of the building (past the small stalls of cobblers and key makers), is the smart-looking:

3. **Shanghai Tang.** This is a reproduction of a Shanghai clothing department store as it might have looked in the 1930s, with gleaming wooden floors, raised cashier cubicles, ceiling fans, and clerks wearing traditional Chinese clothing. This is a great place to shop for typical Chinese goods, from cheongsams to Chinese jackets, as well as funky accessories like Mao watches.

    Return to Des Voeux Road Central and continue west; in about one minute you will come to:

Walking Tour—The Western District

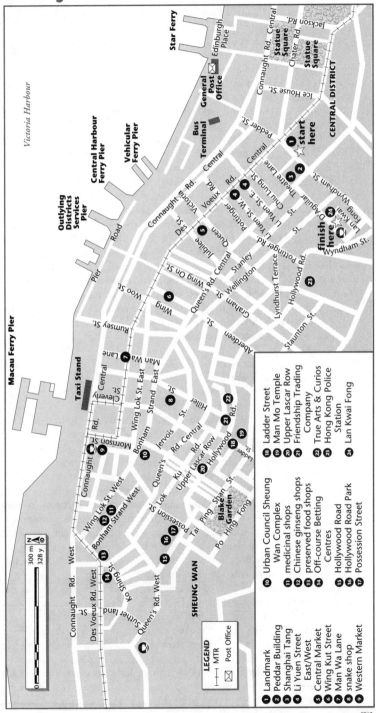

LEGEND

—|— MTR
☒ Post Office

1. Landmark
2. Peddar Building
3. Shanghai Tang
4. Li Yuen Street East/West
5. Central Market
6. Wing Kut Street
7. Man Wa Lane
8. snake shop
9. Western Market
10. Urban Council Sheung Wan Complex
11. medicinal shops
12. Chinese ginseng shops
13. preserved food shops
14. Off-course Betting Centres
15. Hollywood Road
16. Hollywood Road Park
17. Possession Street
18. Ladder Street
19. Man Mo Temple
20. Upper Lascar Row
21. Friendship Trading Company
22. True Arts & Curios
23. Hong Kong Police Station
24. Lan Kwai Fong

Victoria Harbour

Macau Ferry Pier

Star Ferry

Central Harbour Ferry Pier

Vehicular Ferry Pier

Outlying Districts Services Pier

Bus Terminal

General Post Office

Edinburgh Place

Taxi Stand

SHEUNG WAN

CENTRAL DISTRICT

start here

finish here

N
300 m
328 y

2165

4. Li Yuen Street East and **Li Yuen Street West,** two parallel pedestrian lanes that rise steeply to your left and are packed with stalls that sell clothing and accessories, including costume jewelry, handbags, belts, and even bras. If you see something you like, be sure to bargain for it. Walk up Li Yuen Street East, take a right, and then head back down Li Yuen Street West.

Back on Des Voeux Road Central, continue walking west a couple blocks, until (on your left) you'll see the:

5. Central Market, a three-story building that serves as Hong Kong's largest public market for everything from seafood and live poultry to fruits and vegetables. Although it's open from 6am to 2pm and again from 4:30 to 8pm, try to be here in the morning when it's at its busiest, with women buying the day's food for their families and chefs purchasing the daily specials. Following the Chinese penchant for freshness, chickens are killed on the spot, boiled, and then thrown into machines that pluck them. Almost every part of every animal is for sale, including the liver, heart, and intestines. Wicker baskets may contain the discarded horns and skulls of bulls, with even the brains carved out—not for the fainthearted. If all you want to see are fruit and vegetables, head for the second floor.

Central Market also marks the beginning of the 2,600-foot-long hillside escalator that links Central with the Mid-Levels on Victoria Peak. Opened in 1933, it actually consists of a series of escalators and moving sidewalks, with 29 entrances, designed to accommodate commuters who live in the Mid-Levels but work in Central and beyond. As such, the escalators operate downhill from 6am to 10am, and then reverse their direction and go uphill from 10am to 11pm.

Walk several short blocks farther west on Des Voeux Road Central, and on the left you will see:

6. Wing Kut Street, another small lane lined with stalls that sell clothing, handbags, and other accessories for women. Don't forget to look at the small shops behind the stalls, where you will find costume jewelry in a wide range of styles and prices. Many of the shops, however, sell only wholesale.

After walking through Wing Kut Street, take a right. Queen's Road Central will soon curve off to the left, but you'll want to keep walking straight westward onto Bonham Strand East. Soon, to your right, you'll see an interesting street:

7. Man Wa Lane, home since the 1920s of one of China's oldest trades—"chop" or carved-seal making. Made from stone, ivory, jade, clay, marble, bronze, porcelain, bamboo, wood, soapstone, and even plastic, these seals or stamps can be carved with a name and are used by the Chinese much like a written signature. You can have your own chop made at one of the several booths here, with your name translated into Chinese characters. It takes about an hour for a chop to be completed, so you may want to stop by again later after you've finished your walk. You can also have business cards made here with both English and Chinese characters; that takes about a day. Most stalls here are open from 9am to 7pm.

Back on Bonham Strand East, continue westward. Just a few years ago, this area was known for its many snake shops, which did a roaring business from October to February. Now only a few remain, easily identifiable by cages of pythons, cobras, and banded kraits piled on the sidewalk, or by the wooden drawers lining the walls of the shop. Just past Mercer Street is Hillier Street, where you should turn left for the:

8. Snake shop at 13 Hillier St. Eaten as protection against the winter cold and as a cure for rheumatism, snakes are often served in soup. They are favored also for their gallbladders, which are mixed with Chinese wine as cures for rheumatism.

Who knows, you might see a shopkeeper fill a customer's order, by deftly grabbing a snake out of one of the drawers, extracting the gallbladder, and mixing it in yellow wine. The snake survives the operation, but who knows what other fate awaits it. The more poisonous the snake, so they say, the better the cure. The mixture is also believed to be an aphrodisiac.

From Hillier Street, take the next right onto Jervois, walk one block, and then turn right again on Cleverly Street; there you will find open-fronted, family-owned shops selling vegetables, cookware, religious artifacts, joss sticks, and hand-crafted birdcages. Take the first left again back onto Bonham Strand East, where you'll pass a tea merchant's shop, medicinal shops selling dried organic products, and, on the corner of Morrison Street, a rattan shop with handmade wares spilling out onto the sidewalks and hanging from hooks outside the shop. It takes an apprentice three years to learn the skills necessary to become a master rattan maker; the rattan itself comes from a climbing vine found throughout Asia.

Take a right here onto Morrison Street and walk to the end where, on the left, you'll find the handsome:

9. **Western Market.** Built in 1906 and used as a public market until 1989, it escaped demolition when the decision was made to renovate the imposing Edwardian/Victorian red-brick building into a bazaar for shops and artisans. On the ground floor are souvenir and gift shops that sell everything from Chinese seals to children's toys; on the first floor retailers sell bolts of colorful cloth, buttons, clasps, and other sewing accessories.

☕ **TAKE A BREAK** On the top floor of the Western Market is **Mythical China,** a Cantonese restaurant open daily from 11am to 4pm and 6 to 11pm. It offers the usual seafood, chicken, pigeon, pork, and beef dishes in a historical and pleasant atrium setting.

Backtrack on Morrison Street to Bonham Strand East where, across the street, you'll see the:

10. **Urban Council Sheung Wan Complex.** One of Hong Kong's largest neighborhood markets, it features fish and poultry on the ground floor, meats and vegetables on the first floor, and food stalls selling cooked meals on the top floor. The market is at its liveliest before 11:30am.

Exit the market building back onto Bonham Strand East, turn left, and follow the road as it curves around the market's west side. Take the first right onto Bonham Strand West. This is where you'll find the Western District's most interesting enterprises—

11. **Medicinal shops.** Based on the Oriental concept of maintaining a healthy balance between the yin and yang forces in the body, the range of medicinal herbs is startling, including roots, twigs, bark, dried leaves, seeds, pods, flowers, grasses, insects (such as discarded cicada shells), deer antlers, dried sea horses, dried fish bladders, and rhinoceros horns. The herbalist, after learning about the customer's symptoms and checking the pulses in both wrists, will prescribe an appropriate remedy, using perhaps a bit of bark here and a seed there, based on wisdom passed down over thousands of years.

The kings of trade on Bonham Strand are clearly the:

12. **Chinese ginseng shops.** More than 30 varieties of ginseng root are handled in this wholesale trading area. The most prized are the red ginseng from North Korea, white ginseng from North America, and a very rare ginseng that grows wild in the

mountains of northeastern China. Red ginseng is supposed to aid male virility, while the white variety helps to cure hangovers.

At the end of Bonham Strand, turn left on Des Voeux Road West, where you'll see:

13. Shops selling preserved foods. Dried and salted fish, flattened squid, oysters, scallops, abalone, sea slugs, fish bladders, starfish, shrimp, and many other kinds of seafood have been dried and preserved. You can buy bird's nest here, as well as shark's fin, and in winter there's also pressed duck and Chinese sausages made from pork and liver.

At 72–74 Des Voeux Rd. is one of Hong Kong's many:

14. Off-course Betting Centres of the Royal Hong Kong Jockey Club. As the only legal form of gambling in Hong Kong, horse-race betting is so popular that more than 120 such centers can be found throughout the colony doing a brisk business on race days with bettors who do not go to the track. Perhaps you'll want to try your own luck here before continuing west on Des Voeux Road; at shop no. 90 turn left onto Sutherland Street. At the top of Sutherland Street, you may be lucky enough to see some of Hong Kong's remaining streetside barbers. Once plentiful, sidewalk barbers are now going the way of the rickshaw, especially after the recent renovation of this neighborhood; the children's playground here displaced some of the narrow alleys favored by sidewalk barbers. Look for an elderly woman who sets up shop on the sidewalk along busy Queen's Road West, just opposite Sutherland Street. She uses a string to pull out the facial hairs of her customers, an ancient method that few barbers can still perform. Here, at the junction of Queen's Road West and Sutherland, is also a bird shop with hundreds of songbirds, exquisitely crafted wooden and bamboo cages, and tiny porcelain water bowls for sale.

☕ **TAKE A BREAK**   There's no better place for Western food in the Western District than **Sammy's Kitchen,** 204–206 Queen's Rd. West (reached from Sutherland Street by turning right and walking about 2 minutes). A landmark for more than two decades, it's owned by the gregarious and friendly Sammy Yip, who treats foreign guests like royalty. A good place for fresh seafood, steaks, chicken, and house-invented specialties.

From Sutherland Street, turn left and walk east on Queen's Road West; you'll pass several incense shops and, after a minute or so, you'll see a road leading uphill to the right. It's the famous:

15. Hollywood Road, with its strange mixture of shops that sell coffins and funeral items, and furniture and antique shops offering genuine antiques as well as excellent imitations. There are more antique shops concentrated here than anywhere else in Hong Kong, and you'll find everything from woodblock prints and rosewood tables to snuff bottles, porcelain, and round-bellied smiling Buddhas.

First, however, to your left will be:

16. Hollywood Road Park, a pleasant garden oasis with a children's playground, a pond with goldfish, and Chinese pagodas. Stop for a few moments of relaxation before continuing.

After another minute's walk along Hollywood Road, you will soon pass a historic landmark:

17. Possession Street, to your left. There's no need to enter it, but you might be interested to know that it was here that the British first landed in 1841 and planted the Union Jack to claim the island for Britain. At the time, of course, this was part of the waterfront.

After passing more antique and curio shops on Hollywood Road, you'll see to your right (just after shop no. 132–134):

18. Ladder Street, an extremely steep flight of stairs and once a common sight on steep Hong Kong Island. Now, of course, Hong Kong Island has escalators. Just past Ladder Street, on the same side of the street, is the:

19. Man Mo Temple, Hong Kong Island's oldest and most important temple. It was in this area that the movie *The World of Suzie Wong* was filmed. The temple, which dates back to the 1840s and is open daily from 7am to 5pm, is dedicated to two deities: the god of literature (Man) and the god of war (Mo). Mo finds patronage among the members of the police force (shrines in his honor can be found in all Hong Kong police stations)—as well as among members of the underworld. Two ornately carved sedan chairs are kept in the temple to carry the statues of the gods around the neighborhood during festivals; and from the ceiling hang huge incense coils, which burn as long as three weeks, purchased by patrons seeking the fulfillment of their wishes.

If you follow the steps leading downhill opposite Ladder Street, you'll see:

20. Upper Lascar Row, better known as Cat Street, which leads off to the left. For almost a century Cat Street was famous for its antiques, which could be bought for a pittance; now, however, with the new antique shops on Hollywood Road and the nearby Cat Street Galleries, Cat Street offers a fantastic mix of curios and junk. Pleasantly dotted with potted palms, this pedestrian lane is worth a browse for jade, snuff bottles, watches, pictures, copper and brass kettles, old eyeglasses, birdcages, and odds and ends. You can bargain with the vendors who have laid their wares on the sidewalk; most of them do business Monday through Saturday from 11am to about 5pm. You can also bargain at the surrounding antique shops, where prices are rather high to begin with. If you're not an expert, be wary of purchasing anything of value. During my last visit, it seemed that every shop was offering fossilized "dinosaur eggs" for sale. How many can there be?

At the end of Cat Street, return to Hollywood Road, where you should take a left and continue walking toward its eastern end. Here you'll find more chic and upscale antique shops, selling furniture, blue-and-white porcelain, and goods from other countries, including Korean chests and Japanese hibachi. Among my favorites are the:

21. Friendship Trading Company, on the left at 105–107 Hollywood Rd., with its porcelain vases and lacquered boxes, and, just beyond it:

22. True Arts & Curios, 89 Hollywood Rd., a tiny shop packed with all kinds of surprises, from antique children's pointed shoes to porcelain, jewelry, and snuff bottles. It also carries about 2,000 temple wood carvings, most of which are about 100 years old and small enough to carry with you on the plane.

Farther down, at 47 Hollywood Road, just before the elevated walkway, are a couple of ancient-looking hole-in-the-wall shops selling bric-a-brac, old photographs and postcards of Hong Kong (including portraits of women engaged in that ageless profession), snuff bottles, and other interesting stuff. Walk under the elevated people-mover, and just a bit beyond, to the right—on Old Bailey and Hollywood Road—is the:

23. Hong Kong Police Station, originally built in 1864 and expanded in 1919. It's one of Hong Kong's largest clusters of Victorian-era buildings.

Take a left on Pottinger, the first right onto Wellington, and another right on D'Aguilar. This will bring you to Central's nightlife district:

24. Lan Kwai Fong, with its row of bars and restaurants.

☕ **TAKE A BREAK**   The best place to call it a day is in the nightlife district of Lan Kwai Fong, where you'll find such popular bars as: **California,** 24–26 Lan Kwai Fong St., **MadDogs,** 1 D'Aguilar St., and **Post 97,** 9 Lan Kwai Fong St.

WALKING TOUR 3
Kowloon

Start: Star Ferry Terminus, Tsim Sha Tsui.
Finish: Temple Street Night Market.
Time: About 2 hours, not including shopping or visiting museums.
Best Time: Early afternoon, when the Space Museum and the Jade Market are open.
Worst Times: Tuesday, when the Space Museum is closed; Thursday, when the Museum of Art is closed; and Friday, when the Museum of History is closed.

A stroll up Nathan Road through Tsim Sha Tsui and Yau Ma Tei will take you through the heart of Kowloon, past its famous hotels, restaurants, and shops and on to the fascinating Chinese shops and markets in Yau Ma Tei.

A logical tour of Tsim Sha Tsui begins with the Star Ferry since, for more than a century, it served as the only link with Hong Kong Island. Within the terminus itself is the Hong Kong Tourist Association office, where you can pick up free pamphlets, brochures, and maps of Hong Kong. As you leave the Star Ferry concourse, that colonial-looking:

1. **Clock tower** you see to your right, now dwarfed by the new Cultural Centre, is the only remaining part of Hong Kong's old train station, once the final stop for those traveling overland from London on the *Orient Express.*

Straight ahead, past the plaza with its many buses and taxis, is Canton Road, home of several hotels as well as Hong Kong's biggest shopping complex:

2. **Harbour City,** which houses the Ocean Terminal, Ocean Galleries, and Ocean City. Altogether there are 600 shops here, all connected by air-conditioned walkways. Enter it and you might not escape during this lifetime; better save shopping for another day. Instead, turn right and head east along:

3. **Salisbury Road,** which follows the waterfront from Tsim Sha Tsui to Tsim Sha Tsui East. A new promenade hugs the shoreline, a good place for a romantic stroll, especially at night. That huge, modern brick building on your right is the:

4. **Hong Kong Cultural Centre,** the colony's largest arena for the performing arts. Opened in 1989, it boasts a concert hall, theaters, exhibition areas, a cafe, and the:

5. **Hong Kong Museum of Art,** a great place to see Chinese porcelain, bronzes, jade, lacquerware, bamboo carvings, and paintings. Don't miss it.

Just past the museum, on Salisbury Road, is the:

6. **Space Museum,** which is easy to spot because of its white-domed planetarium. The museum is divided into three parts—the Space Theatre's planetarium, where films are projected onto the 75-foot domed roof, the Hall of Space Science, and the Hall of Astronomy. Shows at the Space Theatre are so popular that they often sell out in advance, so you might want to stop off now and buy your ticket for a later performance.

The Space Museum has stolen the view from Tsim Sha Tsui's most famous landmark, the venerable:

Walking Tour—Kowloon

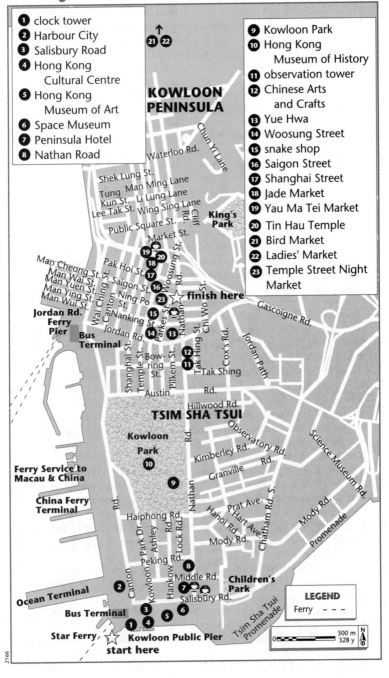

1. clock tower
2. Harbour City
3. Salisbury Road
4. Hong Kong Cultural Centre
5. Hong Kong Museum of Art
6. Space Museum
7. Peninsula Hotel
8. Nathan Road
9. Kowloon Park
10. Hong Kong Museum of History
11. observation tower
12. Chinese Arts and Crafts
13. Yue Hwa
14. Woosung Street
15. snake shop
16. Saigon Street
17. Shanghai Street
18. Jade Market
19. Yau Ma Tei Market
20. Tin Hau Temple
21. Bird Market
22. Ladies' Market
23. Temple Street Night Market

KOWLOON PENINSULA

Chun Yi Lane
Waterloo Rd.
Shek Lung St.
Tung Man Ming Lane
Kun St. Li Lung Lane
Lee Tak St. Wing Sing Lane
Public Square St.
Cliff Rd.
King's Park
Market St.
Man Cheong St. Pak Hoi St.
Man Wai St. Saigon St.
Man Yuen St. Ning Po St.
Man Ying St. Canton
Man Wui St. Nanking
Jordan Rd. Ferry Pier
Bus Terminal
Jordan Rd.
Wai Ching St.
Shanghai St.
Temple St.
Canton St.
Parkes St.
Nathan Rd.
Woosung Rd.
Chi Wo St.
finish here
Gascoigne Rd.
Tak Hing St.
Cox's Rd.
Jordan Path
Bow-ring St.
Pilkem St.
Tak Shing
Austin Rd.
Hillwood Rd.
TSIM SHA TSUI
Kowloon Park
Observatory Rd.
Kimberley Rd. Rd.
Granville Rd.
Science Museum Rd.
Ferry Service to Macau & China
China Ferry Terminal
Haiphong Rd.
Nathan Rd.
Prat Ave.
Hart Ave.
Hanoi Rd.
Mody Rd.
Promenade
Kowloon Park Dr.
Ashley Rd.
Lock Rd.
Hankow Rd.
Canton Rd.
Peking Rd.
Middle Rd.
Children's Park
Ocean Terminal
Bus Terminal
Salisbury Rd.
Star Ferry
Kowloon Public Pier
start here

Tsim Sha Tsui Promenade

LEGEND
Ferry - - -

0 300 m
   328 y

N

2166

7. Peninsula Hotel, right across the street. Built in 1928 and guarded by a fleet of black Rolls-Royces, The Peninsula is Hong Kong's grandest old hotel, with a new tower that restored harbor views to its front-facing rooms. Its lobby, reminiscent of a Parisian palace with high gilded ceilings, pillars, and ferns, has long been a favorite spot for a cup of coffee and people-watching.

☕ **TAKE A BREAK**   Many visitors feel that their Hong Kong stay would not be complete without dropping by for coffee in the **lobby of The Peninsula Hotel.** Music is played from noon to midnight, but the best time to stop by is from 3 to 6:30pm daily, when an English-style afternoon tea is served for HK$135 ($17.55). Otherwise, head for the top floor of the Sheraton Hotel, on the corner of Salisbury and Nathan Roads, where you'll find the **Sky Lounge.** Open from 4 to 11pm daily, this cocktail lounge offers stunning views of the famous harbor. Another good watering hole, without any views but open all day beginning at 8am, is the English pub **MadDogs,** 32 Nathan Road.

Just past The Peninsula Hotel, turn left on:

8. Nathan Road, Kowloon's most famous street. It is also one of the colony's widest, and runs almost 2¹/₂ miles straight up the spine of Kowloon all the way to Boundary Road, the official border of the New Territories. Nathan Road is named after Sir Matthew Nathan, who served as governor at the time the road was constructed. After it was completed, it was nicknamed "Nathan's Folly." After all, why build such a wide road, seemingly in the middle of nowhere? Kowloon had very few people back then and even less traffic. Now, of course, Nathan Road is known as the "Golden Mile" of shopping, because of all the boutiques and shops that line both sides.

You'll pass jewelry stores, electronics shops, optical shops, clothing boutiques, and many others as you head north on Nathan Road. The side streets are also good hunting grounds for inexpensive casual wear, at prices comparable to those of Stanley Market. You'll want to return here to explore this area at leisure. After about 10 minutes (assuming you don't stop to shop along the way), you'll see a mosque on your left, followed by a string of shops called Park Lane Shopper's Boulevard. Behind this boulevard is:

9. Kowloon Park, a good place to bring children for a romp through playgrounds and open spaces. In addition to a water garden, a sculpture garden, a woodland trail, a maze made of foliage, and swimming pools, Kowloon Park is also home to the:

10. Hong Kong Museum of History. Housed in two buildings dating from the 19th century, this museum provides a brief introduction to Hong Kong's past and is well worth a visit.

Continuing up Nathan Road, you will soon reach the Prudential Hotel (222 Nathan Road), which towers above a shopping complex. On the hotel's roof, reached by taking the elevator to the 17th floor, is an:

11. Observation tower 300 feet above the ground, which provides great views of surrounding Kowloon and is open until 7pm.

Back on Nathan Road, be on the lookout for two traditional Chinese-products stores:

12. Chinese Arts and Crafts Ltd., at 233–239 Nathan Rd., an upscale emporium that is popular with tourists, and:

13. **Yue Hwa,** 301–309 Nathan Rd., which caters more to the local Chinese. These department stores sell goods from China, including silk, antiques, porcelain, jade, embroidered tablecloths, and medicinal herbs.

    Once you've passed Yue Hwa, you'll find yourself in Yau Ma Tei. Its name translates roughly as "the place for growing sesame plants," but you won't see any such cultivation today. Rather, like the Western District on Hong Kong Island, Yau Ma Tei offers a look at traditional Chinese life, with shops that sell tea, chopping blocks, joss, bamboo steamers, baked goods, embroidery, herbs, and dried seafood.

    Just past the Yue Hwa store, take a left onto Nanking Street and then a right onto:

14. **Woosung Street.** Here you'll pass restaurants, an herbalist shop, and other family-owned businesses. Near the corner of Woosung and Ning Po Streets is a:

15. **Snake shop,** 80A Ning Po St., which people visit mainly in the winter for snake products to cure their winter ills. Snake soup is a popular winter dish, and snake gallbladder mixed with Chinese alcohol is believed to be a cure for rheumatism and even impotence.

    Continue north on Woosung Street and take a left on:

16. **Saigon Street,** where in succession (on the left side of the street) you'll pass a mahjongg parlor, a shop for herbal teas, and a pawn shop. You'll also pass Temple Street, site of the famous night market (but more on that later). Take a right on:

17. **Shanghai Street,** where you'll pass more traditional shops, the most interesting of which, perhaps, is the shop selling embroidery at 190 Shanghai St. At Kansu Street, underneath the overpass, is the:

18. **Jade Market.** This fascinating market consists of some 400 stalls selling jade and pearls and is open from about 10am to 2pm daily, though some vendors stay until 3:30pm or so if business warrants it. The jade on sale here comes in a bewildering range of quality. The highest quality should be cold to the touch and translucent, but unless you know your jade you're better off just coming here for a look. It's possible to infuse jade with color so that inferior stones acquire the brightness and translucence associated with more expensive stones. If you want a souvenir, get a pendant or bangle, but don't spend more than a few dollars on it. The freshwater pearls are also good buys. Watch how the Chinese bargain—they often do it secretly, using hand signals concealed underneath a newspaper so that none of the onlookers will know the final price.

    Across from the Jade Market is:

19. **Yau Ma Tei Market** and **Reclamation Street,** where all kinds of exotic fruit and fresh vegetables are sold from open-air stalls. This is an interesting area for strolling around.

    North of the Jade Market is a:

20. **Tin Hau Temple,** shaded by banyan trees. This is a popular community temple, its park filled with people playing mahjongg and its inner recesses filled with people asking favors or giving thanks. The temple is open daily from 8am to 6pm.

🍵 **TAKE A BREAK** The **Pearl Seaview Hotel,** located in the heart of Yau Ma Tei at 262 Shanghai St., has a lounge on its 19th floor offering views of surrounding Kowloon. It's open daily from 4pm to 1am; from 4 to 8pm, you can get two drinks for the price of one. **The Eaton Hotel,** 380 Nathan Rd. (just south of Kansu Street), is another good place to stop by for a drink. **Planter's,** just off the hotel's lobby on the fourth floor (enter the hotel on Pak Hoi Street), offers a happy hour daily from 3 to 8pm, with two drinks for the price of one and live music beginning at 6:30pm. Also off the lobby is an outdoor terrace, open noon to midnight for drinks and snacks.

At this point, you may want to go back to your hotel room to rest since Yau Ma Tei's most famous attraction doesn't get under way until after 6pm, with most of the action taking place after 8pm. Otherwise, if you're still feeling energetic, walk north on Nathan Road about 15 minutes, taking a left on Nelson and then a right two blocks later onto Hong Lok Street. Here you'll find the:

21. Bird Market, where hundreds of songbirds are for sale, as well as intricately fashioned birdcages, live crickets, and tiny porcelain water bowls. This place is very Chinese and makes for some great photographs. It's open daily until 5pm. (*Note:* the bird market is scheduled to move by the end of 1996.)

When you reach Argyle Street, turn right, cross Nathan Road, and continue two blocks to Tung Choi Street, home of the so-called:

22. Ladies' Market, where daily from 1 to 10:30pm street vendors sell women's clothing and accessories, including handbags and shoes, and some children's clothing at low prices. You can spend at least an hour here, and pick up some bargains to boot.

The Ladies' Market extends from Argyle to Dundas Street. After exploring this area of Mong Kok, either board the MTR and take it one station south to Jordan or walk back south on Nathan Road to the:

23. Temple Street Night Market, named after the street where it is located. This market, open from about 6pm and busiest from 8 to 11pm, is a wonderful place to spend an evening, with its countless stalls that sell clothing, watches, lighters, sunglasses, sweaters, cassettes, and more. The name of the game is bargaining. There are also many seafood stalls, where you can eat inexpensive meals of clams, shrimp, mussels, and crab. Be sure to follow Temple Street to its northern end past the overpass; in the vicinity of the Tin Hau Temple you'll find palm readers, musicians, and street singers (who favor Cantonese operas and pop songs).

☕ **TAKE A BREAK**   The Temple Street Night Market is famous for its **dai pai dong** (streetside food stalls) that specialize in seafood. You can dine inexpensively here on clams, shrimp, mussels, and crab, sitting at outdoor tables in the middle of the action.

Shopping 8

No doubt about it—one of the main reasons people come to Hong Kong is to shop. According to the Hong Kong Tourist Association (HKTA), visitors spend more than 50% of their money here on shopping, an amount that totals more than HK$15 billion ($1.95 billion) annually. In fact, Hong Kong is such a popular shopping destination that many luxury cruise ships dock longer here than they do anywhere else on their tour. I doubt that there's ever been a visitor to Hong Kong who left empty-handed.

1 The Shopping Scene

BEST BUYS Hong Kong is a duty-free port, which means that imported goods are not taxed in Hong Kong with the exception of some luxury goods, such as tobacco, alcohol, perfume, cosmetics, cars, and some petroleum products. Thus you can buy many goods in Hong Kong at a cheaper price than in the country where they were made. What's more, there is no sales tax in Hong Kong. It's less expensive, for example, to buy Japanese products such as designer clothing, cameras, electronic goods, and pearls in Hong Kong than in Japan itself. In fact, all my friends who live in Japan try to visit Hong Kong at least once or twice a year to buy their business clothes, cosmetics, and other accessories.

Often you can buy products from the People's Republic of China at a lower price in Hong Kong than in China itself. Great bargains include porcelain, jade, cloisonné, silk, hand-embroidery, jewelry, and artwork. You'll also find crafts and goods from other parts of Asia, including Thailand, India, the Philippines, and Indonesia.

Clothing is probably one of the best buys in Hong Kong. If you've looked at the labels of clothes sold in your own hometown, you've probably noticed that many say MADE IN HONG KONG. Both custom-made and designer garments are a bargain in Hong Kong, including three-piece business suits, leather outfits, furs, sportswear, and jeans. Hong Kong is one of the world's foremost producers of knits, and there are also factory outlets and small stores where you can pick up inexpensive fashions for a song.

Other good buys include antiques, shoes, jewelry, furniture, carpets, leather goods, luggage, handbags, briefcases, Chinese herbs, and eyeglasses. Hong Kong is also one of the world's largest exporters of watches and toys. As for electronic goods and cameras, they are not the bargains they once were. Make sure, therefore, to check prices on goods at home before you come to Hong Kong so that you will recognize a bargain. The best deals are in recently discontinued models, such as last year's Sony Walkman.

If you're interested in fake name-brand watches, handbags, or clothing to impress the folks back home, you've come to the right place. Although illegal, fake name-brand goods were still being sold at Hong Kong's night markets during my last visit by vendors who were ready to flee at the first sight of an official. If customs officials spot these fake goods in your bags when you return home, however, they'll be confiscated.

By the way, except for sanctioned areas such as markets, all mobile vendors are being banned from Hong Kong's streets after April 1, 1995. This will greatly change the atmosphere of this business-oriented city, where street hawkers have always been an integral part of everyday life here. It will also mean that you can't pick up that dancing toy bear or writing pen on a spontaneous shopping spree. On the other hand, the city has tried to curb hawkers for many years now by requiring licenses and banning them from certain sections of the city. But that never stopped Hong Kong's entrepreneurial spirit, with illegal hawkers trying to make a sale wherever they could; with one eye they would look for potential sales, and with the other for roving police. Making a rule is easy in Hong Kong; enforcing it is something else.

WHERE TO SHOP   Tsim Sha Tsui has the greatest concentration of shops in Hong Kong. Nathan Road, which runs through Kowloon for 2¹/₂ miles from the harbor to the border of the New Territories, is lined with stores selling clothing, jewelry, eyeglasses, cameras, electronic goods, crafts from China, shoes, handbags, luggage, watches, and more. There are also tailors, tattoo artists, and even shops that will carve your name into a wooden chop (a stamp used in place of a signature for official documents). Be sure to explore the side streets radiating off Nathan Road, especially Granville Road, Cameron Road, Mody Road, and Prat Avenue, all of which abound in small, family-owned clothing stores specializing in silks and casual clothes. There are also department stores and shopping arcades, as well as three huge shopping malls. Harbour City on Canton Road, for example, is gigantic; it is comprised of Ocean Centre, Ocean Galleries, Ocean Terminal, and the new Gateway Shopping Arcade.

For upscale shopping, Central is the place where you'll find international designer labels. The Landmark, Central Building, Prince's Building, Swire House, and Alexandra House boast boutiques selling jewelry, clothing, leather goods and more, with names ranging from A Testoni, Aquascutum, Armani, Cartier, and Chanel to Christian Dior, Ferragamo, Gucci, Hermès, Lanvin, and Tiffany.

Another happy hunting ground is Causeway Bay on Hong Kong Island. In contrast to Tsim Sha Tsui, it caters more to the local market than to tourists, and prices are generally quite low. In addition to small shops selling everything from shoes and clothing to Chinese herbs, there are several Japanese department stores, a Lane Crawford department store, and the China Products store with imports from mainland China. Check the backstreets of Causeway Bay, such as Lockhart Road and Jaffe Road, as well as the area around Jardine's Crescent, an open-air market with cheap clothing, food, and produce.

Another good place to shop for inexpensive fashions is Stanley Market on the southern end of Hong Kong Island, where vendors sell silk clothing, jeans, and casual wear. For shoes, get on the tram and head for Happy Valley; on Leighton Road and Wong Nai Chung Road (near the racecourse) there are rows of shoe and handbag shops.

Antique and curio lovers usually head for Hollywood Road and Cat Street on Hong Kong Island, where everything from snuff bottles to jade carvings is for sale.

Shopping in Tsim Sha Tsui

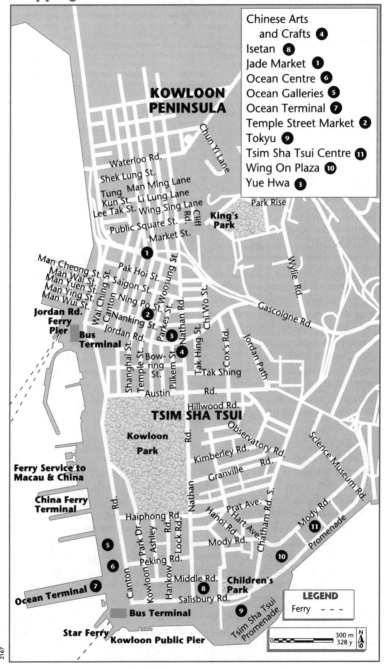

KOWLOON PENINSULA

Chinese Arts and Crafts **4**
Isetan **8**
Jade Market **1**
Ocean Centre **6**
Ocean Galleries **5**
Ocean Terminal **7**
Temple Street Market **2**
Tokyu **9**
Tsim Sha Tsui Centre **11**
Wing On Plaza **10**
Yue Hwa **3**

Waterloo Rd.
Shek Lung St.
Tung Man Ming Lane
Kun St.   Li Lung Lane
Lee Tak St.   Wing Sing Lane
Cliff Rd.
Public Square St.
Market St.
Chun Yi Lane
Park Rise
King's Park

Man Cheong St.
Man Wai St.
Man Yuen St.
Man Ying St.
Man Wui St.
Pak Hoi St.
Saigon St.
Wai Ching St.
Canton
Ning Po St.
Nanking St.
Woosung St.
Parkes St.
Nathan Rd.
Chi Wo St.
Tak Hing St.
Cox's Rd.
Wylie Rd.
Gascoigne Rd.
Jordan Path

Jordan Rd. Ferry Pier
Bus Terminal
Jordan Rd.
Shanghai St.
Temple St.
Bow-ring St.
Pilkem St.
Tak Shing Rd.
Austin Rd.
Hillwood Rd.

TSIM SHA TSUI

Kowloon Park

Observatory Rd.
Kimberley Rd.
Granville Rd.
Nathan Rd.
Science Museum Rd.

Ferry Service to Macau & China
China Ferry Terminal

Haiphong Rd.
Park Dr.
Ashley Rd.
Kowloon Rd.
Hankow Rd.
Lock Rd.
Peking Rd.
Canton Rd.
Prat Ave.
Hart Ave.
Hanoi Rd.
Chatham Rd. S.
Mody Rd.
Mody Rd.
Promenade

Middle Rd.
Children's Park
Salisbury Rd.
Ocean Terminal 7
Bus Terminal
Star Ferry
Kowloon Public Pier
Tsim Sha Tsui Promenade

LEGEND
Ferry – – –

0   300 m
                     328 y

N

2167

Chinese handcrafts are sold in Chinese-product department stores and Chinese arts and crafts shops located on both sides of the harbor.

WHEN TO SHOP   Because shopping is such big business in Hong Kong, most stores are open 7 days a week, closing only for 2 or 3 days during the Chinese New Year. The only exceptions are a few large department stores that close on Sunday, and some Japanese department stores that are closed one day each month. Most stores open at 10am, and remain open until 6pm in Central, 9pm in Tsim Sha Tsui, and 9:30pm in Causeway Bay. Street markets are open every day.

The biggest and best seasonal sale takes place after Christmas and before the Chinese lunar New Year. All the major department stores, as well as shops in many of the huge shopping complexes, hold sales at this time. There are also end-of-season sales in the early spring and early autumn, and some stores feature additional sales in summer, usually in July or August.

WARNING   Hong Kong is a buyer-beware market. Name brands are sometimes fakes; that cheap jade you bought may actually be glass; and electronic goods may not work. To make things worse, the general practice is that goods are usually not returnable and deposits paid are not refundable.

To be on the safe side, try to make your major purchases at HKTA member stores, which display the HKTA logo (a round circle with a red Chinese junk in the middle) on their storefronts. Altogether there are more than 750 member stores, all listed in a directory called "Shopping" that you can get free from the HKTA. This booklet gives the names, addresses, and phone numbers of shops that sell everything from audio-video equipment to musical instruments, clothing, hairpieces, antiques, and wines. Even more important, it lists the sole agents for specific products and brand names, such as Sony, Chanel, or Nikon, along with their telephone numbers. HKTA member stores are required to give accurate information on the products they sell and to respond promptly to justified complaints. If you have any complaints against a member store, call the Membership Department of the HKTA (☎ 852/ 2801 7278) Monday through Friday from 9am to 5pm and on Saturday from 9am to 12:45pm.

GUARANTEES   If you're buying a camera, electronic goods, watches, or any other expensive product, be sure to ask the shopkeeper for a guarantee, which should include a description of the model and serial number, date of purchase, name and address of the shop where you bought it, and the shop's official chop or stamp. Different products and models of the same brand may carry different warranties— some valid worldwide, others only in Hong Kong. Worldwide guarantees must carry the name and/or symbol of the sole agent in Hong Kong for the given product. If you're in doubt, check with the relevant Hong Kong sole agent. And be sure to ask for a receipt from the shopkeeper giving a description of your purchase, including the brand name, model number, serial number, and price for electronic and photographic equipment; for jewelry and gold watches, there should be a description of the precious stones and the metal content.

COMPARISON-SHOPPING & BARGAINING   The cardinal rule of shopping in Hong Kong is to shop around. Unless you're planning to buy antiques or art, you'll probably see the same items in many different shops on both sides of the harbor. And with the exception of department stores and designer boutiques, you'll be able to bargain for your purchase. You most certainly must bargain at all street markets, as well as at many of the smaller, family-owned stores. How much you pay will depend on your bargaining skills and how many items you intend to purchase. Begin your comparison-shopping as soon as you arrive in Hong Kong, so that you can get an idea of the differences in prices. Generally speaking, you can get a better price if you pay with cash rather than by credit card.

SHIPPING   Many stores, especially the larger ones, will pack and ship your purchases home for you. In addition, all upper-bracket and most medium-range hotels offer a parcel-wrapping and mailing service. If you decide to ship your purchase home yourself, the easiest thing to do is to stop by the post office and buy ready-made boxes, which come with everything you need to ship goods home. Packages sent to the United States or Europe generally take 6 to 8 weeks by surface mail and 1 week by airmail. For major purchases, you should buy an all-risks insurance policy to cover the possibility of damage or loss in transit. Since these policies can be expensive, ask whether using your credit card to make your purchase will provide automatic free insurance.

2 Shopping A to Z

The stores listed below are just a few of the thousands upon thousands in Hong Kong. For more detailed coverage, see the booklet "Shopping," which lists some 700 shops that are members of the HKTA.

ANTIQUES

Several of the Chinese-product stores, listed below under "Chinese Crafts & Products," stock antiques, especially porcelain. The most famous area for antiques and chinoiserie, however, is around **Hollywood Road** and **Cat Street,** both above the Central District on Hong Kong Island. This area gained fame in the 1950s, following the 1949 revolution in China which flooded the market with family possessions. Hollywood Road twists along for a little more than half a mile, with shops selling porcelain, clay figurines, silver, and rosewood and blackwood furniture, as well as fakes and curios. Near the western end is Upper Lascar Row, popularly known as Cat Street, where sidewalk vendors sell snuff bottles, curios, and odds and ends. Other buys include original and reproduction Qing and Ming dynasty Chinese furniture, original prints, scrolls, and archaeological items. At the eastern end of Hollywood Road near Pottinger Street is a cluster of chic antiques shops displaying furniture and blue-and-white porcelain, including goods from neighboring Asian countries such as Korean chests and Japanese hibachi. If you're a real antique collector, I suggest you simply walk through the dozens of shops on and around Hollywood Road.

If you cannot tell the difference between originals and reproductions, you would be better off shopping at one of the HKTA member stores. Otherwise, you might want to hire a consultant to help you locate specific items. One such consultant is **Caroline Barkes, D2/5F, University Heights, 42–44 Kotewall Rd., Mid-Levels (☎ 852/2546 8547; fax 852/2857 4114),** who specializes in porcelain and pottery from the Han and T'ang dynasties. She can help buyers avoid unscrupulous dealers; can provide certified appraisal; can arrange for a dating procedure to determine the age of an antique; and can arrange transportation, packing, and shipping. Fees vary according to the service required, beginning at HK$2,500 ($324) for a half day of shopping, plus a 10% commission on whatever you buy, up to HK$250,000. Obviously, her services are for serious collectors, but ultimately she could save you a lot of money if she prevents you from buying a fake product.

Cat Street Galleries

38 Lok Ku Rd., Central. ☎ **852/2543 1609.** Mon–Sat 11am–5:30pm. MTR: Central.

Cat Street Galleries, on Cat Street, houses several individually owned booths of arts and crafts and expensive antiques from the various dynasties.

Charlotte Horstmann and Gerald Godfrey

Shop 104, Ocean Terminal, Harbour City, 3 Canton Rd., Tsim Sha Tsui. ☎ **852/2735 7167.** Mon–Sat 9:30am–6pm. MTR: Tsim Sha Tsui.

This small shop, located in the Ocean Terminal shopping mall on Canton Road, is an emporium of expensive, top-quality Asian antiques. Since the shop itself is rather small, be sure to make an appointment to see the adjoining 10,000-square-foot warehouse. Its stock varies, but Chinese art and jade are well represented; antiques from Indonesia, Thailand, Cambodia, India, and Korea are usually also available.

China Art

15 Upper Lascar Row, Central. ☎ **852/2542 0982.** Mon–Sat 9:30am–6pm, Sun 11am–6pm. MTR: Central.

Located on Upper Lascar Row (popularly known as Cat Street), this family-owned shop is one of Hong Kong's best for antique Chinese furniture, including chairs, tables, and wardrobes, mostly from the Ming dynasty (1368–1644).

True Arts & Curios

89 Hollywood Rd., Central. ☎ **852/2559 1485.** Mon–Sat 10:30am–6:30pm, Sun 2:30–6:30pm. MTR: Central.

This tiny shop is so packed with antiques and curios that there's barely room for customers. Although everything from snuff bottles, porcelain, antique silver, earrings, hair pins, and children's shoes (impractical but darling, with curled toes) are stocked, the true finds here are some 2,000 intricate wood carvings, pried from the doors and windows of dismantled temples and homes. You'll find them hanging from the ceiling and in bins, many of them dusty and grimy from years of neglect. The best ones are carved from a single piece of wood, masterpieces in workmanship and available at modest prices.

CARPETS

Hong Kong is a good place to shop for Chinese, Indian, Persian, and other types of carpets and rugs. For those that are locally made, Tai Ping carpets are famous the world over, produced in Hong Kong with virgin wool imported from New Zealand. The **Hollywood Road** and **Wyndham Street** areas in Central are the best places to search for shops specializing in imported carpets.

Harbour City, the huge megamall at 5 Canton Rd. in Tsim Sha Tsui, is another good place to look, and the shops here include Carpet World and Chinese Carpet Centre. Be sure, too, to check out the Chinese-product stores, which stock hand-knotted wool or silk Chinese carpets.

For Tai Ping carpets, two conveniently located showrooms are in Wing On Plaza in Tsim Sha Tsui East (☎ 852/2369 4061), and the Hutchinson House in Central (☎ 852/2522 7138).

CERAMICS

Chinaware, a fine, translucent earthenware, was first brought from China to Europe by the Portuguese in the 16th century. Its name was subsequently shortened to "china," and Hong Kong remains one of the best places in the world to shop for both antique (mainly from the Manchu, or Ching, dynasty, 1644–1911) and contemporary Chinese porcelain. Traditional motifs include bamboo, flowers, dragons, carp, and cranes, which adorn everything from dinner plates to vases, lamps, and jars. Probably the best place to begin looking for china is at one of the Chinese-product stores, listed below under "Chinese Crafts & Products." If you're looking for contemporary china or replicas, you might want to visit one of the porcelain factories below.

Ah Chow
Block B, Hong Kong Industrial Centre, 489–491 Castle Peak Rd., Cheung Sha Wan, Kowloon. ☎ **852/2745 1511.** Mon–Sat 10am–6pm. MTR: Lai Chi Kok station; then follow the signs for the Leighton Textile Building/Thung Chau West Street.

A small outlet for modern chinaware.

Overjoy Porcelain Factory
1st floor, Block B, 10–18 Chun Pin St., Kwai Chung, New Territories. ☎ **852/2487 0615.** Mon–Sat 10am–6pm. MTR: Kwai Hing station; then take a taxi.

With more than 400 stock designs, dinner services are the specialty. You may also mix and match, or even create your very own design. Sets are usually commissioned for either 6, 8, or 12 diners and take 4 to 6 weeks to complete.

Wah Tung China Company
12th–17th floors, Grand Marine Industrial Building, 3 Yue Fung St., Tin Wan Hill Rd., Aberdeen, Hong Kong Island. ☎ **852/2873 2272.** Mon–Sat 9am–6pm. Bus: 70 from Central.

This is reputedly the largest company specializing in antique porcelain reproductions, especially huge pieces like vases and garden stools.

CHINESE CRAFTS & PRODUCTS

Chinese Arts and Crafts Ltd.
Silvercord Building, 30 Canton Rd., Tsim Sha Tsui. ☎ **852/2375 0155.** Kowloon shops daily 10am–8pm; Yau Ma Tei branch, daily 10am–9pm; Pacific Place, daily 10:30am–7pm; Wan Chai and Central branches, Mon–Sat 10am–6:30pm, Sun noon –6pm. MTR: Tsim Sha Tsui for the Silvercord and Star House branches; Jordan for the Yau Ma Tei branch; Central for the Shell House branch; Admiralty for the Pacific Place branch; Wan Chai for the Wan Chai branch.

In business for more than 30 years, this is the best upscale shop for Chinese arts and crafts and is one of the safest places to purchase jade. You can also buy silk dresses and blouses, arts and crafts, antiques, jewelry, watches, carpets, cloisonné, furs, Chinese herbs and medicine, rosewood furniture, ceramics, Chinese teas, and embroidered tablecloths or pillowcases. It's a great place for gifts in all price ranges.

Other branches include: Star House, 3 Salisbury Rd., Tsim Sha Tsui (☎ 852/2735 4061); 233–239 Nathan Rd., Yau Ma Tei (☎ 852/2730 0061); Prince's Building, 3 Des Voeux Rd., Central (☎ 852/2845 0092); The Mall in Pacific Place, 88 Queensway, Central (☎ 852/2523 3933); and the China Resources Building, 26 Harbour Rd., Wan Chai (☎ 852/2827 6667).

Shanghai Tang
Pedder Building, Theatre Lane, Central. ☎ **852/2525 7333.** MTR: Central.

You are stepping back into the Shanghai of the 1930s when you enter this upscale store with its gleaming wooden floor, raised cashier cubicles, ceiling fans, and helpful clerks wearing classical Chinese jackets. This is Chinese chic at its best, with neatly stacked rows of traditional Chinese clothing ranging from cheongsams and silk pajamas to padded jackets, caps, and shoes. There are even Shanghai tailors on hand to custom-make something for you. You will also find funky accessories and home furnishings, from Mao-emblazoned watches to '30s-style alarm clock remakes.

Yue Hwa Chinese Products

301–309 Nathan Rd., Yau Ma Tei, Kowloon. ☎ **852/2384 0084.** Main store daily 10am–10pm; Park Lane branch, daily 10am– 9:30pm; Nathan Road branch, daily 9:30am–8:30pm. MTR: Jordan for the main store, Tsim Sha Tsui for the other two branches.

Yue Hwa caters to a local clientele with both traditional Chinese and everyday products. The main shop in Yau Ma Tei stocks everything from household goods to clothing, jewelry, arts and crafts, china, medicinal herbs, and even antlers. It was here that I bought some friends a gag wedding gift—Chinese whiskey with preserved lizards in it, all for only HK$25 ($3.25), definitely a bargain. The branch stores specialize primarily in Chinese handcrafts and jewels.

Branch stores include: Park Lane Shopper's Boulevard at 143–161 Nathan Rd. (☎ 852/2739 3888) and at 54–64 Nathan Rd. (☎ 852/2368 9165), both in Tsim Sha Tsui.

DEPARTMENT STORES

It will probably come as no surprise to learn that Hong Kong has a great many department stores. Wing On and Lane Crawford, two upmarket chain department stores, offer a nice selection of clothing, accessories, local and imported designer fashions, gift items, and cosmetics. Japanese department stores have become quite popular with the locals. Causeway Bay has the largest concentration of Japanese department stores. Department store hours are the same for other stores in the area (see "The Shopping Scene," above).

LOCAL DEPARTMENT STORES

Lane Crawford Ltd.

Lane Crawford House, 70 Queen's Rd., Central. ☎ **852/2526 6121.** MTR: Central for the Lane Crawford House main store, Admiralty for the Pacific Place shop, Causeway Bay for the Windsor House branch, and Tsim Sha Tsui for the Nathan Road and Harbour City branches.

This department store, with large clothing departments for the whole family, has branches on both sides of the harbor and is similar to established chain stores in England and the United States.

Other branches can be found at: The Mall in Pacific Place, 88 Queensway, Central (☎ 852/2845 1838); Windsor House, 311 Gloucester Rd., Causeway Bay (☎ 852/2890 9533); 74 Nathan Rd., Tsim Sha Tsui (☎ 852/2721 9668); and Ocean Terminal, Shop 100, Harbour City, 3 Canton Rd., Tsim Sha Tsui (☎ 852/2730 2393).

Wing On

211 Des Voeux Rd., Central. ☎ **852/2852 1888.** MTR: Sheung Wan, Central, Wan Chai, and Tsim Sha Tsui, respectively.

This department store, which is similar to Lane Crawford, offers a wide selection of clothing, jewelry, accessories, and household items.

Other branches can be found at: 26 Des Voeux Rd. Central, Central (☎ 852/2524 7171); Hopewell Centre, 183 Queen's Rd. East, Wan Chai (☎ 852/2529 1060); and Wing On Plaza, 62 Mody Rd., Tsim Sha Tsui East (☎ 852/2723 2211).

JAPANESE DEPARTMENT STORES

Hong Kong Daimaru Fashion Square

Great George St., Causeway Bay. ☎ **852/2576 7321.** Both stores Sun–Thurs 10:30am–9:30pm, Fri–Sat 10:30am–10pm; closed the second Wed each month. MTR: Causeway Bay (both stores).

This department store carries everything from men's and women's fashions, including some designer clothing, to luggage, jewelry, shoes, and cosmetics. Nearby is Daimaru Household Square, at Cleveland Street and Kingston Street, which carries household products such as kitchenware, bedding, and bathroom items, as well as children's clothing, toys, and Chinese antiques. There is also a large grocery department, an inexpensive cafeteria, and a Japanese restaurant.

Isetan

Sheraton Hotel Shopping Mall, Salisbury Rd., Tsim Sha Tsui. ☎ **852/2369 0111.** Daily 10am–9pm. MTR: Tsim Sha Tsui.

Mainly a clothing department store, Isetan carries a nice line of conservative clothing appropriate for business as well as contemporary and fashionable styles. It also stocks shoes, lingerie, ties, belts, cosmetics, and other accessories. It's located next to the Sheraton Hotel.

Matsuzakaya

2–20 Paterson St., Causeway Bay. ☎ **852/2890 6622.** Daily 10:30am–9:30pm; closed the third Thurs each month. MTR: Causeway Bay.

This department store, first established in Japan more than 300 years ago, carries clothing, shoes, handbags, cosmetics, housewares, porcelain, glassware, toys, and cookware. It also features boutiques by Chanel, Fendi, Givenchy, Bally, Nina Ricci, Alain Manoukian, Rosenthal, Wedgwood, Baccarat, and Lalique.

Mitsukoshi

500 Hennessy Rd., Causeway Bay. ☎ **852/2576 5222.** Sun–Fri 10:30am–9:30pm, Sat 10:30am–10pm. MTR: Causeway Bay.

Mitsukoshi is another long-established department store; it first opened as a kimono shop in Japan in the 1600s and is still one of Japan's most exclusive stores. Today it houses the boutiques of well-known designers of shoes, accessories, and clothing, with high prices to match; it also carries lingerie, cosmetics, and household goods.

Seibu

The Mall, Pacific Place, 88 Queensway, Central. ☎ **852/2868 0111.** Sun–Thurs 10:30am–8pm, Fri–Sat 10:30am–9pm. MTR: Admiralty.

One of the largest department store chains in Japan (its Tokyo store is the second-largest department store in the world), this was Seibu's first store to open outside Japan and is a relative newcomer in Hong Kong. An upscale, sophisticated department store targeting Hong Kong's affluent yuppie population, it is the epitome of chic, from its art deco Italian furnishings to fashions from the world's top design houses. More than 65% of its merchandise is European, and 25% is from Japan. The Loft department carries well-designed housewares and gifts, while Seed is the place to go for the latest fashions. Valentino, Kenzo, Paul Smith, and Katharine Hamnett all have boutiques here. The food department is especially good, stocking many imported items that are not available elsewhere in Hong Kong.

Sogo

East Point Centre, 555 Hennessy Rd., Causeway Bay. ☎ **852/2833 8338.** Daily 10am–10pm. MTR: Causeway Bay.

Sogo is much more egalitarian than the other Japanese department stores listed above; its goods are cheaper and its prices lower. Consequently, the store is often packed, filled with families shopping for clothing, toys, furniture, household goods, and electrical appliances.

Tokyu

New World Centre, 24 Salisbury Rd., Tsim Sha Tsui. ☎ **852/2722 0102.** Daily 10am–9pm. MTR: Tsim Sha Tsui.

Tokyu is known for its practical, middle-of-the-road fashions and goods, appealing to both working women and middle-aged homemakers.

OTHER DEPARTMENT STORES

Marks & Spencer

Ocean Centre, Harbour City, Canton Rd., Tsim Sha Tsui. ☎ **852/2730 3163.** Ocean Centre branch daily 10am–8pm; Pacific Place daily 10:30am–8pm. MTR: Tsim Sha Tsui for Ocean Centre, Admiralty for Pacific Place.

Known in Britain for its great prices on clothing and affectionately nicknamed "Marks & Sparks," this import from the United Kingdom has a branch on the Hong Kong side at the Mall, Pacific Place, 88 Queensway, Central (☎ 852/2523 2366).

DESIGNER BOUTIQUES

If you're looking for international name brands and don't care about price, check out the boutiques in the Landmark, Swire House, and Prince's Building, all located in the heart of Central.

The **Landmark,** located on Des Voeux Road Central, is an ultrachic shopping complex, with such shops as Gucci, Tiffany, Polo/Ralph Lauren, Missoni, DKNY, Thierry Mugler, Jean Paul Gaultier, Louis Vuitton, Lanvin, Paloma Picasso, Lalique, and Wedgwood, as well as restaurants. The shops are generally open Monday through Saturday from 9:30am to 6:30pm, Sunday from 11am to 6pm.

Not to be outdone is the **Prince's Building,** on Chater Road, Statue Square, across from the Mandarin Oriental Hotel. It showcases five floors of boutiques, including Dunhill, Cartier, Cerruti, Chanel, Aquascutum, Esprit, Gieves and Hawkes, and Diane Freis. It also has a Chinese Arts and Crafts shop. These shops are open Monday through Saturday from 10am to 7pm.

Meanwhile, across the harbor, **The Peninsula Hotel,** on Salisbury Road in Tsim Sha Tsui, boasts a shopping arcade with such designer boutiques as Charles Jourdan, Kenzo, Hermès, Louis Vuitton, Loewe, Bally, Chanel, Gucci, and Dunhill, to name only a few. Expect to spend a lot of money and you won't be disappointed. **The Regent Hotel** also has a shopping arcade, with concessions for Louis Vuitton, Chanel, Nina Ricci, Lanvin, Salvatore Ferragamo, Bally, Cartier, Diane Freis, Oscar de la Renta, Etienne Aigner, and Donna Karan. Other boutiques are located in Tsim Sha Tsui's huge shopping malls such as Harbour City (see "Megamalls," below).

For **Hong Kong designers,** check out the fashions of Eddie Lau, sold at Chinese Arts and Crafts stores (see "Chinese Crafts & Products," above). Another popular Hong Kong designer, Diane Freis, has outlets in the Prince's Building, the Mall in Pacific Place, Ocean Terminal and Ocean Galleries (both in Tsim Sha Tsui's Harbour City shopping complex), and the Regent Hotel's shopping arcade in Tsim Sha Tsui.

FABRICS

Many tailors stock their own bolts of fabric, but for one-stop fabric shopping with larger selections, the place to go is the **Western Market** on Morrison Street in the Central District. The first floor of this 1906 renovated brick building is lined with shop after shop selling every imaginable type of cloth. The salesmen can advise almost to the inch how much fabric you'll need for any outfit, even if all you have to show them is a drawing. Daily 10am–7pm. MTR: Sheung Wan.

FACTORY OUTLETS

Savvy shoppers head for Hong Kong's factory outlets to buy many of their clothes. Although scattered throughout the territory, the most convenient outlets are in the Central District on Hong Kong Island or Hung Hom and Tsim Sha Tsui in Kowloon. On Hong Kong Island, the best-known building that houses factory-outlet showrooms is the **Pedder Building**, 12 Pedder St., Central. During my last visit I counted almost 50 shops here located on seven floors, including concessions for Chanel, Ann Klein, DKNY, Thierry Mugler, and Moschino, but not all of these shops are factory outlets—many are just regular boutiques with the same merchandise at the same prices as found at their other branches. However, it's convenient to have so many shops in one building and it's fun to just poke around.

On the Kowloon side, there are a few factory outlets in the heart of Tsim Sha Tsui at the **Star House,** 3 Salisbury Rd. (just in front of the Star Ferry), and the **Sands Building,** 17 Hankow Rd. The largest concentration of factory outlets, however, is in Hung Hom, clustered in a large group of warehouse buildings called **Kaiser Estates** on Man Yue Street. Although the Kaiser Estates themselves comprise huge concrete factory buildings, the many outlet shops inside look just like ordinary shops.

Factory outlets sell excess stock, overruns, and quality-control rejects; because these items have been made for the export market, the sizes are Western. Be sure to examine garments inside out. Bargains include clothes made of silk (the latest craze is "washable silk"), cashmere, leather, cotton, and wool, and some outlets have men's clothing as well.

However, you never know in advance what will be on sale, and sometimes the selection is disappointing. What's more, some outlets are indistinguishable from upmarket boutiques, with prices to match. Unfortunately, it seems that some shops simply call themselves "factory outlets" because that's what tourists are looking for. Thus, unless you have lots of time, it may not be worth your while to go to the outlets in Hung Hom in search of a good deal.

For a list of factory outlets along with their addresses, telephone numbers, and types of clothing, pick up the free pamphlet, "Factory Outlets," available at HKTA offices. Most outlets are open from 9 or 10am to 6pm Monday through Friday, and some are open on Saturday and Sunday as well.

FASHIONS

Clothing is one of Hong Kong's best buys, with clothing stores literally everywhere you look. For inexpensive, fun fashion, visit Stanley Market on Hong Kong Island, the many shops and department stores in Causeway Bay and Tsim Sha Tsui, and of course, the megamalls described below. Factory outlets, described above, are also good places to look for bargains.

GIFTS & SOUVENIRS

In addition to the shops here, the Chinese-product stores listed above under "Chinese Crafts and Products," offer a wide array of souvenirs and gifts. Other places to look for souvenirs include hotel shopping arcades, Nathan Road in Tsim Sha Tsui, the Peak Galleria on Victoria Peak, Western Market in the Western District, and the megamalls.

Amazing Grace Elephant Co.
348 Ocean Centre, Harbour City, Canton Rd., Tsim Sha Tsui. ☎ **852/2730 5455.** MTR: Tsim Sha Tsui.

Opened in the 1970s by an American who began selling ceramic elephants from Vietnam, this establishment has since expanded into arts and crafts from China, Thailand, Indonesia, the Philippines, and other Asian countries. Among the beautiful, but expensive, decorations for the home that are offered here are brassware, rattan products, jewelry, clothing, ceramics, and silks.

Welfare Handicrafts Shop

Salisbury Rd. (between the YMCA and the Star Ferry Concourse), Tsim Sha Tsui. ☎ **852/ 2366 6979.** Tsim Sha Tsui branch Mon–Sat 9am–5:45pm, Central branch Mon–Fri 9am–5:30pm, Sat 9am–1pm. MTR: Tsim Sha Tsui, Central branch Central.

Welfare Handicrafts Shops began more than 30 years ago as an outlet for crafts and goods made by Chinese refugees. Today the proceeds go to charity, so I always stop by to see whether there are small items that might make nice stocking-stuffers or presents. Items for sale include T-shirts, porcelain, silk coin purses, pincushions, small cast-iron statues, and other souvenirs.

The Central District branch is situated on the lower ground floor of Jardine House, Shop 7, Connaught Road, Central (☎ 852/2524 3356).

JEWELRY

According to the HKTA, Hong Kong has more jewelry stores per square mile than any other city in the world. Gems are imported duty free from all over the world, and Hong Kong is reputedly the world's third-largest trading center for diamonds. Gold jewelry, both imported and locally made, is required by law to carry a stamp stating the accurate gold content.

Jade, of course, remains the most popular item of jewelry for both visitors and Chinese. It's believed to protect wearers against illness. The two categories of jade are jadeite and nephrite. Jadeite (also called Burmese jade) is generally white to apple green in color, although it also comes in hues of brown, red, orange, yellow, and even lavender. It may be mottled, but the most expensive variety is a translucent emerald green. Nephrite, which is less expensive, is usually a dark green or off-white. In any case, true jade is so hard that supposedly even a knife leaves no scratch. Unless you know your jade, your best bet is to shop in one of the Chinese-product stores, listed above under "Chinese Crafts & Products." For less expensive pieces, visit the Jade Market, described below under "Markets."

Pearls, almost all of which are cultured, are also popular among shoppers in Hong Kong. There are both sea- and freshwater pearls, available in all shapes, sizes, colors, and lusters. For inexpensive strands, check the vendors at the Jade Market. There are also many shops along Nathan Road in Tsim Sha Tsui that retail pearls.

For more information on jewelry, pick up a free pamphlet at an HKTA office called "Shopping Guide to Jewelry," which provides useful information about gold, diamonds, emeralds, rubies, sapphires, jade, pearls, birthstones, and other precious stones. Also included are shopping hints and advice on the care and protection of jewelry.

If you're a real jewelry fan, you'll want to visit the jewelry wholesale outlets in the Kaiser Estate area in Hung Hom. At some outlets, visitors will be asked to register and then will be shown around the factory itself, where they can observe the designs being drawn, learn how the stones are graded, and see the final polishing. After the tour, visitors are taken to the shop that sells finished products. For more information on jewelry outlets, contact the Hong Kong Tourist Association.

MARKETS

Markets offer the best deals in Hong Kong, though a lot depends on how well you can bargain. Be sure to scrutinize the items that interest you carefully, since you won't be able to return them. Check clothing for faults, tears, cuts, marks, and uneven seams and hemlines.

HONG KONG ISLAND

STANLEY   Stanley Market is probably the most popular and best-known market in Hong Kong, and Stanley is a trendy place for foreign residents to live. Located on the southern coast of Hong Kong Island on a small peninsula, it's a great place to buy inexpensive clothing, especially jeans, sportswear, bathing suits, sweaters, casual clothing, and silk blouses, dresses, and suits. During my last visit, shopkeepers were not keen about bargaining, no doubt because tourists come here by the busload. In fact, Stanley is not as cheap as it once was, and many shops are remodeling and becoming more chic and expensive. Still, you're bound to find at least something you're wild about. I buy more of my clothes here than anywhere else in Hong Kong, especially when it comes to cheap, fun fashions; raw-silk suits and silk blouses, skirts, and shorts. I usually walk through the market first, taking note of things I like and which stores they are in, and then I compare prices as I walk through. Most stores carry the same products, so it pays to comparison-shop.

To reach Stanley, take bus no. 6 or 260 from Central's Exchange Square bus terminal near the Star Ferry. The bus ride to Stanley takes approximately 30 minutes. The shops are open daily from 10am to 7pm.

LI YUEN STREET EAST & WEST   These two streets are parallel pedestrian lanes in the heart of the Central District, very narrow and often congested with human traffic. Their stalls are packed with handbags, clothes, scarves, sweaters, toys, baby clothes, watches, makeup, umbrellas, knickknacks, and even brassieres. Don't neglect the open-fronted shops behind the stalls. Some of these are boutiques selling fashionable but cheap clothing as well as shoes, purses, and accessories. These two streets are located just a couple of minutes' walk from the Tsim Sha Tsui MTR station or the Star Ferry. Vendors are open daily from 9am to 7pm.

JARDINE'S BAZAAR & JARDINE'S CRESCENT   The open-air market that spreads along these two streets in Causeway Bay and spills into the surrounding area is a traditional Chinese market for produce, cheap clothing, and accessories, including shoes, costume jewelry, handbags, hair accessories, and children's clothing. Though you may not find something worth taking home, it's fun just to walk around. The nearest MTR station is Causeway Bay, but you can also reach this area easily by tram. It's open daily from 11am to 9pm.

KOWLOON

JADE MARKET   Jade, believed by the Chinese to hold mystical powers, is available in all sizes, colors, and prices at the Jade Market, located on Kansu Street under a flyover in the Yau Ma Tei District. The jade comes from Burma, China, Australia, and Taiwan. Unless you know your jade, you won't want to make any expensive purchases here, but the quality of jade sold here is great for bangles, pendants, earrings, and inexpensive gifts. This market is also recommended for pearls, especially inexpensive freshwater pearls from China. In 1989 I bought two 20-inch three-strand necklaces, one for HK$70 ($9.10) and another with much larger pearls for HK$150 ($19.50). They may not last forever, but they're certainly good buys.

The Jade Market is open daily from 10am to about 2pm, though some vendors stay until 3 or 4pm. It's located near the Jordan MTR station or less than a 30-minute walk from the Star Ferry.

LADIES' MARKET   Tung Choi Street (between Argyle and Dundas Streets) in Mong Kok serves as a lively market for inexpensive women's and children's fashions, shoes, jewelry, sunglasses, watches, and other accessories. The products are geared to local tastes and sizes, but the atmosphere is fun and festive, with plenty of *dai pai dong* food stalls in the evening to feed the hungry. The nearest MTR station is Mong Kok. Vendors are open daily from 1 to 10:30pm.

Night Market

Temple Street in the Yau Ma Tei District of Kowloon is a night market that opens up when the sun goes down. It offers the usual products sold by street vendors, including T-shirts, jeans, watches, lighters, sunglasses, jewelry, cassette tapes, sweaters, luggage, and imitation Lacoste shirts. Bargain fiercely, and check the products carefully to make sure they're not faulty or poorly made. The night market is great entertainment, a must during your visit to Hong Kong.

The night market is busiest from about 8 to 11pm, and is located near the Jordan MTR station.

MEGAMALLS & SHOPPING CENTERS

Hong Kong boasts shopping complexes that are so huge I call them "megamalls." They are open daily, with most businesses operating from 10am to 8pm.

Aside from the ones listed below, other Hong Kong megamalls include the **New Town Plaza** in Sha Tin in the New Territories, and the **Taikoo Shing City Plaza,** located at the Taikoo MTR station on Hong Kong Island.

Harbour City
Canton Rd., Tsim Sha Tsui. MTR: Tsim Sha Tsui.

This is the largest of the megamalls, and probably the largest in Asia. Conveniently located right next to the dock that disgorges passengers from cruise liners and just to the east of the Star Ferry, it encompasses Ocean Terminal, Ocean Galleries, Ocean City, and the Gateway, all interconnected by air-conditioned walkways. Altogether there are more than 600 outlets here, with shops selling clothing, accessories, jewelry, cosmetics, antiques, electronic goods, furniture, housewares, Asian arts and crafts, and much more. There's enough to keep you occupied for the rest of your life, but this is an especially good place to go on a rainy or humid day when you'd rather be inside than out. Some shops are closed on Sunday but otherwise the hours are from about 10 or 11am to 8pm.

The Mall
Pacific Place, 88 Queensway, Central.

Pacific Place is the largest and most ambitious commercial project to hit Central; in fact, it has shifted the city center toward the east. Besides three hotels, Pacific Place has the Mall, with 200 retail outlets and three major department stores (Marks & Spencer, Lane Crawford, and Seibu). Outlets include the Body Shop, Benetton, Crabtree and Evelyn, Esprit, Lacoste, Diane Freis, Yves Saint Laurent, Cartier, Cerruti, Hermès, Hugo Boss, Chanel, and Dunhill. Most shops are open daily from about 10:30am to 8pm.

New World Centre
18–24 Salisbury Rd., Tsim Sha Tsui. MTR: Tsim Sha Tsui.

Located next to the Regent Hotel, this shopping complex has outlets on five floors, with shops selling curios, cameras, Chinese arts and crafts, clothing, accessories, and more. There are also many restaurants.

TAILORS

The 24-hour suit is a thing of the past, but you can still have clothes custom-made in a few days. Tailoring in Hong Kong really began in the 1950s, when tailor families from Shanghai fled China and set up shop in Hong Kong. Today, prices are no longer as low as they once were, but they're often about what you'd pay for a similar ready-made garment back home; the difference, of course, is that a tailor-made garment should fit you perfectly. The standards of the better, established shops rival even those of London's Savile Row—at about half the price. A top-quality man's suit will run about HK$4,500 ($585) or more, including fabric, while a silk shirt can cost HK$500 ($65).

Tailors in Hong Kong will make anything you want, from business suits and evening gowns to wedding dresses, leather jackets, and monogrammed shirts. Some stores will allow you to provide your own fabric, while others require that you buy theirs. Many tailors offer a wide range of cloth from which to choose, from cotton and linen to very fine wools, cashmere, and silk. Hong Kong tailors are excellent at copying fashions, even if all you have is a picture or drawing of what you want.

On average, you should allow 3 to 5 days to have a garment custom-made, with at least two or three fittings. Be specific about what you want, such as lining, tightness of fit, buttons, and length. If you aren't satisfied during the fittings, speak up. Alterations should be included in the original price (ask about this during your first negotiations). If in the end you still don't like the finished product, you don't have to accept it. However, you will forfeit the deposit you are required to pay before the tailor begins working, usually about 50% of the total cost.

With more than 2,500 tailoring establishments in Hong Kong, it shouldn't be any problem finding one. Some of the most famous are located in hotel shopping arcades and shopping complexes, but the more upscale the location, the higher the prices. Tsim Sha Tsui abounds in tailor shops. In any case, your best bet is to deal only with shops that are members of the HKTA or those you have used before. Member shops are listed in the "Shopping" booklet.

Once you've had something custom-made and your tailor has your measurements, you will more than likely be able to order additional clothing later after you've returned home.

TOYS

Even though Hong Kong is one of the world's leading exporters of toys, they seem to be in short supply in Hong Kong itself.

Toys "Я" Us
Shop 003, Ocean Terminal, Harbour City, 5 Canton Rd., Tsim Sha Tsui. ☎ 852/2730 9462. Daily 10am–8pm. MTR: Tsim Sha Tsui.

This is one of the largest, if not *the* largest, toy stores in Hong Kong. A huge department store, it claims to have 20,000 items for sale, including games, sporting goods, hobby goods, baby furniture, books, clothing, and, of course, toys.

VIDEO PRODUCTS

If you're interested in buying videocassette recorders, camcorders/players, laser disc and compact disc videos, laser disc players, or other video-related products, pick up the free pamphlet, "Shopping Guide to Video Products," available at HKTA offices. It gives hints on shopping for these products, lists sole agents in Hong Kong for various brand names, and tells which HKTA member shops sell video products. Prices have increased for these products in the past few years, so be sure to check prices at home before you come to Hong Kong to make sure that what you would like to buy here is really a bargain.

9

Hong Kong After Dark

Nightlife in Hong Kong seems pretty tame when compared with that in Tokyo or Bangkok. With the world of Suzie Wong in Wan Chai now a shadow of its former self, Hong Kong today seems somewhat reserved, rather British, and, perhaps to some minds, yawningly dull. For the people who live here, exclusive clubs are places where expatriates entertain their guests, while the Chinese are likely to spend an entire evening at one of those huge lively restaurants.

Yet it would be wrong to assume that Hong Kong has nothing to offer in the way of nightlife—it's just that you probably won't get into any trouble enjoying yourself. To liven things up, Hong Kong stages several annual events, including the Hong Kong Arts Festival held in January or February, the Hong Kong International Film Festival, which usually occurs in April, and the biennial Festival of Asian Arts, generally sometime in autumn. There are cultural activities and entertainment throughout the year, including theater productions, pop concerts, and Chinese opera and dance performances. In addition, there are plenty of that finest of British institutions—the pub—not to mention sophisticated cocktail lounges, discos, hostess clubs, and topless bars. There's even a nightlife area, so to speak, in the vicinity of Lan Kwai Fong Street and D'Aguilar Street in the Central District, where a modest number of bars and restaurants have added a spark to Hong Kong's financial district. Remember that a 10% service charge will be added to your bill.

If you're watching your Hong Kong dollars, keep in mind that one of the best traditions in the colony is its "happy hour," when many bars offer two drinks for the price of one or else drinks at lower prices. Actually, "happy hours" would be more appropriate, since the period is generally from 5 to 7pm and sometimes even longer than that. Furthermore, many pubs, bars, and lounges offer live entertainment, from jazz to Filipino combos, which you can enjoy simply for the price of a beer. There are also a variety of ways to enjoy yourself at night without spending money—for example, strolling along the harbor waterfront or on Victoria Peak, or browsing at the Temple Street night market.

To find out what's going on, check Hong Kong's two newspapers, the *South China Morning Post* and the *Hong Kong Standard.* Moreover, the two tourist publications, *Hong Kong Magazine* and *Hong Kong This Week,* as well as the "Entertainment" section of the *Official Hong Kong Guide* and the *Hong Kong Diary*, both available at the HKTA, also carry information on what's being shown where. For more information on artistic and cultural events, drop by City Hall on Connaught Road in Central or the Arts Centre on Harbour Road in Wan Chai to pick up a free brochure called "City News."

1 The Performing Arts

The busiest time of the year for the performing arts is the month-long **Hong Kong Arts Festival,** held every year in January or February. This international affair features artists from around the world performing with orchestras, dance troupes, opera companies, and chamber ensembles. Appearing at a recent festival, for example, were the Hong Kong Philharmonic Orchestra, the London Philharmonic, the Empire Brass from Boston, the Hong Kong Chinese Orchestra, the Stuttgart Ballet, the Paul Taylor Dance Company, and the Georgian State Dance Company from the former USSR. City Hall, located in Central just east of the Star Ferry concourse, sells tickets to performances, which are priced from HK$50 to HK$300 ($6.50 to $39). For information about the Hong Kong Arts Festival programs and future dates, call 852/2824 3555.

To obtain tickets for the Hong Kong Arts Festival, as well as tickets throughout the year for classical music performances, rock and pop concerts, theatrical productions, dance, and other major events, contact the **Urban Council Ticketing Office (URBTIX),** which has 18 easily accessible outlets throughout the city. Simply drop by one of the outlets, or reserve a ticket in advance by calling URBTIX at ☎ 852/2734 9009. Tickets reserved by phone must be picked up within 3 days of the order. Major URBTIX outlets include City Hall, 7 Edinburgh Place in Central, open daily from 10am to 9:30pm; the Arts Centre, 2 Harbour Rd. in Wan Chai, open daily from 10am to 8:15pm; and the Cultural Centre, 10 Salisbury Rd. in Tsim Sha Tsui, open daily from 10am to 9:30pm.

PERFORMING ARTS COMPANIES
CHINESE OPERA
Chinese opera predates the first Western opera by about 600 years, although it wasn't until the 13th and 14th centuries that performances began to develop a structured operatic form, with rules of composition and fixed role characterization. Distinct regional styles also developed, and even today there are marked differences among the operas performed in, say, Peking, Canton, Shanghai, Fukien, Chiu Chow, and Szechuan.

The most popular, however, is the Peking-style opera, with its spectacular costumes, elaborate makeup, and feats of acrobatics and swordsmanship. The plots usually dramatize legends and historical events, and extoll such virtues as loyalty, filial piety, and righteousness. Accompanied by seven or eight musicians, the performers sing in shrill, high-pitched falsetto, a sound Westerners sometimes do not initially appreciate.

Chinese opera is immensely popular in Hong Kong, so much so that tickets sell out well in advance, making it almost impossible for tourists to attend performances. If you're still determined to try, contact the HKTA for information on what's playing, or check with one of the tourist publications. You could also ask your travel agent or hotel to try to get you tickets when you first make your travel plans. The Ko Shan Theatre (headquarters of the House of Cantonese Opera) and Lai Chi Kok's Palladium Opera House both stage performances of Chinese opera. Prices usually range from HK$90 to HK$200 ($11.70 to $26).

The Major Concert & Performance Halls

City Hall, Connaught Road and Edinburgh Place, Central District (☎ 852/2921 2840).

Hong Kong Academy for Performing Arts, 1 Gloucester Rd., Wan Chai (☎ 852/2584 1514).

Hong Kong Arts Centre, 2 Harbour Rd., Wan Chai (☎ 852/2877 1000).

Hong Kong Coliseum, 9 Cheong Wan Rd., Hung Hom (☎ 852/2765 9233).

Hong Kong Cultural Centre, 10 Salisbury Rd., Tsim Sha Tsui (☎ 852/2734 2010 for information; ☎ 852/2734 9009 for reservations).

Ko Shan Theatre, Ko Shan Road, near Kowloon City (☎ 852/2334 2331).

Queen Elizabeth Stadium, 18 Oi Kwan Rd., Wan Chai (☎ 852/2591 1347).

CLASSICAL MUSIC

Hong Kong Chinese Orchestra

Performing at the Hong Kong Cultural Centre and City Hall. Tickets HK$50–HK$105 ($6.50–$13.65).

The equally acclaimed Hong Kong Chinese Orchestra features 85 musicians who play a wide range of traditional and modern Chinese instruments, combining them with Western orchestrations.

Hong Kong Philharmonic Orchestra

Performing at the Hong Kong Cultural Centre, 10 Salisbury Rd., Tsim Sha Tsui. ☎ 852/2734 2010. Tickets HK$60–HK$230 ($7.80–$29.85), HK$38 ($4.95) students. MTR: Tsim Sha Tsui.

The Hong Kong Cultural Centre is the home of the Hong Kong Philharmonic, founded in 1975 and performing regularly in the colony from September to June and at other scheduled events throughout the year. Its conductor is David Atherton; guest conductors and soloists appear during the concert season.

DANCE COMPANIES

As for dance, both the **Hong Kong Ballet Company** and the **Hong Kong Dance Company** have extensive repertoires. The Hong Kong Dance Company specializes in the development of Chinese dance in modern forms. Finally, another troupe is the **City Contemporary Dance Company,** which expresses contemporary Hong Kong culture through dance. Performances are often held at the Hong Kong Academy for Performing Arts. Contact the HKTA for the current schedule.

THEATER COMPANIES

Local theater companies include the **Chung Ying Theatre Company,** the **Hong Kong Repertory Theatre,** and the **Hong Kong Drama Club.** They perform at various venues, including City Hall in Central and the Hong Kong Cultural Centre in Tsim Sha Tsui. Prices range from about HK$35 to HK$200 ($4.55 to $25.95).

THEATERS

Fringe Club

2 Lower Albert Rd., Central. ☎ 852/2521 7251. Tickets HK$20–HK$120 ($2.60–$15.60) for nonmembers, including 1-night membership.

Actually a private club which offers a temporary, 1-night membership, the Fringe Club specializes in experimental drama, live music, comedy, and other happenings, from mime to magic shows. At the beginning of each year, the Fringe Club sponsors a 3-week Fringe Festival, open to anyone who wants to perform. Saturdays feature an open mike with free admission beginning at 10pm, when anyone can perform for 10 minutes. Housed in a former dairy farm depot built in 1813, the club (formed in 1984) includes a theater, exhibition space, two rehearsal studios, a pottery workshop, a restaurant, and a bar.

MAJOR CONCERT HALLS & ALL-PURPOSE AUDITORIUMS

City Hall
Connaught Rd. and Edinburgh Place, Central District. ☎ **852/2921 2840.** MTR: Central.

Located right beside the Star Ferry concourse, City Hall's Low Block has a 1,500-seat balconied concert hall, as well as a 470-seat theater used for plays and chamber music.

Hong Kong Academy for Performing Arts
1 Gloucester Rd., Wan Chai. ☎ **852/2584 1514.** MTR: Wan Chai.

Located across the street from the Arts Centre, the academy is Hong Kong's institution for vocational training in the performing arts. It also features regular performances in theater and dance, by both local and international playwrights and choreographers. Its Theatre Block is composed of six venues, including the Lyric Theatre, Drama Theatre, Orchestral Hall, and Recital Hall.

Hong Kong Arts Centre
2 Harbour Rd., Wan Chai. ☎ **852/2877 1000.** MTR: Wan Chai.

Built on Wan Chai's new waterfront of reclaimed land, the Arts Centre hosts the Hong Kong Arts Festival and other international presentations, as well as performances by Hong Kong's own amateur and professional companies. It offers a regular schedule of plays or dances, exhibition galleries, and showings of foreign films. There are three auditoriums: Shouson Theatre, McAulay Studio Theatre, and Lim Por Yen Film Theatre.

Hong Kong Coliseum
9 Cheong Wan Rd., Hung Hom. ☎ **852/2765 9233.** Bus: No. 5C from Star Ferry.

Located on the waterfront near the Hung Hom railway terminus, this 12,500-seat arena has the shape of an inverted pyramid and features rock and pop concerts, ice shows, and sporting events. If you want to see Hong Kong's youth go wild, attend a concert performed by a Cantonese pop-star idol.

Hong Kong Cultural Centre
10 Salisbury Rd., Tsim Sha Tsui. ☎ **852/2734 2010** for information, ☎ 852/2734 9009 for reservations. MTR: Tsim Sha Tsui.

Sandwiched in between the Space Museum and the Star Ferry concourse, the Hong Kong Cultural Centre is the territory's newest and largest arena for the arts. Opened in 1989, this complex boasts both a Western and a Chinese restaurant, exhibition areas, and practice and rehearsal rooms, but its pride is its 2,100-seat Concert Hall, home of the Hong Kong Philharmonic Orchestra. It features a 93-stop, 8,000-pipe

Impressions

Hong Kong illuminated . . . is wonderful. Imagine a giant Monte Carlo with a hundred times as many lights!
—Alfred Viscount Northcliffe, *My Journey Round the World,* 1923

Austrian Rieger organ—one of the world's largest. The stage, set near the center of the oval hall, is surrounded by seating at two levels.

There are also two theaters. The Grand Theatre, which seats 1,750, is used for musicals, large-scale drama, dance, film shows, and Chinese opera. It is fitted with a revolving stage wagon, an orchestra pit for 110 musicians, a five-language simultaneous interpretation system (for conventions and conferences), and cinematic projection equipment. The Studio Theatre, which can seat from 326 to 542 persons, was designed for experimental theater and dance. Its stage configuration can be changed to end, thrust, center, and transverse.

You can learn more about the history of the Cultural Centre and visit the Concert Hall, both theaters, and backstage areas by participating in a 30-minute tour of the Centre, given twice daily at 12:30 and 4pm in both English and Cantonese. Cost of the tour is HK$10 ($1.30) for adults; half price for children, students, and senior citizens. For more information on tours, call ☎ 852/2734 2009.

Ko Shan Theatre

Ko Shan Rd., near Kowloon City. ☎ **852/2334 2331.** Bus: no. 5 from Star Ferry.

A former quarry site, this open-air theater in a large park is preferred for Chinese opera, variety shows, and major film screenings. It seats 3,000 people.

Queen Elizabeth Stadium

18 Oi Kwan Rd., Wan Chai. ☎ **852/2591 1347.** Bus: no. 5, 5A, 90, or 97.

Located near the racetrack in Happy Valley, this 3,500-seat air-conditioned arena sponsors rock concerts and other musical performances.

2 The Club & Music Scene

LIVE MUSIC

Hong Kong does not have jazz, rock, or blues clubs as many other cities do. However, several pubs and discos feature jazz regularly. On the Kowloon side, **Ned Kelly's Last Stand,** an Australian watering hole at 11A Ashley Rd., has long been a fixture in Tsim Sha Tsui with its own in-house band playing Dixieland jazz or swing every night from 9pm. Salsa, soul, and funk are featured most nights of the week at the **Catwalk,** a disco in the New World Hotel on Salisbury Road.

On the Hong Kong side, the **Godown,** located in the basement of the Furama Kempinsky Hotel, offers live jazz every Wednesday from 9pm. The **Fringe Club,** 2 Lower Albert Rd., has an open mike every Wednesday in its Heineken Gallery beginning at 10pm with free admission. Another place to hear music is **JJ's,** located in the Grand Hyatt Hotel, 1 Harbour Rd. in Wan Chai, a huge entertainment center with a disco and bar, as well as a separate area featuring live jazz and blues by a house band. Finally, for jazz on Sunday afternoon, head for the **Dickens Bar,** located in the basement of the Excelsior Hotel, 281 Gloucester Rd., in Causeway Bay, where there's a big-band sound from 3 to 6pm.

Live music is also a standard feature of many hotel cocktail lounges, including the **Sky Lounge** in the Sheraton Hotel, the **Chin Chin** in the Hyatt Regency, and **La Ronda** in the Furama Kempinski Hotel.

For more information on all these establishments, refer to individual listings.

DANCE CLUBS/DISCOS

Disco fever has cooled somewhat in recent years; in its place are karaoke bars, where customers sing into a microphone accompanied by background music. Unlike in Japan where it originated, however, karaoke in Hong Kong is an exclusive thing—karaoke machines are placed in private rooms, which are available for rent, making it a very expensive undertaking.

For those who like to dance, however, there are still some discos that have weathered the years and even a few new ones. Discos in Hong Kong generally charge more on weekend nights, but the admission price usually includes one or two free drinks. After that, beer and mixed drinks are often priced the same.

KOWLOON

Catwalk
In the New World Hotel, 22 Salisbury Rd., Tsim Sha Tsui. ☎ **852/2369 4111.** Cover (including two drinks) HK$120 ($15.60) Sun–Thurs, HK$200 ($25.95) Fri–Sat. MTR: Tsim Sha Tsui.

Decorated in a safari theme, with the black silhouette of panthers slinking along the walls and the markings of cat paws on the floor, this disco also features a separate room with live music offering a mix of salsa, soul, and funk. In keeping with the latest trend, there are also 11 karaoke rooms available for rent. Open Sun–Thurs 9pm–3am, Fri–Sat 9pm–4am.

Falcon Disco
In the Royal Garden Hotel, 69 Mody Rd., Tsim Sha Tsui East. ☎ **852/2721 5215.** Cover (including two drinks) HK$90 ($11.70) Sun–Thurs, HK$175 ($22.75) Fri–Sat. MTR: Tsim Sha Tsui.

A sophisticated disco for dancers who like to dress up, this is the place to go if you want to eat, drink, and dance all at the same place. On the top floor is the Falcon, a refined, English-style pub which offers a roast-beef buffet dinner daily—if you eat here Friday or Saturday, you don't have to pay admission to the disco. The dinner buffet, which costs HK$220 ($28.55) per person, is served daily from 6:30 to 9:30pm. You can save money on drinks if you come for happy hour, Monday through Friday from 4:30 to 8:30pm. The disco is open Sun–Thurs 9pm–2am, Fri–Sat 9pm–3am.

Lost City
Chinachem Golden Plaza, 77 Mody Rd., Tsim Sha Tsui East. ☎ **852/2311 1111.** Cover (including one drink) HK$130 ($16.90) Sun–Thurs, HK$200 ($25.95) Fri–Sat. MTR: Tsim Sha Tsui.

This place is aptly named—it's so huge, with a dozen different venues, that one could get lost indeed. Opened in 1995 as Kowloon's splashiest and swankiest disco, it is quite popular with Hong Kong's young Chinese, with long lines forming outside the front door even before it opens. With the Hong Kong in-crowd as fickle as it is, however, this year's hot spot can just as easily fade into oblivion by next year. At any rate, entering this entertainment complex is rather like entering the lost city of Atlantis; you can wander through a variety of venues offering different forms of entertainment or sustenance, including a disco, karaoke club, a leisure center equipped with golf practice rooms (only in Asia!) and a virtual reality machine, a champagne bar, a traditional-style Hong Kong teahouse, a ballroom reminiscent of Shanghai in the 1940s, a stage with live Broadway-style musical performances, and restaurants. Live music is provided by three different bands. In all, it's kind of like taking a minitrip somewhere, without ever leaving Hong Kong. To help you get in the mood, there's even a cocktail lounge designed to make you think you're at an airport. And you thought you'd seen it all! Open daily 8pm–4am.

The Music Room
In the Kowloon Shangri-La Hotel, 64 Mody Rd., Tsim Sha Tsui East. ☎ **852/2721 2111.** No cover, but after 9pm Fri and Sat there's a minimum drink charge of HK$130 ($16.90) for nonhotel guests. MTR: Tsim Sha Tsui.

This is the place to go if you think you're too old for most discos but aren't quite ready for the rest home. Aiming for an older, more sophisticated crowd, it's designed more for socializing and conversing than for wild partying. Furnished with plush carpets and sofas with a view of the harbor, this disco looks like a living room, and the music, which favors Golden Oldies, is concentrated on the dance floor. Happy hour, from 5 to 9pm, features much cheaper prices for drinks and classical and easy-listening music. Open daily 5pm–2am.

CENTRAL DISTRICT

In addition to the four discos below, **California**, listed below under "The Bar Scene" in the Central District, transforms itself into a disco on Friday and Saturday nights from 11pm to 4am, with a HK$100 ($13) admission.

Club 97

9 Lan Kwai Fong, Central. ☎ **852/2810 9333.** No cover Sun–Thurs, HK$97 ($12.60) Fri–Sat. MTR: Central.

This small disco, decorated in funky "Moroccan" style with black-and-white tiles, mirrors, and tiny lights reminiscent of stars, is fun and usually crowded to capacity. In fact, it's so small that it sometimes feels like a private party—even more so because it's officially a members-only disco. However, nonmembers are allowed in if the place isn't too crowded; plan for a weeknight and maybe even call ahead for a reservation. It's easy to strike up a conversation with your neighbors here, since they are generally a mixture of expatriates and Chinese. The Tea Dance, a gay happy hour, takes place on the first and third Sunday of the month with half-price drinks and again every Friday from 6 to 9pm. Mon–Thurs 9pm–6am, Fri 6pm–6am, Sat 10pm–6am, Sun 10pm–3am.

Judgement A.D.

Basement of Bank of America Tower, 12 Harcourt Rd., Central. ☎ **852/2521 0309.** Cover (including one drink) HK$100 ($13) Sun–Wed, HK$130 ($16.90) for men and free for women Thurs, HK$150 ($19.50) Fri–Sat. MTR: Central.

Ruined Roman pillars and other signs of destruction hint that mankind did not do too well when it came to judgment day, but otherwise the atmosphere here is upbeat, especially during happy hour Monday through Friday from 5 to 8:30pm with a good appetizer table and two drinks for the price of one. After 10pm, a live band plays pop music to a largely Chinese clientele. A separate, circular room serves as a disco Thursday, Friday, and Saturday nights, with soft music beginning at 9:30pm and the harder stuff starting at 11:30pm. Thursday is ladies' night, with free admission and free drinks for women. All in all, a good place to unwind after a day's work in Central. Open Mon–Fri 5 to 8:30pm, Sun–Wed 9pm– 2am, Thurs–Sat 9pm–5am.

Propaganda

30–32 Wyndham St., Central. ☎ **852/2868 1316.** Cover Mon–Wed HK$45 ($5.85), Thurs HK$65 ($8.40), Fri HK$100 ($13), Sat HK$120 ($15.60). MTR: Central.

One of Hong Kong's most popular gay discos, Propaganda is located above the Lan Kwai Fong district and is decorated in a sterile, submarinelike atmosphere, with mazelike corridors and small rooms for intimacy. Come late if you want to see it at its most crowded, but remember that before 10:30pm admission is free Monday through Thursday and almost half price Friday and Saturday, with drinks also half price. Only about 5% of the people who come through the doors are not homosexual, but everyone is welcome. Open Mon–Fri 9pm–3:30am, Sat 9pm– 4:30am.

Yin Yang Club

24–30 Ice House St., Central. ☎ **852/2868 4066.** Cover HK$65 ($8.40) Sun, HK$100 ($13) Mon–Thurs, HK$130 ($16.90) Fri, HK$165 ($21.45) Sat. MTR: Central.

This used to be Hong Kong's most popular gay disco, but smaller crowds have forced management to abandon its exclusively gay focus in an attempt to attract straights as well. At press time, Thursdays and Sundays had been set aside as gay nights, but only time will tell how this will work out. At any rate, don't even think about coming here until after midnight; make this your last stop of the evening. Open Sun–Fri 10pm–3am, Sat 10pm–6am.

CAUSEWAY BAY/WAN CHAI

Jj's
In the Grand Hyatt Hotel, 1 Harbour Rd., Wan Chai. ☎ **852/2588 1234.** Cover (including one drink) HK$155 ($20.15) Sun–Thurs, HK$185 ($24) Fri–Sat. No cover before 8:30pm. MTR: Wan Chai.

This upscale entertainment complex was the first in Hong Kong to offer several diversions under one roof; it is decorated in a style that is part Victorian and part whimsical, giving it an eccentric and playful ambience. There's a main bar, a games room with darts and billiards, a disco, a restaurant serving pizza and sandwiches, and a room with live music featuring jazz, rhythm-and-blues, and hits from the sixties and seventies. This is the place for those who like to move from one scene to the next, without actually having to go anywhere. From Monday through Friday, you can have two drinks for the price of one during happy hour from 5:30 to 8:30pm. Open Sun–Thurs 5:30pm–2am, Fri 5:30pm–3am, Sat 6pm–4am.

Joe Bananas
23 Luard Rd., Wan Chai. ☎ **852/2529 1811.** No cover Sun–Thurs; Fri–Sat HK$110 ($14.20), including two drinks. MTR: Wan Chai.

This is a bar and restaurant that transforms itself into a disco every evening after 9pm. Appealing to Hong Kong's yuppies, it does not allow any military personnel, nor does it allow men with collarless shirts (in other words, no T-shirts). There's dancing Monday through Thursday from 11pm to 5am, on Friday and Saturday from 11pm to 6am, and on Sunday from 11pm to 2am.

3 The Bar Scene

COCKTAIL LOUNGES

The cocktail lounges listed here all have a view—since you're in one of the most romantically beautiful cities in the world, why settle for anything less?

KOWLOON

Sky Lounge
In the Sheraton Hotel and Towers, 20 Nathan Rd., Tsim Sha Tsui. ☎ **852/2369 1111.** MTR: Tsim Sha Tsui.

This plush and comfortable lounge is on the top floor of the Sheraton, affording one of the best and most romantic views of the harbor and glittering Hong Kong Island. There's soft live music in the evenings. Unless you're a hotel guest, from 8:30pm onward there's a minimum drink charge of HK$130 ($16.90) per person. Beer costs HK$48 ($6.25); cocktails, HK$65 ($8.40). Open daily 4pm–1am (to 2am on Fri– Sat).

CENTRAL DISTRICT

Cyrano
In the Island Shangri-La, Pacific Place, 88 Queensway, Central. ☎ **852/2877 3838.** MTR: Admiralty.

This sophisticated lounge is Hong Kong's highest—on the 56th floor with stunning views of the harbor. Decorated in a style reminiscent of the 1930s, it offers live music every night except Sunday from 9pm and a small dance floor. On Friday and Saturday, there's a minimum drink charge of HK$150 ($19.50). Cocktails, averaging HK$75 ($9.75), are a specialty. Open Sun–Thurs 5pm–1:30am, Fri–Sat 5pm–2:30am.

La Ronda Lounge
Furama Hotel (30th floor), 1 Connaught Rd., Central. ☎ 852/2525 5111. MTR: Central.

On the Hong Kong side, this lounge offers spectacular close-up views of Central, the harbor, and Kowloon beyond. Although it's located next to a revolving restaurant, the bar itself is stationary (a blessing, perhaps, if you're drinking). A quartet entertains in the evenings. Cocktails average HK$65 ($8.45). Open daily 5:30–11pm.

CAUSEWAY BAY
Talk of the Town
In the Excelsior Hotel, Gloucester Rd., Causeway Bay. ☎ 852/2894 8888. MTR: Causeway Bay.

Smartly decorated in art deco style, this upscale lounge on the 34th floor offers a fantastic view of the harbor, Kowloon, and Kai Tak Airport, as well as soft live music in the evenings. There's no happy hour, but from 5 to 9pm drinks are cheaper. After 9pm prices go up and there's a minimum drink charge of HK$108 ($14.05) Sunday through Thursday and HK$118 ($15.35) on Friday and Saturday. *Note:* Talk of the Town is due for renovation; call beforehand to see whether it's open. Open Sun–Thurs 5pm–1am, Fri–Sat 5pm–2am.

PUBS & BARS
KOWLOON

Kangaroo Pub
35 Haiphong Rd., Tsim Sha Tsui. ☎ 852/2376 0083. MTR: Tsim Sha Tsui.

This Australian pub with dart boards and televisions often tuned to sporting events is the place to go if you want a beer and fish-and-chips, an Aussie meat pie, samosas, chili, lasagne, grilled chicken, or other items from a mixed menu. Happy hour is from 4 to 7pm, with draft beer going for two for the price of one. Open daily 11am–3am.

MadDogs
32 Nathan Rd., Tsim Sha Tsui. ☎ 852/2301 2222. MTR: Tsim Sha Tsui.

Located underneath the Imperial Hotel, this basement establishment is the Kowloon version of a long-established and popular English-style pub near the Lan Kwai Fong district in Central. Opened in 1990, it looks as though it has been here forever and attracts mainly tourists staying in the many neighboring hotels. Its dress code prohibits running shorts, hats, and sleeveless shirts for men; considering itself animal-friendly, it also prohibits furs. It's a good place to come if you want beer for breakfast, which begins at HK$50 ($6.50) for a pint. Happy hour is from 4 to 7pm daily, with two drinks for the price of one; Wednesday features two-for-one shooters and Thursday features two cocktails for the price of one, all evening. Open Sun–Thurs 8am–2am, Fri–Sat 8am–4am.

Ned Kelly's Last Stand
11A Ashley Rd., Tsim Sha Tsui. ☎ 852/2376 0562. MTR: Tsim Sha Tsui.

This is a lively Australian saloon, with free live Dixieland jazz or swing nightly from 9pm to 2am and attracting a largely middle-aged crowd. It serves Australian chow, including juicy pork sausages with mashed potatoes and onion gravy; stew; liver, bacon, and fried onions; chicken; Australian sirloin steak; hamburgers; and meat pie with mashed potatoes and onion gravy. Happy hour is from 11:30am to 7pm, with cheaper prices for beer. Open daily 11:30am–2am.

Planet Hollywood

3 Canton Rd., Tsim Sha Tsui. ☎ **852/2377 7888.** MTR: Tsim Sha Tsui.

The escalator ride up to this establishment and the music that accompanies it is like the entrance to a theme park, and that theme park is Hollywood. If you're star crazy, this is the place for you; you can gawk at the handprints of Paul Newman, Melanie Griffith, or Patrick Swayze, or such movie memorabilia as the dress worn by Elizabeth Taylor in *The Young Toscanini*, the doll Chuckie from *Child's Play*, the car used by Bruce Lee in the *Green Hornet* TV series, and the cyborg from Schwarzenegger's *Terminator 2*. In case that's not enough, you can even watch TV screens running film clips. A menu offers American food ranging from sandwiches and burgers to pasta and pizza. A strong competitor of the Hard Rock Cafe (See Chapter 5) down the street. Open daily 11:30am–2am.

Rick's Cafe

4 Hart Ave., Tsim Sha Tsui. ☎ **852/2367 2939.** MTR: Tsim Sha Tsui.

Taking its name from the bar in *Casablanca,* this basement oasis features potted palm trees, ceiling fans, and posters of Bogie and Bergman. Although it's more of a bar than a restaurant, it also serves nachos, enchiladas, chili con carne, burgers, fish-and-chips, and other fare. Prices are rather high for what you get, but after 10pm there's a disk jockey and a small dance floor. Beer starts at HK$45 ($5.85) a pint; cocktails at HK$60 ($7.80). Happy hour is from 3 to 10pm (from 6pm to 9pm on Sunday), with two drinks for the price of one. On Friday and Saturday nights from 2 to 5am it's two shots for the price of one. If you take advantage of this, don't count on doing anything the next day. On Friday and Saturday there's a HK$100 ($13) admission, which includes two drinks. Open Mon–Thurs 3pm–3am, Fri–Sat 3pm–5am, Sun 6pm–3am.

Schnurrbart

9–11 Prat Ave., Tsim Sha Tsui. ☎ **852/2366 2986.** MTR: Tsim Sha Tsui.

This is the Kowloon branch of a well-established Central bar, a cozy, small place offering great German beers and German food from a menu which changes weekly. Open daily noon–2am.

Someplace Else

Sheraton Hotel (Basement), 20 Nathan Rd., Tsim Sha Tsui. ☎ **852/2369 1111.** MTR: Tsim Sha Tsui.

This is one of Tsim Sha Tsui's most popular watering holes, especially during happy hour (from 4 to 7pm, with two drinks for the price of one) when it's standing room only. After 10pm, it becomes transformed into a disco, with an admission of HK$108 ($14) Sunday through Thursday and HK$165 ($21.45) Friday and Saturday, including two drinks. This two-level bar/restaurant, decorated with stained-glass lampshades and ceiling fans, has an extensive menu, offering everything from satays, samosas, and tacos to fish-and-chips, spareribs, and hamburgers. Open Sun–Thurs 11am–2am, Fri–Sat 11am–3am.

White Stag

72 Canton Rd., Tsim Sha Tsui. ☎ **852/2375 1951.** MTR: Tsim Sha Tsui.

This English-style pub caters to a mixed clientele of Westerners and Chinese. A nice, quiet place where you can actually hear yourself talk, it sports wooden tables and a few deer heads and antlers. A blackboard announces the choices of the day, which

---

might include corned-beef hash and eggs, lasagne, meat pies, omelets, or soup. There are also fixed-price lunches for HK$60 ($7.80). Beer costs HK$43 ($5.60) and up for a pint, except during happy hour (from 5 to 9pm daily) when it's two for the price of one. On Friday and Saturday nights after 9:30pm, there's free entertainment provided by a Filipino band. Open Sun–Thurs 10am–2am, Fri–Sat 10am–4am.

CENTRAL DISTRICT

Bull and Bear
Hutchinson House, 10 Harcourt Rd., Central. ☎ 852/2525 7436. MTR: Central.

The huge, sprawling Bull and Bear was at the forefront of Hong Kong's English-pub craze, opening back in 1974. Notorious from the beginning, it gets pretty rowdy on weekend nights, attracting everyone from businessmen in suits to servicemen on leave. Since it attracts more men than women, one British expatriate described it as a "meat market." Maybe that's what you're looking for. I can confirm that it's not a particularly comfortable place for a woman alone at night, having had to fight off the attentions of a rather inebriated sailor with tattoos up and down his arms. An alternative is to come for lunch or breakfast. The menu includes chili con carne, steak-and-kidney pie, salads, sandwiches, and daily specials. Happy hour is daily from 5 to 8pm; Tuesday features two cocktails for the price of one. Open Mon–Sat 8am–2am, Sun and hols noon–midnight.

California
24–26 Lan Kwai Fong St., Central. ☎ 852/2521 1345. Disco cover charge Fri–Sat HK$100 ($13). MTR: Central.

Located in Central's nightlife district, this chic bar was once the place to see and be seen—the haunt of young nouveaux riches in search of a definition. Newer establishments have since encroached upon California's exalted position, but it remains a respected and sophisticated restaurant/bar, with silent TV screens showing movies almost everywhere you look. You might consider starting your night on the town here with dinner and drinks—the restaurant is popular for its hamburgers (the house specialty), pizza, pasta, and sandwiches. Happy hour is 5 to 8pm, with two drinks for the price of one. On Friday and Saturday nights from 11pm to 3 or 4am, it becomes a happening disco. Open Mon–Thurs noon–midnight, Fri–Sat noon–3 or 4am, Sun 6–11pm.

Captain's Bar
In the Mandarin Hotel, 5 Connaught Rd., Central. ☎ 852/2522 0111. MTR: Central.

That this refined bar is popular with Hong Kong's professional crowd, especially at the end of the working day, comes as no surprise considering the fact that it's in the Mandarin Hotel. It's a small, intimate place, with seating at the bar or on couches. It's well known for its pints of beer served in aluminum and silver tankards. Live music begins nightly at 9pm; there's even a small dance floor for those inclined to shuffle around. Open daily 11am–2am.

Godown
Hotel Furama Kempinsky (basement), 1 Connaught Rd. (entrance on Chater Road), Central, ☎ 852/2524 2088. MTR: Central.

Recently ensconced in new, more centrally located quarters, the Godown is a long-time favorite. It lost some of its godown (warehouse) atmosphere and decorations in the move, but remains popular for its live jazz on Wednesday from 9pm to 12:30am, during which there's a HK$3 (40¢) surcharge on all drinks. On other evenings you can dance to disco music beginning at 10pm. It's a jovial place to come for lunch as well, when there are fixed-price lunches and a menu offering fish, steaks, Asian dishes, salads, and vegetarian selections, or for happy hour from 4 to 8pm daily with two drinks for the price of one. Open Mon–Sat 9am–2am, Sun 5pm–2am.

Graffiti
44 D'Aguilar St., Central. ☎ **852/2521 2202.** Disco cover charge Fri–Sat HK$55 ($7.15) July and Aug only. MTR: Central.

As its name implies, this place is for those who have a craving to scribble or doodle; crayons are provided on each paper tablecloth. Appealing to a twentysomething crowd of expatriates and Chinese, it offers a menu of such appetizers as onion rings and nachos, a salad bar, and main dishes ranging from sandwiches and burgers to Mexican fare, barbecue chicken, pizza, and pasta. The background music tends toward the beat of disco; on Friday and Saturday nights there's dancing after 11pm, for which a cover of HK$55 ($7.15) is charged only during the months of July and August. Happy hour is Monday through Saturday from 4 to 8pm, and on Friday and Saturday from midnight to 1am, with two drinks for the price of one. Open Mon–Wed noon–midnight, Thurs noon–1am, Fri–Sat noon–3am, Sun 6pm– midnight.

MadDogs
1 D'Aguilar St., Central. ☎ **852/2810 1000.** MTR: Central.

Catering to a mellow crowd of professional people, this is one of Hong Kong's most popular English pubs, with a traditional decor reminiscent of Britain during its imperial heyday. A wide variety of draft beers and scotch malts is offered. It's often packed, especially during happy hour daily from 4 to 8pm and again from 10 to 11pm. The menu goes way beyond typical pub fare, with such offerings as vegetable moussaka, Szechuan chicken, chili, and Singapore stir-fried noodles in addition to the usual fish-and-chips, shepherd's pie, and ploughman's lunch. Incidentally, no shorts or flip-flops allowed; and since the owner is an animal-rights advocate, you must leave your furs at home. Open Mon–Thurs 11am–2am, Fri–Sat 11am–3am, Sun and holidays 10am–2am.

Oscar's
2 Lan Kwai Fong, Central. ☎ **852/2804 6561.** MTR: Central.

This informal cafe/bar doesn't look like much inside, but then, hardly anyone goes inside. Rather, the youthful clientele fetches a beer, which begins at HK$45 ($5.85) for a can, and then stands around outside, giving the scene the atmosphere of a street party. Part of the establishment's success is its happy hour, when beer costs only HK$25 ($3.25) daily from 5 to 8pm and again from midnight to 1am and all day Sunday. A place to meet people. Open Mon–Sat 9am– 2am, Sun noon–midnight.

Post 97
9 Lan Kwai Fong, Central. ☎ **852/2810 9333.** MTR: Central.

With a cheeky reference to Hong Kong's future, this casual cafe is a good place to socialize, relax over a cup of coffee or a drink, or dine on such international fare as deep-fried prawns in a sweet chili sauce, Moroccan-style chicken breast, homemade gnocchi, or seared tuna steak. A smaller menu is offered throughout the night on weekends, making this a good place for a 3am snack. Happy hour is 5 to 7pm daily, with lower prices for drinks. For caffeine freaks, there's a happy hour for hot drinks at half price Monday through Friday from 9 to 11am and again from 3 to 5pm. This is also a good place for breakfast. Open Mon–Thurs 8am–2am, Fri–Sat open 24 hours, Sunday all day until 2am.

Schnurrbart
29 D'Aguilar St., Central. ☎ **852/2523 4700.** MTR: Central.

This is the place to come for German beer on tap, as well as a wide selection of bottled German beers. Popular with German expatriates, it serves sausages, sauerkraut, and other hearty German fare, with a menu that changes weekly. German beer begins at HK$38 ($4.95), except during happy hour (3 to 8pm daily) when the price of drinks is reduced. Open Mon–Thurs noon–1am, Fri–Sat noon–2am, Sun 6pm–1am.

CAUSEWAY BAY/WAN CHAI

Dickens Bar

Excelsior Hotel (basement), Gloucester Rd., Causeway Bay. ☎ **852/2837 6782.** MTR: Causeway Bay.

A classy place with dark-wood paneling, softly lit lamps, and live music from 9pm to 1am, this English pub is especially well known for its jazz band which plays every Sunday afternoon from 3 to 6pm. The pub serves soups and sandwiches, as well as a popular curry buffet lunch available Sunday through Friday from noon to 2pm. Open daily 11am–2am.

Joe Bananas

23 Luard Rd., Wan Chai. ☎ **852/2529 1811.** Cover HK$110 ($14.30) Fri–Sat after 9pm, including two drinks. MTR: Wan Chai.

Under the same management as MadDogs, this is one of the most popular and hippest hangouts in Wan Chai. Called "JB's" by the locals, it's a tribute to the rock, pop, and movie greats of yesterday. Although decorated like an American diner, complete with a jukebox, posters, and music memorabilia, it is unlike a diner in that the dress code prohibits collarless shirts for men, and military personnel are not allowed. This place is a combination bar/restaurant/disco; there is dancing every evening after 11pm, but a cover is charged only on weekends. There is a daily happy hour from 11am until 9pm, during which beer is half price and two cocktails go for the price of one. After 9pm there are daily drink promotionals. Open Mon–Thurs 11:30am–5am, Fri–Sat 11:30am–6am, Sun and holidays 5pm–5am.

Old China Hand

104 Lockhart Rd., Wan Chai. ☎ **852/2527 9174.** MTR: Wan Chai.

This is one of the old-timers in Wan Chai, an informal English pub with a picture of Queen Elizabeth and a lot of kitsch on the walls. A sign warns customers: SORRY, WE DON'T SERVE WOMEN—YOU HAVE TO BRING YOUR OWN. In the tradition of the pub lunch, meals are also served, including steak-and-kidney pie, fish-and-chips, sandwiches, salads, chili con carne, and moussaka. Breakfast is also available. Beer starts at HK$33 ($4.30) and up for a pint. Open Mon–Thurs 7am–2am, Fri around the clock from 7am to 7am, Sat 9am–7am, Sun 9am–1am.

TOPLESS BARS & HOSTESS CLUBS

Hong Kong's world of hostess clubs and topless bars has changed in the past 30 years. Back in the 1950s and 1960s, Wan Chai was where the action was, buzzing with sailors fresh off their ships and soldiers on leave from Vietnam. It was a world of two-bit hotels, raunchy bars, narrow streets, and dark alleyways, where men came to drink and brawl and spend money on women.

Today most of Wan Chai has become respectable (and a bit boring), an area of new buildings, mushrooming high-rises, and Hong Kong's expanding convention center. As for the old nightlife, most of it has moved across the harbor, where it has groomed itself to a higher class, accompanied, of course, by higher prices. Topless bars and hostess establishments still exist, but the Japanese have replaced the sailors and soldiers. Used to high-class hostess bars in their own country, they don't wince at the prices. At any rate, you've been warned.

BBOSS

New Mandarin Plaza, Tsim Sha Tsui East. ☎ **852/2369 2883.** Cover daily 2–9pm HK$380 ($49.35), including two soft drinks or two beers; a hostess HK$240 ($31.15) for 1 hour; beer HK$65 ($8.45). Cover daily 9pm–4am HK$530 ($68.85), including two drinks; a hostess HK$240 ($31.15) for 1 hour; beer HK$130 ($16.90). MTR: Tsim Sha Tsui; then take a taxi.

This 70,000-square-foot hostess club claims to be the largest Japanese-style nightclub in the world. In fact, the place is so big that a full-size, electric replica of an antique Rolls-Royce delivers customers along a "highway" to their seats. There are nightly stage shows, complete with a rotating stage so that everyone gets a chance to ogle the scantily clad performers. There's also a 20-member band and a dance floor large enough for 200 couples. You will be charged according to how long you sit at a table, how many drinks you consume, and how long you entertain a hostess at your table. If you're not careful, you could spend a fortune here. On the other hand, the place is so overdecorated in bows and the color pink, one hour may be all you can stand. Couples are welcome, though single women are not allowed. Prices are lower until 9pm. Open daily 2pm–4am.

Bottoms Up

14 Hankow Rd., Tsim Sha Tsui. ☎ **852/2367 5696.** MTR: Tsim Sha Tsui.

For years this basement establishment had explicit pictures of its namesake at the entranceway. These are now gone in the club's bid for respectability, and it's probably the best place to go if you want a topless joint. Welcoming tourists, couples, and unaccompanied men, Bottoms Up was used as a location shot in the James Bond movie *Man with the Golden Gun*. It features soft red lighting and four round counters with a topless waitress in the middle of each. I suggest that you come during happy hour (from 4:30 to 8:30pm daily), when drinks are cheaper. Open Mon–Sat 4:30pm–3:30am, Sun 5pm–3:30am.

4 Only in Hong Kong

NIGHT TOURS

If you have only one or two nights in Hong Kong, I would recommend that you take an organized night tour. **Watertours** offers more than half a dozen evening tours that combine harbor cruises with various land activities. You can make reservations for these tours through your hotel or by calling Watertours directly (☎ 852/2724 2856, 852/2739 3302, or 852/2367 1970).

The Aberdeen & Harbour Night Cruise, for example, lets participants enjoy a scenic view from Midway up Victoria Peak, followed by dinner on one of the floating Chinese restaurants in Aberdeen. After dinner, there's a cruise on a traditional-style junk with unlimited free drinks. Another recommended tour is the Lei Yue Mun Dinner Cruise, which starts with a cruise on a Chinese junk, followed by a stroll through a wonderful seafood market, where diners traditionally choose their seafood, which is then cooked and eaten as part of dinner at a nearby restaurant.

NIGHT STROLLS

One of the most beautiful and romantic sights in the world must be that afforded from **Victoria Peak** at night. The peak tram, which costs only HK19 ($2.45) round-trip and runs daily until midnight, deposits passengers at the Peak Tower terminal. From the terminal, turn right, and then turn right again onto a pedestrian footpath. This path, which follows Lugard Road and Harlech Road, circles around the peak, offering great views of glittering Hong Kong. Popular with both lovers and joggers, the path is lit at night and leads past expensive villas and primeval-looking jungles. Definitely the best stroll in Hong Kong, it takes about an hour.

On the other side of the harbor, there's a promenade along the **Tsim Sha Tsui waterfront,** which is popular among young Chinese couples.

NIGHT MARKET

If you're looking for colorful atmosphere, head for the **Temple Street Night Market,** near the Jordan MTR station in Kowloon. Extending for several blocks, it has stalls where clothing, accessories, toys, pens, watches, sunglasses, cassettes, household items, and much more are sold. Be sure to bargain fiercely if you decide to buy anything, and be sure to check the merchandise to make sure it isn't going to fall apart in two weeks. This is also a good place for an inexpensive meal at one of the *dai pai dong* (roadside food stalls) which specialize in seafood, including clams, shrimp, mussels, and crab.

But the most wonderful part of the market is its northern end, to the right around the white parking area. There, near the Tin Hau temple, you'll find palm readers and fortune-tellers, as well as street musicians and singers. You'll have to hunt for the tiny alleyway of musicians, where group after group has set up its own stage and is surrounded by an appreciative audience. Cantonese pop songs and operas are among the favorites, and when the musicians do an especially good job they are rewarded with tips. Get there before 9pm to see the musicians.

Otherwise, the night market is in full swing from about 8 to 11pm daily.

MOVIES

The biggest event in the film year is the **Hong Kong International Film Festival,** which takes place in April and May. This festival features a wide variety of films from all over the world.

Films are never far from the minds of Hong Kong residents, since the city is famous in Asia as a center for film production. There are some 30 **cinemas** all over the colony, with tickets costing approximately HK$55 ($7.15). Chinese films are naturally the most popular, especially in the genre of Bruce Lee kung fu movies. There are also showings of the latest Western films. For information on what's playing, check the local newspapers.

MORE NIGHTLIFE SUGGESTIONS

If you're in Hong Kong anytime from September through May on a Wednesday evening, you can go to the **horse races in Happy Valley** or Sha Tin for as little as HK$10 ($1.30). It's standing room only, but you'll be surrounded by betting fanatics and a giant screen displays the races. If you want, you can take an organized trip to the races offered by the Hong Kong Tourist Association; the tour includes a meal, a seat in the Royal Jockey Club members' stand, and racing tips. (For more information, see "Spectator Sports" in Chapter 6.)

Lai Chi Kok, an amusement park near the Mei Foo MTR station and the Sung Dynasty Village in the New Territories, has the usual thrills, and is open every evening until 8:30pm weekdays and 9pm on Saturday and Sunday. Admission is a mere HK$15 ($1.95) for adults and HK$10 ($1.30) for children.

Easy Excursions from Hong Kong

10

Mention Hong Kong and most people think of Hong Kong Island, the shops and neon of Tsim Sha Tsui, and the high-rises of the Central District. What they don't realize is that Hong Kong Island and Kowloon are rather minute in the scheme of things; they comprise only 10% of the entire territory. The New Territories and the outlying islands make up the other whopping 90%.

If you have a day or two to spare, or even just an afternoon, I suggest that you spend it on a trip outside the city in one of Hong Kong's rural areas. Escape the bustle and chaos of the city to one of the colony's small villages in the countryside, especially on the islands, and you'll have the chance to glimpse an older and slower way of life, where traditions still reign supreme and where lifestyles have a rhythm all their own.

1 The New Territories

Before the 1980s the New Territories were made up of peaceful countryside, with duck farms, fields, and old villages. No longer. A vast 389-square-mile region that stretches from Kowloon to the border of China, the New Territories are Hong Kong's answer to its growing population and the refugee crunch. Huge government housing projects have mushroomed throughout the New Territories, especially in towns along the railway and subway lines. Once-sleepy villages have become concrete jungles.

More than one-third of Hong Kong's population already lives in the New Territories, mostly in subsidized housing, and the goal of eventually housing half the population in the suburbs is almost a reality. The New Territories, therefore, are vitally important to Hong Kong, its well-being, and its future. For visitors to ignore the area completely would be shortsighted; many find the housing projects, in some suburbs stretching as far as the eye can see, nothing short of astounding.

If, on the other hand, it's peace and quiet you're searching for, don't despair. The New Territories are so large that not all the land has been turned into housing, and going there is still an interesting day trip—so different from the city itself that it's almost like visiting an entirely different country.

For information on transportation in the New Territories, drop by an HKTA office for a free copy of "Major Bus Routes in the

New Territories," which tells which bus to take, the fare, and where to get off for some of the major destinations. Be aware, however, that it takes time and patience to travel in the New Territories by public bus. Distances are large and the service is slow. If you are going there for the adventure and don't care about inconvenience, great. Otherwise, consider sticking to places easily reached by train or subway, as outlined below.

It is easiest, of course, to leave the driving to someone else, such as the Hong Kong Tourist Association, which offers a number of organized tours of the New Territories. The "Land Between" Tour emphasizes both the rural side of Hong Kong and its urban development, enabling visitors to learn about the lifestyle, customs, and beliefs of the local people. The Heritage Tour covers historic architectural sites spread through Kowloon and the New Territories, including a walled village, 19th-century Chinese mansion, ancestral hall, and temple. For more information on these and other tours offered by HKTA and other companies, see "Organized Tours" in Chapter 6 or contact the HKTA.

THROUGH KOWLOON TO THE NEW TERRITORIES BY MTR

Hong Kong's Mass Transit Railway (MTR) whisks passengers from the heart of Central or Tsim Sha Tsui to the outermost limit of Kowloon and the New Territories in a mere 30 minutes.

YAU MA TEI

A part of Kowloon (not the New Territories), this is the first stop after Tsim Sha Tsui; here you will find both the **Jade Market** and **Temple Street Night Market,** described in Chapter 8 under "Markets." You can reach both markets by taking the MTR to Jordan station.

MONG KOK

If you're a bird lover, as many Chinese are, you might want to visit **Hong Lok Street** with its many shops that sell songbirds (most of which are imported from China) and intricately crafted teak and bamboo birdcages. (*Note:* The Bird Market will move to a new home by the end of 1996; contact the HKTA before making a special trip.) Open daily from 10am to 5pm, it's a 5-minute walk west of the Mong Kok MTR station (take the Nelson Street western exit). Walk westward along Nelson or Argyle Street until you reach Hong Lok Street. If you backtrack and walk eastward on Argyle Street, you'll reach Tung Choi Street in about 10 minutes; this is popularly known as the **Ladies' Market.** Stalls here sell clothing, shoes, and accessories, including scarves, belts, and hats. It's open daily from about 1pm to 10:30pm. (See Chapter 8 for more information.)

MEI FOO

Both the Sung Dynasty Village and Lai Chi Kok Amusement Park are located about a 15- to 20-minute walk from the Mei Foo station. (See Chapter 6 for more information.)

TSUEN WAN

The last stop on the western line of the MTR, Tsuen Wan was a small market town just 100 years ago, with a population of about 3,000 Hakkas and a thriving incense powder–producing industry. Today it is one of the New Territories' largest satellite towns, with a population of almost one million living mostly in housing estates. It's also a convenient jumping-off point for bus trips through the New Territories, especially to the Kam Tin Walled Village (see below).

Just a few minutes' walk from Tsuen Wan Station, the **Sam Tung Uk Museum,** Kwu Uk Lane, Tsuen Wan, New Territories (☎ 852/2441 2001), is actually a restored Hakka walled village. Built in the 18th century by members of the farming Chan clan, it typifies a rural walled village—today it is a tiny oasis of tile-roofed houses in the midst of modern high-rise housing projects. It encompasses four houses that have been restored to their original condition, an ancestral hall, two rows of side houses, and an exhibition hall. On display are farm implements and traditional Chinese furniture, including elegant blackwood furniture. The museum is open Wednesday through Monday from 9am to 4pm; closed January 1, the first 3 days of the Chinese New Year, and December 24–25. Admission is free.

About a 20-minute walk from the Tsuen Wan MTR station is **Chuk Lam Sim Yuen,** popularly known as the Bamboo Monastery. Founded in 1927, it's one of Hong Kong's most spectacular Buddhist monasteries and is famous for its three huge "Precious Buddha" statues.

WONG TAI SIN

Wong Tai Sin is best known for its temple of the same name, a very popular local temple visited by more than 3 million worshipers annually. Although the temple itself dates only from 1973, it adheres to traditional Chinese architectural principles with its red pillars, two-tiered golden roof, blue friezes, yellow latticework, and multicolored carvings. What makes the temple so popular, however, is that everyone who comes here is seeking information about their fortune—from advice about business or horse racing to determining which day is most auspicious for a wedding. Most worshipers make use of a bamboo container holding numbered sticks. After lighting a joss stick and kneeling before the main altar, the worshiper gently shakes the container until one of the sticks falls out. The number corresponds to a certain fortune, which is then interpreted by a soothsayer at the temple. You can wander around the temple grounds, on which can be found several gardens, one hall dedicated to the Buddhist Goddess of Mercy and another to Confucius, and a health clinic with both Western medical services and traditional Chinese herbal treatments. The temple, a 3-minute walk north of the Wong Tai Sin MTR station, is open daily from 7am to 5:30pm. Admission is free, but a donation of about HK$1 (13¢) is expected at the temple's entrance.

SEEING THE NEW TERRITORIES BY KOWLOON-CANTON RAILWAY (KCR)

For years every visitor to the New Territories took the train to the border for a look into forbidden and mysterious China. Now, of course, it's easy to get permission to enter China and the border lookout has lost its appeal—the view was never very exciting anyway. Still, you might want to take the train up into the New Territories just for the experience, as well as for the interesting stops you can make on the way up and back. It costs only HK8 ($1.05) for ordinary class and takes only 30 minutes to go to the end of the line—Sheung Shui.

Leaving every 4 to 10 minutes from the Kowloon railway station in Hung Hom, the Kowloon-Canton Railway (KCR) will take you along 20 miles of track, passing through such towns as Sha Tin, University Station, Tai Po Kau, and Fanling before reaching Sheung Shui—your last stop unless you have a visa to enter China. The train makes a total of 10 stops along the way, enabling you to get out and do some exploring on your own (you can also reach the KCR by taking the MTR as far as Kowloon Tong station and then transferring to the KCR). If I were making a day's excursion of this route, I would first go all the way to Sheung Shui and then stop at

Luen Wo Market in Fanling before heading back south to Sha Tin. After lunch, I would take a taxi to the art gallery at Chinese University and then board a ferry for a cruise through Tolo Harbour.

SHA TIN

This is Hong Kong's prime example of a budding satellite town, with a population approaching 700,000. Fewer than 8 miles north of Tsim Sha Tsui, it's also home to Hong Kong's new and modern **horse racetrack,** as well as a huge shopping mall called the **New Town Plaza,** located next to the Sha Tin KCR station and featuring a 20-minute performance by an illuminated, computer-controlled musical fountain.

The most interesting thing for the tourist here, though, is the **Monastery of 10,000 Buddhas,** located on a hill west of the Sha Tin railway station. It will take about a half hour's energetic walk to get there—with more than 400 steps to climb before reaching the top. The temple was established by a monk named Yuet Kai, who wrote 96 books on Buddhism. He's still at the temple—well, actually, his body is still there. He's been embalmed and covered in gold leaf and sits behind a glass case for all to see. You'll find him in one of the outlying buildings farther up the hill from the main temple. Inside the main temple of the 10,000 Buddhas are more Buddha images than you've probably ever seen gathered in one place. In fact, there are almost 13,000 of them lining the walls, and no two are exactly alike. Also on the grounds is a nine-story pink pagoda. The temple affords a good view of the surrounding countryside.

Where to Dine

The **New Town Plaza,** Sha Tin's huge shopping mall located beside the Sha Tin KCR station, is a good place for a snack or quick meal, with cafeterias, fast-food outlets, and restaurants serving both Western and Chinese fare. For dim sum or Cantonese food, a moderately priced restaurant in New Town Plaza is **Ah Yee Leng Tong** (☎ 852/2691 8515), open from 11:30am to 11:30pm daily. For inexpensive Western fare, head for the **Spaghetti House** (☎ 852/2697 9009), a chain of successful American-style spaghetti and pizza parlors; it's open from 11am to 11pm daily.

Yucca de Lac Restaurant

Ma Liu Shui, Sha Tin. ☎ **852/2692 1835.** Reservations recommended. Rice and noodle dishes and main courses HK$65–HK$130 ($8.40–$16.90). MC, V. Daily 11am–11pm. Transportation: Take a taxi from University or Sha Tin station. CANTONESE.

More than 200 items on the menu here include duck, pigeon, pork, beef, chicken, seafood, and tofu dishes. You might want to try one of the popular pigeon dishes, fried chicken with lemon sauce, diced pork with cashew nuts, or fried fillet of garoupa with green pepper. There's also a Western-fare snack menu. If the weather's nice, you'll want to sit outside on the terrace overlooking Tolo Harbour, which gives the restaurant a slightly European atmosphere.

UNIVERSITY

This stop, which is actually still within the boundaries of budding Sha Tin, serves students going to Chinese University. But your main interest will probably be its art museum and a ferry ride through Tolo Harbour.

The main collection of the **Art Gallery at the Institute of Chinese Studies,** Chinese University, New Territories (☎ 852/2609 7416), is made up of more than 1,000 paintings and examples of calligraphy by Guangdong artists, dating from the Ming period to the present. The gallery also has bronze seals, rubbings of stone inscriptions, jade flower carvings, and Chinese ceramics. There are four levels and a central courtyard with a Chinese garden. Special exhibitions of art on loan from China's museums are sometimes mounted.

The museum is open Monday through Saturday from 10am to 4:30pm and on Sunday and holidays from 12:30 to 4:30pm. It's closed New Year's Eve and New Year's Day, the first 3 days of the Chinese New Year, Easter Sunday, Ching Ming Festival, Cheung Yeung Festival, Christmas Eve, and Christmas Day. Admission is free. To get there, catch a "University" bus from University station, getting off 5 minutes later near the administration building.

University is also where you get off if you want to take a **ferry around Tolo Harbour.** From the station it's a 15-minute walk to Ma Liu Shui, where you board the ferry for a leisurely trip to six villages around the harbor. The ferry leaves only twice a day, at 8:30am and 3:15pm. Since the first ferry may be a little too early and doesn't allow time for you to disembark for sight-seeing, I would suggest taking the afternoon cruise. This ferry makes a stop at Tap Mun at 4:30pm, goes on to some other villages, and then returns to Tap Mun about 50 minutes later. This gives you a little time to do some sight-seeing, but make sure you return to the Tap Mun ferry dock by 5:20pm because there are no hotels here. The ferry gets back to Ma Liu Shui at 6:45pm. The entire round-trip ride costs HK$26 ($3.40) on weekdays and HK$40 ($5.20) on weekends and holidays.

TAI PO MARKET

One of the New Territories' new satellite towns, Tai Po was first settled by Tanka boat people more than 1,000 years ago. Just a short taxi ride from the Tai Po Market KCR station is the newly opened **Hong Kong Railway Museum,** on Fu Road (☎ 852/2653 3339). It is open free to the public every day except Tuesday from 9am to 4pm, and located in what was formerly the Tai Po Market railway station, built in 1913 in traditional Chinese style. Besides the station's original waiting hall and ticket office, the museum displays historic photographs of Tai Po and railway coaches dating from 1911.

From the museum, you can visit the nearby Man Mo Temple by strolling down the century-old lane—Fu Shin Street. The temple, dedicated to the Taoist gods of war and literature, is a popular spot for older residents to gather and play Chinese checkers or simply pass the time. Beside the temple is a bustling market of produce, preserved goods, and seafood.

FANLING

A small farming settlement for several centuries, Fanling is now a huge satellite town. The **Luen Wo Market** in the middle of Fanling (included in the "Land Between" Tour) is interesting if you've never seen a Chinese country market. Covering one square block, this indoor market is a maze of tiny passageways and various stalls selling everything from live chickens to deer heads. There are also vendors of fruit, herbs, goldfish (bred in astonishing varieties and thought to bring good luck), tea, fish, flowers, and soybeans. Many of these vendors also display wares at an open-air market down the street. The best time to visit the market is between 10:30am and noon daily, when it's at its busiest. To get there, take bus no. 78K from the Fanling KCR station for a short ride to Luen Wo Road, which runs right alongside the market.

If you're interested in historic Chinese architecture, you might want to leave the market via taxi for a 10-minute ride to the Tang Chung Ling Ancestral Hall, built in 1525 as the main ancestral hall of the Lung Yeuk Tau clan. Elaborately decorated with wood carvings and murals, it consists of a main building with three halls and two inner courtyards.

SHEUNG SHUI

Once its own market town, Sheung Shui has been swallowed up in the budding satellite town that now spreads out from Fanling. Sheung Shui Heung is an ancient village located about 300 yards north of the main town. Although much of its charm has been lost due to the construction of modern buildings all around, it's still more peaceful than other old villages that are closer to the beaten path. Look for **Man Shek Tong,** a small ancestral hall belonging to the Liu clan, once the most prominent family of the Sheung Shui district. In 1688 as many as 500 members of the Liu clan were living in the district, and Man Shek Tong was erected in 1751 at the height of the clan's power and wealth. Consisting of a long central courtyard with one main hall and smaller halls on both sides, Man Shek Tong is set in a pleasant garden in the middle of the old village; it boasts wood carvings, traditional Chinese mural paintings, and pottery figurines on the ridge of the roof. Unfortunately, you must join HKTA's Heritage Tour (described above) to gain entrance to Man Shek Tong.

OTHER PLACES IN THE NEW TERRITORIES
KAM TIN WALLED VILLAGE

Traveling in the New Territories, you quickly notice women wearing wide-brimmed hats with a black fringe and pajamalike clothing; many of them have gold-capped teeth as well. These women are Hakka, as are most of the farmers of the New Territories. They keep to themselves, preserving their customs and dialect. While most of them hate to have their photographs taken because they think it steals something from their spirit, some will oblige in return for payment. In fact, don't be surprised if you're instantly approached by Hakka women and asked to take their picture— they've learned that it's an easy way to make an extra couple of Hong Kong dollars (be sure to settle on a price before you start clicking away).

At any rate, during the Ming dynasty (1368–1644) some of the Hakka clans in the area of the New Territories built walls around their homes to protect them against roving bandits and invaders. A handful of walled villages still exist today, and are inhabited by the Hakkas. Before visiting any of these villages, stop by the Sam Tung Uk Museum in Tsuen Wan (described above). It will make your visit to a lived-in walled village more enriching. What's more, Tsuen Wan is the logical starting point for such a trip.

Hakka walled villages include Kat Hing Wai, Shui Tau, Kam Hing Wai, Kam Tsin Wai, and Shek Tsin Wai. Of these, Kat Hing Wai is the most famous. Popularly known as Kam Tin, it's home to about 400 descendants of the Tang clan, who built the village back in the 1600s. The village is completely surrounded by 18-foot-thick walls, which provided protection against bandits, rival clans, and wild tigers; and there is only one narrow entrance. A donation of about HK$2 (26¢) is expected; you'll find a donation box located at the entrance. Once inside Kam Tin, you'll find a lane that leads past souvenir stalls to the village's temple and ancestral hall.

To reach Kam Tin, first take the MTR to Tsuen Wan Station. Then board bus no. 51 from the Tai Ho Road overpass (located above the Tsuen Wan MTR station). Your bus will take you over the hills along scenic Route Twisk. Get off at the last stop and then continue walking in the same direction the bus was going. Kam Tin is less than 5 minutes away, on your left.

SAI KUNG

Located on the eastern coast of the New Territories, Sai Kung is the second largest and least populated of Hong Kong's 19 districts and encompasses three county parks. The best way to explore this area is on a do-it-yourself tour with the help of the

Sai Kung Explorer's Guide, available at HKTA offices for HK$28 ($3.65). Complete with a detailed map, recommended walking tours, and explanations of sites and attractions along the way, the small pocket guide is a great way to see rural Hong Kong on your own. Included in the recommended walks is a stroll through Sai Kung Town, a hike through a nature park, and even a trip to a nearby island via ferry.

2 The Outlying Islands

In addition to Hong Kong Island there are 235 outlying islands, most of them barren and uninhabited. Because construction in the New Territories is booming, the islands now offer the best opportunity to see something of rural Chinese life. What's more, they're easy to reach—hop on a ferry in Central and then sit back and enjoy the view.

Three of the most accessible islands are **Lantau, Cheung Chau,** and **Lamma.** Ferries depart approximately every hour or so from the Central District—from new piers built out into the harbor on reclaimed land just west of the Star Ferry. You can purchase your ticket at the piers before departure, but avoid going on Sunday when the ferries are packed with city folks on family outings. The fares are also slightly higher on Saturday afternoon and Sunday, although the most expensive ticket is HK$26.50 ($3.45)—deluxe class on Sunday. Only the ferries to Lantau and Cheung Chau offer deluxe class, which I highly recommend since this upper-deck ticket entitles you to sit on an open deck out back, a great place to sip coffee or beer when the weather is nice and watch the harbor float past. In addition, deluxe cabins are the only ones that are air-conditioned. Otherwise, one-way fares for ordinary class average HK$8 ($1.05) on weekdays and HK$14 ($1.80) on Saturday afternoon and Sunday. Children pay half fare.

On Saturday afternoon and Sunday there is additional limited ferry service from Tsim Sha Tsui's Star Ferry concourse to Lantau and Cheung Chau. The tickets, however, must be purchased in advance at the HYFCO Travel Agency, Shop 3 in the basement of Star House on Salisbury Road, and the service is less frequent. For information, call 852/2730 8608.

For information on ferry schedules, drop by the HKTA for a free copy of timetables. In addition, be sure to pick up a free copy of the "Outlying Islands" leaflet provided by the HKTA. You may also wish to purchase HKTA's *Lantau Island Explorer's Guide* and *Cheung Chau Walking Tour,* both of which cost HK$28 ($3.65) and give detailed information on the sights on both islands. If you plan to do extensive hiking on the islands, inexpensive maps of the trails are available at the Government Publications Centre, located right by Central's Star Ferry terminal.

LANTAU

Twice the size of Hong Kong Island, Lantau is the colony's largest island. But whereas Hong Kong Island has a population of more than a million, Lantau has only about 20,000. County parks make up about half the island, with 43 miles of marked hiking trails. Lantau is an island of high peaks, remote and isolated beaches, small villages, temples, and monasteries. Inhabited since Neolithic times, Lantau has for centuries been the home of people engaged in fishing, salt making, and lime burning.

Taking a ferry from Hong Kong Island (which departs hourly between 7am and 11:15pm, with less frequent departures on Sunday), you'll arrive in about an hour at Silvermine Bay, known as Mui Wo in Chinese. There is a hotel fronting the bay and some fun outdoor restaurants (more on these later), but otherwise there isn't much of interest here. In front of the ferry pier you can catch buses going to other parts of the island, including Po Lin Monastery, Tung Chung, Tai O, Pui O, and Cheung Sha, with departures coinciding with the arrival of the hourly ferry. The exact fare of HK$13 ($1.70) for air-conditioned buses and HK$8.50 ($1.10) for non-air-conditioned buses is required, so come with lots of change. Prices are higher on Sundays and public holidays.

WHAT TO SEE & DO

The most famous attractions on Lantau are the **Giant Tian Tan Buddha** and **Po Lin Monastery,** both situated on the plateau of Ngong Ping at an elevation of 2,460 feet. You can reach both in about 40 minutes by bus from Silvermine Bay, and the Buddha is so huge that you'll have your first glimpses of it en route. More than 100 feet tall and weighing 250 tons, it's the world's largest seated outdoor bronze Buddha and can be seen as far away as Macau (or so it is claimed) on clear days. There are 268 steps leading up to the Buddha itself, but first you may want to stop at the ticket office at the bottom of the steps to purchase a meal ticket, since the other reason people come to Po Lin is to eat. The monastery is famous for its vegetarian lunches, served in a big dining hall (see "Where to Dine" below). Your meal ticket, which specifies the time for your communal meal, doubles as your admission ticket to a small museum inside the base of the statue, but there isn't much to see here. Rather, the best part is the view of the surrounding countryside from the statue's platform.

From here, head to the colorful Po Lin Monastery, largest and best known of the 135 Buddhist monasteries on Lantau. Po Lin (which means "precious lotus") was first established near the turn of the century by reclusive monks; the present buildings date from 1921 and 1970. The ornate main temple houses three magnificent bronze statues of Buddha, representing the past, present, and future; there is a brightly painted vermilion interior with dragons and other Chinese mythical figures on the ceiling. You'll probably want to spend about a half hour wandering through the grounds here.

From Po Lin, you can reboard the bus that will take you back to Mui Wo (Silvermine Bay), with departures every hour. Or, if you want to see more of the island, you can take another bus from Po Lin directly to Tai O (you can also reach Tai O directly from Mui Wo). Upon arriving in Tai O, be sure to check the schedule for buses returning to Mui Wo (buses leave about every half hour). Look, also, for the nearby map of the town.

In my opinion, **Tai O** is Lantau's most interesting village. Inhabited by Tanka fishing people, it wraps itself around the muddy waters of a bay on the west coast of the island. Although parts of the outskirts of town are being developed, the old core of the village has no cars on its narrow, twisting streets, no neon signs, no concrete and steel high-rises. Instead there are one-story wooden houses resting on stilts above the mud of the bay. Squid is hung out to dry beside underwear. Dogs lie asleep in the middle of the road. Life is unhurried and relaxed. You can hear the click-clicking of adults playing mahjongg all day long.

Once the center of Lantau's salt-panning industry, the village is divided in two by a creek, and the only way to get across it is by a flat-bottom boat that is pulled along a rope strung across the water. The women working the boat charge HK$0.50 (6¢) for the trip. There are several temples in Tai O, of which the best known is Kwan Tai on Market Street, dedicated to the god of war and righteousness. Another popular temple is Hau Wong, facing the sea at the end of Market Street. There are also some fish-processing shops and open-fronted stores that sell Chinese herbs, hardware, and, more recently, souvenirs. This is a great little village for just walking around.

If you're interested in old forts, go to **Tung Chung** on the north shore of Lantau (buses go there rather infrequently from Silvermine Bay, but you can walk there from Po Lin Monastery in about 2 hours). Tung Chung was built in 1817 to suppress the opium trade and its ruins today hold six cannons.

As for **beaches,** the two that have weekend lifeguards on duty in the summer, changing rooms, and toilets are Pui O and Cheung Sha. Cheung Sha is the most accessible, a 2-mile-long white sandy beach on the south side of the island, about a 15-minute bus ride from Silvermine Bay.

WHERE TO STAY

Silvermine Beach Hotel
Silvermine Bay, Mui Wo, Lantau. ☎ **852/2984 8295.** Fax 852/2984 1907. 135 rms (all with bath). A/C MINIBAR TV TEL. HK$940–HK$1,290 ($122.10–$167.55) single or double. Discounts available Sept–June, Sun–Fri, and stays of one week or longer. Children under 12 stay free in parents' room. AE, DC, MC, V.

Located about a 7-minute walk from the ferry pier in Silvermine Beach (turn right when you leave the terminal) across the street from a public beach, this is one of Lantau's few hotels and is the most easily accessible. The rooms in the old wing are simple and a bit dull, and there is no elevator to service its three floors. The new wing is slightly more deluxe, complete with elevator and glass sliding doors that open onto tiny balconies. The most expensive rooms are worth it, since they face the ocean and beach across the street. Facilities include an outdoor swimming pool. Its one restaurant, with views of the beach from its outdoor terrace, serves Cantonese and Western dishes.

WHERE TO DINE

Mui Wo Cooked Food Market
Chung Hau Rd., Silvermine Bay. Most menu items HK$25–HK$150 ($3.25–$19.50). No credit cards. Daily 6am–midnight. Take a right from the ferry dock; the market is to your right. VARIED.

This open-air pavilion of food stalls *(dai pai dongs)* offers inexpensive dishes, such as noodles, vegetables, sandwiches, rice dishes, and fresh seafood. Fresh fish, kept alive in tanks in front of each stall, costs about HK$150 ($19.50). This is a good place to wait for the next ferry. If you want, just order a beer for HK$8 ($1.05) and sit at one of the tables next to the water.

Po Lin Monastery
Ngong Ping. ☎ **852/2985 5248** or 852/2985 5113. Fixed-price lunch HK$65 ($8.45). No credit cards. Daily noon–4:30pm. VEGETARIAN.

This dining hall on the grounds of Po Lin Monastery is the most famous place to eat on the island. Only one fixed-price meal is served, which includes soup, vegetarian dishes, and rice. Buy your lunch ticket from the counter at the base of the Giant Buddha; your ticket is for a specific time, at an assigned table. Dining is rather unceremonious, with huge dishes of vegetables, rice, and soup brought to your table. Grab a Styrofoam bowl and chopsticks and help yourself.

Sang Lee Seafood Restaurant
Chung Hau Rd., Silvermine Bay. ☎ **852/2984 8478.** Most menu items HK$38–HK$65 ($4.95–$8.45). AE. Daily 11:30am–11pm. Turn right from the ferry dock and follow the sidewalk next to the water; the restaurant will soon appear on your left, closest to the ferry. SEAFOOD.

Probably the most fun and festive place to dine in Silvermine Bay, Sang Lee is outdoors to boot. It specializes in fresh seafood, including barbecued fish, squid fried with spiced salt, fried rice Singapore-style, steamed fish, crab, and clams. The dishes on the menu are priced at HK$65 ($8.40) and less, but if you choose your meal from the tank holding fish and prawns, expect to pay about HK$180 ($23.40) for two persons for a feast of fresh steamed fish or HK$140 ($18.20) for fresh prawns. The restaurant is open year-round.

Silvermine Beach Hotel

Silvermine Bay, Mui Wo, Lantau. ☎ **852/2984 8295.** Main courses and dishes HK$45–HK$90 ($5.85–$11.70). AE, DC, MC, V. Daily 11am–2:30pm, 6–9:30pm. Turn right from the ferry dock and walk 7 minutes. CHINESE/WESTERN.

This medium-priced hotel, located across from a public beach—just a 7-minute walk from the ferry pier—is your best bet for Western food on Lantau. In nice weather, you can dine on an outdoor terrace with views of the water. Its Western menu lists the generic sandwiches, spaghetti, and steaks found in many restaurants; most economical is the daily fixed-price lunch for HK$83 ($10.75) or dinner for HK$95 ($12.35). The Chinese menu is more extensive and better prepared, with various choices of seafood and chicken, but its specialty is vegetarian cuisine. Especially recommended is the soup of bamboo fungus with shredded vegetables and the fried eggplant with black bean sauce. There are also two fixed-price Chinese meals available for HK$185 and HK$230 ($24 and $29.85).

CHEUNG CHAU

If you have only a few hours to spare and don't want to worry about catching buses and finding your way around, Cheung Chau is your best bet. About an hour's ferry ride from Central with ferries leaving nearly every hour, it's a tiny island (only 1 square mile), but more than 30,000 people live here in a thriving fishing village. There are no cars on the island, making it a delightful place for walking around and exploring.

Inhabited for at least 2,500 years by fisherfolk and serving as a haven for smugglers and pirates until as recently as the 1920s, Cheung Chau still supports a sizable population of fishing families. Junks are built on Cheung Chau after a design hardly changed in centuries, entirely from memory and without the aid of blueprints. The waterfront where the ferry lands, known as the Praya, buzzes with activity as vendors sell fish, lobster, and vegetables. The village itself is a fascinating warren of narrow alleyways, food stalls, open markets, and shops selling everything from medicinal herbs and incense to noodles, rice, haircuts, and—a reflection of the island's increasing tourist trade—sun hats and sunglasses.

WHAT TO SEE & DO

About 3% of Cheung Chau's population live on junks in the harbor, and one of the things to do here is take a *kai do,* or water taxi, past the junks to Sai Wan—it shouldn't cost more than HK$10 ($1.30) and may even be cheaper than that; board it at the public pier next to the ferry pier. I like this harbor more than Aberdeen, and I find it amazing how many families keep dogs aboard their boats. At Sai Wan there's a temple dedicated to **Tin Hau,** goddess of the sea and protectress of fisherfolk. From here it's about a 30-minute walk back to the Praya along Peak Road, one of the main roads on the island. Along the way you'll pass a Chinese cemetery, the Yee Pavilion, built in memory of a local Chinese poet, and Kwan Kung Pavilion, dedicated to the god of war and righteousness.

As for seeing Cheung Chau village, begin with a stroll along the **Praya**—the waterfront promenade right in front of the ferry pier. It's a good place from which to observe the many junks and fishing boats in the harbor. To the right as you leave the ferry pier are several open-air restaurants, as well as the unimaginative-looking Regional Council Cheung Chau Complex, which houses a library, post office, and city market (open daily from 6am to 8pm) with more than 200 stalls that sell everything from fresh seafood to vegetables. On the opposite end of the Praya (to the left as you leave the ferry) are more waterfront restaurants, shops with bicycles to rent, and souvenir shops. After about a 3-minute walk, take a right at the playground onto Pak She Fourth, at the end of which is the **Pak Tai Temple.** Built in 1783, it's dedicated to the "Supreme Emperor of the Dark Heaven," long worshiped as a god of the sea. Inside is an iron sword measuring 5 feet in length that was found by local fishermen and thought to be 1,000 years old, as well as a sedan that is used to carry the statue of Pak Tai around the village during festivals. The most important festival is the Bun Festival, which originated a century ago following a terrible plague; it is famous throughout Hong Kong because of its 50-foot-tall towers of buns. The biggest attraction of the festival, however, is the parade of children who "float" through the streets suspended by hidden wires and rods.

From the Pak Tai Temple, take a left onto Pak She Street, which later becomes San Hing Street. As you walk back to the center of the village, you'll pass open-fronted shops that sell incense, medicinal herbs, provisions, and other local goods and meat. You'll also pass people's homes; their living rooms hold the family altar and their kitchens open onto the street. This is the traditional Chinese home, with the family business and communal rooms on the ground floor and the bedrooms up above.

At the end of San Hing Street, take a left onto Tung Wan Road, which cuts across the thinnest part of the island from the Praya with its ferry to Tung Wan Beach. Here, in the middle of Tung Wan Road, is a gnarled old banyan tree, which is considered to be the dwelling place of the spirit of health and fertility. At the end of Tung Wan Road is **Tung Wan Beach,** the most popular beach on the island.

If you would like to explore more of Cheung Chau, you might consider renting a bicycle from one of several shops on Pak She Fourth Street near the playground and Pak Tai Temple. Bicycles rent for about HK$20 ($2.60) an hour; three-seater pedal carts are available for about HK$35($4.55) an hour. North of the Praya is a broad cycling path that is popular with families.

WHERE TO STAY

In addition to the hotel listed here, there are countless rooms and apartments to rent around the island, with deeply discounted weekly rates. Some of these are also available by the night or weekend. Upon leaving the ferry pier, you'll find several temporary counters and carts set up along the Praya, with vendors offering rooms. Most don't speak English, but they have photographs of all their available properties. Be sure you understand where the room is located (remember, you'll have to walk) and how much it costs, including tax and service charge.

Warwick Hotel

Tung Wan Beach, Cheung Chau. ☎ **852/981 0081.** Fax 852/981 9174. 58 rms (all with bath). A/C MINIBAR TV TEL. HK$1,110–HK$1,350 ($144–$175) single or double. Children under 12 stay free in parents' room. AE, DC, MC, V. Take Tung Wan Road to Tung Wan Beach, about a 7-minute walk from the ferry pier.

If you want to spend a few nights away from the hustle and bustle of Hong Kong, this may be the place to do so. It's located on the south end of Cheung Chau's most popular beach; next to the hotel is a children's playground and a place where you can rent windsurfing boards and paddleboats, and there's an outdoor swimming pool, a pleasant restaurant with outdoor terrace, and a bar. The rooms facing the beach are slightly more expensive, but they're worth it, especially since all rooms have small balconies. If you come during the week or during off-season, ask whether you can be upgraded to a more expensive room. All rooms have hair dryers, radios, and cable TVs with pay movies.

WHERE TO DINE

Amego Cafe
31 Praya St. ☎ **852/2981 0710.** Most menu items HK$8–HK$28 ($1.05–$3.65). No credit cards. Daily 11:30am–11pm. CHINESE/WESTERN.

Easy to find on Cheung Chau's waterfront, to the right as you leave the ferry pier, this air-conditioned cafe serves easy-to-prepare snacks and Chinese and Western dishes, including sandwiches, spaghetti, omelets, hamburgers, fried rice, curries, noodles, ice cream, shakes, and daily specials. Cheap and simple.

Baccarat Restaurant
9A Pak She Praya St. ☎ **852/2981 0606.** Main dishes HK$30–HK$60 ($3.90–$7.80). MC, V. Daily 11am–11pm. Turn left from the ferry and walk along the Praya about 4 minutes. CANTONESE.

On the Praya, the last of several open-air restaurants (located on the corner of Pak She Street beside a playground), this simple spot offers outdoor seating under umbrellas, with a view of the harbor. Its English menu lists a variety of dishes, including deep-fried tofu with red pepper, spareribs with chili sauce, Japanese noodles, beef and pork dishes, chicken, cuttlefish, prawns, steamed fish with chili sauce, sandwiches, soups, and various rice dishes. The chili prawns are great. If you choose, you can buy fresh fish from the market and bring it here to be cooked to your specifications for a fee of HK$20 ($2.60). Your host is manager Larry Cheung, "Fat Larry," who speaks excellent English and is happy to translate any dishes or make recommendations.

Bayview Terrace
In the Warwick Hotel, Tung Wan Beach. ☎ **852/2981 0081.** Main dishes HK$65–HK$135 ($8.45–$17.55). AE, DC, MC, V. Daily 7:30am–10:30pm. Take Tung Wan Road to Tung Wan Beach, about a 7-minute walk from the ferry pier. WESTERN/CANTONESE.

The Warwick Hotel, located on the beach, offers the most sophisticated dining on the island, but its restaurant is rather casual. It consists of two parts: an indoor dining hall serving Cantonese food and an outdoor terrace with a view of the beach that is open all day (in nice weather) for Western food, snacks, and drinks. The Cantonese menu lists the usual seafood, beef, and pork dishes, while the à la carte Western menu has everything from lobster thermidor and grilled chicken to New Zealand lamb chop, grilled tiger prawns, sole, curries, and fried noodle dishes. A fixed-price lunch is available from noon to 2:30pm for HK$85 ($11.05), while a limited snack menu offers hamburgers, sandwiches, satays, ice cream and desserts.

Betty's Garden Cafe Pub
84 Tung Wan Rd. ☎ **852/2981 4610.** Main courses HK$30–HK$90 ($3.90–$11.70); breakfast HK$38–HK$65 ($4.95–$8.45). No credit cards. Wed–Mon noon–midnight. WESTERN.

Located on the village's main passageway between the Praya and the beach, this simple cafe is the local hangout for foreigners and serves European food. Its specialty is British-style pub grub, including a ploughman's lunch for HK$33 ($4.30), toasted sandwiches, sausage or meat pies with "mushy" peas, salads, hamburgers, and curries. Breakfast is served all day. Some of the best things about this place are the outdoor tables and the small beer garden across the street.

Hoi Long Wong Restaurant

Tai Hing Tai Road. ☎ **852/2981 1699.** Main dishes HK$35–HK$160 ($4.55–$20.80). No credit cards. Daily 11am–11pm. CHINESE SEAFOOD.

Located to the right as you leave the ferry pier, this is one of several open-air waterfront restaurants beside the Urban Council market; it has an English menu, as well as open tanks of live seafood from which you can choose your meal. The cooking charge if you choose live seafood is about HK$35 ($4.55) per *catty* (about 1 1/2 pounds). Steamed fish, curried prawns, steamed fresh crab, and steamed lobster with garlic sauce are just some of the dishes available.

King's Cafe

25 Praya St. ☎ **852/2981 0878.** Main dishes and sandwiches HK$10–HK$45 ($1.30–$5.85). No credit cards. Thurs–Tues 11am–11pm. WESTERN/CHINESE.

This simple establishment is on the Praya, to the left as you disembark from the ferry. It serves Western-style food and snacks such as sandwiches and omelets, as well as fried rice and noodle dishes. Although the food isn't great, the prices are l ow, and there are tables and chairs outside where you have a wonderful view of the action on the Praya and the junks anchored close by. For a snack, try a shake or ice cream.

LAMMA

Lamma is the island to visit if you want to do some pleasant hiking or eat fresh seafood on a peaceful waterfront. The closest of the outlying islands and only 45 minutes by ferry from Central, Lamma is Hong Kong's third-largest island, has a population of about 8,000, and is still largely undeveloped. There are no cars on the island, and a 1 1/2- to 2-hour hiking trail connects Lamma's two main villages—Sok Kwu Wan and Yung Shue Wan—both served by frequent ferries from Hong Kong Island. And if it's summer, don't forget to bring your bathing suit, since there are several beaches along the trails.

WHAT TO SEE & DO

Yung Shue Wan, which translates as "Banyan Tree Bay," is Lamma's main town. It used to be small and undeveloped, with old houses and small garden plots, but new houses and shops have sprung up on its hillsides in the past decade, a sizable population of expatriates has settled there, and the town is unfortunately overshadowed by an unsightly power station.

After disembarking from the ferry, follow Yung Shue Wan Main Street and Yung Shue Wan Back Street through town. As you leave town, following signs that read: FAMILY TRAIL and HUNG SHING YEH BEACH, you'll pass vegetable patches and green quilts of neatly cultivated fields that are occasionally watered the old-fashioned way by villagers who balance two watering cans on a pole slung across their shoulders. After about 15 minutes you'll come to one of Lamma's three beaches, **Hung Shing Yeh,** which has changing facilities, showers, toilets, and lifeguards on duty in the summer. If it's hot, it may be hard to resist joining the throngs of families and taking a dip in the water. However, since it's close to that power station, you may want to wait until you reach **Lo So Shing,** which is less crowded and more rustic, or **Mo Tat Wan Beach.**

The path to Sok Kwu Wan resumes on the other side of Hung Shing Yeh Beach, and as you continue hiking, the cement path climbs higher onto barren and windswept hills, finally giving way to lush and verdant valleys and then **Sok Kwu Wan.** The hike takes about 1 1/2 to 2 hours and is a true delight, with great views of the surrounding sea. There's a pagoda about halfway between the two villages. If you feel like hiking farther, pass through Sok Kwu Wan and continue about 20 minutes to the east, where you'll eventually reach **Mo Tat Wan Beach.** There are, however, no lifeguards here. While you're in the area, check out the village of **Mo Tat,** which, at about 400 years old, is the oldest settlement on the island. It consists of a handful of crumbling old houses inhabited mainly by elderly people, and it sits picturesquely inland, amid banana trees and lush countryside.

As for Sok Kwu Wan, it's famous for its open-air seafood restaurants. They're aligned along the small waterfront, extended over the water on stilts; they offer views of the harbor (and, unfortunately, of denuded hills belonging to a cement factory across the harbor). I suggest that you simply walk along the waterfront and choose one that strikes your fancy, but a few specific recommendations are listed below. All restaurants here have tanks of fresh seafood where you can choose the creature that suits your fancy. Fresh seafood is available by the *catty* (one catty is about 1^1/$_2$ pounds). Prices for a catty vary each day, depending on supply and demand. One catty of prawns will cost approximately HK$160 to HK$175 ($20.80 to $22.75), with half a catty usually enough for two people. A catty of lobster will cost about HK$240 to HK$280 ($31.20 to $36.40). If you go all out, meals here will average about HK$250 ($32.50) a person.

WHERE TO DINE

Concerto Inn
Hung Shing Yeh Beach, Yung Shue Wan. ☎ **852/2982 1668.** Main dishes HK$42–HK$57 ($5.45–$7.40). AE, MC, V. Daily 8am–10pm. WESTERN/SNACKS.

Located right on Hung Shing Yeh Beach about a 30-minute walk from the ferry pier in Yung Shue Wan, this new, low-key establishment offers both accommodations and a pleasant cafe, with outdoor seating beside a running fountain and views of a garden and the beach. Its menu is limited, but the restaurant makes a comfortable stop along the hiking trail for a hamburger, sandwich, fish-and-chips, satays, noodles, spaghetti, ice cream, or a beer.

Man Fung Restaurant
5 Yung Shue Wan Main St., Yung Shue Wan. ☎ **852/2982 0719.** Main dishes HK$45–HK$65 ($5.85–$8.40). AE, MC, V. Daily 11am–10pm. CANTONESE/SEAFOOD.

If you start your hike at Sok Kwu Wan and end up hungry on this side of the island, this restaurant is my number-one choice for a meal. Located just a minute's walk from the ferry pier, it offers pleasant outdoor seating right by the water with a view of the sea. Specialties are its fresh seafood straight from the tank, including lobster, prawns, crab, and fish, available at market price (inquire first before ordering). Otherwise, the menu lists pork, beef, chicken, tofu, and vegetable dishes, and there are also pitchers of Carlsberg draft beer and wine from France and Portugal.

Peach Garden Seafood Restaurant
Lot 583, Sok Kwu Wan. ☎ **852/2982 8581.** Small dishes (suitable for two people) HK$45–HK$80 ($5.85–$10.40); medium dishes HK$85–HK$155 ($11.05–$20.15). AE, MC, V. Daily 10am–10pm. CANTONESE/SEAFOOD.

This waterfront establishment is located away from the string of restaurants in Sok Kwu Wan, about a 2-minute walk from the ferry pier (turn left from the ferry). Pleasant and quiet with outside dining and a view of the harbor, it serves seafood Cantonese-style. Try the baked, buttered lobster or spicy squid. There are also fried prawns, crab, fish, scallops, clams, pigeon, and chicken dishes, available in two or three sizes, as well as the usual tanks of the day's catches.

Rainbow Seafood Restaurant

17 1st St., Sok Kwu Wan waterfront. ☎ **852/2982 8100.** Small dishes HK$50–HK$100 ($6.50–$13); medium dishes HK$100–HK$175 ($13–$22.75). AE, MC, V. Daily 10am–10pm. CANTONESE/SEAFOOD.

This is the largest open-air restaurant on Sok Kwu Wan's waterfront, easily recognizable by its whir of ceiling fans and white tablecloths. A member of the HKTA, it offers a menu with photographs of its main dishes, as well as a variety of fresh seafood dishes, including prawns and lobster. A meal for two persons of prawns or lobster averages about HK$200 to HK$300 ($25.95 to $38.95).

Shum Kee Restaurant

26 1st St., Sok Kwu Wan waterfront. ☎ **852/2982 8241.** Small dishes HK$40–HK$70 ($5.20–$9.10); medium dishes HK$60–HK$120 ($7.80–$15.60). AE, MC, V. Daily 11am–11pm. CANTONESE.

This early 1960s eatery offers dining with a view of the water. The least expensive dishes include chicken, beef, pork, and noodle dishes, but no one comes here for those; what patrons prefer are lobster, prawns, crab, and fresh fish, ordered fresh from the water tanks. The house specialties are steamed lobster with garlic, fried prawn with black pepper and spiced salt, and chili crab with black bean.

LOCAL BARS

The Fountainhead

18 Yung Shue Wan Main St., Yung Shue Wan. ☎ **852/2982 2118.** Mon–Fri 6pm–2am, Sat–Sun and holidays noon–2am.

A *gwailo* (foreign) hangout, this air-conditioned bar with tables outside shaded by trees offers beer and snacks.

The Island Bar

6 Yung Shue Wan Main St., Yung Shue Wan. ☎ **852/2982 1376.** Mon–Fri 6pm–2am, Sat–Sun and holidays noon–2am.

Located near Man Fung Restaurant on the waterfront not far from the ferry pier, this is a longtime bar and local gwailo (foreign) hangout. Owned by a Brit who came to Hong Kong more than a decade ago, it's a comfortable place to wait for the next ferry and play darts.

3 China

Hong Kong is a major gateway to the People's Republic of China. Most visitors to the mainland join organized tours that last anywhere from 1 day to several weeks. **Gray Line Tours** of Hong Kong, for example, runs a variety of excursions to China, ranging from 1-day trips to Guangzhou (capital of Guangdong Province) to 5-day trips that include Guangzhou and Beijing in the itinerary. Tours can be booked through most major hotels in Hong Kong. For more information, call 852/2368 7111.

If you want to go to China on your own, **China Travel Service,** 77 Queen's Rd., Central District (☎ 852/2525 2284 or 852/2522 0450), and 27–33 Nathan Rd., Tsim Sha Tsui (☎ 852/2315 7149) can arrange for your visa; it's best to make your visa application at least 3 working days prior to departure. However, there is same-day visa service if you get your application in early in the morning. Visas cost HK$160 ($20.80), except for same-day visas, which cost HK$360 ($46.80). CTS also organizes tours and makes hotel reservations in China. The Central District office is open Monday through Saturday from 9am to 5pm. The Tsim Sha Tsui office is also open on Sunday and holidays from 9am to noon and from 2 to 5pm.

11 Macau

Hanging from China's gigantic underbelly on its southeastern coast, Macau covers all of 6 square miles. It serves as Portugal's last hold-out in Asia, though that will change when the territory reverts to Chinese control in 1999. Portugal's other former Asian strongholds, Goa and Malacca, have long since been claimed by neighboring powers.

According to the 1993 *Guinness Book of World Records,* Macau is the most densely populated territory in the world, with more than 69,000 people per square mile. And yet Macau does not seem crowded. Compared with Hong Kong, it's a small and unpretentious provincial town, reminding old-timers of what Hong Kong used to look like 40 years ago. But with its mixture of Portuguese and Chinese elements, Macau feels different from Hong Kong, different from China, different from anywhere else. Maybe it's the jumble of Chinese signs and stores mixed in with crumbling colonial-style buildings, the temples alongside Catholic churches, the flair of Portugal blended with the practicality of the Chinese. Although Portuguese remained the official language until as late as 1991, 95% of Macau's 400,000 residents are Chinese, which means that you hardly ever hear Portuguese spoken. In fact, you're probably better off with English.

Today Macau is experiencing something of a revival, with the lure of several resort hotels, spanking-new boutiques and restaurants, and increased transportation service to and from Hong Kong and the rest of the world. Macau is changing so rapidly that old-timers are right when they complain that Macau isn't what it used to be—it is, in fact, *more* than it used to be, thanks to a vigorous policy of land rec-lamation that has doubled the size of Macau since the turn of the century. New construction, much of it hideous rows of apartment blocks, has dramatically altered the city's skyline in just five short years. Even greater changes are expected since the opening of Macau's international airport in 1995, which has made Macau more easily accessible for the first time in its history.

Still, Macau makes for an interesting excursion of a day or more, especially if you want to get away from the bustle of Hong Kong after a business trip or strenuous traveling itinerary. It's the ideal place to relax, and although the casinos are undoubtedly a major attraction of Macau, especially for Hong Kong's Chinese, there are also churches, beaches, fortresses, temples, and gardens to explore—but don't expect grand edifices or any of the world's great wonders. If, on the other hand, one of your favorite traveling pastimes is simply wandering through neighborhoods of narrow winding streets and absorbing daily life, Macau is sure to grow on you. What's more, Macau's hotels are much cheaper than their counterparts in Hong Kong, which means that you can live in luxury in Macau for a fraction of what you'd pay in the British colony.

1 Frommer's Favorite Macau Experiences

- **A Pedicab Ride Along Rua da Praia Grande:** Pedicabs are Macau's oldest form of transportation and still occasionally used by the older locals for short distances. Settle on a price before climbing in.
- **A Stroll Around Guia Hill:** If you jog, you'll find the pathway that circles Guia Hill perfect—and even if you don't, this is a great place for a stroll. From the top of the hill, Macau's highest point, you have a panoramic view of the city.
- **Stopping by the Leal Senado:** Macau's most outstanding example of Portuguese colonial architecture has an exhibition room where shows are mounted without much advance notice. Stop by and be surprised.
- **Swimming on Colôane Island:** Two public beaches, Cheoc Van and Hac Sa, feature lifeguards on duty, dining facilities, and public swimming pools.
- **Horse and Dog Races:** Admission to the races in Macau is so cheap it's practically free. And who knows? You could strike gold. A great place to observe a local passion.
- **Observing the Chinese Gambling at the Ornate Floating Casino:** This moored boat is abuzz 24 hours a day with gambling fever. Drop by and observe the Chinese gambling, or try your luck with the slot machines on the upper deck.
- **Dining on Local Macanese and Portuguese Specialties:** African chicken, spicy prawns, sole, and codfish are just some of the culinary treats for the visitor to Macau, at very reasonable prices.

2 A Look at the Past

Macau was born centuries before Hong Kong was even conceived. Portuguese ships first landed in southern China in 1513, and in 1557 Portugal acquired Macau from China. Before long, Macau had achieved a virtual monopoly on trade between China, Japan, and Europe, making the city Portugal's most important trading center in Asia and the Orient's greatest port in the early 1600s.

As the only Europeans engaged in trade in Asia, the Portuguese made a fortune acting as middlemen. Every spring, Portuguese ships laden with Indian goods and European crystal and wines sailed out of Goa, anchored in Malacca to trade for spices, stopped in Macau for silk brought down from China, and then traveled on to Nagasaki to trade the silk for silver, swords, lacquerware, and other Japanese treasures. Using the monsoon winds, the ships returned to Macau to trade silver for more silk and porcelain, then sailed back to Goa where the lacquerware, porcelain, silk, and other exotic Oriental goods were shipped to eager customers in Europe. The complete circuit from Goa and back took several years.

As Macau grew and prospered, it also served as an important base for the introduction of Christianity to China and Japan, becoming a springboard for Jesuit missionaries. Many churches were built, and Asian Christians sought refuge on Macau shores.

Needless to say, because of Macau's obvious prosperity, it attracted jealous attention from other European nations. The Dutch tried to invade Macau several times in the first decades of the 1600s, but they were repelled each time. In response to the threat of invasion, the Portuguese built a series of forts in Macau, several of which still exist.

In the 1630s Japan closed its doors to foreign trade, admitting only the Dutch. This was a great blow for Macau, but the coup de grace came in 1841 when the British established their own colony on Hong Kong Island, only 40 miles away. As Hong Kong's deep natural harbor attracted ships and Hong Kong leapt to the forefront as a base for trade, Macau lost its importance and slowly sank into obscurity.

During the 1970s Macau established a new foothold in the world of trade by producing electronics, clothing, toys, and other items for export. At the same time tourism began to grow; Macau attracted a large number of Chinese gamblers from Hong Kong. In recent years the construction of ever larger resort hotels and apartment buildings has begun to attract more leisure tourists.

On December 22, 1999, Portugal's 400 years of rule will come to an end, and Macau will become a special administrative region of China. Like Hong Kong, Macau will be permitted to have its own internal government and economic system for another 50 years after the Chinese assume control.

3 Orientation

ENTRY REQUIREMENTS

Entry procedures into Macau are very simple. If you are American, Canadian, Australian, Irish, British, or a New Zealander, you do not need a visa for Macau for stays up to 20 days—all you need is your passport. What's more, even though the **pataca** is Macau's official currency, you can use your Hong Kong dollars everywhere in Macau, even on buses and for taxis (though you are likely to receive change in patacas). The pataca is pegged to the Hong Kong dollar at the rate of $103.30 patacas to HK$100; however, on the street and in hotels and shops, the Macau pataca and Hong Kong dollar are treated as having equal value. I suppose, therefore, that you could save a minuscule amount by exchanging your money for patacas, but I have never done so and don't consider it worth the hassle. You may wish to exchange a small amount—say, HK$20 ($2.60)—for taxis, buses, and admission fees, but keep in mind that the pataca is *not* accepted in Hong Kong. For the sake of simplicity, the hotel rates given below are quoted in "HK$," but this could also read "patacas."

VISITOR INFORMATION

IN HONG KONG   Your first stop for information about Macau should be at Hong Kong's Kai Tak Airport; in the arrivals lobby you'll find the **Macau Tourist Information Bureau** counter. The bureau, which is open daily from 9am to 10:30pm, can provide printed material about hotels and sight-seeing in Macau. There's another Macau Tourist Information Bureau at the Macau Ferry Terminal, Room 3704 of the Shun Tak Centre, 200 Connaught Rd., in Central (☎ 852/ 2540 8180). It's open Monday through Friday from 9am to 1pm and 2 to 5pm, and on Saturday from 9am to 1pm. Be sure to pick up a map of Macau, as well as the tourist tabloid *Macau Travel Talk*. If you enjoy do-it-yourself walking tours, be sure to get a copy of the free "Macau Walking Tours" pamphlet, which gives a street-by-street description of several easy hikes.

IN MACAU   There's a **tourist information office** at the new ferry arrivals terminal, open daily from 9am to 6pm. For complete information, however, your best bet is the main **Macau Government Tourist Office,** largo do Senado, 9 (☎ 853/ 397 1115). It's located in the center of town near the Leal Senado, just across from the water fountain, and is open daily from 9am to 6pm. Other tourist information offices are located at Citadel of São Paulo do Monte (Monte Fort) and at Guia Fort and Lighthouse, both open daily from 9am to 5:30pm.

In addition, computerized city guides have been installed at several strategic points around the city; touch-screen technology provides information on sight-seeing, transportation, special events, weather information, and more. You'll find the computers at the ferry terminal, in the foyer of the Leal Senado, and the Yaohan Department Store, as well as in the Hyatt Regency Hotel and Lisboa Hotel.

GETTING THERE
BY BOAT

Located only 40 miles from Hong Kong across the mouth of the Pearl River, Macau is most easily accessible from Hong Kong by boat; for the trip, various companies offer a bewildering array of vessels, including jetfoils, turbocats, catamaran ferries, jumbocats, and high-speed ferries. Most boats depart from the **Macau Ferry Terminal,** located just west of the Central District in the Shun Tak Centre, 200 Connaught Rd., on Hong Kong Island. Situated above the Sheung Wan MTR station, the Shun Tak Centre houses booking offices for all forms of transportation to Macau, as well as the Macau Tourist Information Bureau (on the 37th floor). On the Kowloon side, limited service is available from the new China Hong Kong Terminal on Canton Road, Tsim Sha Tsui, where boats also depart for China.

Tickets can be purchased at either terminal. Jetfoil tickets can also be purchased at any of the MTR Travel Service Centres found at many MTR stations. Holders of Visa, Diners Club, MasterCard, and American Express can also book tickets by calling 852/2859 6569. In Hong Kong information can be obtained by telephoning 852/2859 3333 for jetfoils, 852/2815 3034 for high-speed ferries, 852/2516 9581 for HK ferries, or 852/2789 5421 for turbocats and jumbocats. Confused? If you plan to travel on a weekend or holiday, it's wise to buy round-trip tickets well in advance. Note that the Hong Kong government levies a HK$26 ($3.40) departure tax for those traveling to Macau. Likewise, passengers leaving Macau are charged a departure tax of $22 ptcs or HK$22 ($2.85). The prices below do not include departure tax.

The fastest way to travel is via the sleek **jetfoil,** which departs from Central about every 15 minutes from 7am to 5:30pm in winter and 6pm in summer, and reaches Macau in about 55 minutes. There's even night service, with half-hourly departures from 5:30pm or 6pm until 4am. One-way fares Monday through Friday are HK$110 ($14.30) for first class and HK$97 ($12.60) for economy class; fares on Saturday, Sunday, and holidays are HK$120 ($15.60) in first class and HK$108 ($14) in economy. Fares for night services (after 5:30pm in winter and 6pm in summer) are HK$140 ($18.20) in first class and HK$126 ($16.35) in economy. New on the scene are the **turbocats,** which are roomier than the older modes of transportation and offer luggage space. They depart from Central approximately every half hour between 8am and 5pm and from Kowloon six times a day, with the voyage taking slightly less than an hour and costing HK$97 ($12.60) for economy and HK$197 ($25.60) for first class Monday through Friday, HK$108 ($14) for economy and HK$208 ($27) for first class on weekends and holidays, and HK$120 ($15.60) for economy and HK$220 for first class for four nightly departures.

As for the other modes of transportation, **jumbocats** are catamarans that are slightly larger than jetfoils and reach Macau in about 1 hour. These depart Hong

Kong approximately every half hour from 7:30am to 6pm and cost HK$97 ($12.60) one-way Monday through Friday and HK$108 ($14) on Saturday, Sunday, and holidays. **Catamaran** fares are HK$85 ($11.05) weekdays and HK$100 ($13) on weekends. **High-speed ferries,** with three decks that accommodate 650 passengers, slot machines, and sundecks, reach Macau in about 90 minutes and cost HK$93 ($12.10) for first class, HK$78 ($10.15) for tourist class, and HK$59 ($7.65) for ordinary class on weekdays, rising to HK$116 ($15.10), HK$101 ($13.15), and HK$81 ($10.55), respectively, on weekends and holidays.

If you plan to spend only 1 or 2 nights in Macau, consider leaving most of your luggage at your Hong Kong hotel, or in computer-monitored lockers located at both the Hong Kong Island and Kowloon Macau ferry terminals. Then travel to Macau with only small, hand-carried bags. Otherwise, you could end up paying an extra charge. Passengers on jetfoils, for example, are allowed only one hand-carried bag, not to exceed 22 pounds. One additional piece of luggage may be checked in prior to departure, with charges ranging from HK$20 to HK$60 ($2.60 to $7.80) depending upon its weight. Additional checked-in luggage will be subject to the carrying capacity of the jetfoil. Baggage must be at the check-in counter 15 to 30 minutes prior to the jetfoil's departure. Obviously, your life will be easier if you leave heavy luggage in Hong Kong.

All tickets are for a specific time and cannot be changed. If, however, you've purchased your ticket in advance and then decide you'd like to leave at an earlier time, head for the special queue for standby passengers available at both Shun Tak Centre and in Macau. There is often a good chance that you can get a seat, even on weekends and during peak periods.

BY HELICOPTER

If traveling by boat is not fast enough for you, a helicopter can take you from Hong Kong to Macau in 20 minutes. East Asia Airlines operates 13 round-trips daily between 10:30am and 6:30pm. Fares from Hong Kong are HK$1,176 ($152.70) on weekdays and HK$1,280 ($166.25) on weekends. Bookings can be made in Hong Kong at Counter 8 on the third floor of the Shun Tak Centre (☎ 852/2859 3359).

BY PLANE

Macau's new International Airport opened in November 1995, heralding the birth of Air Macau, the territory's fledgling carrier. No fares had been released at press time, but initial destinations will be within 3½ hours' flying time; possible destinations include: Taipei, Seoul, Bangkok, Malaysia, and Singapore. The airport is located on reclaimed land on Taipa Island and is conveniently connected to the peninsula by a new bridge and bus service. Contact your travel agent or the Macau Tourist Information Bureau for more information.

GETTING AROUND

Macau comprises a small peninsula (site of the city of Macau) and two small islands— Taipa and Colôane, linked to the mainland by bridges.

Because the peninsula is only 2½ miles in length and a mile at its greatest width, you can walk to most of the major sights. Macau's main road is Avenida Almeida Ribeiro; the prettiest walk is along Avenida da República at the tip of the peninsula and on the many back streets of the old city.

If you get tired, you can always jump into one of the 585 licensed metered **taxis,** all painted black and beige and quite inexpensive. The charge is $8 ptcs (85¢) at flagfall, and $1 ptc (13¢) for each subsequent 250 meters (825 feet). Luggage costs

$1 ptc, and there's a surcharge of $5 ptcs (65¢) if you go to Taipa and $10 ptcs ($1.30) to Colôane. There is no surcharge, however, for the return journey to Macau.

There are **public buses** that run daily from 7am to 11:30pm, with most fares $2 to $4 ptcs (26¢ to 52¢). Bus no. 3, for example, travels from the front of the ferry terminal past the Lisboa Hotel to the main street, Avenida Almeida Ribeiro, in the city center and then continues to the Barrier Gate (Portas do Cerco). Buses going to Taipa and Colôcane Islands stop for passengers at the bus stop in front of the Hotel Lisboa, located on the mainland near the Macau-Taipa Bridge.

There are also **pedicabs,** tricycles with seating for two passengers. Even as late as the early 1980s, this used to be one of the most common forms of transportation in Macau, but increased traffic and rising affluence among the locals rendered pedicabs obsolete, and I suppose they will eventually vanish from the city scene much like the Hong Kong rickshaw. Today pedicab drivers vie mostly for the tourist dollar, charging about $75 ptcs ($9.75) for an hour of sight-seeing, but keep in mind that there are many hilly sights you can't see by pedicab. The most popular route is along the Praia Grande Bay around the tip of the peninsula, and back via Rue do Almirante Sérgio. Be sure to settle on the fare, the route, and the length of the journey before climbing in.

Although **bicycles** are not recommended for the narrow city streets and are not allowed on either the Taipa or Colôane bridge, they are a pleasant mode of transportation on Taipa Island. There are several rental shops at Taipa Village near the bus stop, with rates of about $12 ptcs ($1.55) an hour.

And finally, if you want to drive around on your own, you can see Macau by **Moke,** a small, Jeep-like vehicle. Drivers must be at least 21 years old and must have held a driver's license for at least 2 years. Visitors from Australia, New Zealand, the United States, Ireland, and United Kingdom need only a valid driver's license, but Canadians must have an international driver's license. Mokes rent for about $470 ptcs ($61.05) per day Monday through Friday and $490 ptcs ($63.65) per day on Saturday, Sunday, and holidays. They are available from **Happy Mokes,** with locations at the ferry terminal (☎ **853/726868**) and at the New Century Hotel (☎ 853/831212) on Taipa Island. A map of Macau, leaflets, and a guidebook are provided. In Hong Kong, contact the Macau tourist office for more information. *Note: Driving in Macau is on the left.*

FAST FACTS: Macau

Airport   The Macau International Airport, located on reclaimed land on Taipa Island, opened in November 1995. From Hong Kong, however, the most convenient and economical mode of transportation is still by boat.

Area Code   The international telephone country code for Macau is 853. From Hong Kong, dial 001/853 before the number.

Currency   Macau's currency, the pataca, is composed of 100 avos. Coins come in 10, 20, and 50 avos and 1 and 5 patacas. Banknotes are issued for 5, 10, 50, 100, 500, and 1,000 patacas. The Macau pataca is pegged to the Hong Kong dollar at a rate of $103.30 patacas to HK$100; if you're going to be in Macau for only a short time, there's no need to exchange your money into patacas since Hong Kong dollars are readily accepted everywhere in Macau. Hotel rates, in fact, are generally quoted only in Hong Kong dollars. Like the Hong Kong dollar, the pataca is identified by the "$" sign, sometimes also written "M$ or MOP$."

Electricity   Although some older parts of Macau still have 110 volts AC, 50 cycles, the newer sections of Macau, including hotels and the islands, have 220 volts AC, 50 cycles. Outlets accept British-type round or square three-pin plugs. If in doubt, check before using an electrical appliance.

Emergencies   For medical assistance, dial 999.

Language   Both Portuguese and Chinese are the official languages, with Cantonese the most widely spoken language. Hotel and restaurant staff usually understand English.

Police   Call 853/573333 for police.

Taxes   Hong Kong levies a HK$26 ($3.40) tax for departures for Macau; the Macau government levies a M$22 ($2.85) departure tax. Hotels levy a 5% government tax and a 10% service charge on room rates.

Telephone   Telephones in Macau offer international direct dialing, though in your hotel room you may have to go through the hotel operator. International direct-dial calls can also be made from the General Post Office, located at largo do Senado, across from Leal Senado and the Macau tourist office. Note that all telephone numbers in Macau have been changed from five to six digits. For directory assistance, dial 181.

Time   Macau is in the same time zone as Hong Kong.

Water   Macau's water is supplied from China and is purified and chlorinated. However, distilled water is supplied in restaurants and hotel rooms.

4 Where to Stay

Macau is experiencing a building boom, with several new hotels scheduled to open during the lifetime of this book. For current information on new hotels, contact the Macau Tourist Information Bureau.

In addition to the room rates given below (which are the same whether you pay in Hong Kong dollars or in patacas) there is a 10% hotel service charge and a 5% government tax. Except for some of the moderate and inexpensive hotels, most charge the same price for single or double occupancy. Since most of Macau's hotels have reservations facilities in Hong Kong, I've included the Hong Kong reservation telephone numbers when available. For more complete information about hotel restaurants, see "Where to Dine," below.

VERY EXPENSIVE

✪ Hotel Bela Vista

Rua do Comendador Kou Ho Neng, Macau. ☎ **853/965333,** or 852/2881 1288 for reservations in Hong Kong; 800/526-6566 in the U.S. and Canada. Fax 853/965588. 8 rms. A/C MINIBAR TV TEL. HK$2,000–HK$4,300 ($260–$558) double weekdays, HK$2,500–HK$5,550 ($325–$721) double weekends and holidays. AE, DC, MC, V. Free limousine service from ferry terminal and airport.

Like The Peninsula in Hong Kong and The Raffles in Singapore, the Bela Vista is a grand, older hotel—the landmark of a colonial past. Built in the 1890s on the slope of Penha Hill with a commanding view of Praia Grande Bay, the Bela Vista is much smaller than its Asian counterparts on a scale befitting this Portuguese enclave. At various times in the past it has served as a school, a haven for refugees, and a hostel/canteen for British servicemen. Reopening as a hotel after World War II, it gradually slipped into disrepair, but still remained much beloved as a symbol of old-style

Macau Accommodations & Dining

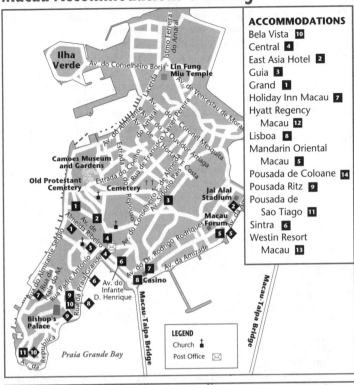

ACCOMMODATIONS

Bela Vista 10
Central 4
East Asia Hotel 2
Guia 3
Grand 1
Holiday Inn Macau 7
Hyatt Regency
   Macau 12
Lisboa 8
Mandarin Oriental
   Macau 5
Pousada de Coloane 14
Pousada Ritz 9
Pousada de
   Sao Tiago 11
Sintra 6
Westin Resort
   Macau 13

LEGEND
Church ✝
Post Office ✉

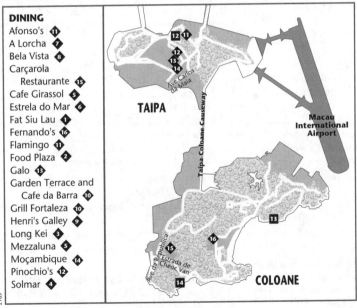

DINING

Afonso's 17
A Lorcha 7
Bela Vista 8
Carçarola
   Restaurante 15
Cafe Girassol 5
Estrela do Mar 6
Fat Siu Lau 1
Fernando's 16
Flamingo 11
Food Plaza 2
Galo 13
Garden Terrace and
   Cafe da Barra 10
Grill Fortaleza 10
Henri's Galley 9
Long Kei 3
Mezzaluna 5
Moçambique 14
Pinochio's 12
Solmar 4

2169

Macau. There was nothing grander than sitting on its spacious veranda, sipping inexpensive Portuguese wine, and watching the world go by.

After several years of restoration, the Bela Vista reopened in 1992 as an exclusive hotel, featuring eight guest rooms under the able management of the Mandarin Oriental Hotel Group. With the historical character and graceful balconied architecture intact, it has been refurbished in the style of a traditional upper-class Portuguese family home, with blue mosaic floors, a sweeping staircase, fireplaces in some of the rooms, Macanese flower motifs, high ceilings, and European still lifes. Each of the eight rooms, identified by a name instead of a number, is decorated in a different style, with a combination of Portuguese and Chinese furniture and fabrics. Five rooms feature verandas with white rattan furniture, palm trees, and ceiling fans—the best of these face the sea. All rooms are equipped with two sinks, a bidet, bathroom scales, shaving/makeup mirror, and room safe. Since the hotel is so small, staying here is almost like staying in a private home. Although there is no swimming pool, guests are entitled to use all health club facilities at the Mandarin Oriental. On the downside, a lamentable land-reclamation project under way is sure to destroy the bella vista this hotel has always enjoyed. Luckily, its lofty position on a hill high above the road and waterfront may preserve at least part of the view.

Dining/Entertainment: The Bela Vista's one restaurant serves Portuguese and Macanese specialties either in a small and intimate dining room or on an outdoor veranda. There's a small, adjoining bar.

Services: Free limousine shuttle to and from the ferry terminal and airport, babysitting, same-day laundry, 24-hour room service.

EXPENSIVE

Holiday Inn Macau

Rua de Pequim, Macau. ☎ **853/783333** or 852/2810 9628 for reservations in Hong Kong; 800/465-4329 in the U.S. Fax 853/782321. 408 rms, 27 suites. A/C MINIBAR TV TEL. HK$900–HK$1,400 ($117–$182) double; HK$1,600 ($202) executive floor; from HK$3,000 ($390) suite. AE, DC, MC, V. Free shuttle bus from ferry terminal and airport.

Opened in 1993, this well-known chain is familiar to North American guests; although the hotel is comfortable enough, it falls short of what you would expect if you've stayed at other Holiday Inns in Asia, where the level of service and facilities is higher than it is in North American properties. The hotel is situated in an area that is being developed between the ferry terminal and downtown (there are no views of the harbor); it's about a 10-minute walk from the main downtown area along Avenida de Almeida Ribeiro. The rooms are somewhat plain and bare, although equipped with satellite TV with in-house movies, coffeemaker, hair dryer, and, on the executive floor, bathroom scales. Like most Macau hotels, it caters largely to gamblers.

Dining/Entertainment: The primary dining facility, open for breakfast through dinner, is Italian. There's also a pub and a 24-hour casino.

Services: 24-hour room service, same-day laundry, nightly turndown, baby-sitting, no-smoking floors.

Facilities: Business center, small indoor swimming pool, sauna, steam room, whirlpool, exercise room, child-care center (open daily 7am–9pm and free for hotel guests).

✪ Hyatt Regency Macau

Estrada Almirante Marquês Esparteiro, Taipa Island, Macau. ☎ **853/831234** or 852/2559 0168 for reservations in Hong Kong; 800/233-1234 in the U.S. and Canada. Fax 853/830195. 322 rms, 19 suites. A/C MINIBAR TV TEL. HK$1,140–HK$1,580 ($148–$205) double; HK$1,700 ($221) Regency Club; from HK$3,200 ($416) suite. Two children under 18 stay free in parents' room. AE, DC, CB, MC, V. Free shuttle bus, or bus no. 28A from the ferry terminal.

If you're looking for a resort getaway with a tropical atmosphere, extensive recreational facilities for the entire family, great restaurants, and comfortable rooms, the Hyatt is a good choice. Located on Taipa Island near the horse-racing track, the hotel adjoins the Taipa Island Resort, a sprawling complex with an outdoor heated pool open year-round, tennis and squash courts, fitness rooms, and more. The guest rooms, which were shipped in units from the United States and then assembled in Macau like pieces of a jigsaw puzzle, have recently been completely renovated and offer all the usual amenities, including satellite TV with pay in-house movies and a voice-mail system. The least expensive rooms face inland toward new apartment construction. The best rooms offer views of the harbor and Macau's rapidly changing skyline. If you really feel like splurging, you might want to stay in the Regency Club, an executive floor that offers free continental breakfast, cocktails, and beverages. The hotel's restaurants are among the best in Macau. In short, you could easily spend days here, unwinding and relaxing. If you feel like exploring or dining on local cuisine, the quaint Taipa Village is only a 15-minute walk away. Note that the swimming pool, aerobics class, and exercise room are free, but there is a charge to use the health spa with its steam rooms, sauna, and Jacuzzi.

Dining/Entertainment: Afonso's specializes in Portuguese food, while the **Flamingo** is a Macanese restaurant with a tropical hot-pink setting and views of a small lake. There's a swim-up bar in the swimming pool, a cocktail lounge with live entertainment in the evenings, a Cantonese restaurant, a popular bar with a 5-to-7pm happy hour, and a 24-hour casino.

Services: Free shuttle to the ferry, airport, and Hotel Lisboa; same-day laundry; 24-hour room service; free newspaper; in-house nurse and doctor on call 24 hours; baby-sitting; no-smoking floor.

Facilities: Outdoor heated swimming pool, children's pool, four tennis courts, two squash courts, fitness center, sauna, steam room, Jacuzzi, massage, hair salon, games room with table tennis and pool tables, business center, a wonderful child-care center (open daily from 10am to 7pm and free when dining at a hotel restaurant, HK$25 [$3.25] for four hours at other times), playground.

✪ Mandarin Oriental Macau

Avenida da Amizade, Macau. ☎ **853/567888,** or 852/2881 1288 for reservations in Hong Kong; 800/526-6566 in the U.S. and Canada. Fax 853/594589. 406 rms, 31 suites. A/C MINIBAR TV TEL. HK$1,200–HK$1,480 ($156–$192) double; HK$1,700–HK$1,900 ($221–$247) Mandarin floors; from HK$3,800 ($494) suite. AE, DC, MC, V. Free shuttle bus from ferry terminal and airport.

A companion hotel of the Mandarin Oriental in Hong Kong and the Oriental in Bangkok, this is one of Macau's most exclusive hotels, but the price is much lower than you'd pay in Hong Kong. It's beautifully designed and elegantly decorated throughout with imports from Portugal, including blue-and-white tiles, chandeliers, tapestries, and artwork. The marble lobby features a carved teak staircase leading up to the second floor, where you'll find the hotel's small but sophisticated casino, with a separate room for slot machines. The guest rooms, equipped with safes, a voice-mail system, and satellite TVs with in-house movies, are decorated in soft pink or green with Portuguese fabrics and natural teak, and the bathrooms are marbled and spacious. The least expensive rooms face inland, while the best rooms (on the top four Mandarin executive floors) face the sea and feature large balconies. Conveniently located about a 7-minute walk from the ferry terminal, the hotel takes advantage of its waterfront location with an outdoor swimming pool right beside the water. Unfortunately, an ongoing land-reclamation project nearby has robbed some rooms of their nice view of the water, not to mention peace and quiet; ask for a room as far away from the construction as possible—on the east end of the hotel.

Dining/Entertainment: Italian cuisine is offered at **Mezzaluna,** the hotel's premier restaurant, small and intimate with views of the water. At the **Dynasty** you can eat dim sum and other Cantonese food, while the **Cafe Girassol** is open 24 hours a day except on Thursday and specializes in Macanese/Portuguese and Asian cuisine, with great breakfast, lunch, and dinner buffets. **Bar da Guia** features a live band every night from 8:30pm except Monday, while the casino is open 24 hours.

Services: 24-hour room service, car rental, doctor on call, baby-sitting, parcel and packing service, same-day laundry and dry cleaning, shuttle bus to the ferry and airport, no-smoking floor.

Facilities: Outdoor swimming pool, sauna, Jacuzzi, massage, tennis courts, exercise room, squash courts, business center, shopping arcade, book kiosk, beauty salon.

Pousada Ritz

Rua da Boa Vista, Macau. ☎ **853/339955,** or 852/2739 6993 for reservations in Hong Kong. Fax 853/317826. 150 rms, 9 suites. A/C MINIBAR TV TEL. HK$1,000–HK$1,580 ($130–$205) double; from HK$2,380 ($309) suite. AE, DC, MC, V. Free hotel shuttle bus or taxi from ferry and airport.

Situated on top of Penha Hill just above the famous Bela Vista Hotel, this Chinese-owned property opened in 1990 as a small, 31-room hotel and then greatly enlarged its facilities with the completion of a new wing in 1995. Its lobby is rather bare, although its marble floor opens onto the Garden Terrace, which offers sweeping views of the Outer Harbour. The more expensive rooms also boast grand views of the sea, and those on the third and fourth floors feature balconies at no extra cost. Rooms are comfortably equipped with TV with in-house pay movies, hair dryer, bathroom scales, clothesline above the bathtub, and the usual amenities.

Dining/Entertainment: Amigo, with its views of the harbor, is the hotel's Western restaurant, serving French, Portuguese, and continental fare. **Lijinxuan** is an elaborately decorated Chinese restaurant offering specialties from Canton, Szechuan, Beijing, and Hunan.

Services: Complimentary shuttle bus, house doctor, baby-sitting, limousine service, same-day laundry, 24-hour room service.

Facilities: Indoor swimming pool, indoor children's pool, sundeck, exercise gym, rooftop tennis court, squash court, whirlpool, sauna, massage, beauty parlor, billiards room, business center, gift shop.

✪ Pousada de São Tiago

Avenida da República, Fortaleza de São Tiago da Barra, Macau. ☎ **853/378111,** or 852/2739 1216 for reservations in Hong Kong. Fax 853/552170. 24 rms and suites. A/C MINIBAR TV TEL. HK$1,300–HK$1,630 ($169–$212) double; from HK$1,800 ($234) suite. AE, CB, DC, MC, V. Free shuttle bus or taxi from ferry and airport.

Built around the ruins of the Portuguese Fortress da Barra, which dates from 1629, this delightful small inn on the tip of the peninsula is guaranteed to charm even the most jaded of travelers. The entrance is dramatic—a flight of stone stairs leading through a cavelike tunnel that was once part of the fort, with water trickling in small rivulets on one side of the stairs. Once inside, guests are treated to the hospitality of a Portuguese inn, with bedroom furniture imported from Portugal and the use of stone, brick, and Portuguese blue tile throughout. The Garden Terrace, shaded by banyan trees, is a great place to while away an afternoon, and most of the rooms, all of which face the sea, have balconies. Unfortunately, this hotel is also plagued by nearby land reclamation, although, according to hotel management, the new land will be used for a garden. The Maritime Museum and A-Ma Temple are within walking distance. This place is a true find, perfect for a romantic getaway.

Dining/Entertainment: The **Grill Fortaleza** is one of Macau's finest and most elegant restaurants, with a drawing-room ambience, serving classic Portuguese and continental cuisine. The **Garden Terrace,** a tree-shaded outdoor patio with glimpses of the sea, serves snacks and light meals until midnight. For drinks, there's the Cascata Bar.

Services: Baby-sitting, same-day laundry and dry-cleaning, medical and dental service, free newspaper, parcel and postal service, room service (7am to 11:30pm), complimentary shuttle to and from the ferry pier on request.

Facilities: Outdoor swimming pool.

✪ Westin Resort Macau
Estrada de Hac Sa, Colôane Island, Macau. ☎ 853/871111, or 852/2803 2015 for reservations in Hong Kong; 800/228-3000 in the U.S. and Canada. Fax 853/871122. 200 rms, 8 suites. A/C MINIBAR TV TEL. HK$1,500–HK$1,900 ($195–$247) double; from HK$4,600 ($597) suite. Children under 19 stay free in parents' room. AE, DC, MC, V. Free shuttle bus from ferry terminal and airport.

Opened in 1993, this is Macau's newest luxury resort hotel, complete with landscaped grounds, two outdoor swimming pools (one of which is a children's pool), an indoor pool, tennis courts, a health club, and Macau's first golf course. Located just a stone's throw from Hac Sa Beach on Colôane Island, it's a bit far from the center of town (about a 15-minute ride from the ferry pier on the hotel's complimentary shuttle bus, with departures every 30 minutes), but the management is betting that most prospective guests are those who want to get away from it all. The hotel, Mediterranean in design and atmosphere, is spacious and airy, with a red terra-cotta tile roof and a comfortable lounge off the lobby which takes advantage of its idyllic setting by providing lots of windows that overlook the sea and by offering live music nightly. To assure tranquillity, there's a separate check-in counter for tour groups.

Constructed in tiers to harmonize with the hillside overlooking Hac Sa Beach, all of the hotel's large rooms face the sea and feature a huge private terrace with plants, rattan or Oriental furniture, room safe, TV with in-house movies, hair dryer, shaving/makeup mirror, and separate areas for showering and bathing. The room rates are based on altitude, with the highest floors (fifth through eighth) costing more.

Dining/Entertainment: Five restaurants and bars, including a Cantonese restaurant with an outdoor terrace overlooking the sea, a coffee shop offering both Portuguese and Macanese food, a Japanese restaurant, and a hotel bar with outdoor seating, all of which have no-smoking sections.

Services: Complimentary shuttle bus, no-smoking floor, 24-hour room service, same-day laundry, baby-sitting.

Facilities: One outdoor swimming pool, outdoor children's pool, indoor pool, eight tennis courts, two squash courts, lawn bowling, jogging lanes, health club, sauna, massage, 18-hole golf course, child-care center (HK$30 [$3.90] per day), games room, table tennis, rental bikes, lobby kiosk, gift shop.

MODERATE

Hotel Guia
Estrada do Engenheiro Trigo, Macau. ☎ 853/513888. Fax 853/559822. 79 rms, 10 suites. A/C MINIBAR TV TEL. HK$540–HK$690 ($70–$90) double; from HK$860 ($112) suite. AE, DC, MC, V. Free shuttle bus or bus no. 28C from ferry terminal.

Located on the slope of Guia Hill below the Guia Fort and Lighthouse and surrounded by traditional colonial architecture, this is one of Macau's more secluded
medium-priced hotels. Opened in 1989, it's small and personable, with a friendly staff
and rooms that range from those facing inland to those with little balconies facing the
sea. The only drawback to its quiet residential location is that it's a bit far from the
action, but a free shuttle bus makes runs every half hour or so to and from the boat
pier and the Hotel Lisboa. Facilities include one Chinese restaurant offering seafood
and specialties from different provinces in China and a disco/nightclub. Room service
is available from 7am to 11:30pm, and there's same-day laundry service. A nearby
jogging path on Guia Hill make this an ideal choice for joggers and walkers.

Hotel Lisboa

Avenida da Amizade, Macau. ☎ **853/577666,** or 852/2546 6944 for reservations in Hong
Kong. Fax 853/567193. 970 rms, 79 suites. A/C TV TEL. HK$790–HK$1,500 ($102–$195)
double; from HK$2,000 ($260) suite. Children under 13 stay free in parents' room. AE, CB, DC,
MC, V. Free shuttle bus or bus no. 28A, 28B, or 28C from the ferry pier.

The Lisboa is in a class by itself. Built in 1969, it's a Chinese version of Las Vegas—
huge, flashy, and with a bewildering array of facilities that make it almost a city within
a city. I always get lost in this hotel. Located near the water, it also has great *fung shui,*
which may explain why its casino is one of the most popular in Macau. You certainly
can't get much closer to the action than the Lisboa; it is very popular among the
Hong Kong Chinese and tour groups from Japan and Australia, making its lobby
rather noisy and crowded. Its casino, one of the largest, never closes, and there are a
bewildering number of restaurants, shops, and nighttime diversions, including the
Crazy Paris Show with a revue of scantily clad European women. One advantage to
staying here is that buses to the outlying islands and other parts of Macau stop at the
front door. As for the rooms, they're located in an older wing, a newer wing, and a
tower that was completed in 1993 (the tower, which added 14 floors, offers the best
harbor views); all of the rooms seem rather old-fashioned and have been decorated
in beige, pink, and orange. Still, this is the place to be if you want to be in the thick
of it. I suspect some guests check in and never leave the premises.

There are more than a dozen restaurants (some open 24 hours) serving European,
Portuguese, Japanese, Chiu Chow, Cantonese, and Shanghainese cuisine; plus
cocktail lounges, bars, a nightclub, and a casino open 24 hours.

Guests enjoy 24-hour room service, same-day laundry, house doctor, money-
exchange banks, complimentary shuttle service, free newspaper on request, and
baby-sitting. The hotel also offers an outdoor swimming pool, sauna and massage,
children's playground, large shopping arcade, electronic games room and billiard
room, a beauty salon, and barber shop.

⑨ Pousada de Colôane

Cheoc Van Beach, Colôane Island, Macau. ☎ **853/882143** or 853/882144, or 852/2540 8180
for reservations in Hong Kong. Fax 853/882251. 22 rms. A/C MINIBAR TV TEL. HK$740–HK$780
($96–$101) double. AE, MC, V. Bus: no. 21A or 25 from Lisboa Hotel.

This small, family-owned property, perched on a hill above Cheoc Van Beach with
views of the sea, is a good place for couples and families in search of a reasonably
priced isolated retreat. More than 30 years old and a bit worn in spots, it's nevertheless a relaxing place, with modestly furnished rooms, all of which have large
balconies and face the sea. There is a small outdoor swimming pool, a children's playground, an outdoor terrace where you can have drinks, and a Portuguese restaurant
which is especially popular for its Sunday lunch buffet. *Note:* The hotel may close at
the end of 1996.

Ⓢ Sintra

Avenida de D. João IV, Macau. ☎ **853/710111,** or 852/2546 6944 for reservations in Hong Kong. Fax 853/510527. 228 rms, 12 suites. A/C TV TEL. HK$640–HK$940 ($83–$122) double; from HK$1,300 ($169) suite. Children under 13 stay free in parents' room. AE, DC, MC, V. Bus: no. 3A or 10 from the ferry terminal.

This moderately priced hotel enjoys a prime location in the heart of Macau, within easy walking distance of Avenida de Almeida Ribeiro (Macau's main street), the Lisboa Hotel, and Rua da Praia Grande. Originally built in 1975 but completely overhauled recently, it looks spanking new; its large rooms are nicely decorated with pastel-colored furnishings and the bathrooms have marble-topped counters. TVs offer in-house pay movies. The higher-priced rooms are on higher floors facing the harbor, but many rooms will probably lose their view once the nearby land-reclamation project is finished. The hotel's one restaurant serves Macanese and Portuguese food, and there is 24-hour room service and same-day laundry.

INEXPENSIVE

East Asia Hotel

Rua da Madeira, Macau. ☎ **853/922433,** or 852/2540 6333 for reservations in Hong Kong. Fax 853/922430. 98 rms. A/C TV TEL. HK$410–HK$520 ($53–$67) twin. MC, V. Bus: no. 3 from the ferry terminal.

This is a good choice for an inexpensive accommodation, located near the Inner Harbour just off Avenida de Almeida Ribeiro in an area filled with local color and atmosphere. More than 60 years old, the renovated hotel features large rooms with tiled bathrooms and complimentary Chinese tea. The least expensive rooms are windowless, so be sure to ask for windows if that's important to you. The rooms on higher floors offer better views.

Hotel Central

Avenida de Almeida Ribeiro, 26–28, Macau. ☎ **853/373888** or 853/372404. Fax 853/332275. 190 rms. A/C TV TEL. HK$310–HK$470 ($40–$61) twin; HK$470 ($61) suite. Weekday discount available. AE, DC, MC, V. Bus: no. 3 from the ferry terminal.

This hotel, right on Macau's main road, first opened about 50 years ago and it looks it. The corridors are narrow and dark; although some of the rooms have been refurbished with new carpets, wallpaper, and furniture, and have tiled bathrooms, most of the rooms are old and run-down, with discolored and peeling wallpaper. Furthermore, some rooms don't even have windows. Before deciding to take a room, ask to see it. Also, be aware that the renovated rooms are more expensive. If possible, try to get a room on the ninth floor; some of these rooms boast balconies with a view over the rooftops to the harbor beyond. The hotel has one Cantonese restaurant and a coffee shop.

Hotel Grand

Avenida de Almeida Ribeiro, Macau. ☎ **853/921111.** Fax 853/922397. 100 rms. A/C TV TEL. HK$550 ($71) twin. Weekday discounts available. AE, MC, V. Bus: no. 3 or 3A from ferry pier.

This hotel, located just off the Inner Harbour not far from the floating casino, has a great 1930s curved facade—classic art deco. The rooms feature high ceilings reminiscent of that era, but otherwise they are dark because of the brown rugs and small windows; the tiled bathrooms are small. The rooms that face the front provide the best view of the Inner Harbour; ask for a room on a higher floor, though making yourself understood may be a problem since most of the staff do not speak English. There's one Cantonese restaurant and a coffee shop.

5 Where to Dine

As a former trading center for spices and a melting pot for Portuguese and Chinese cultures, it's little wonder that Macau developed its own very fine cuisine. The Portuguese settlers brought with them sweet potatoes, peanuts, and kidney beans from Brazil, piri-piri peppers from Africa, chilis from India, and codfish, coffee, and vegetables from Europe. In turn, the Chinese introduced rhubarb, celery, ginger, soy sauce, lychees, and other Asian foods. The result is Macanese cuisine. One of the most popular dishes is African chicken, grilled or baked with chilis and piri-piri peppers. Other favorites include Portuguese chicken (chicken baked with potatoes, tomatoes, olive oil, curry, coconut, saffron, and black olives), bacalhau (codfish), Macau sole, caldeirada (seafood stew), spicy giant shrimp, baked quail and pigeon, curried crab, Portuguese sausage, and feijoada (a Brazilian stew of pork, black beans, cabbage, and spicy sausage). And don't forget Portuguese wine, inexpensive and a great bargain.

Restaurants will add a 10% service charge to your bill.

EXPENSIVE

Afonso's

In the Hyatt Regency Hotel, Taipa Island. ☎ 853/831234. Reservations recommended. Main courses HK$95–HK$150 ($12.35–$19.50). AE, CB, DC, MC, V. Wed–Mon noon–3pm and 7–11pm. Bus: no. 11, 21, 21A, 28A, or 33. PORTUGUESE.

This cheerfully decorated restaurant specializes in traditional Portuguese food, with an emphasis on fresh seafood. It offers daily specials and great appetizer and dessert buffets. Chefs from Lisbon prepare such authentic seasonal dishes as baked codfish with onions and potatoes, sautéed prawns with bacon, beef sirloin with ham and fried egg, and lamb chops marinated with rosemary, garlic, and olive oil. Live music performed by a three-piece band sets the mood in the evenings.

✪ Bela Vista

In the Hotel Bela Vista, Rua do Comendador Kou Ho Neng. ☎ 853/965333. Reservations recommended. Main courses HK$85–HK$150 ($11.05–$19.50). AE, DC, MC, V. Daily noon–3pm and 7–10:30pm. Bus: no. 28B. PORTUGUESE.

The Bela Vista's dining room is much more casual than this elegant hotel would lead you to expect—no need to wear your finest here. Rather, the emphasis is on the food, prepared by a Portuguese chef, and on the great view afforded by the outdoor veranda. If the weather is nice, make a reservation for a table outside—this is what the Bela Vista is all about. From here you can enjoy a seasonal menu that always includes Portuguese antipasto and traditional Portuguese soup, followed by such favorites as African chicken, grilled king prawns, grilled lamb chops in a port wine sauce, or perhaps a seafood stew. During nonmeal hours, you can still drop by for a glass of wine and a sandwich or pastry. There's a small bar adjacent to the dining hall.

Grill Fortaleza

In the Pousada de São Tiago Hotel, Avenida da República. ☎ 853/378111. Reservations recommended. Main courses HK$100–HK$175 ($13–$22.70). AE, CB, DC, MC, V. Daily noon–3pm and 7–11pm. Take a taxi. PORTUGUESE/CONTINENTAL.

Small and intimate, with seating for only 40 diners, this half-oval room with heavy red velvet curtains and a drawing-room ambience was designed to resemble a room in a Portuguese governor's colonial mansion. Offering a view of the water beyond an old tree that was taken into consideration in constructing the hotel, it serves both Portuguese and continental cuisine with a small menu that changes yearly. There are just five appetizers, five soups, and four salads, making it easier to choose. Main courses include such specialties as baked codfish, grilled king prawns served Macanese style, a beef fillet with black pepper sauce and truffles, African chicken, and Macau sole. This is a great place for a romantic dinner or special occasion.

Mezzaluna

In the Mandarin Oriental Hotel, Avenida da Amizade. ☎ 853/567888. Reservations recommended. Main courses HK$135–HK$180; pasta and pizza HK$75–HK$98 ($9.75–$12.70). AE, DC, MC, V. Tues–Sun 12:30pm–3pm and 6:30–11pm. Bus: no. 28A, 28B, or 28C. ITALIAN.

It was a bold move to open an Italian restaurant as a premier restaurant rather than Portuguese/Macanese, long favored by Macau's hotels, but for those looking for something different it's a welcome change. With a modern setting of golds and greens and the casualness of wicker chairs, it offers a limited menu of Neapolitan-style pizzas cooked in a wood-burning stove, pastas, and a dozen main courses ranging from char-grilled chicken served on potatoes with roasted garlic and parsley to grilled tuna served on fennel with chili balsamic dressing. There are three window tables offering views of the water; be sure to reserve one of these in advance.

MODERATE

A Lorcha

Rua do Almirante Sergio, 289. ☎ 853/313193. Main courses HK$50–HK$80 ($6.50–$10.40). AE, MC, V. Wed–Mon 12:30pm–3:30pm and 7–11pm. Bus: no. 1, 1A, 2, 6, 7, or 9.

Just a stone's throw from the Maritime Museum and A-Ma Temple, this is the best place to eat if you find yourself hungering for Portuguese food and you are in this area. Look for its whitewashed walls. Casual yet often filled with business people, it offers stewed broad beans Portuguese-style, codfish in a cream sauce, fried shrimp, clams prepared in garlic and olive oil, and other traditional dishes. Its name, by the way, refers to a type of Portuguese boat, which is appropriate for a colony founded by seafaring explorers.

Caçarola Restaurante

Rua das Gaivotas, 8, Colôane Village, Colôane Island. ☎ 853/882226. Reservations recommended on weekends. Main courses HK$60–HK$82 ($7.80–$10.65). AE, V. Tues–Sun 12:30–3pm and 7:30–10pm. Bus: no. 21A. PORTUGUESE.

This is a tiny two-storey restaurant which is popular with the locals for Portuguese food. Located just off the main square in Colôane Village (Vila Colôane), it offers a small menu that changes daily; some of the frequent specialties are baked codfish with cream, turkey Stroganoff, pork in wine sauce, duck rice, beefsteak Portuguese-style, and ministeak. Other dishes that have appeared on the menu include: bacalhau, stewed squid, grilled octopus, rabbit stew, or, for the more adventurous, "piglet paws stew with chickpea" or "chicken rice cooked in own blood." In nice weather, you may want to sit at one of several tables outside on the balcony.

Café Girassol

In the Mandarin Oriental Macau, Avenida da Amizade. ☎ 853/567888. Dinner buffet HK$140–HK$175 ($18.20–$22.70); lunch buffet HK$120–HK$140 ($15.60–$18.20); breakfast buffet HK$125 ($16.25). AE, CB, DC, MC, V. Fri–Wed 24 hours, Thurs to midnight. Bus: no. 28A, 28B, 28C. PORTUGUESE/ASIAN/CONTINENTAL.

Hungry in the middle of the night after an exhausting evening of gambling? Even if you lost most of your money, you can still enjoy a bite to eat here, with a menu that includes a little bit of everything at reasonable prices, including tandoori, sandwiches, and Macanese specialties. The best time to come, however, is for one of the daily buffets, which changes according to different themes but always offers a variety of Asian and local dishes. Grab a seat by the window and watch the ferries come and go.

Fat Siu Lau

Rua da Felicidade, 64. ☎ **853/573585** or 853/573580. Main courses HK$39–HK$120 ($5.05–$15.60). No credit cards. Daily 11am–midnight. Bus: no. 3. MACANESE.

This is Macau's oldest restaurant (dating from 1903), but its three floors of dining have been renovated in upbeat modern art deco, with a very pleasant color scheme of peach and turquoise blue. Macanese cuisine is served here, including roast pigeon marinated according to a 75-year-old secret recipe; spicy African chicken; curried crab; garoupa stewed with tomatoes, bell pepper, onion, and potatoes; and grilled king prawns.

Fernando's

Praia de Hac Sa, 9, Colôane. ☎ **853/882264** or 853/882531. Main courses HK$55–HK$120 ($7.15–$15.60). No credit cards. Daily noon–9:30pm. Bus: no. 21A or 26A. PORTUGUESE.

For years Fernando's was just another shack on Hac Sa Beach; although outwardly there is nothing to distinguish it from the others (it's the one closest to the beach, to the right below the Coca-Cola sign), a brick pavilion was recently added on the back, complete with ceiling fans and an adjacent open-air bar with outdoor seating (open daily from noon to midnight). There's no air-conditioning (that goes for the kitchen as well), but there is a fireplace for cool weather. The menu is strictly Portuguese and includes prawns, crabs, mussels, codfish, feijoada, veal, chicken, pork ribs, suckling pig, beef, and salads. The bread all comes from the restaurant's own bakery, and the vegetables are grown on the restaurant's own garden plot across the border in China. Only Portuguese wine is served. Very informal, and not for those who demand pristine conditions.

⑤ Flamingo

In the Hyatt Regency Hotel, Taipa Island. ☎ **853/831234.** Reservations recommended Sat–Sun. Main courses HK$55–HK$105 ($7.15–$13.65). AE, CB, DC, MC, V. Daily noon–3pm and 7–11pm. Bus: no. 11, 21, 21A, 28A, or 33. MACANESE/PORTUGUESE.

Decorated in hot pink, this restaurant has a great Mediterranean ambience, with ceiling fans, swaying palms, and a terrace overlooking lush landscaping and a duck pond. The bread is homemade, and the specialties are Macanese and Portuguese dishes, including spicy king prawns with chili sauce, curried crab, African chicken, grilled sardines, and codfish. The garoupa with crab and shrimp in a white sauce is great. There are also beef, lamb, and Oriental selections. Meals here average HK$150 ($19.50)—a great value considering the ambience and the food.

Garden Terrace and Cafe da Barra

In the Pousada de São Tiago Hotel, Avenida da República. ☎ **853/378111.** Main courses HK$75–HK$105 ($9.75–$13.65). AE, CB, DC, MC, V. Daily 7am–11:30pm. Take a taxi. INTERNATIONAL.

The Garden Terrace is an outdoor tree-shaded brick terrace that faces the sea; it's a good place to stop for food if you're walking around the tip of the peninsula (something I do on every visit to Macau). If it's raining, you can enjoy the same menu at the Cafe da Barra, which also provides a view of the water. The menu lists a wide range of Portuguese and Macanese specialties, including African chicken, grilled spicy king prawns, baked Portuguese chicken, and stewed bacalhau, as well as a few choices of curries, spaghetti, and sandwiches costing less than HK$45 ($5.85). There's also a large variety of desserts.

Maxim's Henri's Galley

Avenida da República, 4. ☎ **853/556251** or 853/562231. Main courses HK$48–HK$100 ($6.25–$13). MC, V. Daily 11am–11pm. Bus: no. 6, 9 or 28B. MACANESE/INTERNATIONAL.

Located on the Outer Harbour below the Bela Vista Hotel, this popular establishment is owned by Henri Wong, a jovial and friendly man who used to be chief steward in a galley at sea; he has decorated his restaurant as though he were still aboard ship. The waiters, dressed as stewards, are attentive and there are a few seats outdoors under umbrellas. Specialties of the house include fried Macau sole, African chicken, Portuguese baked chicken, bacalhau, fresh crab curry, spicy giant prawns, steaks, and stuffed crabmeat in its shell, but there are also sandwiches priced at less than HK$45 ($5.85). Expect to spend about HK$100 ($13) for dinner.

Pinochio

Rua do Sol, Taipa Village, Taipa Island. ☎ **853/827128** or 853/827328. Main courses HK$50–HK$100 ($6.50–$13). No credit cards. Daily noon–10pm. Bus: no. 11, 28A, or 33. PORTUGUESE/MACANESE.

Taipa Island's first Western restaurant is still going strong, though some who have known it since its early days claim that the entire atmosphere changed when a roof was added to the original roofless two-story brick warehouse. Specialties include curried crab, prawns, charcoal-grilled sardines, fried codfish cakes, grilled spareribs, roast veal, roast quail, and Portuguese-style cooked fish.

INEXPENSIVE

Estrela do Mar

Travessa do Paiva, 11. ☎ **853/322074.** Main courses HK$39–HK$80 ($5.05–$10.40). AE, DC, MC, V. Daily 11am–midnight. PORTUGUESE/MACANESE.

Located on a side street off Rua da Praia Grande (toward the Bela Vista Hotel), across from the beautiful, pink-colored colonial government palace, this small, unpretentious restaurant serves inexpensive Portuguese cuisine and is a longtime Macau favorite. The menu lists soups, salads, Portuguese or African chicken, Macau sole, roast quail, crabs with curry, spicy fried prawns, pork chops, steak, bacalhau, rabbit, and lamb dishes. You can also dine on sandwiches, omelets, spaghetti, and snacks for less than HK$40 ($5.20). A couple of tables are outside on the sidewalk.

⊛ Food Plaza

In Yaohan Department Store, Avenida da Amizade. ☎ **853/725338.** Main courses HK$20–HK$40 ($2.60–$5.20). No credit cards. Daily 11:30am–10pm. Located across from the ferry terminal. INTERNATIONAL.

This third-floor cafeteria setting resembles the food court of any shopping mall, except that the choices here may be a bit more exotic than what you're used to. Various counters offer Japanese noodles, curry rahmen noodles, yakisoba (fried noodles), sushi fixed-price meals, fried rice, and Indian curries, as well as such familiar dishes as grilled chicken and pizza. Simply walk around until you see something that strikes your fancy—all the food choices are on display along with their prices. If you'd rather dine in a fancier setting with waiter service, there are also a few Asian restaurants on the third floor of the department store.You will find a Japanese teppanyaki restaurant that also offers sukiyaki and shabu-shabu, a Chiu Chow restaurant, and a Bodhi Vegetarian Restaurant; they all provide views of the New Macau–Taipa Bridge and the ferries coming and going. Yaohan is a convenient place to eat if you're waiting for a ferry.

✪ Galo

Rua dos Clérigos, 45, Taipa Village, Taipa Island. ☎ 853/827423 or 853/827318. Main courses HK$38–HK$65 ($4.95–$8.45). AE, V. Daily 11:30am–3pm and 6–10:30pm. Bus: no. 11, 28A, or 33. PORTUGUESE/MACANESE.

A delightful, two-story house in Taipa Village has been converted into this informal and festively decorated restaurant specializing in local cuisines. "Galo" means rooster in Portuguese; look for the picture of the rooster outside the restaurant. Its menu, which includes photographs of each dish, offers such house specialties as Macau crabs, prepared with a mixture of Shanghainese and Macanese ingredients, rather than curry. You might also want to try giant prawns, mussels, African chicken, Portuguese broadbeans, or the mixed grill. In any case, be sure to start out with the sopa da casa (house soup), made from potatoes, red beans, onions, and vegetables simmered in broth from boiled beef and sausages. Delicious!

Long Kei

Largo do Senado, 7B. ☎ 853/573970. Main dishes HK$35–HK$65 ($4.55–$8.40). AE, DC. Daily 11am–11pm. Bus: no. 3. CANTONESE.

If you're in the mood for Cantonese food, this well-known Chinese restaurant is located in the heart of town, right off Avenida de Almeida Ribeiro near the Macau tourist office on the main plaza. The menu lists more than 350 items, including shark's fin, bird's nest, abalone, chicken, frog, duck, seafood, noodles, and vegetable combinations. Most dishes average about HK$35 to HK$45 ($4.55 to $5.85). Try the double-boiled shark's fin with chicken in soup or the minced quail with lettuce.

Moçambique

Rua dos Clérigos, 30–38, Taipa Village, Taipa Island. ☎ 853/827471. Main courses HK$45–HK$65 ($5.85–$8.40). No credit cards. Tues–Sun 12:30–3pm and 6:30–11pm. Bus: no. 11, 28A, or 33. AFRICAN/PORTUGUESE/GOAN.

For a unique dining experience, try this plain and unpretentious spot, located in a century-old building that was once a toy factory (look for it on the side street that runs past Galo). Walk up the creaking wooden stairs to the third floor, with its original high ceiling and African artwork adorning its whitewashed walls. The food is a combination of cuisines with Mozambican, Portuguese, and Goan influences, a reflection of Macau's international history. The menu includes a carrot-cream soup, codfish balls, prawn puffs, samosas, grilled Portuguese sausage, curried prawns, grilled codfish, African-style barbecue chicken, and sarapatel (a Goan dish of chopped pork with Indian spices and rice). All main dishes come with salad, vegetables, or french fries.

Solmar

Rua da Praia Grande, 8–10. ☎ 853/574391. Main courses HK$45–HK$70 ($5.85–$9.10). No credit cards. Daily 11:30am–10:30pm. Bus: no. 3A or 10. PORTUGUESE.

Everyone comes to this typical Portuguese cafe/restaurant to socialize and gossip. One of Macau's old-timers, it is quite informal and has wasted no money on decor. Although specializing in seafood and African chicken, the menu also lists Macau sole, curried crab, Portuguese vegetable soup, prawns in hot sauce, bacalhau, steaks, and of course, Portuguese wines. Often crowded, it's located between the Sintra and Metropole Hotels.

6 What to See & Do
THE TOP ATTRACTIONS

✪ St. Paul's Church
Rua de São Paulo. Free admission. Daily 24 hours. Located in the city center; walk northeast about 10 minutes uphill from Avenida Almeida Ribeiro.

The most famous structure in Macau is the ruin of St. Paul's Church. Crowning the top of a hill in the center of the city and approached by a grand sweep of stairs, only its ornate facade remains. It was designed by an Italian Jesuit and built in the early 1600s with the help of Japanese Christians who had fled persecution in Nagasaki. In 1835, during a typhoon, the church caught fire and burned to the ground, leaving only its now-famous facade. There's a nice view from the top steps of St. Paul's, but if you walk just a few minutes farther uphill you'll have an even grander view from the nearby Citadel of São Paulo do Monte, described below.

Citadel of São Paulo do Monte (Monte Fort).
Free admission. May–Sept daily 6am–7pm, Oct–Apr daily 7am–6pm.

Monte Fort was built by the Jesuits about the same time as St. Paul's to guard the city from Western enemies. Outfitted with barracks, cisterns, and storehouses, it was capable of withstanding a siege for two years. The cannons were used only once, however (in 1622), when Macau was attacked by the Dutch. In its one moment of glory, the fort's cannons fired a shot that landed right on a Dutch powder keg, blowing it to smithereens. At any rate, Monte Fort was largely destroyed by the same fire that consumed St. Paul's, but there are still wall remnants and cannon here, and it has been turned into a public park. It's a few minutes' walk from St. Paul's Church. You'll find a Macau tourist office at its entrance.

Guia Fort and Lighthouse
Guia Hill. ☎ 853/569808. Free admission. Daily 9am–7pm. Bus: no. 6 or 28C; then a 10-minute walk uphill.

This lighthouse, visible from most of Macau, is part of Guia Fort (Fortress of Our Lady of Guia), which occupies the highest point of Macau. Built in the 1630s, the fort was constructed to defend Macau against attacks from China, but because of its height, it proved to be a useful observation post of the harbor as well. In 1865 the lighthouse was added, making it the oldest on the China coast. Also on the grounds of Guia Fort are a small chapel and a tourist-information counter. A jogging path, complete with exercise stations, circles the top of the hill.

✪ Maritime Museum
Rua de S. Tiago da Barra. ☎ 853/595481 or 853/595483. Admission Mon and Wed–Sat, HK$5 (65¢) adults, HK$2 (25¢) children, free, senior citizens; Sun, free for everyone. Wed–Mon 10am–5:30pm. Bus: no. 1, 1A, 2, 6, 7, or 9.

Macau's newest attraction, this excellent museum traces the history of Macau's life-long relationship with the sea. All explanations are in English, Portuguese, and Cantonese, and the museum is ideally situated on the waterfront of the Inner Harbour where visitors can observe barges and other boats passing by. The museum begins with dioramas depicting the legend of A-Ma, protectress of seafarers and Macau's namesake, and continues with models of various boats, including trawlers, Chinese junks, Portuguese sailing boats, and even modern jetfoils. There are also life-size original boats on display, ranging from the sampan to an ornate festival boat. Various fishing methods are detailed, from gill netting to purse seining. The museum

What's Special About Macau

Regional Food and Drink
- Portuguese and Macanese cuisine, including African chicken, bacalhau (Portuguese codfish), spicy giant prawns, feijoada (bean stew).
- Portuguese wine at low prices.

Architectural Highlights
- St. Paul's Church, ruins crowning a hill and Macau's most-photographed building.
- Leal Senado, the most outstanding example of Portuguese colonial architecture in Macau.
- Taipa House Museum, occupying a colonial-style Portuguese home built at the turn of the century.

Chinese Temples
- Temple of Kun Iam Tong, Macau's largest temple and site of the signing of the 1844 Sino-U.S. trade agreement.
- Temple of A-Ma, Macau's oldest temple, dedicated to the goddess of the sea farers; its ornate and colorful buildings spread over the slope of a steep hill overlooking the Inner Harbour.

Gardens
- Lou Lim Iok Garden, a Chinese garden modeled on those in Soochow, with bamboo groves, ponds with carp, zigzag bridge, and pavilion.

Gambling
- Nine casinos, including the Floating Casino (which is popular with the Chinese) and hotel casinos open 24 hours.
- Horse and greyhound racing.

also has nautical equipment and a small aquarium, with tanks of exotic fish and a collection of shells. The museum operates 30-minute boat tours of the Inner Harbour and Outer Harbour aboard a restored fishing junk, with sailings at 10:30am, 11:30am, 3:30pm, and 4:30pm every day except Tuesday and the first Sunday of each month. Cost of the boat trip is $15 ptcs ($1.95), which includes entrance to the museum.

Leal Senado

Largo do Senado. ☎ 853/573500. Free admission. Daily 9am–9pm (exhibition rooms closed Mon).

The Leal Senado, located in the heart of the city just off Avenida Almeida Ribeiro, is considered Macau's most outstanding example of Portuguese colonial architecture. You can enter to see the carved stone plaques, blue-and-white tiled walls, wrought-iron gate, and the public library, as well as an exhibition room to the right of the main entrance that is used for changing exhibits of local interest. During one of my visits, there was a photographic essay of Macau during the last 150 years, providing fascinating insight into the history of the territory. Since admission is free, it's worth stopping by to see what's being shown. Be sure to see the garden at the top of the stairs from the main entry. It features more examples of Portuguese tile, wrought-iron gates, and busts of the poet Luís de Camões (to the left) and Governor Amaral (to the right).

Macau Attractions

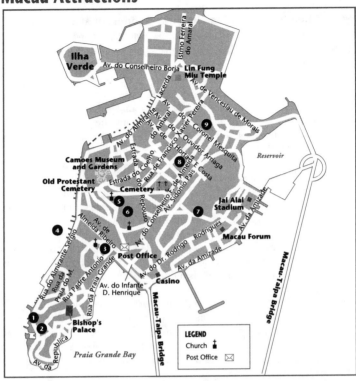

Ilha Verde

Av. do Conselheiro Borja

Istmo Ferreira do Amaral

Lin Fung Miu Temple

Av. de Venceslau de Morais

Av. do Ouvidor Arriaga

Coronel Mesquita

9

Reservoir

Camoes Museum and Gardens

8

Old Protestant Cemetery

Cemetery

Rua de Francisco Xavier Pereira

Estrada do Coelho

Estrada do Repouso

Av. do Conselheiro F. de Almeida

Av. Sidonio Pais

5

6

Jai Alai Stadium

Av. da Amizade

7

Av. de Almeida Ribeiro

Rodrigues

Macau Forum

4

Rua do Almirante Sergio

Rua da Praia do M.

3

Post Office

Av. do Dr. Rodrigo

Av. da Amizade

Rua Padre Antonio

Rua da Praia Grande

Casino

Macau-Taipa Bridge

Macau-Taipa Bridge

Av. do Infante D. Henrique

1

2

Bishop's Palace

Rua da Republica

Av. da

Praia Grande Bay

LEGEND
Church †
Post Office ⊠

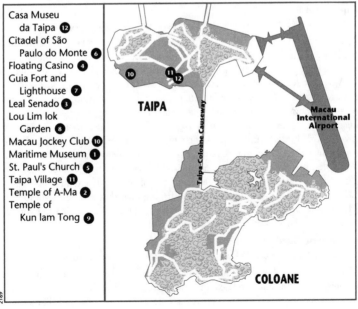

10

11

12

TAIPA

Macau International Airport

Taipa-Coloane Causeway

COLOANE

2169

Temple of Kun lam Tong (Temple of the Goddess of Mercy)

Avenida do Coronel Mesquita. Free admission. Daily 8am–6pm (5pm in winter). Bus: no. 5 or 28C.

Of the many temples in Macau, one of the most important is the Temple of Kun Iam Tong, founded in the 13th century. Its present buildings date from 1627, but the most significant historical event that took place at this largest and wealthiest of Macau's Buddhist temples was the 1844 signing of the first treaty of trade and friendship between the United States and China. The round granite table where the treaty was signed is still here. The stairs of the main temple are guarded by stone lions; although it's said that if you turn the stone ball they hold in their mouths three times to the left you'll have good luck, the lions are now protected from the public by wire mesh. The temple houses images of Buddha representing the past, present, and future, as well as the goddess of mercy (Kun Iam) dressed in the costume of a Chinese bride. She is attended by 18 gold-lacquered figures lining the walls that represent the 18 wise men of China. Curiously enough, the figure on the far left front, with bulging eyes and mustache, is Marco Polo; after he embraced Buddhism, he came to be viewed as one of China's 18 wise men. Behind the temple is a landscaped Chinese garden; it has four banyan trees with intertwined branches, popularly known as the Lovers' Tree. According to local legend, the trees grew from the burial site of two lovers who committed suicide when they were forbidden to marry. But alas, the trees are now dying.

As you wander through the various buildings on the temple grounds, you will notice small funeral rooms with altars dedicated to the newly deceased, complete with photographs of the deceased, offerings of fruit and other food, and paper money to assist the deceased in the afterlife. You may even chance upon a funeral service, in which participants are dressed in white. Please show respect by being quiet and refraining from taking photographs.

Temple of A-Ma

Rua de S. Tiago da Barra. Free admission. Daily 8am–5pm. Bus: no. 1, 1A, 2, 6, 7, or 9.

Another important temple is situated at the bottom of Barra Hill at the entrance to the Inner Harbour, across from the Maritime Museum. It is Macau's oldest Chinese temple, with parts of it dating back more than 600 years. This temple is dedicated to A-Ma, goddess of seafarers. According to legend, a poor village girl sought free passage on a boat, but was refused until a small fishing boat came along and took her on board. Once the boat was at sea, a typhoon blew in, destroying all boats except hers. Upon landing at what is now Barra Hill, the young girl revealed herself as A-Ma, and the fishermen repaid their gratitude by building this temple on the spot where they came ashore. At any rate, the temple was already here when the Portuguese arrived; they named their city A-Ma-Gao (Bay of A-Ma) after this temple. The name has been shortened to Macau now, of course. The temple has images of A-Ma and stone carvings of the Chinese fishing boat that carried A-Ma to Macau. The temple has good *fung shui*, spreading along the steep slope of a hill with views of the water. The uppermost shrine honors Kun Iam.

Lou Lim leoc Garden

Estrada de Adolfo Loureiro. Admission $1 ptc (13¢). Daily 6am–9pm. Bus: no. 2, 5, 9, or 28C.

Macau's most flamboyant Chinese garden was built in the 19th century by a wealthy Chinese merchant and modeled after the famous gardens in Soochow. Tiny, with narrow winding paths, bamboo groves, a nine-turn zigzag bridge (believed to deter evil spirits), and ponds filled with carp, it's a nice escape from the city. If possible, come in the morning, when the garden is filled with Chinese doing tai chi exercises, musicians practicing traditional Chinese music, and bird lovers strolling with their birds in ornate wooden cages.

TAIPA & COLÔANE ISLANDS

And of course, don't forget Macau's two islands—Taipa and Colôane. They are the city's breathing space, Macau's playground, a good place to get away from it all.

Taipa   Closest to the mainland, Taipa was accessible from the mainland only by ferry until 1974, when the Macau-Taipa Bridge was finally completed. Now the second New Macau–Taipa Bridge, constructed for easy access to the new airport, has led to increased development on Taipa, including new apartment blocks. Taipa is also the home of several luxury hotels, Taipa Village with its popular restaurants and colonial architecture, a firecracker factory, temples, the United Chinese Cemetery, a university, and the Macau Jockey Club for horse racing.

For history and architecture buffs, the first stop should be **Taipa Village,** a small village of narrow lanes and alleys and two-storey colonial buildings painted in hues of yellow, blue, and green. Village life is in full view here, with women sorting the day's vegetables on towels in the street, children playing, and workers carrying produce and goods in baskets balanced from poles on their shoulders. There are a number of fine, inexpensive restaurants here, making dining reason enough to come here (see "Where to Dine," above).

But for sight-seeing, the best place to visit is the **Casa Museu da Taipa (Taipa House Museum),** on Avenida da Praia in Taipa Village (☎ 853/827088). It is one of five colonial-style buildings lining the street here which had belonged to Portuguese families at the turn of the century. Combining both European and Chinese designs, the Casa Museu has a large dining and living room, a room for playing cards and other games, and large verandas that face banyan trees and the sea, reflecting the fact that most entertaining in this small colonial outpost took place at home. The home is filled with period furniture, paintings, art, and personal artifacts. The museum is open Tuesday through Sunday from 9:30am to 1pm and 3 to 5:30pm. Admission is free.

The easiest way to reach Taipa Village is via one of the buses that stops in front of the Hotel Lisboa near the bridge on the mainland or by taxi. Bus: no. 11, 28A, or 33.

Colôane   Farther away and connected to Taipa via causeway, Colôane is known for its beaches and pine trees. Two of the most popular **beaches** are Cheoc Van and Hac Sa (which means "black sand"). Both beaches have lifeguards on duty in the summer and windsurfing boards for rent, as well as nearby public swimming pools that are open until 10pm. To reach them, take bus no. 21A from Avenida de Almeida Ribeiro in the city center or from the Lisboa Hotel.

For a bit of greenery, visit **Colôane Park,** a 50-acre expanse with a walk-in aviary, Chinese-style pavilions, botanical garden, a children's playground, a restaurant, and a picnic area. The park, open Tuesday through Sunday from 9am to 5pm in winter and 8am to 9pm in summer, charges $5 ptcs (65¢) for admission to the aviary; entry to the park itself is free. To reach the park, take bus no. 21 or 21A from in front of the Hotel Lisboa or from Avenida Almeida Ribeiro. And finally, you might want to stop by the **Chapel of St. Francis Xavier** to pay homage to this important saint. Located in Colôane Village and built in 1928, it contains bones of Christian Portuguese and Japanese martyrs killed in Nagasaki in 1597 after Japan outlawed Christianity.

For more information on Taipa and Colôane, pick up a free pamphlet from the Macau tourist office called "Macau, Outlying Islands."

GAMBLING

The Chinese so love gambling that it's often said that if two flies are walking on the wall, the Chinese will bet on which one will walk faster. It's not surprising, therefore, that Hong Kong Chinese make up about 80% of the 5.9 million annual visitors to Macau. Since the only legal gambling in Hong Kong are the horse races and mahjongg, you can bet that most of the Chinese come to Macau to gamble, whether it's at the casinos or the tracks.

CASINOS   Altogether there are nine casinos in Macau. Some are fancy, other's aren't, but none of them allows photographs to be taken or allows men to wear shorts. Admission is free.

The most sophisticated casinos are those in hotels—the **Mandarin Oriental, Hyatt Regency, Kingsway Hotel, Holiday Inn,** and the **Hotel Lisboa,** as well as at the **Jockey Club** on Taipa Island. The hotel casinos are open 24 hours and offer black-jack, baccarat, and Chinese games. The Hotel Lisboa, which has the busiest casino, also offers hundreds of slot machines (known, appropriately enough, as "hungry tigers" in Chinese) and roulette. The other casinos, which cater largely to Chinese, include the **Casino Kam Pek,** on Avenida Almeida Ribeiro, the **Jai Alai,** once an arena for jai alai but now a popular casino because it is close to the ferry terminal, and the **Floating Macau Palace Casino,** moored in the Inner Harbour at Rua das Lorchas (near Avenida Almeida Ribeiro). Ornately decorated, the Floating Casino is worth strolling through for a look at Chinese gambling. Open 24 hours, it has slot machines on the top floor.

RACETRACKS   On Taipa Island the **Macau Jockey Club** has its racetrack (☎ 853/821188); it features horse racing most Saturdays and Sundays and some Wednesday evenings from September to June. Transportation is available by both public buses and air-conditioned coaches which depart from in front of the Hotel Lisboa; tickets for the coach and raceway are available in the hotel lobby. The grandstand, which is air-conditioned, charges an admission of $20 ptcs ($2.60). Outdoor public stands are free. Call for more information. Bus: no. 11, 22, 28A, or 33.

For racing of a different sort, check out the greyhound races, held on Tuesdays, Thursdays, Saturdays, and Sundays at 8pm at the **Canidrome,** Avenida General Castelo Branco, located near the border gate with China (☎ 853/574413). Admission ranges from $2 to $5 ptcs (25¢ to 65¢). Bus: no. 3, 4, 5, 6, or 9.

SHOPPING

A duty-free port, Macau is famous for its jewelry stores, especially those offering gold jewelry along Avenida do Infante D. Henrique and Avenida de Almeida Ribeiro. Portuguese wines are another good bargain. In recent years, a number of fashionable clothing boutiques have also opened in the center of town. To my mind, they seem a bit out of place amid the crumbling colonial architecture; in any case, these boutiques can also be found in Hong Kong.

The most significant indication of change was the 1993 opening of Macau's first full-fledged department store, Yaohan—conveniently situated next to the ferry terminal (☎ 853/725338). Modeled after Japanese department stores, Yaohan features four floors of clothing, accessories, cosmetics, jewelry, toys, gifts, electronics, and household goods. It also has a Mister Minit for shoe repairs, an optical shop, a bakery, liquor store, and even a children's playroom with games, rides, and activities fueled by $2 ptcs (25¢) tokens. On the third floor is the Food Plaza, where various counters offer grilled chicken, pizza, Japanese food, snacks, desserts, and drinks. There are also restaurants serving Chiu Chow, vegetarian, and Japanese food. Yaohan is open daily from 11am to 10:30pm.

Index